Lucretia Mott's Heresy

Lucretia Mott's Heresy

Abolition and Women's Rights
in Nineteenth-Century America

Carol Faulkner

PENN

UNIVERSITY OF PENNSYLVANIA PRESS

PHILADELPHIA

Published by
University of Pennsylvania Press
Philadelphia, Pennsylvania 19104-4112
www.upenn.edu/pennpress

Printed in the United States of America on acid-free paper
10 9 8 7 6 5 4 3 2 1

A Cataloging-in-Publication Record in available from the Library of Congress

ISBN 978-0-8122-4321-5

With much love
For my husband
Andrew Wender Cohen

CONTENTS

Heretic and Saint

ON FEBRUARY 11, 1849, LUCRETIA MOTT gave an unusual sermon in her usual place of worship, Cherry Street Meetinghouse in Philadelphia. The petite fifty-six-year-old Quaker minister was one of the most famous women in America. During the previous year alone, she had addressed the first women's rights conventions at Seneca Falls and Rochester, Seneca Indians on the Cattaraugus reservation, former slaves living in Canada, and the annual meeting of the American Anti-Slavery Society in New York City. Yet her audience on that winter day was filled, not with Quakers, African Americans, reformers, or politicians, but with white medical students from Thomas Jefferson Medical College and the University of Pennsylvania Medical School. Many of these students were born in the south. And, although a female medical school would open in Philadelphia the next year, all these students were men.[1]

Her sermon was unique to its time and place. In 1849, Philadelphia was the fourth largest city in the United States, with a population of 121,376. The diverse city was home to the largest population of free blacks in any northern state. It also contained the oldest and most prestigious anti-slavery society in the country, the Pennsylvania Abolition Society, founded by Quakers. With borders touching the slave states of Delaware and Maryland, Pennsylvania was regularly infiltrated by fugitive slaves. Philadelphia's black abolitionists established a Vigilance Committee to aid these fugitives. Mott was a member of two anti-slavery organizations, the Philadelphia Female Anti-Slavery Society and the Pennsylvania Anti-Slavery Society. Both of these interracial organizations denounced slavery as a sin and called for its immediate end.

Yet, despite the presence of this vibrant anti-slavery community, the majority of Philadelphia residents were openly hostile to abolitionism. In the previous decades, the City of Brotherly Love had witnessed multiple race riots. Philadelphia's elites cultivated ties with their southern counterparts. Southern slave owners were welcomed in the city's churches, museums, concert halls, and universities. Philadelphia's free blacks were not.

In order to appeal to these young southern gentlemen, Mott relied on the striking contrast between her virtuous femininity and her anti-slavery radicalism. Walking the streets of Philadelphia, and seeing these young men "separated from the tender care, the cautionary admonition of parents, of a beloved mother or sister," Mott communicated her maternal interest in their lives. She wished to guard their "innocence and purity" against the "allurements" and "vice" of the city. But she did not dwell on the predictable topic of sexual immorality. Instead, she declared, "I am a worshipper after the way called heresy—a believer after the manner which many deem infidel." Mott challenged the medical students to question the received wisdom of organized religion and polite society on the "great evil" of slavery. She prayed that they were "willing to receive that which conflicts with their education, their prejudices, and their preconceived notions." Mott wanted to open their hearts and minds to the degrading and brutalizing reality of plantation slavery. This sermon was not the first, or last, time she addressed white southerners on the topic. Her demure appearance as a Quaker matron enabled her to preach her radical message of individual liberty and racial equality to a wide variety of audiences, including those hostile to her views.[2]

Throughout her long career, Mott identified as a heretic, adopting the term to explain her iconoclasm as much as her theology. In another speech, she declared that it was the obligation of reformers to "stand out in our heresy," to defy social norms, unjust laws, and religious traditions. Her choice of the physical verb "to stand" was deliberate. Mott rejected the idea that the peace testimony of the Society of Friends meant quietism. She told an audience of abolitionists that, "the early Friends were agitators; disturbers of the peace." She advised them to be equally "obnoxious."[3] Lucretia followed her own counsel. She used her powerful feminine voice and her physical body to confront slavery and racial prejudice as well as sexual inequality, religious intolerance, and war. Though she demonstrated enormous personal bravery, she did not advocate violence. Instead, as she did in her sermon to the medical students, she used reason and example to contrast "moral purity" to the "moral corruption" of slavery.[4]

Too often Lucretia Mott is misunderstood as a "quiet Quaker."[5] Scholars have followed the lead of nineteenth-century commentators like Elizabeth Cady Stanton, who wrote that she "worshipped" Mott, regarding her as "above ordinary mortals."[6] Reviled by her opponents, Mott was hailed by her friends as a pious, benevolent, self-sacrificing woman, the perfect nineteenth-century wife, mother, and grandmother. Such perfection has intimidated historians and biographers. Despite her iconic status in the history of the anti-slavery and women's rights movements, there have been only two scholarly biographies of her in the last sixty years. In the most recent biography, *Valiant Friend*, published in 1980, Margaret Hope Bacon argues, "Victorians made a living legend of Lucretia Mott, emphasizing her sweetness and calm." Bacon tried to correct this image, focusing on the repressed anger that drove Lucretia's activism and threatened her health, only to be undermined by her publisher, who proclaimed Mott a "gentle Quaker" on the cover.[7]

Mott's very real devotion to her family further complicates efforts to rescue her from sainthood. In 1884, Anna Davis Hallowell published a joint biography of her grandparents, *James and Lucretia Mott, Life and Letters*. In many ways, Hallowell's instinct to meld the two biographies was correct. The couple's private and public lives were deeply intertwined. Lucretia and James were married for almost fifty-seven years. They had five children who lived to adulthood. James was an important abolitionist in his own right. Very deliberately, however, Hallowell emphasized "the domestic side" of Lucretia Mott. She wanted to "offset the prevailing fallacy that a woman cannot attend to public service except at the sacrifice of household duties."[8] Like other Quaker ministers, Mott's religious calling required her to balance her vocation and her family life. Ironically, her ministry made her more economically dependent than other female activists. Since Lucretia could not accept any pay for preaching, a sin denounced by the Society of Friends in their phrase "hireling minister," she relied on James for financial support.[9] Lucretia was a traditionalist in other ways as well. She used her married name for her entire adult life, for example, even after it became fashionable among other women's rights activists, including her sister Martha Coffin Wright, to include their maiden names. Nevertheless, Hallowell's description of Mott's homemaking skills—particularly in cooking Nantucket delicacies and sewing rag carpets—softens her radicalism.[10]

To borrow one of her favorite terms, Mott has become a "cipher."[11] She used the word to describe women's invisibility in the nation, neither citizen nor chattel. Its other meaning, a code or puzzle, also describes Mott. Unlike many of her fellow activists, including William Lloyd Garrison and Sarah and Angelina Grimké, Mott did not leave a significant body of published writings. She did not keep a diary, except for during one three-month period. The first scholarly edition of her correspondence, *Selected Letters of Lucretia Coffin Mott*, edited by Beverly Wilson Palmer, Holly Byers Ochoa, and myself, reveals letters filled with family news rather than introspection. And she rarely commented on her oppressive public image as a domestic saint.[12]

Without abandoning the private realm, this biography shifts attention back to Mott's public life, and places her at the center of nineteenth-century struggles for the abolition of slavery and women's rights. As a leading abolitionist and women's rights activist, Mott also illuminates the complex personal and political connections between the two movements. With black abolitionists, Mott and her allies in the Philadelphia Female Anti-Slavery Society were among the first and most important advocates of the controversial doctrine of immediatism. Mott was also one of the earliest and most visible supporters of women's rights. When other white female activists prioritized women's suffrage, however, Mott insisted that feminism must include racial equality.[13]

Mott was the foremost white female abolitionist in the United States. An anti-slavery purist who advocated immediate emancipation, moral suasion, abstinence from slave-made products, and racial equality, Mott was in the interracial vanguard of the anti-slavery movement. Historians usually associate this radical position with William Lloyd Garrison, but, in many ways she was more Garrisonian than Garrison himself. One of a small group of women present at the founding meeting of the American Anti-Slavery Society in 1833, Mott's conversion to immediate abolition predated Garrison's by several years. For thirty-six years, she and the white and black members of the Philadelphia Female Anti-Slavery Society urged abolitionists to be uncompromising in their opposition to slavery. Lucretia's remarkable history with this interracial organization provides a crucial correction to recent scholars, who exclude women by privileging the radicalism and egalitarianism of political abolitionists and revolutionaries.[14]

One of the founders of the transatlantic women's rights movement, Mott's deep interest in feminism never trumped her support for abolition or racial equality. The latest studies of the nineteenth-century women's rights movement rightly focus on the racism of most post-Civil War suffragists. This postwar narrative of conflict between feminists and abolitionists also influences the way historians tell the story of the birth of the women's rights movement. According to legend, the meeting of Lucretia Mott and Elizabeth Cady Stanton at the World's Anti-Slavery Convention in London in 1840 precipitated the first women's rights convention at Seneca Falls. In this version, the women's rights movement began with male abolitionists' rejection of Mott and other female delegates to the convention.[15] Rather than a reaction to sexism, however, Mott's recounting of the London convention suggests that women's rights were a logical extension of interconnected humanitarian concerns. She also believed the snub of the female delegates less important than the convention's anti-slavery goals. Eight years later at Seneca Falls, Mott urged convention participants to consider the relationship between women's rights and other reforms, including anti-slavery, prison reform, temperance, and pacifism. After the American Civil War, as other activists split over the Fourteenth and Fifteenth Amendments, she and her allies in the Philadelphia Female Anti-Slavery Society fought segregation on Philadelphia's railway lines and streetcars.

Though Mott's name is inextricably linked to the Society of Friends, her birthright membership only partially explains her involvement in abolition, women's rights, peace, and other reforms. The Society of Friends believed that the divine light of God was in every human being. From their beginnings in seventeenth-century England, this doctrine allowed Friends to accept women as preachers and elders. It also contributed to American Quakers' slow and agonizing rejection of slavery in the eighteenth century. Throughout her life, Mott argued that the inner light was "no mere Quaker doctrine."[16] But her relationship to the Society of Friends was contentious. To her dismay, Quakers tempered their faith in the individual conscience with a series of hierarchical meetings; they also appointed elders and ministers to discipline members. After she was recognized as a minister in 1821, Mott supported the divisive preacher Elias Hicks, who criticized the Quaker leadership for invoking the authority of Scripture over the inner light, abusing their disciplinary power, and betraying their anti-slavery testimony.

The political aftermath of the American Revolution also shaped Lucretia's anti-authoritarianism. On her native Nantucket, Lucretia learned of whaling captains and female ministers who challenged the legitimacy of traditional political and religious powers. While Quaker schools educated her in the evils of slavery, the diverse whaling industry brought Lucretia and her family into contact with the ongoing conflicts over slavery and free labor in post-emancipation Massachusetts. Her religious and political dissent coalesced during a period of protracted schism in the Society of Friends and democratic upheaval in American politics. Following the Separation of 1827, dividing American Quakers into "Hicksite" and "Orthodox," even the more radical Hicksites repudiated Mott's broad attack on all forms of hierarchy, though they never disowned her, fearing her speaking ability might be lost to them. Mott believed she could do more good as a member of the Society of Friends than as a religious come-outer. Preaching the primacy of the inner light, she challenged her fellow Quakers, and all Americans, to break the bonds of sectarianism, elitism, and slavery.[17]

A determined egalitarian, Mott was still human. She was witty, outgoing, and a steadfast friend. She was also overly modest, critical, and stubborn. Though she could not abide division among her allies, she loved a good argument. And Mott was an ideologue. Her allegiance to the founding principles of the American Anti-Slavery Society was unyielding. Much to the annoyance and frustration of other abolitionists, Mott chastised anyone who deviated from these ideals. Her preference for principles over pragmatism had a real—and undoubtedly negative—impact on individual slaves. For example, in 1847, she and the Philadelphia Female Anti-Slavery Society protested British abolitionists' purchase and liberation of Frederick Douglass. Thereafter, the Philadelphia Female Anti-Slavery Society refused to donate any of its considerable funds to buy the freedom of fugitives.[18] Finally, her distaste for the moral compromises involved in party politics made her a poor strategist. She viewed American politics as corrupted by slavery. As a result, she was not particularly interested in the way that political organizing might secure the abolition of slavery or the equal rights of women.

Mott's kind of fame was peculiar to the nineteenth century. A renowned orator, she rarely wrote anything for publication. Like other Quaker ministers, Mott preached extemporaneously, moved by the divine spirit within. Yet as her sermon to the medical students indicates, her reputation extended beyond religious audiences. Mott's effectiveness as a speaker is not always evident in printed versions of her sermons, found in newspapers reports or phonographic (shorthand) transcriptions. Audiences—including Quakers and non-Quakers, Europeans and Americans, southerners and abolitionists, politicians and clergy—flocked to hear this eloquent and feminine woman for her controversial subject matter; many of them responded to her hopeful vision of human progress, from sin, tradition, and slavery to personal morality, equality, and freedom.[19]

Mott spoke before thousands of people, but for much of her life the public repudiated her message. Most early nineteenth-century Americans did not oppose slavery. Most Americans believed racial equality was impossible. And most Americans viewed marriage and motherhood as women's highest and only calling. Mott challenged these political and social orthodoxies of nineteenth-century America, prompting oratorical challenge, public derision, and even mob violence. She was vilified as a heretic and condemned as an ultraist. While Mott embraced these derisive labels, her allies promoted her sainthood, imagining her as a nineteenth-century domestic goddess, an example of their movement's legitimacy. In between these extremes lived the real Lucretia Mott.

CHAPTER 1

Nantucket

In 1855, when Elizabeth Cady Stanton wanted information for a proposed history of the women's rights movement, she asked Lucretia Mott about "Nantucket women." Born in 1793 to Anna Folger and Thomas Coffin, Lucretia spent the first eleven years of her life on Nantucket Island, approximately thirty miles off the coast of Massachusetts. She always considered herself an islander, recalling the "social ties & happy realizations" of Nantucket society; as an adult, Lucretia attempted to recreate this community bound by kinship, religion, and politics.[1] Idealizing Mott's upbringing, Stanton viewed Lucretia's Nantucket childhood as central to her public career as an abolitionist and women's rights activist.

In her typical self-effacing manner, Mott wrote Stanton that "As to Nantucket women, there are no great things to tell." But she proceeded to recount the history of women on the island, beginning with Mary Starbuck, an ancestor who almost single-handedly converted the island's white residents to the Religious Society of Friends in 1702. Though mid-nineteenth-century American culture dictated that women serve as the moral counterpart for the male world of business and politics, Lucretia noted that on Nantucket, "education & intellectual culture have been for years equal for girls & boys—so that their women are prepared to be the companions of men in every sense—and their social circles are never divided." Recalling the experiences of her mother and other wives of sailors, Lucretia stated, "During the absence of their husbands, Nantucket women have been compelled to transact business, often going to Boston to procure supplies of goods—exchanging for oil, candles, whalebone—&.c—This has made them adept in trade—They have kept their own accounts, & indeed acted the part of men."[2] Like Stanton, Lucretia believed these early influences helped her defy the limited domestic and fashionable lives of most middle-class Victorian women. Raised with the communal memory of Mary Starbuck, and the daily observance of Anna Coffin's business acumen, at a young age Lucretia rejected the idea that women were spiritually or intellectually inferior to men.

The material and religious conditions of eighteenth-century Nantucket also shaped Lucretia's views of individual liberty, religious freedom, and the most pressing problem facing the new nation, slavery. Although Quakerism was the dominant religion on the island, the Society of Friends nevertheless provided a framework in which to critique ecclesiastical authority and established religion. Like other seaports, Nantucket was a cosmopolitan society; its boats sailed across the Atlantic and Pacific oceans, trading commodities and consumer goods and facilitating the movement of people and ideas. White settlers on the island used Native American labor for their first ventures in whaling; the industry later turned to free African Americans to staff its boats. The Coffin family's residence on late eighteenth-century Nantucket exposed Lucretia to a range of powerful intellectual currents, from Quaker radicalism to free trade to enlightenment reform. It also introduced her to a set of social questions, most important the place of non-white Americans in the new nation.

*　*　*

If Lucretia spent only eleven years on Nantucket, she nonetheless inherited traditions borne over multiple generations and a century of history. Lucretia's forebears included the first white settlers on the island. One ancestor, Tristam Coffyn, who migrated from England to Massachusetts with his family in 1642, helped organize the purchase of Nantucket. Lucretia's great-great-great grandfather Thomas Macy became the first white resident of the island, when he brought his family to Nantucket from Salisbury, Massachusetts, in 1659. Lucretia's granddaughter and first biographer Anna Davis Hallowell suggested that Macy migrated seeking to improve his economic fortunes. But recent historians emphasize his search for religious freedom, noting that he was a Baptist seeking to distance himself from Puritan authorities in Boston, who charged him with harboring Quakers. These two motivations—religion and finance—remained the island's competing obsessions.[3]

Nantucket's origins as haven for nonconformists made it a "microcosm of religious New England" for the remainder of the seventeenth century. But this tolerance paradoxically allowed it to become more religiously homogeneous after 1700. Lacking an established church, Nantucket was "culturally Quaker" even before the arrival of missionaries like John Richardson to the island. In 1702, Lucretia's ancestor Mary Coffin Starbuck welcomed Richardson into her home. She soon joined the Society of Friends, and then became a preacher herself, converting her large extended family and drawing the island's remaining white inhabitants into the growing meeting.[4]

The Society of Friends first appeared in England in the seventeenth century, during a period of religious reformation that challenged the authority and perceived hypocrisy of the established Anglican church. This quest to recover an authentic Christian past led to the birth of dissenting groups like the Levellers, Diggers, and Puritans. Founded by a young Englishman named George Fox in 1652, the Quakers believed that every human being had the ability to know God, a doctrine known as "the inner light." Rather than relying on the Bible, Fox believed that individuals, through prayer, meditation, and quietness (Quaker meetings were silent until someone was moved to speak), had access to divine revelation. As a result, Quakers had no formal priesthood and they addressed each other as "thee" and "thou," rejecting titles that recognized social hierarchy. From the beginning of the Society, then, women could become ministers and elders.[5]

In order to balance the individualism inherent in Quaker doctrine, George Fox established a system of Monthly, Quarterly, and Yearly meetings to provide counsel and create consensus. Fox also urged meetings to appoint elders to ensure the sound doctrine and deportment of Quaker ministers. Traveling ministers had to prove their good standing by showing a "minute" (or record) issued by their meeting. Quaker egalitarianism had other limits. While women worshipped and preached with men, they were confined to separate and subordinate business meetings well into the nineteenth century. Few African Americans became members of the Society of Friends. If they applied for membership, they faced rejection; if accepted, they sat on segregated benches.[6]

Fox's 1645 refusal to serve in the Puritan leader Oliver Cromwell's New Model Army during the English Civil War served as the basis for the Quaker testimony against war. By 1660 the Society of Friends as a whole had adopted pacifism, arguing that through contemplation of the inner light Quakers had learned that the will of God abhorred war. After the restoration of Charles

II, they informed the king that Divine truth taught only peace: "the spirit of Christ, which leads us into all Truth, will never move us to fight and war against any man with outward weapons, neither for the kingdom of Christ, nor for the kingdoms of this world."[7]

In England and the American colonies, Quakers experienced persecution, as many viewed their doctrines as blasphemous or traitorous. Puritan and British authorities in America imprisoned, whipped, and even executed Quakers for their beliefs. Such extreme persecution, such as the hanging of Quaker convert Mary Dyer in Boston in 1660, prompted dissenters like Lucretia's ancestor Thomas Macy to hide Quakers from authorities. Despite this oppression, the presence of Society of Friends in the colonies grew from the 1650s on. This growth was furthered by the labors of traveling Quaker ministers, or Public Friends, including Fox himself in 1671–72. By 1681, the aristocrat William Penn, a convert to the Society of Friends, had convinced King Charles to give him a colony in the new world to serve as a refuge for Quakers. This colony became Pennsylvania.[8]

Known for their quietude and pacifism, the faith of Nantucket Quakers often stood in stark contrast to their worldly labors: the hunt for whales and harvest of whale oil. Whites soon discovered that the small island could not sustain the growing population of migrants and sheep, and they turned to whaling by the end of the seventeenth century. Whaling was a profitable but gory industry. After harpooning the whale, the seamen lanced the mammal, causing it to choke to death on its own blood. Then they towed the dead whale back to the ship for butchering, a process that lasted several days. During this time, historian Nathaniel Philbrick writes, "the decks were a slippery mess of oil and blood." Confronting the odd image of pacifists slaughtering the planet's largest mammals, Herman Melville described Nantucket's whaling captains as "sanguinary": "They are fighting Quakers; they are Quakers with a vengeance."[9]

Though not unaware of the contrast between the butchery of the whale fishery and the harmony of the meeting, these Nantucket captains exercised their conscience in other arenas. Despite their growing wealth, they condemned brazen display. J. Hector St. John de Crèvecoeur noted in his 1782 *Letters from an American Farmer*, "The inhabitants abhor the very idea of expending in useless waste and vain luxuries the fruits of prosperous labor."[10] Punishments for excess were light. When members did flaunt their material goods, the elders quietly sought an apology. But the problem of extravagance caused significant concern. In 1747, Quaker minister and anti-slavery advocate John Woolman visited the island and suggested that women's de-sire for luxuries provoked men into "acts of extreme and escalating cruelty," namely, the ruthless pursuit of whales.[11]

Significantly, their religious enthusiasm prompted their growing hostility to slave labor. In 1716, Nantucket Monthly Meeting, the local representative body of the Society of Friends, was the first to disavow slavery, an institution that remained legal on Nantucket until 1773 and in Massachusetts until 1783. Though the Society of Friends is known for its early testimony against slavery, throughout most of the eighteenth century many Quakers were ambivalent about abolition. Following an extended effort to achieve consensus, Philadel-phia Yearly Meeting, the most influential meeting in North America, waited until 1754 to issue a statement against slavery. A similar struggle took place among Nantucket Quakers. In 1775, the Nantucket meeting threatened to disown Benjamin Coffin, Lucretia's paternal grandfather, for owning slaves. The warning produced the desired result. In Coffin's subsequent manumis-sion of his slave Rose and her two sons, Bristol and Benjamin, he admitted the practice to be contrary to "true Christianity & divine injunction."[12]

Similarly, the Nantucket Quakers salved their consciences by touting their friendly relationship with the island's native population. Indeed, relations with Nantucket's approximately 3,000 Wampanoag Indians were relatively peaceful compared to those in other settlements in colonial North America, in no small part due to the efforts of Lucretia's forebears. Her great-great-great-great grandfather Peter Folger, known as the "learned and Godly Eng-lishman," served as a missionary on the island during the 1640s and 1650s. Folger then worked as an interpreter for Tristam Coffyn, one of the original purchasers of the island, who carefully cultivated the Wampanaog. Lucretia's granddaughter Anna Davis Hallowell wrote that Coffyn was "regarded as the patriarch of the colony, particularly by the neighboring Indians, with whom he maintained friendly relations from first to last."[13]

Nonetheless, English settlement devastated the Indians. The decline of the native community paralleled the rise of the whale fishery as the dominant industry of Nantucket. The initially collegial trade relationship between white settlers and Native Americans devolved into a complex cycle of credit, debt, and indenture that bound Wampanoag laborers to Nantucket whale boats. In 1746, the Indian community complained of unfair treatment, a charge that town leaders denied. In 1763, an epidemic devastated the Indian popula-tion of the island, reducing their already diminished numbers from 358 to 136, but by then the industry had grown beyond fishing for whales off the

Massachusetts coast to the quest for sperm whales in the South Atlantic, and after 1790 in the Pacific. As the Indian population died off and whaling voyages became longer and less inviting, white ship-owners and captains turned to African Americans and other off-islanders, white and non-white, for their labor force. But if Indians played a declining role in life on Nantucket, their status remained a significant issue for many Quakers, who viewed the native islanders with a mix of concern and condescension.[14]

In addition to Nantucket Quakers' anti-slavery advocacy and sympathy for the Wampanoag, they entertained relative equality among men and women. In most colonial American societies, women were by law and custom subordinate to their husbands. By contrast, on Nantucket, women had a great deal of spiritual and economic autonomy. This freedom flowed in part from the Quaker religion and culture. As Lucretia later recalled, boys and girls received the same education in the island's Quaker schools. And unlike most Protestant denominations in this period, the Society of Friends forbade a professional ministry, allowing anyone, including women like Mary Starbuck and later Lucretia Mott, to become preachers.[15]

But this independence also stemmed from the practical realities of whaling life. Because their husbands were frequently at sea, Crèvecoeur noted that "wives are necessarily obliged to transact business, to settle accounts, and, in short, to rule and provide for their families." Crèvecoeur cited the notorious Kezia Folger Coffin as an exemplar of Nantucket womanhood, contributing to her husband's financial success by her business sense. But as historian Lisa Norling points out, most Nantucketers disapproved of Kezia Coffin's pursuit of personal freedom. She left the Society of Friends after Quakers rebuked her for having a spinnet and for teaching her daughter to play the musical instrument. During the American Revolution, she engaged in smuggling and profiteering to such an extent that she was eventually charged with treason. As Lucretia herself would discover, Quakers might permit women relative independence, but they were far more ambivalent regarding absolute equality.[16]

*   *   *

Lucretia was born on a Nantucket that was recovering from the American Revolution. The island remained neutral during the war, partly because residents opposed violence, but also because they wanted to preserve the whaling industry, which depended on friendly relations with the British. This calculation proved mistaken; both the Americans and the British attacked their ships, leading to the destruction or confiscation of 85 percent of their fleet. On the eve of the revolution, 158 whalers sailed out of Nantucket. By war's end, only 24 ships were left in Nantucket harbor.[17]

Despite the island's official neutrality, many individuals in Lucretia's family took sides. Indeed, her cousin Benjamin Franklin was a leading revolutionary. But other Folgers were British sympathizers. Lucretia's mother, Anna Folger, was known as one of "Bill Folger's tory daughters" (he had six of them). According to Anna Davis Hallowell, William Folger lost his extensive holdings during the war, when colonials seized most of his ships. "Being declared a tory," Hallowell wrote, "he was no favorite with his companions; they liked to tell, at his expense, that the only thing he had ever found in his life was a jack-knife, sticking in a post above his head."[18] William's brother Timothy, who helped Benjamin Franklin chart the Gulf Stream, was charged with treason in 1780 alongside Kezia Folger Coffin (the charges were dropped). Perhaps chastened, Timothy Folger left the increasingly unfriendly atmosphere of Nantucket for Wales.[19]

After the war, Nantucketers quickly buried their loyalist past and seized burgeoning economic opportunities. Surviving his neighbors' enmity, William Folger turned to farming and raising sheep. When he died on Nantucket in 1815, he left a "mansion house" and an estate worth almost $6,000.[20] Lucretia's cousin, renowned whaling merchant William Rotch, was an early victim of revolutionary sentiment, losing his goods at the 1773 Boston Tea Party. Yet, after the war, Rotch was among the first to sail into British harbors flying the American flag. As the whale oil trade with Britain foundered during the Revolution, William Rotch conceived of a plan to sell seal skins to China. In 1785, his ship the *United States* returned from the Falkland Islands with 13,000 seal skins, Nantucket's first venture in the China trade. This initiative later proved fateful for both the Coffin and Folger families.[21]

By the time Lucretia's mother married her childhood sweetheart, Thomas Coffin, in 1790, Nantucket had begun to rebuild its economy. Thomas's older half-brother, Micajah Coffin, helped his brother begin his career as a mariner and merchant. One of Thomas's earliest voyages was in the ship *Lucy*, which sailed from Nantucket in 1785. In 1790, Micajah bought the 160–ton brig *Lydia* for £720, allowing Thomas to buy a 1/8 stake in the ship for an investment of £78. The brothers estimated that the *Lydia* could carry 800 barrels of sperm whale oil. With the oil priced at $1.08 per gallon in 1790, at 31.5 gallons per barrel, the *Lydia* could bring home a gross revenue of $35,280, equivalent today to $659,000.[22]

Thomas Coffin had reason to be optimistic about his fortunes; his decision to name his second daughter Lucretia, after an ancient Roman heroine, rather than giving her a family name, may have reflected his political hopes for the young republic. But in contrast to Thomas's private dreams, in 1793, the year of Lucretia's birth, Nantucket's cohesive Quaker community was disintegrating. Seeking economic opportunities elsewhere, many residents left the island, including Lucretia's Rotch cousins, who had all moved to New Bedford by 1795. Nantucket Monthly Meeting tried to prevent the exodus and recover the sense of community by withholding minutes for transfer to another meeting, necessary if a Quaker moved from an area bounded by one monthly meeting to another.[23] But the Quaker elders were also partly responsible for the growing disaffection of their fellow islanders. From 1754, when three members were disowned for grazing more than their fair share of sheep on the Nantucket commons, the number of disownments by the meeting grew exponentially. Nantucket Monthly Meeting disciplined only 90 members before 1770; in the following decade the meeting disowned 227 members. And the record disownments continued.[24]

Led by the clerk of the women's meeting, Sarah Barney, this local purge was part of a broader reformation in American Quakerism, and American Protestantism in general, which aimed to rid the society of sin. Often referred to as the "Great Awakening," this spiritual renewal, characterized by the ministries of Jonathan Edwards and George Whitfield, preceded the revolutionary politics of the late eighteenth century. But while other evangelical denominations like the Methodists sought converts by preaching individual salvation from sin, the Quakers aimed both to purify their discipline against worldly encroachment and, ironically, to protect their community from dissolution.[25]

Notably, the elders targeted marriage out of meeting (in other words, to non-Quakers). Though membership in the Society of Friends was easily achieved through birth or a statement of faith and desire for membership, out-marriage was a violation of Quaker discipline. As historian Lisa Norling notes, the meeting disproportionately targeted female Quakers who embraced new romantic ideas by marrying for love rather than duty to family or community. Nantucket's Quaker elders viewed young women's romantic sensibilities as dangerously individualistic.[26]

Although she was never a sentimental person, this era in Nantucket Quakerism made an indelible impression on Lucretia. She agreed with the reforms inspired by early Quaker abolitionist John Woolman, who rejected the growing materialism of American society. His testimony against slavery included a refusal to use any products of slave labor, such as the indigo dye used in clothing. But throughout her life she strongly opposed the Society of Friends' marriage policy, which condemned not only interfaith matches, but also the Quakers who approved or attended them. In an 1842 letter, Lucretia complained "Our veneration is trained to pay homage to ancient usage, rather than to truth, which is older than all. Else, why Church censure on marriages that are not of us?—on Parents conniving? On our members being present at such &c.? Oh, how our discipline needs revising—& stripping of its objectionable features."[27] Throughout her life, Mott criticized those who represented man-made rules as Divine truth, using religious authority to enforce their private interests and personal opinions.

As Quaker elders suppressed dissent at the turn of the nineteenth century, so too did Nantucket families, with lasting impact on Lucretia. She recalled her grandmother, Ruth Coffin Folger, as equally strict with her grandchildren. On one visit to her grandparents' home, Ruth informed Lucretia that because she had misbehaved, she would not be allowed to go on a hayride with her grandfather. Lucretia remembered this incident forty years later, writing to her sister and brother-in-law that, "What I had done left no impression, but her unkindness I couldn't forget."[28] Perhaps frustrated by their authoritarian streak, Lucretia never bonded with her Folger grandparents. Though both lived more than a decade into the nineteenth century, no correspondence with her mother's parents survives.

Lucretia's nagging memory of her grandmother's discipline shows how the larger crisis in religious authority on Nantucket influenced her views. In the letter recalling the incident, Lucretia wondered, "When shall we learn that retaliation is never in imitation of [']Him who causeth his sun to shine on the evil & on the good'?" Mott continued, criticizing Orthodox believers for crying "heresy" at every sign of religious progress, a favorite theme of hers, in this case referring to the controversial sermons of Unitarian radical Theodore Parker. As Nantucket's elders exerted their power, they not only prepared the ground for migration to friendlier shores, but also inspired dissenting voices, then and a generation later.[29]

Economically, the family prospered. Thomas Coffin continued to work with his brother Micajah, and their ship the *Lydia* made a number of profitable voyages in the 1790s. Captained by Micajah's son Zenas Coffin, who at his death left the largest individual fortune in Nantucket history, the *Lydia* sailed to the whaling grounds off the coast of Brazil in 1793–94. Though it is not recorded how much whale oil the *Lydia* brought back, a later voyage to Brazil procured 1,000 barrels.[30] By 1797, Thomas had earned enough money to purchase a large, elegant house on Fair Street for his growing family, which included Lucretia, her handicapped older sister Sarah or Sally (as was typical in this period, the family rarely mentioned her), and younger sister Eliza. As Nathaniel Philbrick points out, "where a person lived in Nantucket depended on his station in the whaling trade." While shipowners and merchants lived up the hill from the wharves on Pleasant St., captains lived on Orange Street, with its magnificent view of the harbor.[31] Fair Street lay between the two, perhaps indicating Thomas's aspirations.

While Thomas pursued his various business interests with Micajah Coffin, Anna, like many Nantucket wives, kept a small store selling "East India goods" (one street in Nantucket was known as Petticoat Lane in honor of this tradition). She operated the store from the left front room, while the right front room—the parlor—hosted many gatherings of the six Folger sisters and visiting Quaker preachers. The absence of their husbands and the requirements of their stores led many Nantucket women, including Coffin, to undertake trips to the mainland "to exchange oil, candles, and other staples of the island, for dry goods and groceries." Hallowell described these trips as "serious undertakings," if not quite so serious as a whaling voyage.[32]

In 1801, Anna Coffin opened her parlor to visiting Rhode Island Quaker minister Elizabeth Coggeshall. The previous year, Thomas Coffin had embarked on an extended voyage to the Pacific on the ship *Trial*. Coggeshall talked to Anna, Lucretia, and her siblings, who now included three-year-old Thomas and one-year-old Mary, "on the importance of heeding the inward monitor, and of praying for the strength to follow its directions."[33] This visit influenced Lucretia in two important ways. First, it cemented her commitment to the inner light, or individual conscience, above all other forms of religious and temporal authority. Though basic to Quaker principles, this belief became increasingly controversial over the course of the nineteenth century as Quakers, guided by the influence of evangelicalism, turned more to Scripture and church doctrine for authority.

Second, Lucretia was curious about Coggeshall's association with the infamous Hannah Barnard. In 1798, Coggeshall and Barnard embarked on a religious mission to England, which led to Barnard's 1802 disownment for

her rational, some said "deist," interpretation of Quaker theology. As Mott
later recalled, Barnard had been censured because "when she had preached
against war, as never having been prosecuted by the command of the Divinity, she had been accused of denying the authenticity of the Scriptures; and
whereas Jesus had faith in Moses, therefore she denied Jesus, and was an
infidel." In the view of English Quakers, Barnard's peace sermon challenged
a literal interpretation of the Old and New Testaments. The controversy surrounding Barnard's visit to England reverberated throughout American
Quakerism, paving the way for the Hicksite split of 1827, during which the
Society of Friends divided into two factions not only over the place of the
Scriptures and the inner light in Quaker belief, but also over the growing
power of the elders and the propriety of doing business with slavery.[34]

Though Coggeshall expressed her uneasiness with Barnard's views, her
visit to Nantucket brought Lucretia into vicarious contact with a female
minister who was not afraid to challenge the Quaker elders or their growing faith in the Bible, and who became an example for the young girl. This
influence was reinforced when Lucretia later attended Nine Partners Boarding School in Hudson, New York, run in part by Barnard in the 1790s. Yet
Barnard's story also suggested the costs of female dissent. Anne Mott, Lucretia's mother-in-law, sent her various papers relating to Hannah Barnard's
disownment, including "Hannah Barnard's creed, opposed to any 'scheme
of salvation.'" After reading (and undoubtedly rereading) them, Lucretia
passed these papers on to other Friends until they were lost.[35]

Like all Quaker children in Nantucket, Lucretia also learned to hate slavery and admire the economic principles underlying the whale fishery. At
Quaker school in 1797, she first saw British abolitionist Thomas Clarkson's
widely distributed image of the packed slave-ship *Brookes*, which made such
an impression that she told her children and grandchildren about it. First
printed by the thousands in 1789, the diagram, showing 482 slaves crowded
into a ship for transport from Africa to Jamaica, remained a powerful weapon
in the anti-slavery movement. The image probably arrived in Nantucket via
a Quaker ship captain. Nantucket's close economic ties to Britain intersected
with religious ties to English Quakers, who dominated the anti-slavery movement there. Alternatively, British sailors may have passed on copies of the
image to their American counterparts when socializing in port.[36]

Likewise, Lucretia's reader, Quaker Priscilla Wakefield's *Mental Improvement*, encouraged children's empathy by offering lessons on slavery in the
context of amusing and instructive discussions of natural history. Originally

published in London at the height of the British campaign to abolish the slave trade, the first American edition was published in Nantucket's sister port, New Bedford, in 1799. Written as a conversation between the fictional Harcourt family and their orphaned friend Augusta, the book sought to "excite the curiosity of young persons" regarding how cloth, paper, glass, metal, and other common objects were made. Appropriately for Nantucket's schoolchildren, *Mental Improvement* began with a discussion of whaling. When Augusta asks Mr. Harcourt why men undertake such dangerous voyages, he replies that they do it to earn a living, noting that whaling not only supplies Europe with candles and oil, but also encourages free trade and friendship among nations, "by which each party may reap advantage by interchanging the superfluous produce of different climes, and exercising the mutual good offices of love and kindness."[37] When the Harcourts' son Henry asks about sugar, Mr. Harcourt replies that it is farmed by "negro slaves," "snatched from their own country, friends, and connections, by the hand of violence, and power." After hearing Mr. Harcourt's account, the children conclude to abstain from all goods produced by slave labor, including sugar, rice, coffee, and calico, as had hundreds of thousands of British citizens. Sophia Harcourt, the oldest daughter, proposes to discuss maple sugar as a substitute for cane, describing the maple tree as a potential weapon against slavery: "A tree so various in its uses, if duly cultivated, may one day supply us with sugar; and silence the arguments of the planters, for a continuation of the slave trade."[38]

Though slaves were rare on Nantucket by the late eighteenth century, Lucretia and the other children on the island did have contact with free blacks. African Americans increasingly made up the crews of Nantucket whaling vessels (her uncle Micajah asked a New Bedford colleague to find him four African American sailors for the *Lydia* in 1801), making them part of the fabric of everyday life on the island. By the beginning of the nineteenth century, Nantucket town had an established black neighborhood, known as New Guinea. Lucretia's mother Anna Folger Coffin borrowed some of her many colorful and practical sayings (for instance, "Handsome they that handsome be") from a black man named Pompey. Anna also referred to "Black Amy," who lived with Lucretia's grandmother Folger, who "didn't like to be *told* to do, what she was just going to do." As the story suggests, in the Folger household, African Americans filled traditionally subordinate roles as servants and laborers, if not slaves. Yet even though "Black Amy" was a domestic servant, she had the luxury of grousing. Within the Folger household, whites and blacks, employers and workers, had thus negotiated the terms of free labor. Anna and her children recognized in Amy's complaint the desire for autonomy and respect. Years later, Anna Folger Coffin joined Lucretia at the founding meeting of the American Anti-Slavery Society.[39]

*   *   *

At the age of ten, Lucretia had a common but nevertheless traumatic experience, when the family believed her father had been lost at sea. Fearing the dangers of whaling voyages, Thomas Coffin had been anxious to abandon the business for some time. In 1788, off the coast of the French colony of Martinico (Martinique), Thomas reported to a passing ship that, "he had lost his mate and four hands, and when he left the coast, he had only one man able to keep the deck." In 1790, Thomas fitted the *Lydia* for whaling only after he and his brother Micajah concluded they could not succeed trading with France or England.[40] In 1800, Coffin followed the inspiration of William Rotch and turned to the China trade in South American sealskins, a line hardly less lucrative than whaling. In 1799, Mayhew Folger, Anna Coffin's younger brother, had captained one of the first ships solely devoted to sealing, the *Minerva*. On this one voyage, Folger and his crew accumulated 87,000 skins, gathered by clubbing the mammals to death. Though the practice was vicious, the profits were enormous: Folger brought back $40,000 from this trip (unsurprisingly, by 1807, when Folger commanded the *Topaz*, the seals had disappeared and he had to look for new sealing grounds).[41]

In 1800, Coffin invested in the ship *Trial* (or *Tryall*) with Moses Mitchell, Paul Gardner, Jr., and Thomas Starbuck. Mitchell and Gardner were members of the Richard Mitchell family, which had "a controlling interest in virtually all of Nantucket's ventures to China." Captained by Coffin, the *Trial* headed for the Juan Fernández island group off the coast of Chile. But rather than killing the seals themselves, Lucretia's biographer and granddaughter Anna Hallowell claimed, the crew allegedly "bought" skins in the Straits of Magellan and sent them to China by another ship. Whether an invention of Coffin's squeamish great-granddaughter, or an expression of Coffin's Quaker principles, the decision to send an initial load of seal skins on to China guaranteed the voyage's profits.[42]

This decision proved wise when the Spanish authorities in Valparaiso arrested Coffin the next year, condemning his vessel, charging a "violation of neutrality." In the 1790s, Spanish seizure of American ships was a common occurrence. The Spanish did not allow any foreign trade in their American colonies, though between 1796 and 1800 they allowed neutral ships from countries like the United States to bring goods owned by Spanish merchants into their ports. Nevertheless, extensive illegal trading persisted. Spain's enemy Britain pierced their defenses, seeking to turn the Spanish colonies into a market for their manufactured goods. American whaling vessels, whose Nantucket captains combined their close economic ties to Britain with increasing distrust of imperial and religious authority, may have aided their efforts. While the Spanish authorities suspected U.S. ships of bringing contraband into their ports (often under the guise of distress), the Americans suspected the Spanish of merely wanting to loot their ships. Often, the Spanish suspicions proved true. In 1801, Captain Swain of the *Mars* (another ship owned by the Mitchells and Paul Gardner, Jr.), tried to smuggle $2,000 worth of luxury goods into the port of Callou. Captain Swain's cargo was seized, though the ship was sent on its way. In 1808, Lucretia's uncle Mayhew Folger's ship, the *Topaz*, was also condemned on its way back from Pitcairn Island, where he had discovered the survivor mutineers of the *HMS Bounty*.[43]

Seeking to recover his investment in the *Trial*, Coffin stayed in Chile for three years, only returning when the courts ruled against him a final time. When he arrived home in Nantucket, "he learned that his family had heard nothing of him for more than a year, and had believed him lost."[44] During that time, Anna and her children undoubtedly hoped for Thomas's return. As time passed, however, they came to accept their lot as a familiar one in a whaling community, and began to grieve his passing. Anna and ten-year-old Lucretia, who took on the responsibilities of an eldest child, probably worried what would happen to the family without the economic support of a husband and father.

Ecstatic at their father's return, Lucretia and her sisters and brother begged Thomas Coffin to tell and retell the story of his journey. Like Captain Swain, Coffin may have believed he had been "robbed, plundered, and put into prison, set at liberty and ordered to leave the country without ever finding out what we had done to cause them to treat us in this manner." But, strikingly, the trip only enhanced the family's sense of tolerance. After boarding with a family in Valparaiso, Thomas Coffin offered a "warm-hearted defense of the Catholics of South America" on his return. He also taught his children to say "good morning" and "good night" in Spanish.[45] Coffin's return imbued the young Lucretia with a sense of optimism that came in handy in the long battle against slavery; Frederick Douglass later described one of her speeches as among the most "hopeful" he had ever heard.[46] More speculatively, the loss of her father's ship may have convinced Lucretia to privilege morality over profit. Throughout her adult life, Lucretia insisted her Quaker brethren renounce the consumption of and trade in slave goods like cotton and sugar. She aimed at replacing Melville's "sanguinary," greedy Quaker with something more consistent.

Even after her father's return, the seizure of the *Trial* brought the Coffins into the political and legal struggle to dismantle slavery and elevate free labor in northern states. In 1804, Stephen and Joshua Hall sued Thomas Coffin, Paul Gardner, Jr., and Thomas Starbuck for $200 in damages following the *Trial*'s confiscation. The plaintiffs, the Halls, had not sailed on the *Trial*, but their indentured servant James Mye, of Mashpee Wampanoag and free African American ancestry, had been hired by Coffin and his partners for 1/100th of the ship's profits, also known as a lay. After the court of Common Pleas ruled against them, the ship's partners appealed to the Massachusetts Supreme Court. The Halls asserted that Coffin had only pretended to hunt seals, intending instead to "take on board" and trade illicit (probably British) goods in the Spanish colonies of South America, knowing full well that his ship might be condemned. Deceived by Coffin, the Halls had thus been "wholly deprived of the expected and stipulated benefits and profits of a hundredth part of the skins which might have been acquired and sold aforesaid, and have lost the time, labor and service of the said James Mye from that time to this."[47]

As with whaling and sealing, Quaker traders managed to reconcile their religion to their business. Though the discipline of the Society of Friends forbade "fraudulent trade," this testimony did not prevent Quakers like Swain (or possibly Coffin) from smuggling, especially in a foreign land. The disciplinary assertiveness of Quaker elders on Nantucket, combined with the politics of the American Revolution, made many sea captains ambivalent about any authority except their own. And given their economic experiences during the Revolution, most Nantucket merchants abhorred any restrictions on their ability to trade. In their attempts to traffic with Spanish colonies, they became early missionaries of free trade, recently popularized by Adam Smith, deliberately violating Spain's mercantile restrictions in favor of their economic interests.[48]

Ultimately, the case rested not on the intricacies of international trade but on state laws regarding the status of Native Americans and the nature of indentured labor. In their appeal, Coffin and his partners cited a 1789 Massachusetts law placing the Mashpee Indians under the care of overseers and guardians. As the court interpreted the law, only the board of overseers of the poor had the power to apprentice Indian children. The guardians of the Indians, answerable to the overseers, also had the right to bind out impoverished Mashpee children. The Hall brothers produced a 1793 apprenticeship agreement between their father and the guardians of the Mashpee that bound Mye for the next ten years, until he reached age twenty one. Upon his death, Joshua Hall, the father, assigned his wife and sons "all right and title conveyed to him by the indenture to the service of James Mye." The Supreme Court ruled strongly in favor of Coffin and his partners. The judges objected to the Hall brothers' assumption of the terms of an indenture that they had not personally signed. They ruled the assignment "a nullity." But, the judges continued, even if the Hall brothers did have a formal indenture agreement with the Mashpee guardians, "they would not have had the right to send him [Mye] to the south pole, to the end of the globe, in their service." The court speculated that the guardians might have had this right, but then only if instruction in navigation was part of the agreement.[49]

In the decision, the judges, and by extension Coffin and his partners, objected to the idea that a person's labor (indeed the entire individual) could be owned by another, to the extent that labor could be traded, inherited, or hired out. In the view of the court, the Halls' proposed attempt to profit from James Mye's labor was akin to slavery. In challenging this illegal indenture, Coffin, Gardner, and Starbuck aided the triumph of free over slave labor in the North.[50] Whether young Lucretia was aware of her father's actions, the issues in *Hall v. Gardner*—race, native rights, slavery, patriarchal authority—remained at the very forefront of her consciousness until her death over seven decades later.

Lucretia's father's victory reflected the growing connection between Quaker interests and Quaker politics. As many historians have noted, Friends were the "vanguard of the industrial revolution"; their principled stance against slavery was conveniently attuned to their economic interests.[51] Nantucket crews were paid in shares, so if the ship's owners lost money, as in the case of the *Trial*, the sailors did as well. And, though whalers hired sailors of color, crewmen like Mye often bunked in segregated and cramped quarters and ate inferior rations.[52] Stranded in Chile, the *Trial's* crew were forced, like Thomas Coffin, to make their way home. Yet the freedom granted by *Hall v.*

Gardner allowed the young man of color to gain a measure of economic and personal independence. Mye's descendents were able to buy property after working as mariners and carpenters along Cape Cod. By 1850, Mye's son and namesake could proclaim his prosperity by purchasing a daguerreotype of himself wearing a top hat, frock coat, vest, and bowtie.[53]

The ordeal of the *Trial* ended Thomas Coffin's seafaring career and marked the conclusion of Lucretia's childhood on Nantucket. In 1804, Thomas moved his family to Boston, leaving behind the anxious life of the sea for a potentially more stable career as a merchant. He continued his business relationship with his brother, selling oil and candles that Micajah delivered to Boston, buying bricks to be sent back to Nantucket, or advancing funds to Micajah's associates.[54] In doing so, the Coffins became part of the larger migration from Nantucket in the early national period, joining the Rotchs and others who sought more economic opportunity, and perhaps greater religious freedom, elsewhere.

The move was more difficult for Lucretia than for the younger Coffin children. She left behind family, friends, and a place where she felt at home, whether on the wharves and beaches, or in the cobblestone streets and wood frame buildings. Anna Davis Hallowell wrote that her grandmother "always seemed to regard this first home with an affection different from that which she felt for any subsequent dwelling-place. In after years she taught her children, to the third generation, to cherish its traditions." Included in these Nantucket traditions, according to Hallowell, were "simplicity, moderation, temperance, and self-restraint in all material things" and "abhorrence of falsehood and injustice."[55] Though Lucretia never lived on the island again, she visited at least seven times, with her visits increasing in number as she got older. It was on Nantucket that she developed her conscience. Lucretia's education continued at Nine Partners Boarding School, where she became part of a larger family of Quaker reformers.

CHAPTER 2

Nine Partners

IN 1806, AT THE AGE OF THIRTEEN, LUCRETIA COFFIN left the common schools of Boston for Nine Partners Boarding School in Dutchess County, New York, about 200 miles west. Nine Partners provided Lucretia and other girls with an extraordinary education, giving her skills superior to those of most men at that time. But the school offered more than book learning; it further exposed her to the tensions between Quaker simplicity and prosperity, their anti-slavery testimony and the slave economy, their peculiarity and their connections to the larger society. In the spirit of eighteenth-century reformers, Quaker educators tried to purify their religion without losing members. Yet the balance between authority and the individual conscience was difficult to maintain. One's inner light might just as easily counsel rebellion as obedience, a problem for the school, the Society of Friends, and indeed for a liberal republic like the United States. As Lucretia grew from gifted student to teenaged teacher, from spirited adolescent to young wife, she was ideally placed to question the authority society bestowed according to age, gender, race, and faith.

After their move to Boston in 1804, Thomas Coffin and his family had prospered. Initially establishing a home on Milk Street, in 1806 the family moved to a house in the more desirable neighborhood of Green Street. The following year, Thomas purchased a brick house on Round Lane, later renamed William Street, for $5,600. His warehouse, located on Central and then Long Wharf, the largest of eighty wharves in the commercial city, was doing very well. Long Wharf accommodated large ships, carrying goods from up and down the eastern seaboard as well as from across the Atlantic and Pacific oceans.[1] Coffin had the means to send three of his children to

Quaker boarding school. Lucretia and her younger sister Eliza attended Nine Partners, while Thomas, Jr., went to Westtown in Chester County, Pennsylvania. Though the Nine Partners tuition was only £26 per year, this expense was a luxury most families denied their female children.[2]

Living only two years in Boston, Lucretia never identified with the city that would become a hotbed of radical abolitionism in the 1830s. After the religious homogeneity of Nantucket, Boston must have seemed a profoundly un-Quaker city. In the colonial period, Puritan Boston was known for its persecution of Quakers such as Mary Dyer. By the time the Coffins moved there, the city had become increasingly diverse and cosmopolitan, but it was still dominated by the established Congregational church.[3]

Lucretia's parents wanted to give their children a "guarded" Quaker education. Whatever their disagreements with Nantucket Monthly Meeting, Quakers such as the Coffins would have been worried about the impact of these outside influences on their children. In response to these concerns, Quaker boarding schools like Westtown and Nine Partners, near Poughkeepsie, were located in rural settings far from the temptations of the city.[4]

Founded by New York Yearly Meeting in 1796, Nine Partners offered "useful & necessary learning" and immersion in the religious culture of the Society of Friends. The founders of Nine Partners feared that Quaker children were not learning the history or principles of the Society of Friends, and as a result had become "prey to the Custom of the World and its habitudes." Seeking to prevent a new wave of disownments, Nine Partners School sought to discourage materialism and inculcate the Quaker doctrines of "obedience to the inward Principle of Light & Truth" and "Silence & Attention."[5]

Though it depended on income from tuition, Nine Partners accepted impoverished pupils. Quaker educators worried that poor children might abandon the religion to achieve economic success. In its place, the members of the school committee offered themselves as examples of pious upward mobility. As educator and Nine Partners founder James Mott, Sr.—grandfather of Lucretia's future husband—remarked to his colleague Joseph Tallcot, "I am willing to own, that a proper degree of what some call the world's polish, or, in other words, a remove from that rusticity that the children of some Friends manifest, is not incompatible with a religious character."[6] Like Nantucket Quakers, Mott believed that Quaker peculiarity should not stand in the way of success in business or education.

Most important for Lucretia, Nine Partners, following Quaker religious practice, was coeducational. Following the Revolution, female education expanded in the country at large. American educators viewed women as having an essential role in the new republic in raising their children to be virtuous citizens. As Benjamin Rush, a signer of the Declaration of Independence, stated, "The equal share that every citizen has in the liberty and the possible share he may have in the government of our country make it necessary that our ladies should be qualified to a certain degree, by a peculiar and suitable education, to concur in instructing their sons in the principles of liberty and government." But such calls for female education were not calls for equality. Rush wanted to educate women to be "republican mothers," capable of raising virtuous male citizens. Until the 1820s, when Emma Willard's Troy Female Seminary began instructing women in advanced subjects like math and science, most girls attended separate schools offering curriculums that included embroidery, drawing, and other feminine skills.[7]

At Nine Partners, male and female students received the same education in reading, writing, math, accounts, and grammar, but the curricula were not identical. Nine Partners was surrounded by a working farm, and the school's plan called for classes to include "Business & Domestic Employment" suitable to the age of the student. Business and domestic training were implicitly segregated by sex. Only girls enrolled in the sewing classes. Girls and boys also learned and lived in separate classrooms and quarters "to prevent any improper familiarities." As in Nantucket, however, Quakers viewed entirely distinct spheres for men and women as unnatural. So despite rules discouraging contact, no doubt instituted in part to appease parents, the school's founders welcomed "innocent & cheerful intercourse" among students under the appropriate supervision.[8]

The school's board, made up of male and female members of New York Yearly Meeting, was a *Who's Who* of the Quaker elite. Lucretia first met abolitionist Elias Hicks, whose ministry divided the Society of Friends in the 1820s, when she was a student at Nine Partners. Hicks was a founding member of the school committee. Before her disownment in 1802, Hannah Barnard, the "deist" pacifist female preacher, also served on the board, as did her traveling companion Elizabeth Coggeshall. Quaker educators James Mott, Sr., and Joseph Tallcot were longstanding members of the committee, and both served as superintendent of the school.[9]

Mott, Lucretia's future grandfather-in-law and the superintendent of Nine Partners during her attendance, profoundly influenced her. Under his direction, the school's plan called for teachers to be kind and affectionate with their students, using "as little chastisement" as possible. Mott articulated his views for a larger audience in 1816 in *Observations on the Education of Children; and Hints to Young People on the Duties of Civil Life*. He advised parents to avoid both overindulgence and severity in raising their children. In Mott's view, "when the dread of punishment predominates, the disposition is generally artful," a position articulated by critics of slavery as well as opponents of corporal punishment. Instead, he advised parents to treat the child as a companion and to teach by example: "the necessity and propriety of practicing on all occasions, the most scrupulous integrity, liberality, fair dealing, and honour, consistent with the rule of doing unto others, on all occasions as they would be done unto, ought to be early and forcibly inculcated, by precept and example." Mott extended his insights on childrearing into public life, where he urged young people "to remember others, and fulfill the obligations we are under of doing good." Like other Quakers, Mott advocated modesty, moderation, and charity, but he also preached democracy. He believed in respecting others by avoiding bigotry and condescension.[10]

James Mott, Sr.'s egalitarian approach to education was not unusual in the age of revolution. His pamphlet was one entry in a flood of child-rearing tracts published during the first two decades of the nineteenth century. Influenced by John Locke and other philosophers, these experts argued that children too had inalienable rights that should not be abused. Instead of physical discipline, they advised parents to use psychology and reason to teach their children the essential values of morality, self-control, and good citizenship. British writer Maria Edgeworth urged parents to practice preventive methods rather than creating unreasonable restrictions. For example, she suggested parents place valuable china and tempting sweets out of reach. Teach habits of obedience, she recommended, by asking children to do things they were already inclined to do. Once children were old enough, parents should use reason. In this way, Edgeworth wrote, "children, who have for many years experienced, that their parents have exacted obedience only to such commands as proved to be ultimately wise and beneficial, will surely be disposed from habit, from gratitude, and yet more from prudence, to consult their parents in all the material actions of their lives."[11] Despite the proliferation of such advice books, Lucretia especially valued Mott's words. Later, as a new wife and mother, she corresponded regularly with her husband's grandfather. She read his "instructive" and "useful" book when it was published, and later reread it when she had a house full of young children.[12]

As Anna Coffin prepared Lucretia and Eliza for the journey to Nine Partners, she followed the school's guidelines for simplicity. Each girl packed 2 bonnets, 1 cloak, 2 gowns for winter and 2 for summer, 4 handkerchiefs to wear around her neck, 4 shifts, 4 pairs of stockings, and 4 aprons. The girls brought no books or money, as the school discouraged inappropriate reading material and class distinctions among students. The school also advised parents not to demand frequent visits from their children. The school committee regarded such visits as disruptive to the education of their students and potentially dangerous to their model Quaker community. Just a few decades earlier, Quaker reformers had accused parents of encouraging their children's desire for material rather than spiritual happiness. Indeed, returning students might bring worldly influences, or, alternatively, lose the "polish" that Nine Partners wished to instill. The Coffins carefully followed the school's instructions; Lucretia and Eliza not only missed the birth of their youngest sister Martha in 1806, they did not go home for two years.[13]

Nine Partners provided Lucretia and Eliza with a substitute family of like-minded Quakers. Lucretia recognized the school's reader, *Mental Improvement*, and the illustration of the slave-ship *Brookes*, from her school days on Nantucket, but she was also exposed to new ideas. Despite the school committee's concern that their students read only Quaker authors or the Bible, Susanna Marriott, a British Quaker in charge of the sewing room, introduced Lucretia and her peers to the didactic poetry of William Cowper. Lucretia quoted Cowper's most famous poem, "The Task," from memory throughout her life, applying its criticism of blind adherence to social norms to the problem of slavery and women's rights:

> Such dupes are men to custom, and so prone
> To reverence what is ancient, and can plead
> A course of long observance for its use,
> That even servitude, the worst of ills,
> Because delivered from sire to son,
> Is kept and guarded as a sacred thing.

Importantly, Cowper also wrote anti-slavery poems, which Marriott, an abolitionist, probably shared with her students. "The Negro's Complaint" began,

> Forced from home and all its pleasures
> Afric's coast I left forlorn
> To increase a stranger's treasures
> O'er the raging billows borne.

The image of the African being taken from home for the profit of another appealed to this Nantucket Quaker, who disapproved of the accumulation and display of wealth for its own sake. Another Cowper poem, "Pity for Poor Africans," reinforced Priscilla Wakefield's admonition to boycott slave produce:

> I pity them greatly, but I must be mum,
> For how could we do without sugar and rum?
> Especially sugar, so needful we see;
> What! Give up our desserts, our coffee, and tea?

Marriott later taught New York suffragist and reformer Emily Howland, who likewise credited Marriott for introducing her to the anti-slavery movement.[14]

As the founders intended, Lucretia's instructors taught Quaker doctrines, of which opposition to slavery was one. Students learned how the Society of Friends differed from other Christian denominations:

> We decline the use of ordinances, viz. baptism and the sacrament,
> believing that worship can be acceptably performed in silence; that
> war and oaths are unlawful; that no human appointment can qualify
> a person to preach the gospel; and our ministers receive no pay for
> preaching.

They acknowledged and defended their peculiarities of "plainness of dress, simplicity of language, and avoiding complimentary expressions," and their belief that all days of the week were equally holy.[15]

The Society of Friends believed in religious and human progress, and part of this progress was the recognition of slavery as wrong. Students at Nine Partners were drilled in the success of the British abolition movement, which by 1807 had succeeded in abolishing the slave trade (the United States followed suit in 1808). The example of British abolitionist Thomas Clarkson taught Lucretia and other students that "zeal and perseverance, in a right cause, seldom fail of success." Students also learned that many Quakers continued to use the products of slave labor, and attributed this lapse, as did Cowper, to the "bias of custom." But they learned the immorality of slave products from their teachers. James Mott Sr. limited his family's consumption of sweets to maple sugar, produced without the aid of slaves.[16]

Students also studied the Bible, but Friends disagreed over the appropriate place of Scripture and the inner light in their discipline. Joseph Tallcot, former superintendent of Nine Partners, promoted the reading of the Bible in all schools, Quaker and non-Quaker alike; most Protestants in early nineteenth-century America accepted the wisdom of this position without question. Other Quakers, however, believed that the Scriptures were subordinate to the inner light. Abigail Mott, a member of the Nine Partners school committee, wrote: "attend still more to that divine principle in your own hearts . . . it is by submitting to the teachings of this inward monitor, that we both learn, and are enabled to fulfill, our duty to God and to one another."[17] In the ensuing decades, such divisions among Friends grew increasingly important. Like most American Protestants, Lucretia and other Quakers had a deep familiarity with the Bible, reciting passages from memory. But they declined to allow their knowledge to become veneration, as it had among mainstream Protestants.

Such immersion in Quaker values shaped students into devoted believers, but it also provided the basis for the individual subjectivity that had threatened religious unity throughout their history. For fun, Lucretia and her friends played "meeting," as other American children might play church or school, imitating the women's meeting for discipline by monitoring their schoolmates' behavior. Such games trained young women for leadership in the Society of Friends, and reinforced the individual moral authority of the inward monitor. Following their conscience, each Quaker student had the ability—even the duty—to take a position on issues of pedagogy and doctrine. As a result, her education gave Lucretia a sense of agency and purpose that led her to clash with her Quaker teachers.[18]

Nine Partners struggled with one of the signal questions of post-Enlightenment reform, namely how best to replace the punishment of the physical body with the discipline of the mind. Eighteenth-century British utilitarian Jeremy Bentham argued that prisons could control convicts more efficiently if they arranged their cells in a circle with a jailer at the center. Believing themselves watched at all times, prisoners would feel compelled to behave. Bentham saw his so-called "Panopticon" as humane innovation that reduced the need for brutal punishments. Though inspired by the same premises, Quakers took a very different approach. In Philadelphia, reform-minded Friends built the Walnut Street Prison in 1790, which had workshops for lesser criminals, but sixteen individual cells for harder cases. These inmates were given Bibles and kept in solitary confinement, not as punishment, but to encourage contemplation and redemption. The problem with these approaches soon became apparent. Authorities relied less on corporal punishment, but observation encouraged paranoia and guilt, while solitude induced insanity.[19]

Lucretia's experience at Nine Partners led her to question this—in the words of philosopher Michel Foucault—"perfect exercise of power." James Mott, Sr., advised teachers at the school to confine children as punishment, but urged that "they ought always to be confined in sight, and never where there is a danger of their being affrighted." But despite the superintendent's instructions, Lucretia saw one male student locked in a dark closet and given only bread and water as sustenance. She was so disturbed by this that she violated rules separating boys from girls, and "contrived to get into the forbidden side of the house where he was, and supply him with bread and butter under the door." Lucretia later commented on the Philadelphia prison system, "There has always seemed to me great cruelty in doing such violence to a man's social nature, to say nothing of the effect on the nervous system, as to place him in solitary confinement." Convinced of the moral capabilities of every individual and fearing for the impact of punishment on the criminal, Lucretia advocated persuasion as means of inducing good behavior.[20]

Lucretia became increasingly aware of the tension between authority and rebellion. In the winter of 1809, she would have learned that her uncle, Captain Mayhew Folger, had discovered the sole surviving mutineer from the HMS *Bounty*, John Adams, also known as Alexander Smith.[21] In 1807, Captain Folger's sealer, the *Topaz*, departed Nantucket for the South Pacific and eventually Canton (now Guangzhou). The first part of his voyage was relatively uneventful. Folger placed two members of his crew in stocks and irons, but otherwise the crew remained in good order. Then the *Topaz* met bad weather, and after two months of rough passage the crew docked in Tasmania for repairs and provisions. Island-hopping looking for seal grounds, Folger headed for Pitcairn, where he discovered the *Bounty* mutineer, who presented him with the *Bounty*'s compass and chronometer. Off the coast of Chile, the Spanish seized the *Topaz* and took it to Valparaiso, where Folger saw his brother-in-law's brig, the *Trial*, still sitting in the harbor and passed word to a British officer of Adams's presence on Pitcairn. While Folger waited, 21 of his 49 crewmen deserted, and he went into debt trying to support the rest. In 1809, a full year after his discovery of the *Bounty* mutineer and the subsequent seizure of his ship, Folger finally recovered the *Topaz* from the Spanish and won $44,000 in damages.[22] Though Mayhew Folger was a ship captain like William Bligh, he clearly sympathized with the *Bounty*'s rebellious crew, calling Adams a "worthy man."[23] From Folger, Lucretia learned that rebellion was a legitimate response to undeserved and arbitrary power. If authority was necessary for the safety of a ship (or society), then it had to be tempered with kindness, morality, and justice.

In the protective politically and theologically liberal community of Nine Partners, the teenage Lucretia Coffin blossomed. She was smart and vivacious, a petite young woman with a striking brow, large bright eyes, and brown hair. Lucretia's radiant personality enabled contemporaries to describe her as attractive and even beautiful. She excelled in school, and by 1808 she was working as an assistant to Deborah Rogers, the head female teacher. Nine Partners was initially intended for students from ages seven to fourteen, but the previous year, possibly for financial reasons, the school decided to allow older students to continue. Since fifteen-year-old Lucretia had mastered the academic subjects available, she moved into teaching. Outside dame or finishing schools, female teachers were still unusual in the United States. As historian Joan M. Jensen notes, "Quakers were not the only women to teach but they were among the first." Two decades later, Catharine Beecher pioneered teaching as a profession for all women. The transition Mott made from student to teacher became commonplace. Thirteen-year-old Harriet Beecher (later Stowe) entered her older sister's Hartford Female Seminary in 1824, becoming a teacher in 1829.[24]

As an assistant teacher, Lucretia formed close friendships with other instructors at Nine Partners. Her friend and future sister-in-law Sarah Mott, granddaughter of superintendent James Mott, Sr., described the "good times" they had at school: "there are several teachers & assistants on each side & after the cares of the day, we can enjoy an hour or two of fine converse around the sitting room fire, with a double relish." Like Lucretia, Sarah became a teacher, but she was close in age to her pupils, whom she described as "lovely girls, who interest every feeling of my heart for them." In addition to Sarah Mott, Lucretia's school chums included Sarah's cousin Phebe Post (later Willis).[25]

Despite the wishes of the founders, this social and intellectual camaraderie sometimes included romance, as it soon did for Lucretia and James Mott, Sarah's twenty-year-old brother, another teacher at the school. A tall, blond, blue-eyed but reserved junior male teacher, James already knew Lucretia through his sister Sarah; Lucretia had visited their home on Long Island during a school vacation. Drawn to her passion and her intelligence, James invited Lucretia to join a French class that he and other teachers organized, where their flirtation deepened.[26]

James and Lucretia met and fell in love during a transitional period in American courtship. For most of the eighteenth century, parents exerted enormous influence over their child's choice of spouse. But after the American Revolution, young people gained more autonomy, choosing their mate based on love and mutual attraction with little parental interference. Because of their emphasis on the inner light, members of the Society of Friends emphasized the importance of individual choice and true love much earlier than other American Protestants.[27]

Yet James and Lucretia undoubtedly sought their parents' approval before their courtship progressed. As in other parts of the religion, the Society of Friends sought to balance individualism with the authority of the meeting. Historian Barry Levy describes Quaker marriage discipline as a "spiritual obstacle course." Quakers disapproved of premarital sex (which could lead to disownment), so early in their relationship young couples were instructed to notify parents and other senior Friends of their intentions. If these elders approved, the couple announced their engagement to their meeting, which then undertook an investigation of the match that could last as long as two months. Of course, the marriage discipline also included harsh rules for marrying outside meeting or otherwise disobeying the community. The Coffins and Motts approved the union from the beginning; Thomas Coffin had, after all, already entrusted his daughter to the Mott family.[28]

Teaching alongside her future husband, Lucretia expressed her first frustration at sexual inequality. In 1805, when he was seventeen, James Mott, Jr., became an assistant teacher. By May 1807 he was making £70 per year as a teacher at Nine Partners, but Deborah Rogers, the head female teacher, made only £40 per year. One year later, Mott was making £100 per year, while Lucretia, as Deborah Rogers's assistant, worked without pay. Only in 1809 did Rogers receive a raise to £100, but by that time James earned £250. James's salary may have reflected nepotism rather than sexism, but Lucretia clearly saw the gap as an example of male privilege. The outraged Lucretia "resolved to claim for myself all that an impartial Creator has bestowed."[29]

If Lucretia had already shown signs of rebelliousness, her choice of partner was conventional. Five years older than Lucretia, James Mott was raised in North Hempstead, Nassau County, then known as Cowneck. Due to the insular Quaker world of Long Island, probably similar to that of Nantucket, James's parents' were distant cousins, direct descendants of Adam Mott, a Quaker who settled in Hempstead in 1655, and his second wife Elizabeth Richbell, whose family owned the first land patent to Mamaroneck, in

Westchester County, directly across Long Island Sound. James's father Adam Mott was the son of Sarah Willis and Adam Mott, Sr. Anne Mott, James's mother, was the daughter of Mary Underhill and James Mott, Sr.

Like their neutral pacifist coreligionists on Nantucket, Long Island Quakers struggled during the American Revolution. Adam Mott, Sr., a farmer, was robbed by colonials and commanded by the British to furnish their army with wood. James Mott, Sr., a prosperous merchant in New York City prior to the Revolution, bought a mill in Mamaroneck, where he retreated from the British-controlled city in 1776. But his daughter Anne vividly recalled life in Westchester County during the Revolution, when she hid cattle from thieves and concealed the profits from coffee hidden in her father's mill.[30]

Slavery also played a prominent role in James Mott's family history. According to Lucretia's granddaughter, the family genealogist, "most Friends" on Long Island held slaves prior to the American Revolution. New York Yearly Meeting prohibited slaveholding in 1774, but, as historian Graham Hodges writes, in an area with a large African American population of 21,000, "New York Quakers lagged behind their brethren elsewhere in the colonies in shedding their commitment to slaveownership." The natural rights ideology of the Revolution helped further anti-slavery sentiment. Black New Yorkers participated in revolutionary uprisings and put pressure on their owners to free them. British influence also may have prompted Quakers to manumit their slaves. In Virginia in 1775, British commander Lord Dunmore issued his famous proclamation offering freedom to slaves who fought for the king. By 1776, the British army, supported by black soldiers, occupied New York City. As Hodges notes, "New York under British rule became an emporium for black freedom." Accordingly, in 1776, James's paternal great-grandmother Phebe Willets Mott Dodge, known as Grandmother Dodge, a traveling minister in the Society of Friends, freed her slave Rachel, after years of "concern of mind on account of holding negroes in bondage."[31] Dodge's act was the first manumission in Westbury (Long Island) Monthly Meeting. In 1778, Dodge's neighbor and friend Elias Hicks, then thirty years old, freed a slave named Ben. These belated manumissions still put Quakers ahead of their fellow New Yorkers, who instituted a gradual emancipation plan in 1799. On July 4, 1827, the state of New York released all slaves in its jurisdiction. But liberty remained unattainable for many former slaves. The children of Sojourner Truth, a former slave from Ulster County, were bound as apprentices as late as 1851.[32]

In 1785, James's parents Adam and Anne Mott married in Mamaroneck.

After their wedding, they lived with Adam's parents while he ran a flour mill in what is now Port Washington. Their second child and first son James was born in 1788. By 1790, they were living on their own on a farm near the mill. According to their great-granddaughter, Anna Davis Hallowell, the Motts prospered: "The simple, frugal, diligent habits of this rural life; the kindly, gentle manners and self-watchfulness inherited from many Quaker ancestors, added to much intellectual culture and refinement, made a model household."[33] As on Nantucket, religious beliefs seemed to further, rather than impede, Quaker ability to prosper. Adam and Anne Mott strictly followed Quaker guidelines for simplicity in dress and manner and were respected members of their religious community. Adam served as clerk of the Westbury men's meeting for business, while Anne served as clerk of the women's meeting. In 1803, the family moved to Mamaroneck to live on a farm adjacent to that of James Mott, Sr., becoming partners in his mill. But Jefferson's 1807 embargo of Britain and France caused the family some financial difficulty, and so young James became a teacher at Nine Partners.[34]

According to Lucretia, James Mott, Jr., "was never in his element" as a teacher, as he preferred not to be the center of attention. Once Lucretia and James decided to make their life together, Lucretia arranged for the couple to live with her family in Philadelphia, where they had moved in 1809. Thomas Odiorne, a Massachusetts native who brought the new and booming business in cut nails to Pennsylvania, had invited Thomas Coffin, whom he probably met through his second wife, Mary Hussey of Nantucket, to run one of his manufactories outside Philadelphia. Coffin invested $20,000 of his own money in the concern, and initially the factory, at French Creek in Chester County, did well, with sales reaching $100,000 per year. Coffin also continued his career as a merchant, establishing a commission, or wholesale, business in the city. Though James had no special experience with business, Thomas Coffin helped his daughter by inviting his son in-law to become a partner in the venture with an investment of $3000.[35]

Philadelphia had long been the hub of the Society of Friends in America, and the Coffins and Motts felt comfortable in the City of Brotherly Love, where Quakers still had significant, if declining, influence. Important for Lucretia, Philadelphia was home to a prominent anti-slavery movement, as well as the largest community of free blacks in the northern states. The most important anti-slavery society in the country, the Pennsylvania Abolition Society, had been founded in Philadelphia in 1775, five years before Pennsylvania became the first state to abolish slavery. Founded by Quakers, the organization grew to include prominent lawyers, politicians, and business-men. Benjamin Franklin served as the society's president in the 1780s. In the ensuing decades, Philadelphia became a "city of refuge" for blacks flee-ing slavery from below the Mason-Dixon Line. The Pennsylvania Abolition Society offered legal assistance to these fugitives and otherwise promoted the end of slavery through moderate legal and political means. As a con-sequence, by 1810, people of African descent numbered 9,656, 10.5 percent of the total population of 91,877. James Mott joined the Abolition Society; Lucretia did not. Such organizations were closed to women and African Americans, and Lucretia's new life as a wife, mother, and schoolteacher, left her little time for activism. But the city put her in contact with slavery and anti-slavery in ways that her childhood in Nantucket and adolescence in New York had not.[36]

In 1810, James wrote to his parents of his plans to make his connection to the Coffin family permanent. Of going into business with Thomas Coffin, he shared his reasoning: "when we take into view that the business here is an established one, and the person with whom connected, a man of experience and prudence, I believe you will say with me that this is the most eligible." Like many young businessmen, James took into account Thomas Coffin's reputation in the community. In a credit economy, economic success was built on such personal ties. He also informed his parents that he and Lucretia had decided to announce their intention to marry in their monthly meeting, setting off the period of inquiry by the meeting. Both parents gave their final approval, and James and Lucretia declared their engagement to their fellow Friends on February 20, 1811. Though James expressed his anxiety, he "felt as calm and composed during the whole operation as if I had been speaking before so many cabbage stumps."[37]

After their monthly meeting investigated the suitability of the match, James and eighteen-year-old Lucretia were married on April 10, 1811, in Pine Street Meeting House, with both families in attendance. Like other Quaker couples, the two were married in a ceremony without a presiding minister to "consecrate or legalize the bond." Instead, they stood before the meeting and vowed to be "loving and faithful." Though it would become fashionable for nineteenth-century feminists in other denominations to drop the promise of obedience in marriage vows, there was no such clause in the Quaker ceremony because there was no, in Lucretia's words, "assumed authority or admitted inferiority; no *promise of obedience*." "Their independence is equal," she con-tinued, "their dependence mutual, and their obligations reciprocal."[38]

Yet the backdrop for egalitarian Quaker marriages was a patriarchal marriage relation established by English and American common law. No matter how progressive her vows, Lucretia Mott was officially a *feme covert*. As an unmarried *feme sole*, she had enjoyed an independent legal status and the right to control her earnings. But after her wedding her husband became her legal, financial, and political caretaker. Mott and other married women were "covered" by their husbands.[39]

Lucretia and James shared a deep physical as well as emotional connection throughout their marriage. Under the close supervision of Lucretia's parents, they may have kissed or shared some physical intimacy before their marriage, but they probably did not have sex. Though premarital pregnancy rates spiked in this period of American history due to a transition in courtship practices, Lucretia did not give birth until a very respectable sixteen months after her wedding. Their sexual relationship lasted for many years. She had her sixth and last child at age thirty-five, when she and James celebrated their seventeenth anniversary. Lucretia and James were together constantly, so few letters survive to document their relationship. But after James's death in 1868, a devastated Lucretia refused to sleep in the bedroom they had shared. She once described her feelings for James as "perfect love."[40]

The young couple's anticipation of owning a "house of their own" faltered as their early marriage coincided with a turbulent economy. Jefferson's embargo, intended to insulate America from the turbulence of the Napoleonic Wars, had hurt many northeastern merchants. The growing possibility of war between the U.S. and England furthered the economic disruptions. As James reported to his parents, "Many failures have taken place, and no doubt many more will. All confidence is destroyed, and those who have money keep it in their own hands."[41]

These economic troubles also affected the whaling industry, prompting a visit from Lucretia's uncle, Mayhew Folger, and his family. In addition to sharing his complete adventures on the *Topaz*, Folger introduced the Coffins and Motts to "Ohio fever." With business in Philadelphia stagnant and war with England begun, many looked to Ohio as a place of opportunity. In 1812, Thomas and Anna Coffin traveled to Massillon, Ohio, to consider moving there permanently. Though the Coffins returned to Philadelphia, Folger decided to relocate, living there until his death in 1828. James considered migrating with the Folgers as he searched for a way to provide a "comfortable living" for his family. Instead of heading for Ohio, however, James, pregnant Lucretia, and their daughter Anna, born in August 1812, moved to

Mamaroneck in early 1814, where James worked at his Uncle Richard Mott's mill. After six months, the young family, including their new son Thomas Coffin Mott, born in July 1814, returned to Philadelphia, where James found work in a wholesale plow store. James and Lucretia's anxiety over their finances was partially relieved by their joy over their growing family.[42]

Even when distracted by domestic concerns, Lucretia and James always paid close attention to race relations in Philadelphia. Despite the city's reputation for anti-slavery, the situation of free blacks was far from equal. In a brief moment of racial cooperation during the War of 1812, white Philadelphians asked African American men for help in fortifying the city against potential British invasion. But whites also feared that the free black population would increase as the city became a destination for fugitive slaves. In January 1815, James wrote to his parents that southern Quakers and slaveholders had begun to bequeath slaves to Philadelphia Quakers and the Pennsylvania Abolition Society in an effort to free them. James was "undecided"—torn between the possibility of determining the "future situation of blacks in the Southern States" and violating Quaker testimony against slaveholding. A careful man, James believed that Quakers needed to consider this moral dilemma before deciding whether it was acceptable to own slaves, even if ownership was only a means to free them. James and Lucretia were also aware of the Northern Liberties mob that burned down a black church later that year, presaging the racial violence that characterized antebellum Philadelphia.[43]

Meanwhile, the financial problems of Thomas Coffin and James Mott grew worse. Coffin lent some money to a friend, John James, who defaulted on the loan. As Coffin spiraled into debt, his reputation suffered. Lucretia later recalled that her father's accounts "were disputed by the Odiornes, because of their inability to pay." When Thomas died suddenly from typhus in February 1815, he left his family thousands of dollars in debt and in the midst of a lawsuit. As James Mott wrote, "my business is suddenly changed." In addition to the four members of their nuclear family, Lucretia's mother Anna Coffin, her older sister Sarah, and younger siblings Thomas and Mary continued to reside with them (her sister Eliza had married Philadelphia merchant Benjamin Yarnall in 1814). In order to support the family, Anna opened a small store as she had on Nantucket, while James continued to search for a meaningful career, working as a bookkeeper for Philadelphian John Large at a salary of $750 per year; he would eventually earn $1,000 a year in the same position. Despite having two young children in the house, Lucretia also contributed to the family's income, teaching in a Quaker school affiliated with

Pine Street Meeting, where students paid $7 per quarter to attend. In April 1817, the school had ten students.[44]

Though the family rebounded quickly after Thomas Coffin's death, they soon faced another tragedy. In the spring of 1817, Lucretia and her son Thomas came down with high fevers. Lucretia survived, but their "active, fat, and rosy-cheeked" darling Thomas died at the age of two years and nine months. His last words were "I love thee, mother." Lucretia, weak from the same illness, was bereft. James wrote platitudes to his parents about the "inscrutable wisdom" of the Almighty and endeavoring "patiently to bear the stroke," but Lucretia never resigned herself to little Thomas's death. Her grief prompted a religious awakening that would eventually lead her into the ministry. Rejecting the pessimistic Christianity that saw humans as sinners with little ability to comprehend the divine, Lucretia believed that all individuals had the ability to know and understand God's plans. Though medicine had not yet progressed to the point that it could have cured her son, she believed that reason and science, rather than superstition, were the answer to the world's ills. This powerful belief allowed her to return to teaching soon after little Thomas's death. She only stopped teaching when another daughter, Maria, was born in 1818.[45]

At twenty-five, Lucretia was a loving wife and mother and a devout member of the Society of Friends. But her "guarded" Quaker education at Nine Partners had also prepared her to be an independent actor in conflicts that would soon divide the nation: the province of religion in a society rapidly disestablishing its churches, the place of slavery in a free country, and the status of women as citizens in a republic that did not grant them full rights. Nine Partners also introduced Lucretia to a broader Quaker community, stretching from Nantucket to New York to Philadelphia. But this close-knit religious group was about to come apart. Following Tommy's death, Mott sought spiritual and intellectual solace. Her personal search brought her into the heart of the social and religious conflict that severed the Society of Friends in America.

CHAPTER 3

Schism

LUCRETIA MOTT BEGAN HER LONG CAREER as a Quaker minister at Twelfth Street Monthly Meeting in Philadelphia. In 1818, a year after her son Thomas's death, she rose and prayed publicly for the first time. In her sweet and melodious voice, Lucretia appealed for strength to enable Friends to stand firm against the enticements of the larger world: "As all our efforts to resist temptation and overcome the world prove fruitless, unless aided by Thy Holy Spirit, enable us to approach Thy Throne, and ask of Three the blessing of Thy preservation from all evil, that we may be wholly devoted to Thee and Thy glorious cause."[1] After her death, Mott's meeting remembered her adherence to "the simple faith of the society." They recalled her ability to quote from Scripture and her emphasis on "practical righteousness" and "the sufficiency of divine law." These circumspect women avoided mention of their own passionate opposition to Mott's sermons over the course of her ministry.[2]

In 1819, during one of her first trips as a visiting Friend, Lucretia traveled with Sarah Zane to Virginia, to attend Quarterly Meeting at Hopewell, twenty-four miles southeast of Richmond. There she met Edward Stabler of Alexandria, a regular clerk of Baltimore Yearly Meeting and friend of the increasingly divisive minister Elias Hicks. At Baltimore Yearly Meeting, Stabler had a reputation for convening a close circle of six allies to stay up all night discussing strategy, an effective way to influence the direction of debate in the larger body. Mott had a similar experience, noting that "He is one of the very interesting men. We lodged at the same house, and sat up very late to hear him talk." Mott also observed the surrounding countryside, writing "the sight of the poor slaves was indeed affecting." The Virginians she met reassured her of the contentment of the slaves, citing kind treatment from their masters, but Lucretia's Quaker education taught her to question such pleasantries.[3]

In 1821, at age twenty-eight, Mott became an approved minister in the Society of Friends. Though any Quaker could speak in meeting if moved by the spirit, monthly meetings recorded the names of especially gifted preachers in their minutes. By issuing a minute, they also authorized these ministers to preach at distant meetings. The Society of Friends recognized female ministers regardless of age, marital status, or number of children, valuing their spiritual talents over their familial obligations. And most female Quakers typically found their calling in their twenties. For example, Elizabeth Coggeshall, the traveling minister who visited the Coffins on Nantucket, had been married three years when she was recognized as a minister at age twenty-six.[4]

A typical female preacher in many ways, Lucretia soon distinguished herself from her peers. By 1825, Quakers in Philadelphia knew her for her "peculiar testimony" on "female elevation" and "woman's responsibility as a rational and immortal being." One man remembered that Lucretia "was in the practice of introducing the subject in social circles and in her public communications."[5] Quakers were surprised by her pronouncements because advocates of women's rights were rare in the 1820s. Lucretia's focus on the female sex suggested her transformation over the course of the decade from a respectable Quaker minister, wife, and mother to a controversial dissenter, social critic, and activist.

Mott's identity as a minister and reformer was forged in the context of an internal Quaker controversy over the ministry of Elias Hicks, culminating in the Schism of 1827. Hicks and his allies, known as Hicksites, preached the importance of the inner light, criticizing Quaker elders for abandoning this fundamental doctrine, abusing their power of disownment, and compromising with the world. Hicks's opponents, known as evangelical or Orthodox Quakers for their strong theological and associational ties to mainstream evangelical Protestants, advocated the twin authorities of the Bible and Quaker leadership. Intersecting with the larger social and cultural turmoil of the 1820s, the Hicksite doctrinal schism overlapped with divisions wrought by class, slavery, and democracy. This decade witnessed not only the rending of the Society of Friends in the United States, but conflicts between free thinkers, religious liberals, and Evangelical Christians, revolutions in transportation and communications, the rise of Jacksonian democracy, preliminary skirmishes over women's status, and the birth of immediate abolitionism.[6]

Though her granddaughter later wrote that Mott only reluctantly separated from Twelfth Street Meeting and Philadelphia Yearly Meeting, it is
more likely that she was an enthusiastic Hicks partisan from the beginning.
As historian Larry Ingle observes, the elders, or overseers, of Philadelphia
Yearly Meeting were disturbed by young ministers in their purview "eagerly
adopting and just as eagerly preaching the sentiments of Elias Hicks." Mott
was undoubtedly one of these young preachers. On one occasion, two female
elders from Twelfth Street Meeting visited Mott to inform her that Friends
felt uncomfortable with some of the language used in her sermons. What did
she mean by referring to Quakers' "*notions* of Christ"? Mott replied that she
had been quoting from William Penn: "Men are to be judged by their likeness
to Christ, rather than their notions of Christ." While Mott's response satisfied the elders this time, they became increasingly critical of the way Hicks's
allies used Penn and other early Quakers to justify their doctrines. Hicksite
and evangelical Quakers both struggled to prove that they were the authentic
and legitimate body of the Society of Friends.[7]

Equally suggestive is the Motts' longstanding personal relationship with
Elias Hicks. Lucretia confirmed that Hicks was "the same consistent exemplary
man that he was many years ago" at Nine Partners Boarding School. Like James
Mott, Hicks was from Long Island, born in Hempstead in 1748. Hicks married
a fellow Quaker, Jemima Seaman, and moved to her family's farm in Jericho.
As a farmer, he developed a deep skepticism of the market economy and industrialization, helping poor white and black neighbors in his community survive
the American Revolution by selling produce at low prices (according to one
source, he refused to sell to the rich). In 1778, the same year he freed his slave
Ben, Hicks was recognized as a minister in the Society of Friends.[8]

By the 1820s, Hicks's criticism of slavery, the market economy, and the
Quaker elders linked him to the Democratic radicals of the Workingmen's
Party in nearby New York City. Barnabas Bates, a correspondent of Hicks,
was one of these spiritual and political fellow travelers. Originally from
Rhode Island, Bates moved to Manhattan in 1824 and began publishing a
newspaper called the *Christian Inquirer* to promote "Free Inquiry, Religious
Liberty, and Rational Christianity." In 1828, Bates became an organizer for
the Workingmen's Party and also joined other Anti-Sabbatarians to oppose
evangelical efforts to legislate Sunday as a day of rest. Hicks shared Bates's
opposition to Sabbath laws, arguing that they violated "the Liberty of Conscience guaranteed by our free constitution to all its Citizens."[9] An adamant
egalitarian, Bates also opposed both high postage rates and slavery. In 1830,

following Hicks's death, he delivered a eulogy to the African Benevolent Societies of New York City. Bates remembered Elias Hicks as "among the first that brought the subject [of slavery] frequently and forcibly before the members of his religious society."[10]

In 1811, Hicks had published an influential pamphlet that reflected the core of his anti-slavery principles, *Observations on the Slavery of the Africans and their Descendants*. Written as a series of questions and answers, the pamphlet showed slavery's incompatibility with both America's commitment to equality and Quaker testimony against war. Hicks began by affirming that every man is "a moral agent (that is free to act)." African Americans were deprived of their inalienable freedom at birth, he argued, when "they are taken in a state of war, and considered by the captor as a prize." Most important, Hicks described purchasers and consumers of slave goods as supporting and encouraging the institution. He concluded that "no man who is convinced of the cruelty and injustice of holding a fellow creature in slavery, can traffic in, or make use of the produce of a slave's labour."[11] For the rest of his career, Hicks placed "free produce" at the center of Quaker anti-slavery testimony. By this time Friends had severed all direct ties to the peculiar institution, but Hicks believed that until they abjured slave products Quaker testimony was incomplete, and their "hands stained with blood."[12]

Hicks's pamphlet on slavery caused little debate until Quakers began questioning his other theological views. Phebe Willis (not to be confused with Lucretia's school friend, Phebe Post Willis), a member with Elias Hicks of Jericho Monthly Meeting, called upon Hicks to clarify his views on the Bible in writing. On May 5, 1818, Hicks wrote Willis that the Scriptures, as they have been interpreted, "have been the cause of four-fold more harm than good to Christendom." Citing Quaker founder George Fox, Hicks viewed "the light and spirit of truth in the hearts and consciences of men and women, as the only sure rule of faith and practice." These views would have scandalized most American Christians, but Hicks was surprised at the negative response he got from Quakers. In another letter to Willis, Hicks denied that these statements deviated from his previous sermons or beliefs; he had always condemned "professors of Christianity" for idolizing the Bible. Ingle notes that these letters dropped like a "bombshell" in the midst of the Society of Friends. Indeed, Hicks's replies set off a wave of recriminations, polemics, and pamphleteering among Quakers and non-Quakers alike.[13]

Trends within the Society of Friends made Hicks's statements more troubling to the elders than they might have been at the beginning of his ministry. In both England and the U.S., evangelical Christianity was undergoing a period of revivalism known as the Second Great Awakening. In the U.S., revivalism coincided with religious disestablishment, which prompted denominations such as the Baptists and Methodists to compete with previously state-supported religions for potential converts, especially women, through a vibrant proliferation of charitable voluntary societies. At the same time, prosperous Quaker businessmen and merchants began to drop their opposition to worldliness. Particularly in Philadelphia, the wealthy Quaker leaders saw themselves as similar to other Protestants, basing their doctrines on the Bible, establishing a clear hierarchy to rule the religion, and joining Bible, tract, missionary, Sabbath, and temperance societies to establish their place in mainstream American culture. These respectable elders wanted to remove any taint of disrepute from their religion, which had been associated with dangerous dissenters in the colonial period. One sign of this change was the decision by Philadelphia Yearly Meeting in 1806 to disown those who denied Christ's divinity or a literal interpretation of the Bible. By the 1820s, the Philadelphia elders were exerting their power on a regular basis, targeting Hicks and his supporters.[14]

The elders took special exception to Hicks's sermons on free produce, which they rightly perceived as attacking both their piety and their business practices. In October 1819, Hicks preached at Pine Street Meeting in Philadelphia, where Lucretia had taught school and married James. Pine Street Meeting was now the spiritual home of Jonathan Evans, leader of the evangelical Quakers, who had retired from the lumber industry in 1817, having accumulated a fortune of $43,000. During the American Revolution, he had served a short jail term for refusing military service, and for a time he abstained from slave products. But by 1819 Evans had given up on free produce as too cumbersome in an economy so closely tied to slavery. In his sermon, Hicks remarked that Friends who had previously embraced free produce and had now fallen away were little better than "thieves and murderers." When Hicks asked permission to preach on the same subject to the women's meeting, Evans initially rejected his request, but eventually the men's meeting gave permission. Still, Evans found another way to demean Hicks. While Hicks was delivering his sermon to the women, Evans proposed adjourning the men's meeting. Hicks returned to an empty room, leading his supporters to complain bitterly about Evans's rudeness. This infamous adjournment was not the only time that the two men disagreed over free produce. On at least two other occasions, Hicks's sermons prompted a protest from Evans.[15]

In the period leading up to the schism, Lucretia became more openly critical of the power of the elders. In a letter to James Mott, Sr., she bemoaned the
"departure from simplicity of Quakerism as reflects trade, with the consequent embarrassment attendant thereon," adopting Elias Hicks's perspective
on the wealth and worldliness of the prominent Quakers in her city. She later
referred to Jonathan Evans as "the Pope of that day."[16] Mott's disapproval
of their heavyhandedness was also reflected in her concern over a series of
disownments in 1822. Two daughters of Rebecca Paul, a "poor widow" and a
minister in the Society of Friends, were excommunicated for marrying outside meeting, the Quaker phrase describing an interfaith marriage. From her
childhood on Nantucket, Lucretia had viewed this type of repudiation as an
unnecessary abuse of power. But the Philadelphia elders pushed their authority farther than Nantucket's Quaker leaders. The elders heard a complaint
against Paul herself for "conniving" to arrange the marriages of her children.
In the end, Philadelphia Monthly Meeting disowned Rebecca Paul. Mott described this case as "trying" and wondered if there could be "improvement
in the Discipline relative to out-goings in marriage."[17] Two years later, Lucretia witnessed the disownment of her youngest sister Martha, who married
Captain Peter Pelham, a War of 1812 hero and one of Anna Coffin's paying
boarders.[18]

These internal troubles spilled beyond the borders of the Society of
Friends beginning in 1821, in a series of inflammatory letters printed under
pseudonyms in the *Christian Repository*, an evangelical newspaper published
in Wilmington, Delaware, later published as a book titled the *Letters of Paul
and Amicus*. The correspondents were Eliphalet Gilbert (Paul), a prominent
Presbyterian minister, and Benjamin Ferris (Amicus), one of the leaders of
Hicks's sympathizers in Wilmington. Gilbert's goal was to prove that Quakers were not Christians, but infidels, deists, atheists, and Unitarians. He
started by condemning the Quaker belief in the inner light as *"superior to
the sacred scriptures,"* referring to Elias Hicks as an example of this Quaker
heresy. The exchange, which went on for two years, horrified evangelical
Quakers not only because Gilbert accused all Quakers of "holding doctrines
and practices inimical to the principles of the Gospel," but because Benjamin
Ferris's defense of the Quakers adopted Hicks's views rather than their own.
As a result, the correspondence won approval from Hicks's allies like Mott,
who later recommended Ferris's letters to Irish Friends.[19]

The *Letters of Paul and Amicus* show the clashing worldviews of evangelical Christians, in the midst of expanding their Protestant empire, and

the "liberal views" of many Hicksite Quakers, Unitarians, and free thinkers. Benjamin Ferris, writing as Amicus, defined the age as "distinguished by a Spirit of Free Enquiry," pointing to the individual duty and ability to seek religious truth. In contrast, he singled out Lyman Beecher, the famous minister and leader of the Second Great Awakening, as "intending to establish a Calvinistic influence in this country," noting the establishment of seminaries and colleges under Beecher's control. In addition to violating the separation of church and state, Ferris viewed missionaries and other "hireling ministers" as examples of greed and corruption; he referred to them as "MERCENARY CLERGY."[20] Gilbert responded that free enquiry must inevitably lead to the Scriptures, the doctrine of the Trinity, and the network of Bible, Sabbath, tract, and missionary societies. He cited the "astonishing, numerous, and extensive revivals of religion" taking place in the country as evidence of the truth of his position. And he complained of Quakers' "*indiscriminate opposition to all ministers of the gospel.*"[21] In reply, Ferris referred to Bible societies and revivals as "carnal" rather than "spiritual" manifestations of religious belief. Like Hicks, Ferris viewed custom and tradition as poor arguments for religious doctrine.[22]

The debate between Gilbert and Ferris revealed one of the principal dividing lines in American religion: slavery. Gilbert criticized the Society of Friends for its opposition to missionary societies. In reply, Ferris argued that missionary efforts were "ill timed." Using India as an example, he pointed out that missionaries had only succeeded in subjecting "Hindoos" to "political slavery" and "religious domination." And while Gilbert and other missionaries labeled South Asians heathens and idolaters, Ferris argued that "the love of God is extended to *all* his rational family." Finally, Ferris contrasted evangelical benevolence in foreign lands to their neglect of the homegrown problem of slavery. Christian missionaries, he wrote, were unwilling "to extend this divine government through our own land. Here we see *One million five hundred thousand* of our fellow creatures unjustly held in a degrading bondage, which is entailed on their innocent posterity."[23] Gilbert, in turn, noted his own opposition to slavery, but argued that slavery was not a religious issue: "A man, on mere principles of humanity and sound policy, may be as strongly opposed to oaths, slavery, and war, as any of your society can be, yet be a deist or an atheist. What should hinder? Your opposition to these civil and political evils, therefore, does not prove you a *Christian* society." Gilbert's statement reflected the views of most mainstream Protestants, who desperately sought to avoid involvement in the debate over slavery. Yet as the

Philadelphia elders worked to position their sect in the evangelical tradition, the exchange between "Paul" and "Amicus" further distinguished Quakers from other Protestants. As Lucretia recalled, the Philadelphia Meeting for Sufferings, a standing committee charged with governance, issued a disclaimer and protest against Benjamin Ferris.[24]

The harsh reaction of the Philadelphia leadership provoked new entries into the ongoing pamphlet war, with Quaker women playing a central role in these theological and political battles. Phebe Willis was the first to publicly question Hicks's views on the Bible. Anna Braithwaite, a British traveling minister closely associated with evangelical Quakers in her home country, entered the American fray with a vengeance. Braithwaite's style was both confrontational and aristocratic—she traveled in a fine carriage with a female servant beside her—and thus guaranteed to alienate the Hicksites. She made three trips to the United States during the controversy; the first visit was in 1823, when she sought an interview with Elias Hicks. Unsurprisingly, the two sides disagreed about Braithwaite's motivations. Evangelicals described Braithwaite as "unprejudiced"; the Hicksites criticized her intention "to bring the American people into all the glorious *consistency* of the *Mother Church* [London Yearly Meeting]."[25]

Anna Braithwaite's published account of her interview with Hicks was intentionally provocative, casting Hicks as a heretic and a crank. According to Braithwaite, Hicks claimed that the Bible was unnecessary. He denied the account of creation in Genesis. He also questioned the doctrine of the Atonement, asking her "whether she could suppose the Almighty to be so cruel as to suffer Jesus Christ to die for our sakes." He demonstrated the same broad and scandalous conception of spirituality as Benjamin Ferris, asserting that "the heathen nations, the Mahometans, Chinese and Indians bore *greater evidence* of the influence of Divine light, than professing Christians." Finally, according to Braithwaite, Hicks testified to the absolute universality of the inner light, stating "the fullness of the Godhead was in *us* and in every blade of grass."[26]

Elias Hicks's defense, written as a letter to Dr. Edwin Atlee, a Philadelphia ally, indicated his distance from the evangelical position. Though he acknowledged the importance of Scripture among Christians, he reiterated his belief in the inner light: "we ought to bring all doctrines, whether written or verbal, to the test of the Spirit of Truth in our own minds, as the only sure director relative to the things of God." And he remained skeptical of the Atonement as the test of Christian faith. In an introduction to the published version of the letter, Hicks's friends further linked the minister to William Penn, who had also been "egregiously slandered, reviled and defamed by pulpit, press and talk, terming him a blasphemer, seducer, Socian, denying the Divinity of Christ and what not."[27] They saw Hicks as protecting the Society of Friends from those who had been "too easily uniting with the prevalent spirit of the world." His allies did not hold back from their own controversial assertions, referring to the Bible as a false idol, a "gilded *household God*."[28]

Quaker minister Priscilla Hunt of Indiana served as Hicks's female counterpart. She preached on similar topics and drew large crowds in Philadelphia in 1822 and 1823. In one sermon she declared, "I have seen the Gospel trumpet laid down in this city. False alarms have been sounded here and believed. True alarms have been sounded and not believed."[29] Like Hicks, she emphasized the inward light, which she called "the *monitor* in the *breast*." But her preaching (and her popularity) drew the ire of the elders. In response to one sermon at Pine Street Meeting, William Evans, son of Jonathan Evans, rose and stated, "These are not the doctrines of our religious Society." After this rebuke, Priscilla Hunt kneeled to pray, and the rest of the meeting rose in unity, with the exception of William and Jonathan Evans. The meeting then ended in an "agitated fashion."[30] When Hunt returned to speak at Arch Street and Pine Street Meetings, she faced similar opposition. But she was welcomed at Green Street Meeting, a stronghold for Hicks, and at Mott's Twelfth Street Meeting. Lucretia later referred to her as a "great minister." Evans justified his behavior by suggesting that Hunt had been reprimanded for unsound doctrine by her home meeting. But one Hicksite later testified, "it was not the business of elders in Philadelphia to condemn an individual unheard, and thus publicly proscribe her; which that opposition manifested was calculated to do."[31]

With women as crucial players, the character and authority of female ministers became an issue in the Hicksite controversy. Evangelical Quakers saw Hannah Barnard, whose disownment figured so prominently in Lucretia's childhood, as a Quaker Eve, precipitating the fall. Thomas Eddy, a leading Quaker and founder of the American Bible Society, claimed that before Barnard's trip to England the Society of Friends was united in "love and amity," but her "deist" sermons on the Scriptures, the Atonement, and the divinity of Christ divided Quakers. Eddy cited Barnard as a direct predecessor to Elias Hicks.[32] Female ministers presented a problem for evangelical Quakers because their equal presence further distinguished the Society of Friends from mainstream denominations. For example, Presbyterian minister Eliphalet

Gilbert, writing as Paul, viewed female preachers as another Quaker heresy. "Paul" described the pen of "Amicus" as like a "scolding woman's tongue" and female Quaker ministers as "frothy" and "ignorant."[33]

All Quakers agreed on the right of women to be ministers, but they disagreed about which women had received genuine inspiration. Evangelical Quakers defended Anna Braithwaite as "innocent" and a victim of "calumny and persecution." Hicksites saw her as "shameful and unprincipled," "violent," and deluded.[34] Evangelical Quakers described Ann Shipley, a witness to Anna Braithwaite's conversation with Elias Hicks, as a "worthy minister," while Hicksites doubted her authorship of a letter supporting Braithwaite's account.[35]

As a consequence, the mistreatment of female ministers became one of many points of contention between evangelical and Hicksite Quakers. In 1826, the Hicksite-dominated Green Street Meeting succeeded in having several evangelical holdouts, including Ann Scattergood and Mary Taylor, removed as ministers. The Orthodox or evangelical Quakers later referred to this action as "oppressive and arbitrary" as well as ungentlemanly.[36] Similarly, the Hicksites complained of the Evanses' treatment of Priscilla Hunt, deploring their hostile "reception of a virtuous female stranger."[37]

Most historians consign female Quakers to a minor role in the split, yet women's participation was evident during every stage of the conflict. In 1826, Anna Braithwaite and another British Friend, Elizabeth Robson, appeared at Philadelphia Yearly Meeting and, according to Lucretia, "had full opportunities to relieve their minds, and we had much preaching."[38] Robson returned to Philadelphia in 1827 and, after requesting an audience with the men's meeting, preached for close to an hour against the unsound doctrines of Hicks and his allies.[39]

After the acrimonious 1827 Yearly Meeting adjourned, a struggle ensued for the loyalty of women. Hicksite men were particularly concerned about the influence of British evangelicals on the women's meeting. When Ann Jones, another English Friend, proposed appointing a committee to determine the state of the ministry, Hicksite men saw it as an attempt to derail the separation. Their anger at Jones turned on the women's meeting, and they suggested that the women had exceeded their authority. At Green Street Monthly Meeting, which had already broken its connection to Philadelphia Quarterly Meeting, Orthodox minister Ann Scattergood tried to lead a "rump" women's meeting, only to have several men interrupt to bring out their wives.[40] Despite Hicksite men's concerns, women were among Hicks's most important partisans. In addition to Priscilla Hunt and Lucretia Mott, Esther Moore, wife of Hicksite Dr. Robert Moore of Easton, Maryland, remained true to Hicks throughout the controversy.[41]

The Hicksite and Orthodox Quakers offered two competing models of womanhood. The Hicksites' egalitarianism, closely linked to democratic ferment and free thought, produced Hannah Barnard and Priscilla Hunt, dynamic preachers liberated from the constraints of religious orthodoxy and middle-class domesticity. The Orthodox Quakers celebrated a more reserved female piety as exemplified by the private Ann Shipley or the haughty Anna Braithwaite. Within the bounds of propriety, Orthodox Quakers and their evangelical allies encouraged women to expand their benevolent presence in the public sphere, as missionaries, exhorters, fundraisers, and volunteers. In 1829, this mainstream ministerial embrace of female moral power inspired Catharine Beecher, daughter of Lyman Beecher, to embark on the first mass petition campaign among women. Beecher argued that women's religious "influence" should be exerted to raise sympathy and awareness of the plight of the Cherokee, the target of removal efforts led by Democratic President Andrew Jackson.[42]

Any chance of unity among Philadelphia Quakers ended with the 1827 Yearly Meeting. After the split, the Orthodox Philadelphia Yearly Meeting retained most of the property and assets, but counted only 9,009 members to the 17,000 strong Hicksites. Both sides filed lawsuits to gain control over meetinghouses and schoolhouses. They also issued pamphlets to win the hearts and minds of fellow Quakers. The Orthodox, staking their place firmly in the Protestant evangelical mainstream, referred to the Hicksites as a new and distinct sect, made up of "libertines" advocating "wild ranterism." They condemned the Hicksites' disregard for doctrine, and viewed the separation as a result of Hicksite unwillingness to follow "strict morality" or "religious obligations."[43] The Hicksites, on the other hand, adopted the democratic language of the time. They invoked their "inalienable right" to religious liberty, calling the measures of the Philadelphia elders "oppressive." Instead, they promoted "the blessings of a Gospel Ministry unshackled by human authority."[44] With intentional symbolism, Hicksites held a meeting in June 1827 in Carpenters' Hall, where the Continental Congress first met. This convention gave birth to Cherry Street Meeting, where the Motts worshipped after the separation.

The bitter rupture of Philadelphia Yearly Meeting spread quickly through American Quakerism. News of the split traveled to Aurora, New York, where

Anna Coffin and the newly widowed Martha Pelham were teaching school. Lucretia's youngest sister had already been disowned for marrying out of meeting, but Scipio Meeting promptly disowned Anna Coffin, who sided with the Hicksites. Yearly Meetings in Baltimore, Indiana, New York, and Ohio soon suffered their own fractures.[45]

*   *   *

Though Mott followed these theological debates intently, her family required her physical presence and emotional attention. Lucretia had children at regular intervals throughout the decade. After the birth of her daughter Maria in 1818, there was a gap of a few years as she explored her calling as a minister. This deliberate spacing of children suggests Lucretia participated in a larger demographic transition among American women, who limited their family size from an average of seven children to an average of 3.5 children over the course of the nineteenth century. In 1823, Lucretia had a son, also named Thomas. Two more daughters followed: Elizabeth in 1825, and Martha (known as Pattie) in 1828. In the nineteenth century, pregnancy was a dangerous proposition. While Lucretia survived her pregnancies, her younger sister Mary Temple died in childbirth in 1824. Her older sister Sarah had died from a fall earlier that year. These births and deaths undoubtedly intensified Lucretia's reaction to the social and spiritual unrest of the separation.[46]

Like other Quakers, Lucretia and James experienced the split on a very personal level. The Motts withdrew their oldest daughter Anna from Westtown School, now affiliated with the Orthodox. Lucretia's sister Eliza was married to Benjamin Yarnall, son of Ellis Yarnall, a vocal partisan for the Orthodox in Philadelphia. When Eliza decided to ally with the Orthodox, Lucretia worried that she might lose her sister and closest female friend in the city. The friendship between Lucretia and Eliza survived the schism, but not all relationships did. James Mott's mother Anne Mott chose the Orthodox, a sign of the bitter division Hicks's ministry caused in Jericho Monthly Meeting. As Anne grew increasingly alienated from her son, the frequent letters between Long Island and Philadelphia declined dramatically, devastating Lucretia and James. The choices prompted by the split were neither easy nor simple.[47]

The Hicksite split also served as Lucretia's political baptism. In the wake of the schism, the Motts permanently altered their economic choices, moral judgments, and intellectual allegiances. Henceforth, both James and Lucretia Mott cut all ties to slavery, inspired by new calls for immediate emancipation. But Lucretia's identification with Hicks's theology also extended to a broader interest in free thought, political radicalism, and liberal religion. Amidst the wreckage of the Hicksite split, Lucretia emerged as an outspoken and divisive minister.

Elias Hicks's sermons on free produce occasioned hard choices for James, her husband. His sermons, painting Orthodox business practices as signs of economic and spiritual corruption, offended Philadelphia elders and inspired his followers. Living on the economic margins of the market economy, many Hicksites rebelled against the combined wealth and power of the elders, embracing free produce in part to call attention to elite Quakers' intimate ties to slavery. As he struggled to establish himself in business and support his growing family, James Mott shared an economic status similar to other Hicksites. But by 1826 he owned a cotton commission business. His success prompted a new wave of anxiety and soul-searching. American cotton, on its way to market dominance as "King Cotton," was produced by slaves, a task made more efficient and profitable by the 1792 invention of the cotton gin. James's commissions were a point of contention between the usually harmonious couple. Lucretia confessed to her mother-in-law, "I would be much better satisfied, if they could do business that was in no wise dependent on slavery."[48]

Lucretia's unyielding stance on free produce reflected her growing belief in its potential as a tool to end slavery. Long convinced of the truth of Hicks's testimony, she was further stirred after reading a pamphlet by British Quaker Elizabeth Heyrick, titled *Immediate, Not Gradual Abolition; Or, An Inquiry into the Shortest, Safest, and Most Effectual Means of Getting Rid of West Indian Slavery*, published in Philadelphia in 1824. Heyrick intended to reenergize the British anti-slavery movement, which had succeeded in outlawing British involvement in the Atlantic slave trade in 1807. She condemned the cautious and conciliatory efforts since embraced by politicians and moralists; gradualism, Heyrick proclaimed, only increased indifference to the plight of the slave. Instead, she called for the *immediate* abolition of slavery. To accomplish this, Heyrick proposed boycotting the products of slavery, primarily sugar from the West Indies, an effective tactic that had been embraced by approximately 400,000 British men and women in the 1790s. She celebrated the "astonishing effects of human power," arguing that "The hydra-headed monster of slavery, will never be destroyed by other means, than the united exertion of *individual opinion*, and united exertion of *individual resolution*."[49]

After its publication, Heyrick's pamphlet circulated extensively in the city, exciting "much feeling and interest." Elias Hicks's allies formed a ready audience; even some Orthodox Quakers adopted free produce principles. Middle-class women also embraced Heyrick's arguments. Not only did Heyrick provide a striking example of women's individual power, but American women were well aware of the historic link between household economy and political change. While British women formed the backbone of the earlier anti-slavery boycott, American women had provided the precedent by replacing British goods with homespun during the American Revolution. Mott agreed with Heyrick's statement that "when there is no longer a market for the productions of *slave labour*, then, and not *till then*, will the slaves be emancipated." But she also responded to Heyrick's message of personal power and individual purity, or "the consciousness of sincerity and consistency,—of possessing '*clean hands*,' of having 'no fellowship with the workers of iniquity.'"[50] For Mott and other Quakers, abstinence was another way to reject worldliness and maintain their testimony regarding slavery, plain living, and the authority of individual conscience.

Soon after reading Heyrick's pamphlet, Mott banned slave produce from her home, much to the dismay of her husband and children. In 1830, when Hicksite Quaker Lydia White opened a free produce store, "the first establishment exclusively of this character," at 86 North Fifth Street, Lucretia immediately began purchasing her groceries and dry goods there.[51] But, as her granddaughter later wrote, "free calicoes could seldom be called handsome, even by the most enthusiastic; free umbrellas were hideous to look upon, and free candies, an abomination."[52] These hardships prevented free produce from winning a large following. Later writers derided advocates of the boycott as irrelevant, sentimental, and even "crackbrained."[53]

Though boycotting sugar or cotton did little to pressure American slaveholders, the formation of a community dedicated to abstinence formed the basis for an interracial movement of men and women united in their revulsion for the peculiar institution. The publication of Heyrick's pamphlet signaled the beginning of a new, more radical phase in American abolitionism. After his move to Philadelphia, James Mott, as an up and coming Quaker businessman, had joined the respectable, all-white, all-male Pennsylvania Abolition Society, serving as the society's secretary in 1822 and 1823. The moderate Pennsylvania Abolition Society pursued political lobbying to restrict slavery and legal means to free fugitive slaves. In an 1815 letter to his parents, James had noted that a slaveholder bequeathed forty slaves to the organization, presumably to get around restrictive manumission laws in southern states.[54] Two years later, the American Colonization Society proposed another gradual alternative to these slaveholders by encouraging them to emancipate their slaves and send them as colonizers and missionaries to Africa. African Americans in Philadelphia, led by wealthy sail maker James Forten, opposed the American Colonization Society's plan. Three thousand individuals, including Forten, attended a protest meeting at Rev. Richard Allen's Mother Bethel African Methodist Episcopal Church. They resolved that as "our ancestors (not of choice) were the first successful cultivators of America, we . . . feel ourselves entitled to participate in the blessings of her luxuriant soil, which their blood and sweat manured."[55] The Motts' letters from this period do not mention arguments for or against colonization. By the late 1820s, however, James and Lucretia were ardent opponents of the American Colonization Society.

Further inspired by Hicks's free produce sermons and the publication of Heyrick's pamphlet, reformers created an interracial network of anti-slavery societies in Philadelphia. In 1827, while he still traded in cotton, James Mott helped found the Free Produce Society of Pennsylvania to disseminate information on where to buy free "Cotton, Rice, Sugar, Molasses, Tobacco" and to encourage its consumption. Its Quaker organizers believed their efforts would diminish slavery.[56] Quaker women formed a sister-society, the Female Association for Promoting the Manufacture and Use of Free Cotton. These societies, like the Pennsylvania Abolition Society, included only white members, but free produce encouraged connections across the color line. African Americans formed the Colored Free Produce Society in 1830 and the Colored Female Free Produce Society in 1831. Like their white counterparts, the free black members of these societies argued that, "every individual who uses the produce of slave labor encourages the slave-holder, becomes also a participator in his wickedness." Robert Purvis, the wealthy son of a South Carolina slaveholder and an African American woman, was one of the founders of the Colored Free Produce Society. Within a year, the handsome Purvis married Harriet Forten, daughter of James Forten.[57] It is likely that the Motts first met Purvis, who became a close friend, through these free produce societies. And, as with so many white abolitionists, relationships with African Americans may have accelerated the Motts' radical rejection of slavery. By 1830, under pressure from his wife and friends, James Mott abandoned his cotton business to deal in wool, a potentially risky financial decision for a man with five children.[58]

Yet even as some Hicksites embraced free produce, others rapidly retreated from the more radical implications of Hicks's ministry. In 1828, Scottish freethinker Frances (Fanny) Wright began a lecture tour of the United
States, speaking in cities including Baltimore, Philadelphia, and Wilmington. Three years earlier, Wright had founded a mixed-race communitarian
society in Nashoba, Tennessee. She had proposed to gradually emancipate
slaves by offering them the opportunity to work toward their freedom. After
Nashoba failed due to poor management and accusations of free love, she
edited Utopian socialist Robert Dale Owen's *New Harmony Gazette*.[59] Wright
also had strong ties to the Workingmen's Party (often called the "Fanny
Wright Party"). Detractors referred to her as the "Red Harlot of Infidelity"
for her radical politics, anti-clericalism, and rejection of marriage. According
to Mott, Wright lectured on topics with broad appeal, such as "knowledge"
and "education," but she also addressed subjects close to the hearts of most
Hicksites. Wright railed against slavery, intolerance, "the hired preachers of
all sects, creeds, and religions," and "financial and political corruption." Like
Elias Hicks, Fanny Wright aroused the outrage and fear of prominent evangelicals. Lyman Beecher worried that Wright's audiences, filled with "females
of respectable standing in society," might be led astray by her message.[60]

One group of prominent Hicksites acted swiftly to sever all connections
in the public mind between their beliefs and Wright's. As clerk of Wilmington Meeting, Benjamin Ferris, better known as Amicus, led the disownment
of Benjamin Webb, editor of the *Delaware Free Press*, for printing articles
supporting Wright's views and those of other freethinkers such as Robert
Dale Owen. At least five others were also disowned for "Ultraism." Lucretia
was outraged. These individuals, she proclaimed, were among the "most active, benevolent citizens." Lucretia and James entered an "indignant protest"
against these intolerant and "arbitrary measures," at the risk of losing their
own status among their fellow Hicksites.[61]

As her co-religionists grew more conservative, Mott began reading more
radical works. By 1827, Lucretia had read Mary Wollstonecraft's controversial *Vindication of the Rights of Woman*, originally published in 1792. Wollstonecraft argued that women's current status reflected not only their legal
and political subordination but also their "notions of beauty," "their fond-
ness for pleasure," and their consequent objectification. In its place, Wollstonecraft offered equal education and intellectual development: "I wish to
persuade women to endeavor to acquire strength of both mind and body,
and to convince them that the soft phrases, susceptibility of heart, delicacy

of sentiment, and refinement of taste are almost synonymous with epithets of weakness."[62]

Wollstonecraft's Enlightenment thought appealed to Mott's political and religious sympathies. Like a good republican, she rejected the trappings of aristocracy, closely linked to women's taste for fashion and adornment. And as a Quaker radical, she was out of place in a society that increasingly valued white women's sexual purity, submission, and domestic isolation. By the 1820s, *Vindication* was out of print in the United States. Many Americans condemned Wollstonecraft as a "blood-stained Amazon," a symbol of dangerous rebellion against the political, religious, and sexual order. But Mott celebrated both Wollstonecraft and Fanny Wright, decrying the "denunciations of bigoted Sectarianism." Mott referred to *Vindication* as one of her "pet books": "From that time it has been a centre table book, and I have circulated it, wherever I could find readers."[63]

Mott also began reading liberal theologians outside the Society of Friends. In 1831, she encountered the published sermons of William Ellery Channing, leader of the Unitarian movement. Channing, a Harvard graduate and the pastor of the Federal Street Church in Boston, rejected the Calvinism of New England Congregationalism in favor of a more positive interpretation of human nature and the individual relationship to God. He defined God as benevolent, and, like the Hicksites, criticized the doctrine of the Atonement: "This system used to teach as its fundamental principle, that man, having sinned against an infinite Being, has contracted infinite guilt, and is consequently exposed to an infinite penalty."[64] Instead, he emphasized individual agency, echoing the Quaker doctrine of the inner light. In "Honor Due All Men," Channing wrote "The Idea of Right is the primary and the highest revelation of God to the human mind. . . . [The individual] begins to stand before an inward tribunal, on the decision of which his whole happiness rests; he hears a voice, which, if faithfully followed, will guide him to perfection." Finally, he viewed this individual sense of right as an equalizer, "which annihilates all the distinctions of this world." In fact, Channing's vision so clearly corresponded to Mott's own that in her own notes quoting "Honor Due All Men" she inserted the Quaker phrase "inward monitor" in place of Channing's "inward tribunal."[65]

In Boston, Channing influenced another important American woman, Elizabeth Peabody. In 1825, the twenty-one-year-old teacher began attending Channing's Federal Street Church. The minister and parishioner struck up an uncommon friendship and intellectual collaboration based on their

discussions of liberal theology. As biographer Megan Marshall argues, Elizabeth Peabody "had read and studied her way out of the Calvinist doctrine of
original sin." Channing confirmed her ideas and encouraged her intellectual
development; in turn, she copied Channing's sermons for publication, secur-
ing his legacy. Over the course of her career as a teacher, writer, bookstore
owner, and editor of the *Dial*, Elizabeth Peabody "ignited" the intellectual
and literary movement known as Transcendentalism. She also coined the
term. Peabody adapted poet Samuel Coleridge's word "transcendental" to
name the philosophy, which, like Hicksite Quakerism, emphasized the ability of every individual to grasp the Divine, unmediated by ecclesiastical authority or the Scriptures.[66]

As these powerful liberal ideas gained influence in Boston, Mott experienced a disappointing regression among Hicksites in Philadelphia. In 1830,
Mott became clerk of the Hicksite Philadelphia Yearly Meeting of Women.
After the split, the London Yearly Meeting endorsed the Orthodox, refusing
to recognize the Hicksites as members of the Society of Friends. In 1828, when
the Hicksites appealed their case to British Friends, they were denounced as
"separatists." In 1830, they proposed to try again. The new epistle sought to
"open the channel of Christian intercourse" between the (Hicksite) Philadelphia Yearly Meeting and the London Yearly Meeting. The Hicksites made their
case for recognition, warning that the British decision threatened to remove
London Yearly Meeting "from religious communion with [upwards of] eighteenth thousand of your fellow-professors of the gospel of Christ." Further,
they described the Orthodox as usurping "power over the many, subversive
of our established order, and destructive to the peace and harmony of society." But the authors also attempted to assuage British Friends by professing
their belief in the "history of the birth, life, acts, death, and resurrection of the
holy Jesus" as written in the divinely authored Bible. Anna Davis Hallowell
wrote that Lucretia objected to "any statement in the nature of a declaration
of faith, other than the 'inward light,'—the divine light in the soul,—which
she regarded as the cardinal doctrine of Friends." As a result, after serving
her function as clerk and reading the letter to the women's meeting, she ve-
hemently opposed the epistle. Despite Mott's disapproval, the women's meeting endorsed the letter and Mott, along with John Comly, clerk of the men's
meeting, signed it. Their efforts to appease English Quakers were futile, as the
epistle was returned unread with the word "mendacity" written on it.[67]

The position of clerk was a sign of Mott's growing status in the Society of
Friends, but she signaled her independence when she spoke out against the

epistle. Tested in the Hicksite split, her commitment to the inner light and individual moral authority became central to her ministry. At age thirty-seven, after giving birth to five living children, Mott was poised to become the most prominent Quaker minister of her time. Nevertheless, she continued to clash with the Hicksites over their "retrograde" views on liberal theology, slavery, and women's rights.[68] Versed in Penn and Hicks, as well as Wollstonecraft, Channing, and Fanny Wright, Mott looked beyond the borders of the Society of Friends to make sense of the problems of slavery, inequality, and religious intolerance. And she identified the principle obstacle to human progress as slavery.

CHAPTER 4

Immediate Abolition

LUCRETIA'S DAUGHTER WROTE THAT HER CHILDHOOD HOME fulfilled the "prophecies of amalgamation" in the minds of their neighbors. In the 1830s, racial mixing, whether in private homes, churches, or voluntary associations, was rare and taboo. Yet when her daughter penned those words, Lucretia had a house full of white and black visitors, including a fifteen-year-old Haitian boy who sat in her front window all day. Quakers and reformers knew Lucretia as a generous host. The Motts regularly welcomed out of town guests, and held dinner parties attended by anywhere from ten to fifty people. Even as her politics grew more radical, Lucretia was celebrated for her skills as a wife and mother. This domestic prowess allowed Lucretia to maintain an aura of gentility as she defied social convention by inviting whites and blacks to her home. Her most frequent guests were Robert and Harriet Purvis, but other friends in the anti-slavery movement such as the Fortens could also be found at her dinner table.[1]

Lucretia's willingness to practice as well as advocate racial equality confirmed her as a critical outsider in American society. Her belief in individual authority in matters of religion threatened the evangelical Protestant establishment. Her vocal support for women's intellectual, spiritual, and social equality rejected emerging cultural norms assigning men and women separate spheres. And, by the 1830s, Mott's embrace of immediate abolition endangered the social and economic order of the country. Mott contributed her distinctive voice to the anti-slavery cause, giving women a visible but contested place in the burgeoning abolitionist movement.

In June 1830, Lucretia and James received a fateful visit from a young newspaper editor, William Lloyd Garrison. He told them a troubling story about the growing ability of the slave power to limit the individual rights of all Americans, white and black. The twenty-four-year-old had just been released from Baltimore Jail, after serving forty-nine days of his six-month sentence for libel. The previous year, Garrison had entered into partnership with Benjamin Lundy, editor of the Baltimore anti-slavery newspaper the *Genius of Universal Emancipation*. In its pages, Garrison had charged Francis Todd, a wealthy merchant from Garrison's hometown of Newburyport, Massachusetts, with using his ships to transport slaves for Baltimore slave-trader Austin Woolfolk, another frequent target of the newspaper editors. In addition to defending his reputation, Todd and his ally Woolfolk wanted the lawsuit to shut down the *Genius of Universal Emancipation*, and in this they succeeded. Garrison saw the case as an attempt "to stifle free inquiry, to dishearten every effort of reform, and to intimidate the conductors of newspapers."[2]

The lawsuit signaled growing national tension over the issue of slavery. From Garrison's perspective, politicians and financial elites in the North and South were conspiring to strengthen slavery's grip on American society. In addition, the country was in an uproar over the recent publication of *Walker's Appeal, in Four Articles; Together with a Preamble to the Coloured Citizens of the World*. Like his brethren in Philadelphia, David Walker, a free black man living in Boston, opposed colonization. Walker intended "to awaken in the breasts of my afflicted, degraded and slumbering brethren, a spirit of inquiry and investigation respecting our miseries and wretchedness in this *Republican Land of Liberty!!!!!!*" But his incendiary language also struck fear into the hearts of white Americans. Walker warned of God's judgment on whites for keeping African Americans in a state of ignorance and degradation. Invoking the American Revolution, he implied that this situation might soon come to a bloody end: "had I not rather die, or be put to death, than to be a slave to any tyrant, who takes not only my own, but my wife and children's lives by the inches? Yea, would I meet death with avidity far! far!! in preference to such *servile submission* to the murderous hands of tyrants." While the *Genius of Universal Emancipation*, under Lundy's leadership, was too moderate to publish the pamphlet, Garrison wrote that the South's reaction, severe censorship, showed that "the boasted security of the slave states is mere affectation, or something worse."[3]

Radicalized by his experience in Baltimore, Garrison learned from Benjamin Lundy that he might find a sympathetic audience at the Motts' house. Lundy and the Motts moved in the same network of Hicksites, free produce advocates, and freethinkers. A moderate who supported a gradual end to slavery, Lundy nevertheless offered a space for the publication of more radical ideas. In addition to Garrison, in 1829 Lundy hired a young Quaker poet named Elizabeth Margaret Chandler to edit the "Ladies' Repository" section of his paper. Chandler encouraged women to get involved in the anti-slavery cause in two ways. First, she argued that women should abstain from the products of slave labor. Next, Chandler suggested women venture beyond this domestic "exertion" to form "societies for the publication and distribution of tracts and pamphlets" so that the "feelings of many hitherto unthinking persons [will be] aroused into detestation of a system which is a source of so much misery." Chandler wrote approvingly of both the Female Association of Philadelphia for Promoting the Manufacture and Use of Free Cotton and Lydia White's free produce store.[4] Though she confined her own involvement to writing, Chandler, and by extension Lundy, endorsed female social activism, a controversial position at a time when women's voluntarism was largely limited to religious and charitable organizations. And while Lucretia didn't agree with everything she read in the *Genius of Universal Emancipation*, such proposals appealed to her, and earned her financial support.[5]

The Motts quickly arranged a public meeting for Garrison in the city. A passionate and persuasive writer, Garrison was still an awkward public speaker, and he read his manuscript word for word. Lucretia, by now an experienced orator, advised Garrison to take some lessons from Quaker ministers, who always spoke extemporaneously: "William, if thee expects to set forth thy cause by word of mouth thee must lay aside thy paper and trust to the leading of the spirit."[6] This initial meeting not only established their friendship, but provided a foundation for their future political alliance. Mott wrote of Garrison that "there are few my contemporaries whose characters I more revere." Garrison was similarly admiring. In a letter to his wife, he described Lucretia as a "bold and fearless thinker." He later wrote that "If my mind has become liberalized in any degree (and I think it has burst every sectarian trammel),—if the theological dogmas which I once regarded as essential to Christianity, I now repudiate as absurd and pernicious,—I am largely indebted to James and Lucretia Mott for the change."[7]

Elizabeth Heyrick's pamphlet had introduced the concept of immediate abolition, but William Lloyd Garrison turned this idea into a social movement. A combination of factors—the publication of *Immediate, Not Gradual Abolition*, growing doubts about colonization, the formation of free produce societies, and distribution of David Walker's pamphlet—created an interracial audience for a more radical anti-slavery stance, defining slavery as both an individual and a national sin. Upon his return to Boston, Garrison began publishing his newspaper the *Liberator*. Unlike Lundy, who advocated gradual approaches to ending slavery, Garrison now rejected moderation, writing "I *will be* as harsh as truth, and as uncompromising as justice." Garrison also proclaimed his egalitarianism in the masthead: "Our Country is the World—Our Countrymen are Mankind." Supported in part by African Americans in Boston, the *Liberator* condemned colonization and promoted both immediate emancipation and racial equality. But as both Garrison and Mott soon found out, many white Americans were hostile to their views.

For most white Americans, immediate abolition posed the specter of social chaos and bloody vengeance. Two years after David Walker issued his *Appeal*, some of these fears came to fruition. In Southampton County, Virginia, an enslaved man named Nat Turner led a violent uprising against slavery. Beginning on August 22, 1831, Turner and his men killed his nine-year old owner, Putnam Moore, and Moore's parents, Sally and Joseph Travis. Over the course of the next two days, Turner's band, made up of approximately seventy free and enslaved blacks, killed fifty-five whites. The Virginia militia led the violent suppression of the rebellion, which culminated in Nat Turner's execution on November 11, 1831. Commentators in both the North and South held Garrison and his newspaper partially responsible for the uprising. Garrison described himself as a pacifist, "a Quaker in principle," but he set the tone for radical abolitionists' response to slave rebellions and anti-slavery violence. Garrison saw the revolt, and its bloody outcome, as a warning to white Americans, who should respond by ending the oppressive institution of slavery. In other words, the violence of slavery resulted only in more brutality.[8]

Nat Turner's revolt further mobilized radical abolitionists in the North. In Philadelphia, women donated money to support the embattled *Liberator*. They also organized a campaign to petition Congress regarding the wrongs of slavery. Ultimately, Mott and over two thousand other "female citizens of Philadelphia and its vicinity" petitioned Congress to "act to the extent of their power in removing this evil." In signing this petition, Mott and other women drew on the recent precedent of female petitioning against Cherokee removal, an effort led by evangelical Catharine Beecher. But while Beecher's petitions proposed to channel women's moral and religious influence on behalf of Native Americans, Mott's petition invoked women's status as citizens, who had a constitutional right to petition their legislators. Philadelphia women acknowledged that politicians may find their petition "intrusive," but they softened their entrance into the political arena by noting "we approach you unarmed; our only banner is Peace." Like subsequent anti-slavery petitions, the women who signed focused on the abolition of slavery in the nation's capital and other areas where Congress had legal jurisdiction.[9]

Meanwhile, Garrison directed his energies toward forming a national organization dedicated to the immediate abolition of slavery. The founding convention of the American Anti-Slavery Society (AASS) was held at the Adelphi Building in Philadelphia in December 1833. The convention signaled the delegates' final break from colonization and other gradual schemes of abolition. The interracial body also reflected the new organization's commitment to racial equality as well as immediatism.[10] Approximately seventy men and women attended from all over the northeast; delegates from Philadelphia included James Mott, Robert Purvis, Hicks's ally Edwin Atlee, and African American barber and dentist James McCrummell (sometimes spelled Mc-Crummill), among others.

While the official delegates and signatories to the convention's Declaration of Sentiments were exclusively men, Mott and at least seven other women attended the convention. Several of these women were Lucretia's immediate family members: her mother, Anna Folger Coffin; her youngest sister Martha, now married to David Wright, who was visiting from Aurora, New York; and her oldest daughter Anna, who had recently married Edward Hopper, a twenty-one year old lawyer and son of Isaac T. Hopper, a Hicksite Quaker, who, like Lucretia, had referred to Orthodox Quaker leader Jonathan Evans as a "pope." At the convention, they were joined by three other Quaker women: Hicksite Lydia White, owner of the first free produce store; Hicksite Esther Moore, who had moved with her physician husband from Easton, Maryland, to Philadelphia; and Orthodox Quaker Sidney Ann Lewis, an advocate of free produce, who later opened her own shop.[11] All of these women were white, but it is possible some African American women attended. Out-of town abolitionists boarded with local families, including the Motts. One of these delegates invited the Coffin and Mott women. Since other abolitionists boarded with black Philadelphians, they too may have invited their hostesses.

Lucretia boldly interceded in the debates at the convention. As Edwin Atlee read the Declaration of Sentiments, composed by Garrison and a committee that included Quaker poet John Greenleaf Whittier and Unitarian minister Samuel J. May, Lucretia offered two suggestions. First she proposed that references to "Divine Revelation" and the Declaration of Independence be transposed, to read "With entire confidence in the over-ruling justice of God, we plant ourselves upon the Declaration of our Independence and the truths of Divine Revelation as upon the EVERLASTING ROCK." With this statement, abolitionists identified themselves as Americans committed to the egalitarian principles of the Declaration of Independence, but they also claimed the higher authority of Divine law. Lucretia also helped craft a phrase expressing abolitionists' firm commitment to the ultimate truth of abolition: "We may be personally defeated, but our principles never."[12]

Her participation in the convention violated the period's gender and racial norms. Outside of Quaker meetings, the sight of a woman speaking publicly to a "promiscuous" audience of men and women was a rare event. Delegates to the convention remembered Lucretia's comments long after. Robert Purvis recalled that Lucretia's "beautiful face was all aglow." After Lucretia used the word "transpose," James Miller McKim, a young delegate from Carlisle, Pennsylvania, twisted around in his seat to catch a glimpse of the woman who knew the meaning of the term. While Lucretia's participation surprised the delegates, the very existence of an interracial anti-slavery convention scandalized Philadelphians. The young anti-slavery movement had already inspired violent opposition, such as the attacks on Prudence Crandall's school for African Americans in Canterbury, Connecticut. As a result, the convention took the precaution of posting a guard outside the building on Fifth Street. Still, some local philanthropists, fearing retribution, refused to participate. Their refusal prompted another short speech by Mott, who argued "right principles are stronger than great names. If our principles are right, why should we be cowards?"[13]

Under Mott's influence, the American Anti-Slavery Society's declaration set out the basic assumptions of the emerging abolitionist movement. The declaration compared abolitionists to the patriots of the American Revolution, but noted their rejection of "all carnal weapons for deliverance from bondage; relying solely upon those which are spiritual." As a result, their method of resisting slavery was to contrast "moral purity to moral corruption" and to "overthrow prejudice by the power of love." In addition, members of the American Anti-Slavery Society agreed that "no compensation should be given to the planters emancipating their slaves—because it would be a surrender of the great fundamental principle, that man cannot hold property in man." Finally, the declaration included a statement of support for free produce: "We shall encourage the labor of freemen rather than that of slaves, by giving a preference to their productions." The declaration reflected the same "purity of motive" that had captured Lucretia's attention in Heyrick's pamphlet.[14]

Four days later, Mott and the other female spectators helped to found the interracial Philadelphia Female Anti-Slavery Society (PFASS), which would outlive every other women's anti-slavery group in the United States. Mott remembered that "at that time I had no idea of the meaning of preambles, and resolutions, and votings." But her ignorance, exaggerated to emphasize the newness of their venture, had as much to do with religion as it did sex. Mott was clerk of the Philadelphia Yearly Meeting of Women, with over a decade of experience in the internal politics of the Society of Friends. But Quakers determined doctrine by consensus rather than votes. Outside of the Society of Friends, her experience was limited to one "colored" convention (probably one of the Annual Conventions of Colored Americans, held in Philadelphia from 1830–1832) and the founding meeting of the American Anti-Slavery Society. The women asked James McCrummell, a member of Philadelphia's black elite and a signer of the American Anti-Slavery Society's Declaration, to chair the meeting, the only time in the organization's history that such a measure was taken. Their choice of McCrummell also explicitly linked the Philadelphia Female Anti-Slavery Society to the American Anti-Slavery Society, further attesting to their commitment to racial equality.[15]

The meeting appointed a committee composed of white and black women, including Mott, Margaretta Forten (daughter of James Forten), Sarah McCrummell (James McCrummell's wife), Esther Moore, and Lydia White, to write the organization's constitution. Submitted on December 14, the constitution stated that "slavery, and prejudice against colour, are contrary to the laws of God, and to the principles of our far-famed Declaration of Independence." Article 1 noted the society's intentions to distribute accurate information about slavery, "dispel prejudice against color," and improve the condition of free African Americans. Article 10, added to the constitution in January 1834, demonstrated the women's years of commitment to free produce, recommending "that the Members of this society should, at all times and on all occasions, give the preference to free produce over that of slaves believing that the refusal to purchase and use the products of slave labour is one of the most efficient means of abolishing slavery."[16] Their language echoed Heyrick's, showing the continuing influence of her emphasis on the potential of individual moral power to end slavery.

Like other voluntary societies, the Philadelphia Female Anti-Slavery

Society had a president, corresponding secretary, treasurer and other officers to run the organization. Hicksite Esther Moore was named the organization's first president. Lucretia was the first corresponding secretary, and, after she was succeeded by the gifted Mary Grew, she served a short stint as president before becoming a regular member of the Board of Managers. Abba Alcott, mother of the young Louisa May Alcott, whose husband Bronson was teaching at the nondenominational Germantown Academy, was on the original Board of Managers. While white women dominated the official positions, African American women usually held at least one office. Margaretta Forten was the society's first recording secretary.[17]

One historian astutely describes the Philadelphia Female Anti-Slavery Society as "cliquish." Though its membership eventually exceeded two hundred women, a core group ran the society and determined its direction. Kinship, as well as friendship, bound these members together. Charlotte Forten, wife of James, along with her daughters, Margaretta Forten, Sarah Forten, and Harriet Purvis, were all members. Grace Bustill Douglass, an Orthodox Quaker and wife of the successful black barber Robert Douglass, joined with her daughter Sarah, a schoolteacher. By 1836, Mott's two oldest daughters, Anna and Maria, were active in the organization. Women in the Philadelphia Female Anti-Slavery Society also shared similar economic status. Both white and black members came from the middle and even elite classes of Philadelphia society. Some of the white and black women worked as school teachers, but other members did not need to rely on paid employment. African American members were especially unusual in this regard, as most free black women in Philadelphia were among the poorest residents of the city, working primarily as domestic servants, laundresses, or street vendors.[18]

The Philadelphia Female Anti-Slavery Society represented a breakthrough for women's activism. Though female anti-slavery societies proliferated in the coming years, the society was one of only a handful in existence in 1833. The mingling of black and white women stoked the fear of social equality and even "amalgamation," that is, miscegenation. And women's entrance into the often violent debate over slavery soon provoked a crisis over women's proper place in the public arena.

While the city of Philadelphia was home to a large and vibrant community of free blacks, some of whom were prosperous by any standards (James Forten and Robert Purvis both had fortunes of $100,000), the era of Jacksonian democracy saw an assault on their status. Black Philadelphians endured routine violence, including race riots in 1834, 1835, and 1837. Following the

August 1834 riot, which killed one, injured numerous others, and destroyed forty-four black-owned churches and buildings, Lucretia and James visited a damaged neighborhood and estimated the property losses at $5,000–6,000. The destruction prompted their friends Robert and Harriet Purvis to buy a country home in Bristol Township. Then, when Pennsylvania revised its constitution to expand voting rights for white men in 1838, the state simultaneously disenfranchised African American men. Robert Purvis and other free blacks argued that the new constitution "laid our rights a sacrifice on the altar of slavery," in order to win favor from southern states. This loss of their citizenship further endangered the uneasy freedom of the state's African American population, now lacking the political power to resist further attacks on their civil rights. Reminding readers of the fugitive slave clause in the U.S. Constitution, Purvis asked, "Need we inform you that every colored man in Pennsylvania, is exposed to be arrested as a fugitive from slavery?"[19]

In this intense period, Lucretia and the members of the Philadelphia Female Anti-Slavery Society met monthly, undertaking three main tasks. First, in order to disseminate information about slavery, they donated money to support the American Anti-Slavery Society and subscribed to newspapers like the *Liberator* and the *Herald of Freedom*, edited by New Hampshire abolitionist Nathaniel P. Rogers. They also sponsored public lectures, including one by British abolitionist George Thompson, whose scheduled appearance in Boston in 1835 incited a mob. Similarly, American activists, such as Samuel J. May, Robert Purvis, James Forten, Jr., Charles C. Burleigh, and Benjamin Lundy, regularly addressed the society's meetings. Second, in order to improve the condition of blacks in Philadelphia, the Philadelphia Female Anti-Slavery Society established a committee to visit African American schools and offer aid. By 1838, the Philadelphia Female Anti-Slavery Society had taken on financial responsibility for the school run by member Sarah Mapps Douglass. Finally, the Philadelphia Female Anti-Slavery Society continued the work begun by Philadelphia women in 1831, petitioning Congress to abolish slavery in the District of Columbia and the territories, and to outlaw the interstate slave trade. One such petition declared slavery "a sin against God, and inconsistent with our declaration that equal liberty is the birth-right of all."[20]

The Philadelphia Female Anti-Slavery Society also encouraged women to join the anti-slavery movement and to take on more public roles. In her initial role as corresponding secretary, Lucretia exchanged letters with women in other young anti-slavery societies, such as Lucy Williams of the Brooklyn, Connecticut, Female Anti-Slavery Society, who sought advice from an "elder" in the movement.[21] In their own state, the Philadelphia Female Anti-Slavery Society published an address "To the Women of Pennsylvania" describing their "duty as a citizen of the United States" to leave the "hallowed precincts of the home" for the "halls of Congress." They urged women to circulate and sign anti-slavery petitions. Adopting a strategy used by other anti-slavery women, the Philadelphia Female Anti-Slavery Society drew attention to free women's obligations to enslaved women: "Yes, although we are *women, we* still are citizens, and it is to *us, as women,* that the captive wives and mothers, sisters and daughters of the South have a particular right to look for help in this day of approaching Emancipation."[22] When Angelina Grimké, the daughter of a prominent South Carolina slaveholding family and a new member of the society, became an agent of the American Anti-Slavery Society, the first woman to hold such position, the Philadelphia Female Anti-Slavery Society issued a public statement of approval. Describing Grimké's path as a "new field of labor," they acknowledged that she would receive "not only the sneers of the heartless multitude, which are the portion of every faithful abolitionist, but grave charges of infractions of the laws of female delicacy and propriety." The Philadelphia Female Anti-Slavery Society urged anti-slavery societies around the country to give her "your support, your sympathy, and your prayers."[23]

Angelina Grimké's 1836–37 public speaking tour, which included an address to the Massachusetts Legislature, provoked immediate backlash. Congregational ministers in Massachusetts issued a Pastoral Letter that denounced women who adopted the male role of "public reformer" as "unnatural," and recommended that churches close their doors to female speakers. Catharine Beecher, daughter of the eminent evangelical and colonizationist Lyman Beecher, published an *Essay on Slavery and Abolitionism, with Reference to the Duty of American Females.* Addressed to Angelina Grimké, the essay condemned female anti-slavery societies and petition campaigns (despite Beecher's own activism on behalf of the Cherokee), instead advising that women use their influence not to "exasperate" but "for the purpose of promoting a spirit of candour, forbearance, charity, and peace."[24]

In Philadelphia, Benjamin Lundy's new journal, the *National Enquirer,* printed a series of responses to Catharine Beecher from "L." "L" was undoubtedly a member of Philadelphia's abolitionist community, and may have been Lucretia Mott. While Lucretia did not usually write for publication—she did not believe she had any particular talent for it—she did occasionally publish short letters or articles in anti-slavery newspapers. And as a defender of Angelina Grimké's right to speak out against slavery, Mott believed that Beecher merited a thorough rebuttal. In her first article, L denied that coloni- zationists could properly be considered abolitionists. She defended William Lloyd Garrison from Beecher's aspersions and suggested Beecher herself was a member of the "half-way" or "neutral" party (unacceptable to uncom- promising Garrisonians). L also denied that the tactics of abolitionists were dangerous, inciting "envy, discontent, and revengeful feelings" in the black community. Instead, L pointed out that black abolitionists were "universally acknowledged to be kind, respectful, sober, and forgiving, and above slander, even from Miss Beecher."[25]

Shortly after L began publishing her articles, Lundy printed Angelina Grimké's responses to Beecher. Grimké defended the anti-slavery movement as the ultimate "school of morals in our land." She argued that individuals had rights as moral beings, and that while the slave's rights had been "plundered," his "right and title to himself is as perfect now, as is that of Lyman Beecher." Grimké made the same argument on behalf of her sex: "My doctrine then is, that whatever it is morally right for man to do, it is morally right for woman to do."[26] Grimké defined equality as inherent to every human being, echo- ing Quaker belief in the inner light and William Ellery Channing's "Idea of Right." L probably concluded that Grimké's response was much more ef- fective than her own, as she stopped publication of her series. Still, not all Garrisonians agreed with Grimké's assessment of women's "right" to speak against slavery. As abolitionists deliberately and repeatedly violated the na- tion's racial and sexual order, the outcry intensified.

*   *   *

As the controversy over women's role in the anti-slavery movement grew, Mott took her place on the national stage. After the separation, Mott's skills as a preacher made her an important ambassador from Philadelphia Friends to Quakers across the country. In 1833, she and her school friend Phebe Post Willis, a cousin of James from Long Island, traveled on a religious mission through New York and Massachusetts, ending in Mott's birthplace of Nan- tucket, where Quakers were in a "tried state" following a series of disown- ments, further reverberations from the schism in Philadelphia. Despite these tensions, Mott relished her time with Phebe, writing "sisters could not have harmonized more entirely." But the Orthodox journal *The Friend* pointed out that Lucretia was traveling under false pretenses by claiming she represented the Society of Friends. Classifying Mott as a Hicksite, they argued "the Society of Friends are in no way responsible for her doctrines or movements." ("Have you seen how I am posted in 'The Friend'?" Mott asked Willis).[27]

Though she still had young children, Lucretia's calling meant that she was frequently away from home. In May 1834, after several of her children had recovered from scarlet fever, Lucretia left on a three week journey to Southern Quarterly Meeting. Anna Coffin lived with the Motts and helped with domestic duties, as did Lucretia's older daughters. Nevertheless, James experienced her departure as an emotional as well as a practical trial, writing, "I am not a whit better reconciled to a separation than I was a year ago,—but must make the best of it." The following spring Mott commented that "I have been less from home this winter than for several years past," a turn of phrase that suggested she had traveled quite a bit. But the demands of childrearing also declined in the coming years. In 1836, eight-year-old Martha and eleven-year-old Elizabeth went to a school run by Anthony Sharp in Mt. Holly, New Jersey, where Lucretia's cousin Rebecca Bunker was a teacher. In October of that year, eighteen-year old Maria married Edward M. Davis, a Quaker merchant, member of the Young Men's Anti-Slavery Society of City and County of Philadelphia, and, in 1838, one of the founders of the Pennsylvania Anti-Slavery Society, a state-wide organization affiliated with the American Anti-Slavery Society.[28] Lucretia approved whole-heartedly of both her sons-in-law, who were as devoted to abolition as the rest of the family.

In 1836, in response to the emergence of female anti-slavery societies across New England and the mid-Atlantic, the Boston Female Anti-Slavery Society (BFASS) suggested the formation of an executive committee to oversee the various groups. Benjamin Lundy praised the idea, writing "Much good would doubtless result from the united exertions, of such minds as those of A. E. Grimké, Lucretia Mott, Mary Parker, Mary Clarke [sic], M. W. Chapman, L. M. Child" and others. Parker, Maria Weston Chapman, and Lydia Maria Child were all members of the Boston society, while Mary Clark hailed from the Concord, New Hampshire, Ladies Anti-Slavery Society, founded in 1834. While the Philadelphia Female Anti-Slavery Society approved the proposal, anti-slavery women from Maine to Pennsylvania disagreed about what they could and should do to end slavery. An executive committee offered the possibility of a female alternative to the American Anti-Slavery Society. But some women suggested they preferred to integrate the American Anti-

Slavery Society, and still others remained skeptical of the utility of a national organization.[29]

As a compromise, abolitionist women held a national Anti-Slavery Convention of American Women, which in Lucretia's view marked the beginning of the women's rights movement. The convention took place in New York City from May 9–12, 1837. Seventy-one women from seven states came to "interest women in the subject of anti-slavery" but also to discuss the propriety of women speaking, writing, and petitioning against slavery. Lucretia chaired the meeting, and she and Grace Douglass of the Philadelphia Female Anti-Slavery Society were named as vice presidents. Mary Grew and Sarah Pugh, also of the Philadelphia Female Anti-Slavery Society, served as secretaries. In total, twenty-two women traveled from Pennsylvania, including Douglass's daughter Sarah Mapps Douglass and Mott's daughter Anna Hopper.[30]

Angelina Grimké and her older sister Sarah both offered resolutions on women's duties in the anti-slavery cause. Lucretia spoke in support of these resolutions, and years later remembered almost to the word Angelina Grimké's statement on women's sphere:

> Resolved, That as certain rights and duties are common to all moral beings, the time has come for woman to move in that sphere which Providence has assigned her, and no longer remain satisfied in the circumscribed limits with which corrupt custom and a perverted application of Scripture have encircled her; therefore that it is the duty of woman, and the province of woman, to plead the cause of the oppressed in our land, and to do all that she can by her voice, and her pen, and her purse, and the influence of her example, to overthrow the horrible system of American slavery.

Angelina Grimké's resolution prompted "animated debate." And though it passed, it did not pass unanimously. Some female delegates took the unusual step of placing their names on record as disagreeing with Grimké's language.[31] Two parts of the resolution were especially controversial. Most women at the convention considered themselves Christians, and unlike Mott, were reluctant to assign women's status to a "perverted application of Scripture." But delegates also disagreed about women's duty to use her voice, a blatant violation of women's assigned role as a peaceful, benevolent, and most importantly, private influence.

Many male abolitionists worried that the issue of women's rights might distract members from the primary goal of ending slavery. As Angelina Grimké composed her reply to Catharine Beecher, Sarah Grimké began writing her *Letters on the Equality of the Sexes*. Mott later referred to Sarah Grimké's book as the "best Work after Mary Wollstonecraft's Rights of Woman." While John Greenleaf Whittier called the Grimkés' public labors "noble," he expressed concern about their new role as "controversial writers." Whittier asked, "Does it not look, dear sisters, like abandoning in some degree the cause of the poor and miserable slave"? In comparison, he called women's suffering a "trifling oppression."[32]

Meanwhile, newspapermen mocked the Anti-Slavery Convention of American Women, contending that women were naturally and biologically suited to domesticity. Instead of describing the convention's officers as president or vice presidents, anti-slavery editor Col. William Leete Stone referred to them as "governesses" in the pages of the *New York Commercial Advertiser*. Calling the gathering "ludicrous," Stone highlighted women's inadequacy for the task: "The spinster has thrown aside her distaff—the blooming beauty her guitar—the matron her darning-needle—the sweet novelist her crow-quill;—the young mother has left her baby alone to nestle in the cradle—and the kitchen maid her pots and frying pans—to discuss the weighty matters of state—to decide upon intricate questions of international polity—and weigh, with avoirdupoise exactness, the balances of power."[33]

Opposition to women's activism also came from weightier quarters. At the convention, anti-slavery women united around their right to petition, but this right had recently come under attack by pro-slavery forces in Congress. The previous year, the House of Representatives passed the first of an annual series of "gag rules." From 1836–1844, instead of reading and acting on the memorials of their constituents, Congressmen tabled all anti-slavery petitions. Abolitionists protested this violation of first amendment rights, but women in particular watched as their sole political right evaporated. As Angelina Grimké argued, "we regard every effort in Congress to abridge this sacred right, whether it be exercised by man or woman, the bond or the free, as a high-handed usurpation of power, and an attempt to strike a death-blow at the freedom of the people."[34] Mott and the other Philadelphia delegates returned from the convention resolved to defy the gag rule. The Philadelphia Female Anti-Slavery Society printed two thousand petition forms, divided up the state by county, and circulated "To the Women of Pennsylvania."[35]

After the first Anti-Slavery Convention of American Women, the Philadelphia Female Anti-Slavery Society issued another public statement of support for Angelina and Sarah Grimké. They affirmed Angelina's resolution that "the time has come for woman to move in that sphere which Providence has assigned her." They also encouraged the two women to "persevere." But the negative public reaction to Angelina Grimké's lectures also prompted the women of the Philadelphia Female Anti-Slavery Society to reflect on "on the present state of the Anti-Slavery cause, the danger from false brethren, the necessity of reading & investigating, that we may be able to act understandingly on the important questions of the day." Rejecting compromise or diplomacy on controversial issues, the women suggested that rather than asking what course will be "universally approved," they would ask: "What is Right?"[36]

By 1837, Mott and her allies had built a small but influential movement dedicated to the goals of eradicating slavery and racial prejudice. The lofty principles of equality, liberty, love, and moral purity had united radical abolitionists. Yet the Philadelphia Female Anti-Slavery ended the year pondering the "present state of the anti-slavery cause" and their "false brethren." The proliferation of female anti-slavery societies, Angelina Grimké's public notoriety, and the Anti-Slavery Convention of American Women had illuminated previously hidden political differences among abolitionists. Though Mott and the Philadelphia Female Anti-Slavery Society affirmed their commitment to principle, other abolitionists confronted the limitations of a strategy based on moral suasion.

CHAPTER 5

Pennsylvania Hall

ON NOVEMBER 7, 1837, A MOB murdered anti-slavery newspaper editor Elijah Lovejoy in Alton, Illinois. Lovejoy's death shocked eastern abolitionists. They expected the violence—after all, mobs had already destroyed three of Lovejoy's printing presses. But Lovejoy's decision to use arms to defend his fourth press unsettled allies of the American Anti-Slavery Society. Lucretia and the Philadelphia Female Anti-Slavery Society expressed the views of most Garrisonians. While they blamed the system of slavery for the violence that destroyed both northern and southern homes, they deplored Lovejoy's methods. Carnal weapons, the Philadelphia Female Anti-Slavery Society declared, "are not the proper means for advancement of our cause."[1]

Two days after the news of Lovejoy's murder arrived in Philadelphia, abolitionists celebrated the raising of Pennsylvania Hall. Both workmen and stockholders enjoyed a temperance and free produce feast at Ellis & Longstreth's carpenter shop.[2] Philadelphia's abolitionists had built the hall at a cost of $40,000, or $926,000 today. The board of managers, led by President Daniel Neall, a Hicksite Quaker dentist, raised money by issuing two thousand shares at $20 apiece; the Philadelphia Female Anti-Slavery Society was among the stockholders.[3] Abolitionists' unity at this dinner disguised political differences that soon tore apart the American Anti-Slavery Society. As the Whig Party challenged former President Andrew Jackson's Democrats for dominance, many abolitionists viewed party politics as a means to achieve anti-slavery goals. Abolitionists continued to struggle with the woman question. And, faced with mob violence, some abolitionists began to question the moral strategy of Garrisonians. Confronted with these challenges to moral purism, Mott chose principles over political pragmatism.

To inaugurate Pennsylvania Hall as a "Temple of Freedom," abolitionists planned a week of events beginning May 14, 1838. They prided themselves on erecting one of the "most commodious and splendid" buildings in the city, at the corner of Sixth and Haines Streets. The lecture hall could hold 3,000 people, with meeting rooms available for smaller gatherings. Design highlights included gas lighting and a ventilator at the center of the ceiling that was shaped like a sunflower with "gilt rays." At the center of the sunflower was a concave mirror, "which at night sparkled like a diamond." Over the stage was an arch inscribed with the words "Virtue, Liberty, and Independence." The opening day included speeches against Cherokee removal, colonization, and, of course, slavery. Female abolitionists planned to hold their second Anti-Slavery Convention of American Women later that week.[4]

Though participants tried to emphasize their unity, the speeches and debates at Pennsylvania Hall indicated important ideological and tactical differences. The mixed-sex (or promiscuous) audience included both black and white members, but William Lloyd Garrison complained that no African Americans sat on the stage. He saw this oversight as either "wicked prejudice" or "fear of giving public offence," moral weaknesses that demonstrated "a squeamishness with regard to coming out boldly in favor of the doctrine of *immediate* emancipation."[5] Some abolitionists present, such as John Greenleaf Whittier, who had just moved to Philadelphia to edit the Pennsylvania Anti-Slavery Society's newspaper the *Pennsylvania Freeman*, argued for using the political system to end slavery. Whittier proposed a resolution that male abolitionists "hold our right of suffrage sacred to the cause of freedom." Garrison viewed the political process as leading to unacceptable compromises. He declared, "Honesty before policy! Justice before expediency! Innocency before union!"[6]

While Garrison worried that abolitionists were not radical enough, the crowd gathering outside the hall raged that they were too extreme. Had Garrison called George Washington a "robber and man-stealer"? Was a white woman who had married a black man about to address the promiscuous audience? Indeed, fears of amalgamation riled the mob. The New Orleans *True American* later reported that "One pretty woman (white) was seen seated between two black fellows with woolly heads. Men were seen gallanting black women to and from the Hall." From this *"tabernacle of mischief and fanaticism,"* another southern newspaper reported, "the descendant of Ham or

Africa" emerged "side by side, with some of the fairest and wealthiest daughters of Philadelphia."[7]

The rumor of an interracial marriage referred to the wedding of Angelina Grimké and white abolitionist Theodore Dwight Weld. The couple married on May 14, the opening day of Pennsylvania Hall, in the Philadelphia home of the bride's sister. Weld pledged to love, honor, and cherish Angelina. He also vowed to recognize her "equality." Rejecting the legal power of husband over wife, he "abjured all authority, all government, save the influence which love would give to them over each other as moral and immortal beings."[8] Even in the Quaker city, the ceremony transgressed standards of sexual and racial propriety. After the Welds' unusual vows, "a colored Presbyterian minister" prayed, "followed by a white one." Their guests included "several colored persons" including former slaves owned by the Grimké family. As Sarah Grimké reported, "we thus had an opportunity to bear our testimony against the horrible prejudice which prevails against colored persons."[9] Quaker doctrine prevented Mott from attending an interfaith marriage featuring "hireling" ministers, but she rejoiced in the couple's "connubial bliss." And she wholeheartedly concurred with their defiance of public opinion.[10]

Around the city, gossips spread tales of race mixing, while posters denounced the convention as a threat to the nation. Calling all citizens to Pennsylvania Hall, one placard read: "Whereas a convention for the avowed purpose of effecting the immediate abolition of slavery in the Union is now in session in this city, it behooves all citizens, who entertain a proper respect for the right of property, and the preservation of the Constitution of the United States, to interfere, *forcibly* if they *must*, and prevent the violation of those pledges heretofore held sacred." The violence began on the first day, when rocks hurled at the building broke a window. Then, in an obviously threatening manner, men outside the hall began to inspect the gas pipes. By Wednesday night, the crowd yelled and screamed, hurling brick-bats and other "missiles" at the building. Inside, Angelina Grimké Weld, the woman who had supposedly married a "negro," told the audience "Hear it—hear it. Those voices tell us the spirit of slavery is here, and has been roused to wrath by our abolition speeches and conventions."[11]

The violence outside the hall tested the egalitarianism of the frightened men and women inside. Although most Philadelphia abolitionists "freely admitted" that they let African Americans sit anywhere in the hall without "molestation," some ran from accusations of amalgamation. Lucretia later reported to her son-in-law Edward M. Davis that Dr. Joseph Parrish tried to edit the official minutes of the Anti-Slavery Convention of American Women to exclude a controversial resolution "relating to social intercourse with our colored brethren." Mott had supported the resolution, offered by Sarah Grimké, that "it is the duty of abolitionists to identify themselves with these oppressed Americans, by sitting with them in places of worship, by appearing with them in our streets, by giving them our countenance in steam-boats and stages, by visiting them at their homes and encouraging them to visit us, receiving them as we do our white fellow citizens."[12]

Some female abolitionists also balked at sexual equality. Juliana Tappan, an abolitionist from New York City and secretary of the second Anti-Slavery Convention of American Women, had proposed a resolution vowing to continue petitioning "until the slave shall go free, or our energies, like Lovejoy's, are paralyzed in death." Willing to be martyred for the cause, the Anti-Slavery Convention of American Women nevertheless refused to allow men in their meetings because of fears that it was improper. Following addresses to the mixed assembly by Angelina Grimké Weld and Abby Kelley on Wednesday night, Mott, speaking as vice-president of the Anti-Slavery Convention of American Women, informed the audience that these speeches were not sponsored by the women's convention, but that she hoped "such false notions of delicacy and propriety would not long obtain in this enlightened country."[13]

On Thursday afternoon, May 17, Mott addressed the anti-slavery women regarding the previous night's riot. The meeting was smaller due to fears of more violence. African American women in particular worried that they might become targets of the mob's anger over racial mixing. Unlike the white women present, their sex did not protect them. White men, reluctant to rough up respectable middle-class white women, would not blanch at doing the same to black women. Lucretia urged the women present to be "steadfast," advising them not to be "alarmed by a little *appearance* of danger." But despite these confident words, Mott admitted it was a "searching time": "I believe I was strengthened by God. I felt at the moment that I was willing to suffer whatever the cause required." During the meeting, the women remained calm, despite being surrounded by a mob filling the doors and threatening to enter the room.[14]

After they adjourned, Mott and the others had to pass through the crowd, now in the thousands. Angelina Grimké Weld proposed that they link arms with the African American women present in order to protect them, and so they did. One woman noted the "vile" and "hideous countenances" of the men and boys, "fellows of the baser sort." As the mob shouted "incendiary, violent, and abusive" insults like "Down with the Quaker, down with the nigger's friend," the women exited the building.[15]

The Anti-Slavery Convention of American Women was the last group to meet in Pennsylvania Hall. Vowing not to defend the hall by force, the managers appealed to the mayor for justice, citing "the laws of our country" and the Constitution. But Mayor John Swift, a Whig, needed a majority of voters in the upcoming election. The unsympathetic politician told the abolitionists that all he could do was make a speech. Swift appeared at the hall, and, after designating the mob his "policemen," received three hearty cheers from the crowd. Now numbering approximately 15,000 individuals, the mob commenced the attack after the mayor departed. Over 100 individuals forced open the doors, and after placing a pile of papers on the stage, set fire to them. To insure the destruction of the building, the men then turned the gas pipes toward the flames. In a few hours, the building was completely consumed.[16]

After burning Pennsylvania Hall to the ground, the mob turned its attention to other symbols of amalgamation. The mob headed first for the Motts' new home at 136 North Ninth Street, where eleven white and black delegates to the convention were staying. While the Motts and their friends waited patiently in the parlor, the mob seized on a more vulnerable target, heading for a "colored orphanage" on Thirteenth Street near Callowhill. The violence lasted for two more days, with African American buildings, like Mother Bethel Church on Sixth Street, suffering the brunt of the damage. Still, in the mind of the mob, Lucretia remained an enticing representative of the threat of racial equality. On Friday, after the Anti-Slavery Convention of American Women held its final session at Sarah Pugh's school, the Motts got word that the crowd planned to attack their house. As "an excited throng" ran up Race Street, a young man succeeding in diverting the crowd by yelling "On to Mott's" then leading them up Race, past Ninth Street.[17] One guest, Maria Weston Chapman of Boston, was so upset by the violence that she suffered a "brain fever."[18]

The destruction of Pennsylvania Hall also caused lasting harm to the anti-slavery movement. After the fire, Angelina Grimké and Theodore Dwight Weld ended their brilliant careers as anti-slavery lecturers. In the pages of the *Pennsylvania Freeman*, Whittier also documented numerous examples of the "unavoidable friction of the mighty moral machinery of the American Anti-Slavery Society." Abolitionists disagreed over theology, human government, and nonviolence. After Mayor John Swift's defeat, they debated the merits of the ballot box and a third party devoted to abolition. But the problem of female abolitionists remained one of the most divisive.[19]

Despite the tragedy, Mott and the Philadelphia Female Anti-Slavery Society decided to host another Anti-Slavery Convention of American Women. The traumatized women reconvened in June 1838, and Lucretia reminded them of their commitment to abolishing slavery and racial prejudice: "At the request of Mrs. Mott the preamble to our Constitution was read, upon which she commented with much feeling, thereby strengthening the hands and cheering the hearts of some who were well nigh fainting." This resolve was necessary, as a few months later the women were evicted from their usual meeting room when the owners refused to rent to them any longer. The women adjourned to Sarah Douglass's school. A similar problem occurred when they tried to find a location for the next Anti-Slavery Convention of American Women. Mott reported that "we have applied for several places of worship—those of Friends as well as others have so far been refused to us." Mott and the other women ended up holding the convention on May 1–3, 1839, in the Pennsylvania Riding School on Filbert Street.[20]

Due to the previous year's violence, the presence of African American women at the convention became an issue again. Pressured by "timid" reformers like Dr. Parrish, white women worried about the possibility of another mob. African American members also expressed concern about the danger of another public mixed-race assembly in the heart of Philadelphia. Addressing the fears of members, Lucretia called upon members of the Philadelphia Female Anti-Slavery Society to look into their own hearts for prejudice and to pray for its extinction. The white and black women resolved to encourage the attendance of their "colored sisters" at their monthly meetings as well as at the upcoming convention. The Philadelphia Female Anti-Slavery Society appealed to African American women not because of declining black membership, but rather in response to the violence directed at interracial meetings. They affirmed their right and duty to hold these gatherings, whatever the risk to their physical bodies or their social respectability (a hard won status for even the most elite African American women).[21]

Outside the small circle of the Philadelphia Female Anti-Slavery Society, Philadelphia's new mayor expressed concern over the women's behavior at the upcoming convention. Did white and black women plan to walk to the Riding School and enter together? Would black women participate in the convention as equals? Mott responded that "it was a principle with us, which we could not yield, to make no distinction on account of color."[22] Indeed, after the convention the Philadelphia Female Anti-Slavery Society resolved to combat racism anew. Members issued an Address to American Women on Prejudice. They also divided up the city, with two members assigned to different African American neighborhoods. They proposed to visit families, organize meetings, and to help raise African Americans out of "degradation, ignorance, and poverty." In its *Sixth Annual Report*, the Philadelphia Female Anti-Slavery Society reminded readers of the importance of eradicating racial prejudice. Racism, members concluded, was "crushing" the black population.[23]

The voices of anti-slavery women who preferred to integrate existing male institutions had grown stronger, further limiting the size of the 1839 meeting. Lydia Maria Child informed Mott that she thought female conventions were like "half a pair of scissors"—ineffective. Abby Kelley, the Massachusetts abolitionist who had made her first speech to a "promiscuous audience" the previous year, argued that female conventions were unnecessary. Mott, who had never worried about speaking to a mixed assembly, agreed with them in part. But she also saw the uses of female societies, arguing "that our Conventions have done something toward bringing woman to a higher estimation of her powers." Though some women wanted to join male associations, it was not clear that men would let them. In 1839, the American Anti-Slavery Society debated whether women could serve as delegates to their annual convention. The following year, after Abby Kelley was elected to the American Anti-Slavery Society business committee (charged with determining the "business" of the meeting), the national society split, with prominent abolitionist Lewis Tappan leading the exodus to form a new organization, the American and Foreign Anti-Slavery Society.[24]

The Pennsylvania Anti-Slavery Society included female abolitionists with less controversy, appointing Mott to the business committee at their annual convention in Norristown in May 1839. From then on, the working relationship between the Philadelphia Female Anti-Slavery Society and the Pennsylvania Anti-Slavery Society was extremely close. Mott, Sarah Pugh, Mary Grew, and several other white members regularly served in official positions in the state society—as members of the business and executive committees, or as secretary or treasurer of the organization. Significantly, the women of the Philadelphia Female Anti-Slavery Society wielded financial influence as well. Like other female abolitionists, the society held an annual fair, raising hundreds, if not thousands, of dollars for the cause each year. They used this money to subscribe to anti-slavery newspapers, to distribute anti-slavery publications, and to support the state and national society. Both white and black members were fully involved in the planning and execution of the fair. In 1844, the Philadelphia Female Anti-Slavery Society published an appeal for donations to the fair, noting that all the money raised would go into the treasury of the Pennsylvania Anti-Slavery Society. Among the signers were Sarah M. Douglass, Harriet Purvis, Hetty Burr, Esther (or Hester) Reckless, and Margaretta Forten.[25]

The Pennsylvania Anti-Slavery Society was almost entirely dependent on the fundraising abilities of the women in the PFASS, but only a small group of white women served in an official capacity in the state organization. The state society may have been less welcoming to African American women, who observed that "even our professed friends have not yet rid themselves" of racial prejudice.[26] In addition, like many middle-class white women, black women may have felt uncomfortable taking a public role in a mixed-sex organization. Indeed, most women in the Philadelphia Female Anti-Slavery Society did not participate in the official business of the state society, preferring to work with other women.

Even as the American Anti-Slavery Society and the Pennsylvania Anti-Slavery Society integrated women into their organizations, the Philadelphia Female Anti-Slavery Society resolved to continue as a female organization, rejecting proposals to change their name or merge with a male society in Philadelphia. Mary Grew, the female society's long-standing corresponding secretary, was reluctant to adopt any measure that might interfere with the special "nature" of the Philadelphia Female Anti-Slavery Society, sustained over a decade of labor. She described the organization as "true to the highest form of anti-slavery principles" and "clear-sighted" in times of "darkness and perplexity."[27] Mott also viewed the society as an important source of ideological and emotional strength. The society's longevity can be attributed in part to members' continuous self-examination of their purpose, their goals, and their beliefs.

In the face of violent opposition to their movement, Garrisonian abolitionists rejected the use of "carnal weapons" against slavery, not only force, but also politics. Like the issue of women's participation, "non-resistance" also caused conflict in the American Anti-Slavery Society, contributing to the schism in the movement. In 1838, William Lloyd Garrison founded the New England Non-Resistance Society to advocate civil disobedience. He used the pages of the *Liberator* to promote nonviolence as well as anti-slavery, and John Greenleaf Whittier, among others, complained that the introduction of even "collaterally connected" issues was inappropriate for an anti-slavery newspaper. Whittier's fears came to life when James Gordon Bennett, editor of the *New York Herald*, denounced the American Anti-Slavery Society for welcoming "the Non-Resistants, Infidels, Socialists, Atheists, Grahamites, Pantheists, and all the disaffected materials afloat on the bosom of society." As Bennett's litany of insults indicated, critics discerned something far more disturbing than mere pacifism. Non-resistants refused to vote or hold elected office, arguing that the American political system rested on the violence of slavery, capital punishment, a standing army, and militias. Outsiders viewed Garrison as embracing an anarchical "no government" position, but his rejection of the vote also disturbed many abolitionists, who saw politics as one path to ending slavery. By 1840, these former allies founded the Liberty Party, with Pennsylvania abolitionist Thomas Earle, who was married to Mott's cousin Mary Hussey, as the vice-presidential nominee.[28]

Unlike her relative Thomas Earle, Lucretia applauded the New England Non-Resistance Society as the new vanguard of Quaker pacifism. In September 1839, she traveled to Boston to attend the society's annual meeting, and addressed the gathering several times. Mott wrote that "The words of truth & soberness were spoken forth there and the meeting altogether was of deep interest to me—On one account, more so than our first Anti-Slavery Convention—That *women* were there by right."[29] But some leaders of the Hicksite Society of Friends condemned Mott's participation in both the anti-slavery and non-resistance movements. George F. White, a New York minister, led the attack. Lucretia described him as a "Hicksite Priest" who assailed Unitarians, "Abolitionists, Non-Resistants & Temperance men." White, like a growing number of Hicksites, was disturbed by Quaker participation in worldly organizations. White saw such interfaith organizations as threatening to repeat the events leading to the great separation, when Orthodox Quakers cooperated with "hireling ministers" in benevolent associations. He warned Quakers against associating with ministers from other religions as "their vine was as the vine of Sodom & their grapes bitter." But his attack was also personal, focusing with vituperative intensity on Mott. White traveled to Philadelphia to preach at Cherry Street, her home meeting. In his sermon, he complained of Mott's trip to Boston to attend the meeting of the Non-Resistance Society, when she had violated social norms by traveling without a male escort (something Lucretia did on a regular basis):

What did woman want in the name of rights, but liberty to roam over the country from Dan to Beersheba spurning the protection of man—to traverse the streets & lanes of the City—to travel in stages and steamboats by day Lines & night Lines without a male protector—for himself before he would submit to the dictations of an imperious woman, he would traverse the earth while there was a foot of ground to tread upon & swim the rivers while there was water to swim in.

White delivered this message up and down the east coast. Mott might have been able to dismiss him as insane—"His theology is dark & mysterious—contradictory and absurd"—but for the fact that he posed a serious threat to her membership in the Society of Friends. She wrote that she was "cast down in view of what awaits the Society—if this spirit of judging and condemning is not arrested." Mott too interpreted these events in light of the Hicksite split, when Elias Hicks' anti-slavery testimony brought down the wrath of Orthodox Friends.[30]

White returned to Cherry Street Meeting repeatedly, causing a "spirit of division." His ministry confounded one member of the meeting, William Adams, an abolitionist who wrote approvingly of Lucretia's preaching in his diary: "What else but the divine arm of power can support her, and enable her to declare unsophisticated truth with such boldness, convincing her hearers of the truths of the Gospel, in all its simplicity, stripped of its forms and ceremonies." Adams described White as taking a "tried path" and his sermons as "singular." But during another visit, White won him over with an "impressive sermon" opposing "the present mode of abolitionists, in persuading southern slaveholders to liberate their slaves; but it is said he abstains entirely from products of slave labor."[31]

This division between radical abolitionists favoring nonsectarianism and those who advocated a closed Quaker approach also surfaced in the Philadelphia Yearly Meeting of Women Friends. White's ally Rachel Hicks, another New York minister, prompted dissension in her regular visits to Philadelphia Yearly Meeting. In 1841, for example, with Hicks in attendance, the women of the Philadelphia Yearly Meeting worried that "slander" had disrupted the "love and unity" of the society. In a standard review of their adherence to the principles of the society (presented as queries), some of the women present expressed concern "that we may be faithful to our testimony against an hireling ministry," a concern directed toward abolitionists, many of whom were paid for their lectures. Mott's involvement in the anti-slavery movement exposed her to these charges even though she did not accept remuneration. In response to this subtle attack, those who embraced an immediate end to

slavery suggested that not all members were faithful to the society's testimony against slavery. Mott wrote to Phebe Post Willis, a member of New
York Yearly Meeting, "As to Rachel Hicks if she preaches as she did when
last here, I cannot feel much interest in her meetings . . . I wish thou would
tell her so!" This understatement belied the trouble brought by the combined
labors of White and Hicks. The following year, Philadelphia Quakers refused
to give Lucretia a minute to travel as a minister.[32]

Lucretia's close friend, the abolitionist lecturer Charles C. Burleigh, known
for his eccentric long hair and beard, described the tension between Mott and
White as the hottest topic of conversation since the burning of Pennsylvania
Hall. Burleigh purposely linked the two attacks (one physical and one verbal)
to show that this was no mere internal Hicksite debate, but rather one in a
line of charges against abolitionists by the "enemies of our holy enterprise."
Indeed, Lucretia told her friend Phebe that White had criticized her for being
too "wrapped up" in Garrison. But Lucretia, like Charles Burleigh, embraced
this identification with the founder of the American Anti-Slavery Society. In
the coming years, she positioned herself as an important partisan of Garrisonian abolitionism, based on the pure moral power expressed in the American
Anti-Slavery Society Declaration of Sentiments and the Philadelphia Female
Anti-Slavery Society constitution.[33]

Mott's resistance to these enemies transformed her national reputation
into an international notoriety. On March 5, 1840 the *Pennsylvania Freeman*
scolded "Most Shameful!" The previous month, Lucretia had visited Delaware on a religious mission. Fifty-seven-year-old Daniel Neall and his new
bride (and second wife), Lucretia's fifty-three-year-old cousin Rebecca Bunker, traveled with her. At Smyrna, the newspaper reported, "a rumor of their
being abolitionists had preceded them, and some threats of disturbance were
made." After preaching, Lucretia and the Nealls returned to their lodgings,
only dodging a "few harmless missiles." But as they sat around the fireside, a
"low fellow" entered and demanded that Daniel Neall accompany him back
to Smyrna. According to the growing mob outside, they knew Neall as president of Pennsylvania Hall and as an advocate of "disorganizing doctrines."
When Neall refused to leave, the crowd dragged him out by force. Lucretia
wrote that Rebecca "was not inured to Mobs as some of us are—she shook,
as with an ague from head to foot." Mott and the others chased after Neall,
and when they caught up to the mob, the tiny, ninety-two-pound minister
confronted them. Lucretia recalled, "I plead hard with them to take me as
I was the offender—if offence had been committed, & give him up to his

wife—but they declined saying 'you are a woman & we have nothing to say to you.'—to wh. I answered 'I ask no courtesy at your hands on accot. of my sex.'" The mob tarred Neall's coat, added a few feathers for good measure, and then rode him on a rail before releasing him. Afterward, both Neall and Mott addressed the crowd. Lucretia called them "a respectful mob," writing that they "listened to all I said."[34]

The tale of the Delaware mob spread rapidly through the anti-slavery community. Boston abolitionist Anne Weston, sister of Maria Weston Chapman, asked for more details, so Lucretia recounted the "old story" in May. Soon after, she and James sailed for England, where they planned to attend the World's Anti-Slavery Convention. At a tea party in London, British abolitionists asked Mott to tell her version again. Despite the friendly audience, the tensions that wracked the American anti-slavery movement—over female abolitionists, racial equality, nonviolence, politics, and religion—had traveled across the Atlantic with her. After Lucretia remarked that she traveled to Smyrna with a "minute" from her monthly meeting, British Quaker Josiah Forster interrupted to voice the Orthodox complaint: "she was not a member of the Society of Friends, and could not be recognized by them as such."[35] As events in London made clear, the anti-slavery movement was divided from within and assailed from without.

CHAPTER 6

Abroad

THE WORLD'S ANTI-SLAVERY CONVENTION OF 1840 transformed history, further dividing the abolitionist movement and connecting Lucretia with a young Elizabeth Cady Stanton. Yet Mott's very public trip to London as the "leader of the delegate women from America" was shaped in part by private concerns over money problems and poor health.[1] In September 1838, anti-slavery lecturer Charles C. Burleigh reported to his friend Miller McKim that the Penn Factory "was burned to the ground, & in it, part of the machinery, a considerable quantity of wool, & some manufactured goods." James Mott owned one quarter of the business, and Burleigh estimated his losses at $20,000, about $500,000 today. James was despondent. The family (with Charles as a regular guest) feared that they might lose their home at 136 North Ninth Street, which would have forced them to move in with their daughter Anna, her husband Edward Hopper, and their baby, Lucretia. Now forty-five years old, Mott proudly described her first granddaughter, known as "Lue," as "forward and smart." In May 1838, Maria and Edward Davis also had their first child, Anna (Mott's biographer Anna Davis Hallowell). Mott was moving into a new stage of life.

Though their two oldest daughters were established and secure in their own households, James and Lucretia still faced an uncertain financial future. The country had just emerged from the speculative crisis known as the Panic of 1837. Indeed, the economy would not fully recover from the resulting depression for another four years. James Mott owed money, Burleigh reported, and had no means to pay his debts since the fire. Nevertheless, Burleigh ended the letter on a positive note: "But I can hardly believe that he—known as he is as a man of sterling integrity—will fail to receive from his creditors the same favour which he shows to those who owe him—& I hope we shall by & by see clear sky, cloudy as the prospect now seems."[2]

Most of Burleigh's letter was devoted to Lucretia's reaction to the economic setback. "Our good 'mother' bears all like the noble woman she is—but though noble, she is still woman," he told Miller. As this statement suggests, Charles was especially interested in the tension between her "calm & quiet courage" and "heroic bearing," manly attributes in the early republic, and her feminine obligations to her husband and family. Charles had witnessed her bravery in the "trying times" of the Pennsylvania Hall mobs. But, he wrote, "I have never before seen her exhibit so fully the excellent woman & the true Christian as now." This excellent woman, Charles declared, was self-sacrificing, "in refusing to sink under it, in counselling, consoling & encouraging others, in combating her own sadness & tendency to gloom, that she may remove her husband's." Burleigh knew that Miller McKim was a sympathetic audience for his adoring description of Lucretia. "She evidently feels deeply, & as evident is it to one who observes her attentively," Charles wrote. Then, he asked, "do you wonder that I so observe her?"[3]

Both Miller McKim and Charles Burleigh viewed Mott as a mentor, a "mother" to abolitionist radicals. Both men were born in 1810, which made them seventeen years younger than Lucretia and only two years older than her daughter Anna Hopper. But their close relationship to Mott was based on more than maternity. They idealized her as a woman, an activist, and an intellectual sparring partner. McKim first met Mott at the founding convention of the American Anti-Slavery Society in 1833. A native of Carlisle, Pennsylvania, McKim was training to be a Presbyterian minister at the time, and he was ordained in 1835. But from the moment they met, Lucretia challenged the young evangelical's religious faith. A great lender of reading material, she gave him Quaker abolitionist John Woolman's *Journal* as well as *Causes and Evils of Contentions Unveiled in Letters to Christians* by Noah Worcester, a pacifist Congregationalist minister and former editor of the *Christian Examiner,* a Unitarian periodical. She told Miller "I want thee to have done with calling Unitarian rationalities—'icy philosophizing.'" Instead, Lucretia wrote, "It is quite time we read & examined the Bible more rationally in order that truth may shine in its native brightness." When McKim renounced the doctrine of the Atonement, leading to his removal for heresy in 1838, Mott rejoiced that he burst the "fetters of Presbyterianism." She happily reported that he was growing "more & more a Quaker."[4]

McKim's spiritual awakening also enabled Lucretia to play matchmaker, facilitating his engagement to Sarah Speakman, a Quaker from Chester County. After a secret courtship, Lucretia convinced Sarah's father, Micajah Speakman, to support the interfaith marriage. McKim enjoyed this intellectual and personal scheming as much as Lucretia. He reportedly told her, "Mrs. Mott you are the greatest radical I ever met with." McKim's phrasing suggests his amusement that a woman—a married woman—could be such a subversive.[5]

Born in Plainfield, Connecticut, Charles C. Burleigh came from a family with anti-slavery convictions. He first became active in the movement when he wrote an article defending Prudence Crandall's school, where his sister worked as a teacher. Charles gave up a career as a lawyer to become an anti-slavery lecturer, a calling in which he excelled. During an 1836–37 lecture tour of Pennsylvania, he endured "being laughed at, called fanatic, lunatic, and everywhere receiving brickbats, rotten eggs, &c," but his speaking skills contributed to the formation of sixty new anti-slavery societies in the state. In 1840, Burleigh became editor of the *Pennsylvania Freeman*, replacing John Greenleaf Whittier. Lucretia valued Burleigh's talents, informing Maria Weston Chapman that he was needed to prevent the crisis then dividing Boston's abolitionists from happening in Philadelphia.[6]

But like other abolitionists Lucretia disapproved of Charles's appearance; he wore his shirt collar turned down, like Lord Byron, and had "a profusion of auburn or reddish hair hanging in ringlets down his shoulders; while a huge beard of the same colour fell upon his breast." She commented that his failure to shave and cut his hair was no "*small*" matter—if it renders him, with all his powerful mind & happy gift of speech, less effective as the slave's appellant."[7] Despite her doubts about his appearance, Lucretia played "Match-Maker" for Burleigh as well, encouraging his courtship of Gertrude Kimber, daughter of Emmor Kimber, a disowned Quaker and founder of the experimental Kimberton School in Chester County, which Lucretia's sister Martha as well as her youngest daughter Pattie attended. Charles Burleigh and Gertrude Kimber married in 1842. When Miller teased Lucretia about her involvement in Charles's love life, she responded "What can I do, if you young people will come to me, whispering in my ear, your hearts best affections. You cant expect one of my temperament, to hear with coldness & indifference."[8]

This extended family of anti-slavery radicals and religious liberals sustained the Motts through their financial crisis. By November 1838, Lucretia wrote that James's renunciation of the cotton business had also been a sound financial decision: "Jas. feels very differently now with regard to his business, he is doing well with wool & we feel as if all would prove for the best." Even with the upturn in James's prospects, largely due to increased demand from wool manufacturers, the Motts could not afford a trip to Europe, unlike their well-traveled daughter and son-in-law, Maria and Edward M. Davis. As a result, Mott's Nantucket connections also proved crucial. When James and Lucretia decided to attend the World's Anti-Slavery Convention in London in 1840, a distant relative, Elizabeth Rodman, helped pay for the journey. Rodman, a liberal "New Light" Quaker, was the daughter of William Rotch, the successful New Bedford whaling merchant. Joseph Warner of Philadelphia also donated money toward their passage. Such fundraising was not uncommon for Americans who made the journey. Women in anti-slavery societies in Maine and Rhode Island raised money to fund the trip of African American abolitionist Charles Lenox Remond.[9]

While the Motts' financial condition had improved, friends and relatives also expressed concern for Lucretia's health. In 1838, with a house full of guests for the opening of Pennyslvania Hall, her daughter Maria wrote that Lucretia was feeling "poorly" and had stayed in bed instead of going to meeting. Her ill health persisted, so much so that her family encouraged her to make the trip to England, thinking that the ocean voyage might do her good.[10] Mott probably suffered from one of her many bouts of dyspepsia, an illness she battled through much of her adult life. A digestive disorder, the most common symptom of dyspepsia is stomach pain, but other symptoms can include bloating, burping, nausea, and vomiting. This chronic indigestion may be associated with a feeling of fullness or loss of appetite. Nineteenth-century doctors recommended exercise, fresh air, travel, light meals, and daily "slapping" or "kneading" of the stomach and bowels.[11] Lucretia's low weight (92 lbs.) may be partly attributed to this sickness.

The reasons for Mott's illness are unclear. Biographer Margaret Hope Bacon sees Lucretia's stomach problems as a physical manifestation of her anger at the world's injustices. Nineteenth-century doctors viewed dyspepsia as a product of mental anxiety, exhaustion, or over-excitement.[12] Certainly anti-slavery factionalism and criticism from Quakers like George F. White taxed Lucretia, who preferred to build consensus. Mott's family also attributed it to her "carelessness" of her own health. She was relentless in her attendance at religious and reform meetings, traveling immense distances, often in great discomfort, to participate in a national convention or yearly meeting. James especially worried about his wife's health, writing that in her "go-ahead-ativeness" to speak against the oppression of others, Lucretia was committing "voluntary oppression." James's choice of the incongruous Yankee term "go-ahead-ativeness" associated Lucretia with other ambitious Americans, examples of the "spirit of progress" sweeping the nation. Newspapers and commentators frequently used the characterization to describe her contemporary Cornelius Vanderbilt, the steamboat and railroad tycoon. An unlikely pair, Vanderbilt singlemindedly pursued his economic interests, while Mott focused her energy on the nation's morals. In using this label, James thus highlighted another possible explanation for Lucretia's illness, the contradiction between her irrepressible drive and the modest standards of Quaker womanhood.[13]

With humor as well as exasperation, James described a typical day in his wife's life, in which she received numerous callers "high & low rich & poor, for respect, advice, assistance, encouragement &c." These visitors, James noted, think she can "do anything & everything." Then, she went out to visit the sick and afflicted. Every Sunday, Lucretia traveled to Quaker meetings within the purview of Philadelphia Yearly Meeting, holding two meetings herself, in which she preached "*heresy & infidelity*" as well as slavery and abolition. She often arrived home as late as 11 p.m. Similarly, Mott's sister Martha Wright wrote, "I do believe if she let slavery to its chance, forswore 'mental feasts' and quarterly meetings,—let woman's rights, tight-lacing and the study of anatomy alone . . . that her health would be as good as ever." Mott was sympathetic to their diagnosis, but stubbornly refused to alter her schedule. Her family's only response was gently to mock her enthusiasm, hoping to prod a change in behavior. James also made sure he traveled with her when he could.[14]

When contemplating the trip to Great Britain, then, Lucretia was not particularly concerned with her health. Instead, she wanted to attend the "Grand Convention." "What an interesting event it will be!" Lucretia declared to Miller McKim. Reeling from criticism by Hicksite Quakers and upset by infighting among abolitionists, she was optimistic about this world convention.[15] As they had earlier in the century, American activists looked to the British for leadership. In 1834, England had abolished slavery in its colonies, instituting a period of apprenticeship to ease the transition to a free labor society. By 1838, Britain's former slaves had won their freedom. The next year, the newly formed British and Foreign Anti-Slavery Society announced the World's Anti-Slavery Convention to promote "the universal Abolition of Slavery and the Slave-Trade." In the invitation to abolitionists across the Atlantic, the British and Foreign Anti-Slavery Society urged that sectarian and party feelings be overcome in order to consider "moral, religious, and pacific" means to end slavery.[16]

But how American abolitionists responded to the invitation depended on their position on the recent divisions in the American Anti-Slavery Society. The "new organization," the American and Foreign Anti-Slavery Society (linked explicitly by name to its British counterpart), sent a contingent of male delegates, mostly ministers and politicians. But several organizations sent female representatives. Lucretia traveled as a delegate of Garrison's American Anti-Slavery Society, the Philadelphia Female Anti-Slavery Society, and the American Free Produce Association, an organization founded in 1838. She also had a certificate from her Monthly Meeting, authorizing her to speak in Quaker meetinghouses, and she represented the Association of Friends for Promoting the Abolition of Slavery.[17] In total, eight American women made the journey to England. Other delegates from the Philadelphia Female Anti-Slavery Society included Mary Grew, the corresponding secretary, Sarah Pugh, the society's president, Elizabeth Neall, daughter of Daniel Neall, and Abby Kimber, a teacher and daughter of Emmor Kimber. Three female delegates traveled from New England: Ann Greene Phillips, cousin of Mary Grew and wife of abolitionist orator Wendell Phillips; Abby Southwick, who had attended the 1838 Anti-Slavery Convention of American Women as a delegate from Massachusetts; and Emily Winslow, who traveled with her father Isaac Winslow, a Quaker merchant from Portland, Maine. After learning of the impending arrival of the American women, the organizing committee of the British and Foreign Anti-Slavery Society sent out another call in February 1840, specifying its preference for "gentlemen" as delegates. This set the tone for the convention to come, suggesting that the British and Foreign Anti-Slavery Society was decidedly biased toward its American namesake.[18]

Mott sailed from New York City on May 7, 1840, on the ship *Roscoe*. Despite her father's journeys across the Atlantic and Pacific Oceans, this was Lucretia's first trip overseas. Sensing that the trip was a significant moment in her life, she kept a diary of her three months abroad, the only time that she bothered to write a journal. Mott's diary reflects the rushed and newsy style of her letters to family and friends; she lists the events and people of each day, only recording her emotional and intellectual reaction in a terse or wry aside. On board, the Motts traveled with a large party of abolitionists, including the other female delegates from Philadelphia; Mary Grew's father Henry Grew, a member of the Pennsylvania Anti-Slavery Society and an independently wealthy Baptist minister originally from Birmingham, England; Isaac and Emily Winslow; Abby Southwick; and George Bradburn, a Unitarian minister, agent of the American Anti-Slavery Society, and Nantucket representative to the Massachusetts Legislature. As Mott recorded in her diary, the company entertained themselves by conversing on "slavery with West-Indians, particularly a Dr. McKnaught,—on Theology with Sectarians,—on Politics with Tories and haters of O'Connell [the Irish emancipator]." The "West-Indians" were white planters and former slaveholders. Unsurprisingly, Mott wrote, there were "No conversions." During the rough voyage, Mott also visited the steerage passengers, who were suffering from a measles outbreak.[19]

After a twenty-day passage, the ship docked in Liverpool on May 27. Since the convention was not due to begin until June 12, the Motts, in their first trip abroad, had time to see the country and visit English Quakers and like-minded reformers along the way. After stopping overnight in the port city, and meeting with William Rathbone, a former Quaker, the Motts traveled to Manchester. There, they toured a textile mill and attended a Quaker meeting where the "orthodox faith" was preached. In Birmingham, they visited a pin factory, after which they traveled to Stratford upon Avon, Oxford, and Windsor, finally arriving in London on June 5. Mott's response to the traditional English tourist highlights reflected her Quaker and republican skepticism of theater, aristocracy, and high church Protestantism. Mott noted that she had failed to cry on Shakespeare's grave, and she labeled the "chauntings" of the boy's choir in the Windsor chapel "ridiculous."[20]

Lucretia and James expressed the deepest interest in British industrialization, and they visited factories throughout their stay in the British Isles. As a convert to free produce, James identified English hypocrisy on the issue of slavery, observing "Liverpool is the great market from which the large manufacturers are supplied with the slave-grown cotton of the United States. Thus while the people of Great Britain, at a cost of twenty millions sterling, have abolished slavery in their colonies, they purchase annually from twelve-fifteen millions of the slave-stained cotton of [our] country." The Motts were also interested in the similarities and differences between English "wage slavery" and American chattel slavery. In Manchester, Lucretia wrote in her diary that the women and children working at the mill looked better than she expected, hardly a ringing endorsement.[21]

After arriving in the capital, the Motts roomed at Mark Moore's boarding house, No. 6 Queen Street Place, Southwark Bridge, Cheapside. Other American guests included Henry Stanton, a political abolitionist associated with the American and Foreign Anti-Slavery Society, and his new bride, future women's rights leader Elizabeth Cady Stanton. By marriage, the twenty-five-year-old Elizabeth was on the opposite side of the American anti-slavery divide, but she gravitated immediately toward Lucretia. Stanton later described her as a "revelation of womanhood." The two women discussed all Mott's favorite subjects, everything from Elias Hicks and the inner light to phrenology (the "science" of reading the contours of the skull), Unitarianism, and Mary Wollstonecraft. In Stanton, Mott won a devoted convert. Elizabeth recalled:

> It seemed to me like meeting a being from some larger planet, to find a woman who dared to question the opinions of Popes, Kings, Synods, Parliaments, with the same freedom that she would criticize an editorial in the *London Times*, recognizing no higher authority than the judgment of a pure-minded, educated woman. When I first heard from the lips of Lucretia Mott that I had the same right to think for myself that Luther, Calvin, and John Knox had, and the same right to be guided by my own convictions, and would no doubt live a higher, happier life than if guided by theirs, I felt at once a new-born sense of dignity and freedom; it was like suddenly coming into the rays of the noon-day sun, after wandering with a rushlight in the caves of the earth.[22]

Lucretia also felt an immediate connection to the younger woman. She described Elizabeth Stanton in glowing terms as "bright, open, lovely," noting "I love her now as one belonging to us." Her feelings for Elizabeth even extended to "her Henry" whom Mott never accepted as a "New-Organizationist." Though she met Elizabeth for the first time in London, Lucretia had known Henry Stanton since 1834, when, as one of the abolitionist "rebels" from Lyman Beecher's Lane Seminary in Cincinnati, Ohio, he had traveled to the American Anti-Slavery Society annual meeting, stopping at James Forten's house in Philadelphia on the way.[23]

In London, the dispute between the American women and the British and Foreign Anti-Slavery Society erupted immediately. With control over the transatlantic anti-slavery movement at stake, conversations revolved around two interconnected issues: recognition of the American female delegates and the "Hicksite" affiliation of James and Lucretia Mott. On the day after their arrival, Joseph Sturge, a British Quaker, called on the women and "begged submission of us to London Committee." At a tea party later that day, Mott reminded British abolitionists of the pioneering efforts of free produce advocate Elizabeth Heyrick, but failed to persuade them to include women in the upcoming convention. Two days later, Josiah Forster, another British Friend, pulled James aside to tell him that the English refused to recognize the Motts as Quakers due to the "dangerous tendency" of their doctrines. James and Lucretia were upset and frustrated by this display of "bigotry" and "ignorance."[24] These exchanges reflected two competing visions of the anti-slavery movement. Mott and other Garrisonian abolitionists viewed immediatism as breaking the chains of slaves, women, and other oppressed groups, exposing the false authority of slaveholders, politicians, and clergy. In contrast, the British and Foreign Anti-Slavery Society and its American counterpart defined themselves as influential, seeking access to the halls of power rather than its overthrow.[25]

Lucretia and the other American women did find allies among the British. Though Mott's theology may have shocked Anna Isabella Milbanke, better known as Lady Byron, Quaker Elizabeth Pease, and future suffragist Anne Knight, they all supported the right of the American women to participate. And, after dining at their evangelical nemesis Anna Braithwaite's house, Mott wrote that she was surprised to find her "more liberal toward us than we expected." She also discovered that Braithwaite's children had become Episcopalians, perhaps accounting for her softer attitude. In general, however, Mott failed to arouse much activist energy among British women. After one meeting with female abolitionists, she wrote "found little confidence in women's action either separately or con-jointly with men, except as drudges—some sectarian zeal manifested."[26]

The female delegates also received support from male abolitionists, including the Irish leader Daniel O'Connell, who had secured the "emancipation" of Irish Catholics, or their right to sit in the British Parliament. O'Connell initially opposed the admission of women to the World's Anti-Slavery Convention, but after the meeting opened Mott appealed directly (and publicly) to O'Connell as "one of the most distinguished advocates of universal liberty" to state his views on their exclusion. In his published response, O'Connell described the denial of female delegates as an "injustice," reflecting the "cowardice" of the convention's organizers. He also offered praise for American women, who "have persevered in our holy cause, amidst difficulties and dangers, with the zeal of confessors, and the firmness of martyrs; and, therefore, emphatically, they should not be disparaged or discouraged by any slight or contumely offered to their rights." Other male supporters included John Bowring, William Ashurst, and a reluctant George Thompson, all of whom spoke in their favor on the convention floor.[27]

Despite some manifestations of support, the women from Pennsylvania were resigned to their exclusion. Indeed, they concluded not to present their credentials to the British and Foreign Anti-Slavery Society, a controversial decision. But the Pennsylvania women did write a formal protest, which diplomatically acceded to the London organizers while at the same time indicating their opinion that the committee had violated appropriate procedure. Sarah Pugh, president of the Philadelphia Female Anti-Slavery Society, signed the protest. Born to a Quaker family in Alexandria, Virginia, in 1800, Pugh and her family moved to Chester County, Pennsylvania, three years later. After her mother, Catharine Pugh, opened a dressmaking business in Philadelphia, she sent Sarah to Westtown Boarding School. Pugh joined the Motts' Twelfth Street Meeting, where she also taught school. After the great separation, however, she resigned from Twelfth Street Meeting and declined to join a Hicksite meeting. "I join not the ranks of the other party," Pugh wrote, "for, however much I admire some of their principles, and love many of their members, I am not a sectarian." Like Mott, this schoolteacher judged people by their actions, and her assessment of British Quakers was harsh. Pugh later described their opponents as "aristocratic Quakers" who were "jealous" of Lucretia's influence. The Pennsylvania protest acknowledged the "kind attentions" of the British but expressed "regret" at the resolutions passed by the British and Foreign Anti-Slavery Society Committee regarding the credentials of the women from Massachusetts. Pugh and the other women pledged their cooperation, but only to "the just objects of the Convention, to whom it is presumed will belong the power of determining the validity of any claim to a seat in that body."[28]

The convention opened at Freemasons' Hall the following day, and Mott and the American women took their place in a special section, separated from the other delegates by a bar. Wendell Phillips, a staunch Garrisonian and devoted husband, intervened in the convention's proceedings to present the credentials of the female abolitionists from Massachusetts. Just as the Pennsylvania women's protest had implied, Phillips proposed that the convention as a whole, rather than the London organizing committee, determine who would be accepted as delegates. The ensuing debate among male delegates combined praise for women's efforts with a desire to limit what work women might do in abolishing slavery. For example, Reverend John Burnet, of the Congregational Union of England and Wales, hailed the usefulness of female abolitionists. "But," he said, "it is quite another thing to clothe them with office." Not only was this British custom (or "English Usage," as Mott termed it) embraced by many of the American abolitionists present, but these abolitionists largely agreed that women's subordinate place was ordained by God. Henry Grew, the father of PFASS delegate Mary Grew, declared that seating women would violate "the ordinance of Almighty God, who has a right to appoint our services according to his sovereign will." Mott noted his "inconsistency" and described the ensuing discussion as "rather noisy—the result cheered, unworthily—were told it was common in England." At the end of the day, an overwhelming majority of the convention had voted to exclude female delegates.[29]

Elizabeth Cady Stanton and her feminist ally Susan B. Anthony later asserted that "The movement for woman's suffrage, both in England and America, may be dated from this World's Anti-Slavery Convention." As they describe in the multivolume *History of Woman Suffrage*, after the rowdy debate over women's inclusion, Mott and Stanton decided to convene a women's rights meeting when they returned to the United States: "As Lucretia Mott and Elizabeth Cady Stanton wended their way arm in arm down Great Queen Street that night, reviewing the exciting scenes of the day, they agreed to hold a woman's rights convention on their return to America, as the men to whom they had just listened had manifested their great need of some education on that question."[30]

Yet Lucretia did not record this conversation with Stanton in her diary, nor did James mention it in his published account of their journey *Three Months in Great Britain*. This absence illustrates the two women's different understandings of the wellspring of women's rights. Looking back many years later, after the successful war against slavery, and the disappointing exclusion of women from voting rights guaranteed in the Fifteenth Amendment, Stanton's exaggeration of their conversation illustrated the importance of abolitionist rejection to the history of the women's rights movement.[31] By contrast, Mott's neglect indicated her focus at that moment on the anti-slavery movement. Her support for women's rights flowed less from her outrage at exclusion than her notions of individual liberty and common humanity.

In fact, Mott's stance drew criticism from other female abolitionists. When William Lloyd Garrison arrived several days late for the convention, he, Charles Lenox Remond, Nathaniel P. Rogers, and Rhode Island Quaker William Adams, all credentialed delegates, decided to sit with the women behind the bar. Rather than embrace their action, Lucretia had greeted them "with joy & sorrow too." She reasoned with them, hoping to change their minds, but "found them fixed."[32] From Massachusetts, Abby Kelley wrote to complain that Lucretia had "sacrificed *principle* at the altar of Peace." Lucretia accepted the criticism: "I have sometimes shrunk from a defence of our rights, when others have gone forward & stood in the breach—& I am very willing to crown such with laurels that I may not deserve." But she did not think that any principle had been sacrificed. Mott's position most closely resembled George Thompson's, who "dreaded" the rancor of the debate over seating women. While she did not agree with him that the issue was an "abstraction," she did believe it interfered (with little chance of success) in the business at hand. Instead, Lucretia "gave some rubs on our proposed exclusion," agitating on women's behalf when she could.[33]

After the first, and most famous, day at the World's Anti-Slavery Convention, delegates gathered for ten more days, considering speeches and resolutions on the international slave trade, the appropriate relationship between the Church and slavery, "Mohammedan" slavery, slavery in East India, colonization, the results of emancipation in the West Indies, and other topics. Mott attended the convention every day, following the debates closely.[34]

Lucretia paid particular attention to the discussions of free produce, a moral conviction and strategy to which she remained committed. On June 20, members of the convention debated a resolution recommending "the disuse of slave-labour produce . . . as far as practicable." As Mott noted in her diary, few were there to support it. Henry Grew, a member of the American Free Produce Association, was absent. James Mott was too "discouraged" to mount a defense. Baptist minister and "new organizationist" Nathaniel Colver, of Tremont Temple in Boston, opposed the resolution as inexpedient. As a result, delegates finally agreed to form a committee to examine possible sources of free produce as a replacement for the earlier resolution. Mott was appalled. She raged against Colver's hypocrisy, writing "N. Colver told how tender he was once on the subject, how he gathered his little ones about him, and explained to them the cruelty & wickedness of such participancy," but then "he too discovered self-denial was not easy & gave it up & his children full of latitude & spoil & the gain of oppression." After his speech, Colver "sallied forth" to the bar, behind which the rejected female delegates sat, and invited Mott to speak "if the spirit moves you." Not only did he profanely invoke this Quakerism, but his presumption of granting her permission to speak was condescending. In protest, Mott sat in silence, instead writing in her diary that, "Our Free Produce society will have to double their diligence & do their own work—and so will American abolitionists generally—& especially women."[35]

At every opportunity, Mott enjoyed provoking Colver, who was also boarding at Mark Moore's. In one exchange, after Colver pronounced "Women constitutionally unfit for public or business meetings," Lucretia reminded him "that the colored man too was said to be *constitutionally* unfit to mingle with the white man." Mott crowed, "He left the room angry." Recalling her trip to London two years later, Mott expressed her affection for all the different factions, including British Quakers and new organizationists, as long as they retained "sympathy for the suffering bondsman." But there was one exception, she wrote, in the bigoted Nathaniel Colver.[36] In the *History of Woman Suffrage*, Stanton deliberately portrayed Colver at his most grotesque: "the Rev. Nathaniel Colver, from Boston, who always fortified himself with six eggs well beaten in a large bowl at breakfast, to the horror of his host and a circle of æsthetic friends, stood his ground to the last—his physical proportions being his shield and buckle, and his Bible (with Colver's commentaries) his weapon of defence."[37]

In the end, the convention passed several measures supporting the "general axiom, that free-labour is more profitable to the employer, and consequently cheaper, than slave-labour." Mott criticized these resolutions for appealing to "avarice" and neglecting individual "moral power." Unlike the abstract economic laws promoted by the World's Anti-Slavery Convention, she viewed abstinence as a profoundly egalitarian response to slavery. Every individual had the ability to choose free produce, thus liberating themselves from the grasp of slavery even as they furthered its abolition. Despite the American Anti-Slavery Society's initial support for free produce, by this time even William Lloyd Garrison had grown weary of its rigors. During one conversation in London, Mott wrote that she was "sorry" to learn of his "inconsistency" on the subject. Mott and her fellow delegates from the Philadelphia Female Anti-Slavery Society remained among its most devoted adherents.[38]

On June 22, the convention moved to the Friends meetinghouse on Grace Church Street. Here, Mott and the other female delegates sat in the balcony. In her diary, she wrote "didn't like being so shut out from the members." That night, James Mott, Wendell Phillips, George Bradburn, William Adams, Isaac Winslow, and other allies of the American women finalized their official protest to the convention. The male delegates pointed out six interrelated errors in the convention proceedings: the "limited character" of the delegates, the predominance of the "will of the few" (the London Committee), the disregard for the rights of the American delegates, the abuse of power by the London Committee, "the deference to custom and usage" contrary to the "principle of the whole Anti-Slavery movement," and the violation of free speech by the convention's organizers. This protest, like the ones that had preceded it, criticized the hypocrisy of a "World's" convention (or, in the preferred language of the British, a general convention) that discriminated against female abolitionists. When the men offered the protest to the convention on June 23, Nathaniel Colver "impudently" moved to lay the protest on the table, effectively blocking any discussion. Though the London Committee had relented and allowed women to sit on the floor for the final proceedings of the convention, Mott left the meeting "disgusted" that the convention voted with Colver and tabled the protest.[39]

After the convention (and the London Committee's authority) ended, Mott addressed an anti-slavery tea held at a meeting hall named the Crown & Anchor. The five hundred people in attendance heard speeches by Garrison, Henry Stanton, Remond, and George Thompson. William Crewdson, a former Quaker, chaired the meeting and announced that "L.M. is confidently expected to make the next speech." As she rose to speak, the Rev. John Scoble stood and said he had some *important* remarks to make first. But the gathering drowned him out with cries of "No! No!—Mrs. Mott." Before she began, Mott slyly apologized for the relative *"unimportance"* of her remarks, and then, given the convention's failings, offered a speech on free produce. As she ended her lecture, Josiah Forster stood up to remind the audience that she was not a Quaker, but he too was shouted down by the audience with cries of "down, down, order, order, shame, shame." The mistreatment of the American women had won them new defenders.[40]

Furthermore, religious radicals in England supported Mott's view that "sectarian proscription," as well as "English Usage" and "American New Organization," had led to the their exclusion. James Fuller, an English Quaker and farmer living in Skaneateles, New York, informed the Motts that "the secret of it was that so many of us were not of their faith—that it was announced in the London Yearly Meeting that we were coming, and they were put on their guard." William Howitt, British Quaker and author of *A Popular History of Priestcraft in All Ages and Nations*, wrote, "It is pitiable that you were excluded on the plea of being women; but it is disgusting that, under that plea, you were actually excluded as heretics. That is the real ground of your exclusion, and it ought to have been at once proclaimed and exposed by the liberal members of the Convention."[41] Indeed, in their accounts of the trip, James and Lucretia paid special attention to the words and actions of Friends in the British Isles. Wealthy Quaker banker Samuel Gurney held several parties at his house during and after the convention. Though the Motts later attended one of these gatherings, Gurney first discouraged their presence, as "where there were young people they were afraid of our principles."[42]

The Motts remained in London for another two weeks before continuing on their tour of the British Isles. During that time, they socialized and visited Sir John Soanes's museum and the British Museum. Mott enjoyed the former's "economy of space" and "beautiful paintings," but she described the British Museum as too big with "so much to see that the eye is wearied." The Motts also went to see the crowd gathered at Newgate prison to witness the execution of the valet François Benjamin Courvoisier, who had, in a sensational crime, murdered his employer Lord William Russell, brother of the future prime minister. Mott described those who supported capital punishment as "abusive;" when they left London for Birmingham, she and James attended a lecture by Unitarian minister George Harris opposing the death penalty. Lucretia also addressed the crowd of 2,500 people and received cheers for her speech. "So much for English Usage," she commented. From Birmingham, they, along with Sarah Pugh and Abby Kimber, traveled to Bath, Manchester, and then Liverpool, where they set sail for Dublin.[43]

In Ireland, the Motts were struck by the poverty of the country, which they attributed in part to British colonial rule. They saw crowds of beggars almost everywhere they went. James wrote, "The contrast between the rich and poor was more striking than in any other place we visited." He observed that most of the "aristocracy" lived in Dublin, spending their days visiting and riding. Instead, the Motts asked their host Richard Webb to take them to the "Liberties," the poorest neighborhood in the city. In the countryside, James noted that most of the field labor was performed by women, who worked without shoes or hats to protect them (again, with no outcry from those touting English custom). But, he asked, is "all this poverty, filth, and degradation" "as bad as our slavery"? No, he concluded, "for our slavery is all this and more." Both situations, he wrote, "need reparation, and both will get it." The Motts visited Irish Quakers and abolitionists, including Webb, a printer, and his wife, Hannah, and Richard Allen, a cotton merchant, and his wife, Ann. These Irish Friends sympathized with the Motts' theological and political views. At the Webbs' home, they were joined by Garrison and Nathaniel P. Rogers, on an anti-slavery lecture tour trying to win allies for the American Anti-Slavery Society. The Webbs, in particular, had become "Garrisonized to the backbone" at the World's Anti-Slavery Convention.[44] The Motts corresponded with these transatlantic allies long after their departure from Ireland, writing about common friends, theological debates, the anti-slavery movement, and their mutual interest in the reforms of the day.

From Ireland, the Motts traveled to Scotland, where they met up with their old friend the Edinburgh phrenologist George Combe and his wife Cecilia.

The Motts had met Combe in Philadelphia in 1838, when he was in the midst of a successful lecture tour of the United States. Indeed, Combe's lectures and books popularized phrenology, a discipline that claimed the grooves and bumps of the cranium were the key to human personality. Believing phrenology a true science, capable of revealing the laws of nature, Mott and other advocates also saw it as contributing to the progress of humanity. Combe himself was involved in anti-slavery, prison reform, and educational reform. However comic the pseudo-science of head reading may seem today, its emphasis on the study of physical characteristics rather than religious faith marked it as enlightened. For both Combe and Mott, phrenology offered the possibility of individual moral development through self-knowledge. In a letter to Combe, Mott expressed her wish that the "truths of Phrenology" "could find entrance into the Church & Theological schools, as a substitute for the dogmas & hidden mysteries there instilled & given forth, in the name of Christianity." Such sentiments echoed her frustration at the superstitions used to explain the death of her first son as "God's will."[45]

Of course, it did not hurt that Combe gave Lucretia complimentary readings. In his account of his lecture tour, *Notes on the United States of North America: During a Phrenological Visit 1838–9–40*, Combe described the Motts as the most "estimable" people he had met: "To the soft delicacy of a refined and accomplished woman, Lucretia Mott adds the clear and forcible intellect of a philosopher." Mott returned the compliment, describing the American phrenologists Orson and Lorenzo Fowler as his inferiors. She also praised his best-selling book *Constitution of Man* (1835) as a "breaker of images": "it is now perceived that Religion, or the Salvation of Man, consists not so much in believing a miracle, & subscribing to a mystery, as in acting out a principle, and conforming to an eternal & unvarying law."[46]

Despite her preference for Combe, when Orson Fowler came to Philadelphia, she, James, and her sister Eliza Yarnall, allowed him to "read" their heads. Mott found the readings accurate, though she did not like "the flattery they intersperse in the characters." Since Fowler's reading described her as "censorious," hardly a flattering assessment, perhaps she accepted this diagnosis. Mott's head also apparently demonstrated her "strong adhesiveness & moral principles—know your own faults & notice those of others—cannot keep quiet and see things go wrong." In addition, he noted her "considerable temper but well governed—moral indignation strong & irrepressible." She was also "rather disposed perhaps to extremes," had "a disposition and ability to reason," and was a "good mimic" with a "quick perception of the ridiculous." Finally, Fowler concluded, Mott "lay stress upon life rather than doctrine, are liberal rather than sectarian."[47] This last assessment conformed clearly to Mott's own sense of herself. A partisan player in the internecine struggles of Quakers and abolitionists, Mott nevertheless saw her opponents as bound by sectarianism. At times, her extreme "moral principles" clashed with her "liberal" outlook.

After visiting the Combes, the Motts traveled to Glasgow, where they were invited to a meeting of the Glasgow Emancipation Society. One outraged newspaper reported that the guests were treated rudely on their arrival: "no places were appointed on the platform for Mr. and Mrs. Mott—no invitation was given to them to address the assembly!" After this snub, their Unitarian friend, the Rev. George Harris, invited Lucretia to speak at his church. A crowd filled the building on August 9. Lucretia spoke for two hours, holding "a delighted audience in breathless attention." Like other Quaker ministers, Mott always spoke extemporaneously, and, as a result, no copies of her speeches and sermons exist except those transcribed by journalists or published in convention proceedings. Only a few of her speeches and sermons were published as separate pamphlets. In this case, the London *Christian Pioneer* published an account of her speech in Glasgow, which was then reprinted in the *Liberator.*[48]

Mott began her speech by thanking the audience for the opportunity, reminding those filling the pews that she had been denied elsewhere because of her sex and the prejudices of the Society of Friends in England. She urged that the "enlarged, and beautiful, and exalted views, which she and the Unitarian brethren entertained, could be embraced and felt by all; and she was happy in believing such views were spreading and would continue to spread, till all mankind, from their holy influence, would become one large family." But Mott also feared the lack of moral courage and the influence of "mammon-worshippers" in the world. She spoke against war and capital punishment and also addressed the issue of women's rights:

> She defended, on Scriptural grounds, the right of women to speak in public; spoke of the imperfect education which women too commonly received, which consequently debarred them from occupying their proper places in society; called upon her sisters to look to this, and embrace every opportunity of gaining knowledge on every subject; not to be content with a little reading, a little writing, and a little sewing; to brush away the silken fetters which had so long bound them—no longer

content to be the mere toy or plaything of man's leisure hours, but to fit themselves for assuming their proper position, in being the rational companions, the friends, the instructors of their race.

Like her other sermons, Mott's speech drew not only on the Bible but on her voracious reading in everything from the early Quakers to Wollstonecraft to Combe. She ended with a denunciation of the "evils and abominations" of slavery, and a "beautiful and fervent" prayer for its extinction.[49]

After Mott's speech, new enemies emerged. Local Quakers, including William Smeal, John Smeal, William White, and John Maxwell, published a disclaimer in the Glasgow *Argus*, declaring: "we deem it right, on behalf of the Society of Friends residing in Glasgow, to inform the public that we hold no religious fellowship with Lucretia Mott, nor with the body in the United States (called Hicksites) to which she belongs; they not being recognized by the Society of Friends in the United Kingdom." Furthermore, they wrote, "we do not wish to be in any way identified with, or considered responsible for any sentiments that Lucretia Mott may have uttered." The disclaimer prompted a furious James Mott to publish a letter of his own. He noted that the men had not even been present at the lecture. "Are you afraid of being robbed of your good name?" James asked the men, "or are your doctrines of such an evanescent character, that they are in danger of vanishing before the sunshine of truth?"[50]

After the heated atmosphere of Glasgow, the Motts returned to George Combe's house and then visited Abbotsford, the country home built by Sir Walter Scott. The author of *Ivanhoe* had a large following in the United States. Southern slaveholders in particular saw themselves as heirs to the knightly culture of chivalry described in Scott's novels. As a result, Scott's mansion was an obligatory stop for American tourists since it opened to the public in 1833. Even the skeptical Lucretia was moved by its charms, describing herself as "much interested." There, the Motts met not only Mrs. Purdie, the "widow of Scott's trusty servant Tom," but also a slave owner from Georgia who was touring the estate. As always, Lucretia engaged the man in a conversation about the peculiar institution. The planter "tried to convince us the slave was better off than the working man in England & Ireland—not succeeding—begged off." Afterward, the American abolitionists and the slaveholder traveled together to Dryburgh Abbey. The Georgia planter rowed the anti-slavery women across the River Tweed, good naturedly commenting that he "was glad to do what he could to bring us over to the *other side*."[51]

Such direct and personal engagement with slaveholders was not unusual for Mott, who believed it was her duty to persuade each and every slave owner of the moral truth of immediate abolition. Indeed, every time she met a slave-holder in her travels she ruthlessly broached the subject. On one trip from New York to Philadelphia, Mott met a planter from Edisto Island in South Carolina. Mott gave the slave owner, Charles Miller, a copy of the American Anti-Slavery Society's Declaration of Sentiments. After Miller informed her that he paid his slaves, Mott "told him that such as he were the strongest sup-porters of the slavery, because they gave, by their humane example, a false credit to the system." The slaveholder was so struck by her remarks that he called on her in Philadelphia. Lucretia proceeded to take him to a Quaker meeting, to James Forten's, and finally to the home of her fellow Philadelphia Female Anti-Slavery Society member Esther Moore, "who addressed him with all her eloquence."[52] Lucretia viewed such individual conversions as im-portant even though they were only a small part of the abolitionists' propa-ganda campaign. As stated in the Declaration of Sentiments, she wanted at all times and on all occasions to expose the moral corruption of slavery.

The Motts returned to London once more before their trip home. On the way, they stopped in Tynemouth to visit an ailing Harriet Martineau, the British writer and Unitarian who had written favorably about the American anti-slavery movement in an article titled "The Martyr Age of the United States." In London, the Motts' party again crossed paths with Elizabeth and Henry Stanton. Lucretia and Elizabeth went to visit an "Infant School" run by Samuel Wilderspin, a friend of George Combe. Mott wrote that the school was "not equal to our expectation & hopes—felt much for the poor little chil-dren in Spitalfields." Stanton, revealing the philosophy of parenting with which she raised her seven children, apparently wanted "to remove them [the children] in Omnibuses to Hyde Park to romp & play."[53]

Lucretia also visited the studio of Benjamin Robert Haydon, the art-ist commissioned to paint the World's Anti-Slavery Convention. Her diary entry—"saw picture—talked with him"—hid what must have been a tense in-teraction. James and Lucretia sat for Haydon, as did a number of the Ameri-can abolitionists. While James appeared among the delegates in the finished painting, Lucretia discovered she was merely a tiny blurred image in the back-ground. Haydon's diary explains the artist's decision. After meeting Lucretia, Haydon wrote, "I have found her out to have infidel notions, and resolved at once, narrow-minded or not, not to give her the prominent place I first in-tended. I will reserve that for a beautiful believer in the divinity of Christ."[54] Lucretia's beliefs excised her from the visual record of the convention.

The Motts departed Liverpool on August 26 on the *Patrick Henry*. This packet ship was larger than the *Roscoe* at 880 tons and 159 feet long. Captain

Joseph C. Delano, of New Bedford, Massachusetts, was a businessman as well as a sailor, and he owned 1/8 of the boat. Both Lucretia and James made note of the twelve cabin passengers and the 140 in steerage (including 3 stowaways and 1 infant born during the voyage). Luckily for these passengers, the twenty-nine-day journey to New York was not as rough as the trip to England. Mott again engaged the slaveholding passengers in debate; she wrote that they "didn't relish the discussion of the subject." James concluded that the trip had succeeded in its aim, contributing as it had to the restoration of his wife's health.[55] But the story of the World's Anti-Slavery Convention did not end when the Motts landed in New York. American abolitionists continued to discuss and debate what had happened in London for many months to come, profoundly altering the landscape of their movement.

*   *   *

In Philadelphia, the proceedings of the World's Anti-Slavery Convention, reprinted in *Pennsylvania Freeman*, hardened Garrison's allies, who supported immediate abolition and racial equality as well as women's rights and nonresistance, against his opponents. After their return, on October 8, Mott, Mary Grew, and Sarah Pugh offered an official, and relatively mild, "Report of the Delegates" to the monthly meeting of the Philadelphia Female Anti-Slavery Society. The report recounted their arrival in London, the decision of the "Executive Committee" of the British and Foreign Anti-Slavery Society, and their own resolution to withhold "their claim to membership." But the three women also praised the convention. They noted that not everyone had opposed their admission, offering an alternative vision of what might have been: "In their eyes, the anti-slavery platform was large enough to admit the lovers of truth and freedom, of every nation or sect, or sex, or color." They acknowledged the "bright hopes" focused on the convention. Indeed, the convention had provided important leadership on the relationship between the church and slavery, advising all Christians that it was their duty to exclude slaveholders from fellowship. "Its influence will be felt throughout the American church," the women wrote. They concluded that "although it was not, in its own estimation, or in truth, a *World's Convention*, yet it was a Convention that shall bless the world."[56] The report reflected that the authors had attended the convention as abolitionists first and foremost.

At its annual meeting that same month, the American Free Produce

Association, composed of abolitionists, Hicksites, and Orthodox Quakers, addressed the failure of the World's Anti-Slavery Convention to take strong action on abstaining from slave-produced goods. Mott conveyed her own disappointment in the delegates' "weak" and "unsound" arguments against abstinence, noting that the women present could "have defended the cause of truth."[57] Since the American Free Produce Association had nominated both men and women to attend the World's Convention, members passed resolutions denouncing women's exclusion. Henry Grew, father of Philadelphia Female Anti-Slavery Society corresponding secretary Mary Grew, found himself in the uncomfortable position of having to explain his own actions in London. In a letter to the *Pennsylvania Freeman*, Henry Grew argued that he had not betrayed the American Free Produce Association by failing to supports its female representatives. He claimed that his beliefs on the segregated and divinely ordained spheres of men and women were unrelated to his commitment to free produce.[58]

These divisions among Philadelphia abolitionists were relatively minor compared to the bitter feud between the Garrisonian abolitionists of the American Anti-Slavery Society and the ministers and politicians affiliated with the American and Foreign Anti-Slavery Society. In July, the *Pennsylvania Freeman* had printed a letter from its former editor, John Greenleaf Whittier, now living in his hometown of Amesbury, Massachusetts, expressing his sorrow at the schism in the American Anti-Slavery Society. But Whittier also noted his sympathies for the new organization; indeed, his name was on the American and Foreign Anti-Slavery Society's list of officers.[59] After the delegates returned, Whittier wrote another letter to the editor praising the World's Anti-Slavery Convention and condemning its critics. Any criticism of the London convention, he wrote, gave ammunition to proslavery forces. Whittier denounced the outrageous behavior of Garrisonians such as newspaper editor Nathaniel P. Rogers, who had called British abolitionists more despotic than American pro-slavery mobs. In his poetic fashion, Whittier compared Rogers's "fervid, imaginative, electric-sparkling abolitionism" to the "quiet Quakers, sturdy impassive country gentlemen, begowned clergymen, and Baroney M.P.'s sitting down to the work of abolishing slavery." This goal, Whittier concluded, "might be attained without subscribing to our Yankee doctrines of equality or sexless Democracy."[60]

Two weeks later, the *Freeman* printed a response to Whittier, probably authored by his successor and Mott's friend Charles C. Burleigh. The author observed that Whittier's letter was based on a false assumption; after all, Philadelphia abolitionists had not condemned the convention outright. But their circumspection did not mean the convention was entirely free from criticism: "We cannot bestow unqualified commendation on a body of abolitionists that violates the rights of a portion of its own properly constituted members, and of those whom such members were sent to represent."[61] The article also defended Rogers, balking at Whittier's comparison of American and British abolitionists. The British reformers, the author pointed out, never had to face a furious pro-slavery mob.

Such exchanges in the pages of the *Freeman* forced Philadelphia abolitionists to make choices between the new and old organization, between politics and principles. Whittier proposed that abolitionists should focus single-mindedly on slavery, leaving all other extraneous issues aside. In his view, non-resistance and the rights of women were not only a distraction, but they tainted and ultimately hindered the anti-slavery cause. Instead, sober, thoughtful, and influential men, such as the Quakers, clergymen, and Members of Parliament described in his letter, should pursue the end of slavery through the accepted (and, significantly, male) channels of the political system. But Mott saw anti-slavery, peace, and women's rights as part of the same reform impulse to liberate the individual from the bonds of tradition, custom, and organized religion. Her support for free produce was one aspect of this radical individualism. She believed that individuals must free themselves from the sin of slavery before they presented a consistent moral example to the world. Through example and persuasion, by contrasting their own purity to the corruption of slavery, Lucretia believed that reformers could succeed in abolishing slavery and racism. Whittier might have described her position, like that of Nathaniel P. Rogers, as idealistic, unrealistic, and dangerous.[62]

Over the next two decades, with some important exceptions, Lucretia and other Philadelphia abolitionists remained united in the Pennsylvania Anti-Slavery Society and the Philadelphia Female Anti-Slavery Society, both of which retained their allegiance to the American-Anti-Slavery Society. Mott's example was undoubtedly a crucial factor in the choices of Philadelphia's reformers. These organizations further refined the strategy of moral suasion, at the same time narrowing their ideological platform. Despite Elizabeth Cady Stanton's later claim that she and Mott conceived the idea of a women's rights meeting in London, Mott did not follow a direct path from the World's Anti-Slavery Convention of 1840 to the Seneca Falls Women's Rights Convention in 1848.[63] Other matters needed tending first. In that time, Mott devoted herself to the abolitionist cause, further troubling her relationship with the Society of Friends. But she also pursued her wide vision of reform in other arenas.

Figure 1 (above).
Thomas and Anna Folger
Coffin.

*Courtesy Nantucket Historical
Association.*

Figure 2 (right).
James and Lucretia Mott,
circa 1842.

*Courtesy Friends Historical
Library, Swarthmore College.*

Figure 3 (above).
Pennsylvania Hall. *Courtesy Library Company of Philadelphia.*

Figure 4 (below).
The destruction of Pennsylvania Hall. *Courtesy Library Company of Philadelphia.*

Figure 5 (above).
James Miller McKim.
*Courtesy Massachusetts
Historical Society.*

Figure 6 (right).
Charles C. Burleigh.
*Courtesy Massachusetts
Historical Society.*

Abby Kimber   *Emily Winslow*   *Mary Grew*

Elizabeth Neall   *Abby Southwick*   *Sarah Pugh*

Figure 7. Delegates to the World's Anti-Slavery Convention. From top left, Abby Kimber, Emily Winslow, Mary Grew. From bottom left, Elizabeth Neall, Abby Southwick, Sarah Pugh. *Courtesy Massachusetts Historical Society.*

Figure 8. Prominent female activists. Mott is surrounded by (clockwise from top) Harriet Beecher Stowe, Abby Kelley Foster, Lucy Stone, Lydia Maria Child, Antoinette Brown Blackwell, and Maria Weston Chapman.

Courtesy The Schlesinger Library, Radcliffe Institute, Harvard University.

Figure 9 (right).
Robert Purvis.
*Courtesy Massachusetts
Historical Society.*

Figure 10 (below).
Roadside.
*Courtesy Friends Historical
Library, Swarthmore College.*

Figure 11 (left).
Lucretia Mott.
Courtesy Friends Historical Library, Swarthmore College.

Figure 12 (below).
Camp William Penn.
Courtesy Library Company of Philadelphia.

Figure 13. Maria Mott Davis, Anna Davis Hallowell, Lucretia Mott, and her
great-granddaughter Maria Hallowell, circa 1878.

Courtesy Friends Historical Library, Swarthmore College.

CHAPTER 7

Crisis

ON NOVEMBER 5, 1840, the *Pennsylvania Freeman* reported that Lucretia Mott had addressed a few remarks to a recent meeting of the Female Vigilance Committee "in such a manner that her hearers wished they had been extended." Associated with David Ruggles's New York Vigilance Committee, the Philadelphia Vigilance Committee, founded in 1837, assumed responsibility for hiding, feeding, clothing, and finding transportation for runaways. Robert Purvis was president of the Philadelphia Vigilance Committee as well as a member of the Pennsylvania Anti-Slavery Society, while Philadelphia Female Anti-Slavery Society members Hester Reckless, Sarah McCrummell, and Margaretta Forten were active in the female auxiliary.[1]

If Mott received a warm reception from the African American women of the Female Vigilance Committee, she had become a divisive figure in the wake of the World's Anti-Slavery Convention. Mott's fame (or infamy, in some circles) grew. In the face of ideological and strategic challenges to Garrisonian abolitionism, Mott became a pure partisan. She battled other members of the Philadelphia Female Anti-Slavery Society over whether to aid fugitive slaves, consume free produce, or endorse third party politics. Meanwhile, she engaged in her own delicate balance between her expansive interest in women's rights and her commitment to abolitionism.

Amid this crisis in the anti-slavery movement, Lucretia focused her critique on the close relationship between American religion and slavery. In a strategy known as "come-outerism," many abolitionists—especially female abolitionists—left denominations that failed to denounce the sin of slavery. In contrast, Mott fought attempts to have her censored or disowned, choosing to remain a Quaker. Though her decision confounded her allies, it did not prevent Mott from becoming a leading critic of the church's corruption. But these conflicts also exacted a further toll on her physical and mental health.[2]

After the London convention, Mott assumed a new leadership role in the national anti-slavery movement. In early 1841, she addressed the state legislatures of Delaware, Pennsylvania, and New Jersey. No copies of her speeches exist, but she reported that, "respectful audience was granted while I plead [sic] the cause of the oppressed."[3] She also held anti-slavery meetings on the road, addressing two large audiences in a Harrisburg courthouse and one in Smyrna, Delaware, the town where she and Daniel Neall were attacked. At least one member of the old mob was present, but he left the building after she began speaking. Lucretia and James discovered the man's nefarious intentions when they saw that a linchpin had been removed from their carriage. After replacing the linchpin, they sought refreshment and rest in a local inn, but were turned away by the proprietor. However frightening, such abuse further reinforced Mott's view of abolitionists as true Christians. As she noted in a sermon a few years later, "Jesus taught the heresy of that age, and it was his opposition to the cherished forms and creeds of the day that constituted his greatest offense."[4]

Later that year, Mott delivered a "public religious address" to a large audience at Marlboro Chapel in Boston. Her sermon brought together many of the issues that she had advocated at the World's Anti-Slavery Convention, including nonsectarianism, women's rights, abolition, and free produce. She began by praising her interdenominational audience, free from the "distinctions which prevail in professing Christendom." Indeed, Mott believed that the "truth of God" could only be realized by abandoning "educational prejudices and sectarian predilections." She affirmed her faith in the "inner sense which all possess" not as a "Quaker tenet" but a "universal obligation." Rejecting biblical sanction for women's silence, Mott addressed their rights: "I long for the time when my sisters will rise and occupy the sphere to which they are called by their high nature and destiny." She also touched on slavery, war, intemperance, materialism, and the "vices of society." For Mott, American society represented a "field white to the harvest." "Who can look at the crimes and sufferings of men, and not labor for reformation?" she asked. "Let us put our own souls in their souls' stead, who are in slavery, and let us labor for their liberation as bound with them." Mott called on her audience to examine their personal relationship to slavery. "We all have a part of the work to perform, for we are all implicated in the transgression," she told them.[5] She believed individual rejection of the pervasive sin of slavery was at the heart of abolition.

Remarkably, Lucretia also took her message directly to the slaveholding South, a region notoriously hostile to any expression of anti-slavery views. During the winter of 1842–43, she traveled through Delaware, Maryland, Virginia, and Washington, D.C., addressing large audiences, including 3000 people in Richmond. Mott told the *Pennsylvania Freeman* that she was pleased with the progress of anti-slavery sentiment in the region, aided by the presence of southern Quakers. She even made a few converts, including a little girl who handed her a donation, and new subscribers to the *Pennsylvania Freeman* and the *National Anti-Slavery Standard*, published by the American Anti-Slavery Society. One slaveholder helped her organize a meeting that included "a number of colored people and some slaveholders, and a patient audience was given to the plain truths spoken on the occasion." In response to her trip, other slaveholders hinted that Mott's only protection from "all violence" was her sex.[6]

Denied an audience in the Capitol Building, Mott delivered an anti-slavery sermon in the Unitarian Church in Washington, D.C., on January 15, 1843. Thirty legislators, many of them southerners, were in the standing-room-only crowd. They listened "with strict attention, and apparent admiration to the eloquence and sublimity of the language of this little woman" with only some "murmurings among them."[7] The topic of Mott's sermon was "Righteous exalteth a Nation, but sin is a reproach to any people." She blamed the continued presence of sin on the fact that "Men have been taught that they were more prone to evil than to good." Mott preferred the positive view of humanity advocated by Unitarian minister William Ellery Channing, who before his death in 1842 had risked his reputation to speak out against slavery, "appealing to the intelligence of the people" on "the most unpopular topic of the day." She too was "aware of the place I stand." Mott believed it was her duty to raise the issue of slavery, even to an unfriendly crowd. "Is there not a fear as regards the question of slavery, a fear to permit it to be examined?" she asked.[8]

Mott wanted her allies and opponents to come together "in a christian spirit," thus breaking down the "petition walls" of "prejudice, sectarian, and sectional jealousies." Indeed, Lucretia believed slavery was not a sectional but a national problem: "we are all verily guilty concerning our brother." This free produce advocate told her audience that "the manufacturers of the north, the consumers of the various commodities of southern productions, are implicated in this matter, and while the sweets of this system are found upon our table we are partakers of other men's sins." While this sentiment may have appealed to the southerners present, she also advised these politicians that "political arrangements," or compromises, deals, and laws, were only temporary fixes for the sin of slavery. Instead, Mott suggested bringing Christianity out of the churches and seminaries into daily life in order to transform the morals of the country. "Let our fruits test the purity of our profession," she advised, "and when we are making these contracts by which we are enriching ourselves, let us look whether we are not indulging ourselves in extravagance in life to such an extent as to bring misery and woe upon others." Listening in the audience was transcendentalist Ralph Waldo Emerson, who likened her sermon to the "rumble of an earthquake."[9]

Believing that part of her mission in the capital was to "interest those in power on the subject of emancipation," Mott called on two politicians on opposite sides of the issue, President John Tyler and Congressman John Quincy Adams. Given that Tyler was a Virginia slaveholder and later a leading secessionist, he might have been dismissive, but Mott reported that the President "professed some interest," and advocated colonization. During the conversation, Mott contradicted every position Tyler advanced. When the Virginian praised an address on slavery issued by the Baltimore Yearly Meeting, Mott disparaged it as "calculated to set the slave-holder's conscience too much at ease." President Tyler was relieved when Lucretia departed. "I should like to hand Mr. Calhoun over to you," Tyler told her, referring to the fierce proslavery senator from South Carolina. When Mott visited Adams, the former president, opponent of the gag rule, and lawyer for the Africans captured on the slave-ship *Amistad*, she found him discouraged. Mott concluded "Our hopes of success must rest not on those in power, but on the common people, whose servants they are."[10]

These national appearances did not distract Mott from the work of the Philadelphia Female Anti-Slavery Society. In the aftermath of the split in the American Anti-Slavery Society, members disagreed how best to advance abolition and racial equality. While some blacks, like Robert Purvis and William Whipper, founded interracial organizations such as the American Moral Reform Association, others preferred to keep their institutions under their own control. To improve the condition of African Americans in Philadelphia, the PFASS had taken an interest in black schools, assuming financial responsibility for the school of member Sarah Mapps Douglass. But in 1840 Douglass withdrew her school from the society's management. In a letter to

Sarah Pugh, Douglass explained that she had given financial control to the Philadelphia Female Anti-Slavery Society in order to escape the shadow of its founders, James Forten and her mother Grace Douglass. She lamented that "for the sake of a living, I had parted with that for which we had so long toiled," her autonomy. The interracial Philadelphia Female Anti-Slavery Society too regretted Sarah Douglass's decision to withdraw the school, but bade her continued "prosperity and usefulness."[11]

Despite Douglass's demand for independence, she and her school retained a close relationship with the Philadelphia Female Anti-Slavery Society. The society met regularly in Douglass's schoolroom, for which it paid rent. Douglass continued as the society's librarian and a regular member of its fair committee. In 1849, a committee consisting of Mott and Sarah Pugh determined that the small number of students did not justify the rent, preferring their money go to supply the "general wants of the anti-slavery enterprise in Pennsylvania." Even then, Sarah Douglass declared herself "satisfied" with the society's course, and began the hunt for another schoolroom. The Philadelphia Female Anti-Slavery Society praised her in its annual report, noting that the school "is conducted with ability, and is of great value to the class of persons for whose benefit it was instituted." And long after, Sarah Douglass continued her affiliation, indicating that the struggle over her school was less consequential than some historians have suggested.[12]

The Philadelphia Female Anti-Slavery Society's decision to cut ties with Douglass's school reflected the reorientation of their priorities. The internal debate began when Philadelphia's Vigilance Committee solicited donations from the larger community of abolitionists during the 1840s. The society minutes noted a $10 donation to the Philadelphia Vigilance Committee in March 1841. In September, Hester Reckless appealed to the society for more aid, reporting that in one month the Vigilance Committee had aided 35 fugitive slaves. In response, the society resolved to pay quarterly dues to support it. Vigilance Committee members continued to alert the society to a steady stream of runaways and the need for aid. In October and November 1842, the Committee assisted almost 100 "travelers."[13]

Though the Philadelphia Female Anti-Slavery Society regularly voted to contribute to the Vigilance Committee, the place of the Underground Railroad in the anti-slavery movement provoked disagreement. In 1846, Esther Moore, the organization's first president, resigned in order to work with the Vigilance Committee. The minutes of the meeting note that "This gave rise to a discussion as to how far these mere branches of the Anti-Slavery cause had claims on Abolitionists for their support. The general expression seemed to be 'These things ought ye to do, and not to leave the other undone.'"[14] Ironically, though popular audiences often associate Mott with the Underground Railroad, she defined vigilance and anti-slavery societies as distinct endeavors, with different goals. In other words, aiding fugitives was an important task, but not "properly anti-slavery work" that could destroy slavery "root and branch."[15]

Mott articulated this perspective for a national anti-slavery audience. In 1844, she wrote a rare short article titled "Diversities" for the *Liberty Bell*, a book published annually by Boston abolitionists in conjunction with their annual fair. Mott's article celebrated "the diversity of operations" in the anti-slavery movement, including those focused on purifying the church, electing anti-slavery politicians to office, abstaining from slave produce, fighting racial prejudice, and aiding fugitive slaves. But, she argued, each branch must "be careful lest he be engrossed with his favorite department in the great work." "Rather," Mott suggested, "let our main and most vigorous exertions be directed to the overthrow of the outrageous system of American slavery."[16]

The attempt to regulate members' enthusiasms and beliefs prompted a larger exodus from the Philadelphia Female Anti-Slavery Society over the course of the decade. As historian Jean R. Soderlund describes, during the 1840s the society adopted a "more restrictive ideological position." Members like Esther Moore chose not only between anti-slavery societies and vigilance committees, but also between free produce and the inexpensive fruits of slavery, and between moral power and political action. Significantly, the organization lost only one African American member in that decade, demonstrating that differences on these issues did not fall along racial lines. And members reassured themselves that the loss of members was not a reflection on their direction: "The smallness of our meeting no cause for discouragement. Reformers will always be a small minority as they are always progressing."[17]

After the World's Anti-Slavery Convention, many abolitionists followed William Lloyd Garrison in abandoning the cause of free produce as "a waste of time and talent" with "no practical benefit" for the slave. Only a minority of black and white abolitionists continued to advocate abstinence, including leading members of the Philadelphia Female Anti-Slavery Society such as Mott, Harriet Purvis, Mary Grew, and Sarah Pugh, who believed that hypocrisy threatened the success of their crusade. But even though their constitution contained a clause on free produce, the society had trouble passing resolutions reinforcing it. In 1842, the society tabled Mary Grew's proposal that "it is the duty of abolitionists immediately to abstain from the use of the products of slave labor." By 1848, however, Lucretia's remarks on free produce caused no debate, largely because many doubters had resigned their membership to pursue other anti-slavery strategies.[18]

Activists also disagreed about whether to participate in electoral politics. In 1842, the Philadelphia Female Anti-Slavery Society passed two controversial resolutions. The first affirmed the society's commitment to moral suasion at the expense of political action, resolving "that in the work of abolishing slavery, we rely not on the efficacy of physical force, or political parties, but on moral power, or the use of those weapons, which operated on the heart & on the conscience." The second resolution advocated a doctrine known as "disunionism," which challenged the legitimacy of government support for slavery. Passed after heated debate, the final version read, "that we acknowledge no allegiance to any national compact or legislative enactment which sanctions slavery or contravenes any principle of right." Frustrated by the direction of the society, Susan Grew, Mary's half-sister, resigned in 1847 to join a society more "sympathetic to the Liberty Party," the main political vehicle for abolitionists, founded in 1840.[19]

Their support for ideological moral purity led the women of the Philadelphia Female Anti-Slavery Society to clash with the larger anti-slavery movement. In early 1847, a controversy among American reformers erupted after British abolitionists bought the freedom of abolitionist Frederick Douglass, who had published his *Narrative* in 1845. The initial announcement of the deal in the *Pennsylvania Freeman* laid out the contradiction between Douglass's "freedom" and abolitionist "principle."[20] Two months later, a Philadelphia Female Anti-Slavery Society resolution denounced the purchase as "an implied acknowledgment of the master's right of property in human beings." Lucretia and her colleagues not only condemned this deviation from the society's Declaration of Sentiments, they also questioned it as strategy, arguing that Douglass's effectiveness as an abolitionist lay in his bondage. The purchase, they wrote, took "from him one of the strongest claims to the sympathy of the community . . . weakening the bond that connects the *suffering slave* with the *free man*."[21]

One of the leading spirits behind this resolution, Lucretia's concern for theoretical "consistency" was turning her into an ideologue. In an 1846 article in the *Liberty Bell*, titled "What Is Anti-Slavery Work," Mott argued that buying the freedom of slaves was "misdirected benevolence" and "indirect support of slavery." Mott admitted that for years "my sympathy was so wrought upon by the cases of peculiar hardship . . . that, without much reflection, I contributed my mite toward the purchase of slaves." But, after further reflection, she realized that such money spent by abolitionists only furthered the institution. Mott urged that abolitionists' attention be directed at the "whole class" of slaves, not just a "few isolated cases."[22] At an 1846 meeting of the Pennsylvania Anti-Slavery Society, when a colleague stood up and asked for contributions so a young man in the audience could buy his daughter, who was about to be sold south, Mott objected. Then, the *Pennsylvania Freeman* reported, she "read a passage from the Declaration of Sentiments of the American Society condemning compensation."[23]

In taking this stance, Mott advanced what she saw as the purest form of immediate abolitionism, but her disregard for the individuality of slaves was as troubling to her contemporaries, including William Lloyd Garrison, as it is today. Despite her humanitarianism, Mott was a committed activist, not a gentle Quaker. She believed the primary goals of abolitionists should be ending slavery and racial prejudice, and that the best way to accomplish these ends was to present a consistent moral example. Any deviation, such as wearing cotton produced by slaves or purchasing a slave's freedom, not only acknowledged the legitimacy of slavery, but also furthered the economic and political life of the institution. Buying slaves, even to free them, accepted the slaveholders' definition of slaves as property, dehumanized objects to be bought and sold.

Mott's anti-slavery purism coexisted, sometimes uneasily, with her devotion to women's rights and other causes. In the middle of the decade, Mott gravitated toward issues of women's health, sexual exploitation, poverty, employment, and motherhood. Yet she did not see women's rights as compromising her principal goal of abolishing slavery. Her children were now almost fully grown, a fact that freed her to pursue a variety of causes. More important, she viewed slavery and sex, as well as intemperance and war, as interconnected struggles. Mott's willingness to deviate from her ideological convictions signaled her expanding political interests.

In 1841, Mott and her daughters attended a controversial lecture series on female anatomy and physiology by Mary Gove, a disowned Quaker. Lucretia wrote that many of the "intelligent class" of Quaker women attended. She noted that, "I had long wished that subject properly presented to Females." But Orthodox Quakers and other critics shocked by a public discussion of female biology opposed Gove's lectures. Lucretia concluded, "the more I heard her slandered the more it became a principle with me to countenance her efforts."[24]

Mott's interest in women's health and sexuality extended to African American women. She was an enthusiastic booster of the Moral Reform Retreat in Moyamensing, established by the American Moral Reform Association to aid "intemperate colored women." In 1842–44, this organization helped seventy-two women "addicted" to alcohol and licentiousness. Mott convinced the Philadelphia Female Anti-Slavery Society to donate $30 to aid this charity. She also urged the *Pennsylvania Freeman* to stop printing "dry essays on disputed points," instead offering "items of interest" such as the Moral Reform Retreat. Lucretia argued that the retreat "ought to receive all the aid that abolitionists can afford." Of course, this perspective contradicted her strict definition of anti-slavery work published in the *Liberty Bell*, hypocrisy attributable to her growing involvement in women's issues.[25]

As war loomed in Oregon and Texas, Mott became an even more visible advocate for peace, tying women's responsibility as mothers to the larger goal of ending violent conflict. In June 1846, two thousand women in Exeter, England, appealed to their counterparts in Philadelphia for aid in preventing war over the Oregon territory. Mott drafted a reply "befitting the intelligence of woman." She argued it was "the duty of Women, to look with an attentive eye upon the great events which are transpiring around them." Rejecting the view of women as inherently peaceful, Mott argued that war grew from "the seed sown by his mother's hand, when in his childish hours she gave him tiny weapons, and taught him to mimic war's murderous game." Invoking eighteenth-century notions of Republican motherhood, she advised women to instill "the principles of justice, mercy, and peace" in their children. More than three thousand women signed Mott's address, which was forwarded to Exeter by William Peter, the British consul.[26] Though the nation avoided war with Great Britain, Congress responded to President Polk's claim that Mexican forces had invaded American territory by declaring war on Mexico in May 1846. The next year, Lucretia complained to George Combe that it was a "disgrace" "that we are engaged in a War of aggression & conquest with a neighboring weak and comparatively defenceless Nation!" Like other abolitionists, Mott saw the war as an effort to enlarge slave territory. "Slave-holdg. Rulers are in the ascendant," she advised Combe.[27]

In 1846, Lucretia became president of Northern Association for the Relief and Employment of Poor Women, an organization she had founded with other Quaker women two years earlier. She stayed in this position for the next twenty years. The objects of the association's charity were women, white and black, "whose circumstances prevent their earning a subsistence in any other way; such as the aged, the sick, and infirm, and widows with families of small children." The association employed these women to sew a variety of garments, quilts, shawls, and comforters, which they then distributed to the needy or sold from their offices or through sister-organizations like the Rosine Association, founded in 1847 to bring prostitutes into contact with "respectable" women, find them suitable employment, and thus end the moral stigma attached to individual prostitutes. Initially paying 25 cents per day, by 1848 the Northern Association concluded to pay by the piece. That same year it moved to a building at 242 Green Street, which it then purchased.[28]

The Northern Association's rules reflected middle-class distaste for the poor as well as a feminist critique of women's position in society. The organization made sure to distinguish between the "industrious" poor and those "disposed to live upon charity." The rules instructed employees to be temperate, punctual, clean, and neatly dressed. The Northern Association also discouraged any expression of discontent from their clients: "The women are to be satisfied with the work given them and the price paid and obey all the instructions of the matron and committee."[29] Nevertheless, the members understood that women's poverty was based on their social, legal, and economic dependency. Prefiguring what late twentieth-century activists called the "feminization of poverty," the Northern Association described female clients as "crushed, broken down, and dejected by adverse circumstances." Acknowledging the limits gender placed on their own lives, its 1849 corporate charter stipulated that only single women could be legal members. This clause protected the Northern Association from the legal or economic demands of husbands.[30]

Like the Philadelphia Female Anti-Slavery Society, the Northern Association became a family project. Lucretia's son-in-law Edward Hopper was the association's lawyer. James Mott made frequent donations, as did their children. Her daughter Elizabeth and cousin Rebecca Bunker Neall also joined.[31]

As Lucretia welcomed the contributions of her extended family, she faced significant changes to her household. In 1843, she sent her youngest daughter, fourteen-year-old Pattie, to Kimberton Boarding School. In July 1845, at the age of twenty, Elizabeth married Thomas Cavender, a farmer and abolitionist. Lucretia did not fully approve of the match. Though he was active in the Pennsylvania Anti-Slavery Society, Cavender defined himself as a political abolitionist and disapproved of the Motts' allegiance to the American Anti-Slavery Society. During their courtship, Lucretia wrote to her sister Martha that she was "resigned to any turn wh. that intimacy may take" "knowg.

that tastes differ—& that *our* liking would not secure mutual happiness."[32] Thomas Mott was now a partner in his father's struggling wool commission business. After a secret courtship, twenty-two-year-old Thomas married his first cousin Marianna Pelham, Martha's daughter by her first marriage, in July 1845, a week after his sister's wedding. The match was scandalous not only because of the blood relationship but also because Marianna had previously been engaged to a Philadelphia Quaker named Rodman Wharton. Lucretia was disappointed in the match, but she loved Marianna. Well aware of Quaker policy on marriage between first cousins, she was also prepared for Thomas's subsequent disownment by Cherry Street Meeting.[33]

Despite Lucretia's reservations, the two marriages in the summer of 1845 provided a much-needed cause for celebration. The previous year, her health had suffered a relapse. After an exhausting season of meetings, when she and James crossed the Delaware River "eleven times in as many weeks, through the winter, after 10 oclock in the evening," Lucretia suffered an "inflammation of the lungs." At the same time, in March 1844, her seventy-three-year-old mother, Anna Coffin, was "seized" by bilious pleurisy, a disease of the lungs similar to pneumonia. She died in a few days. Lucretia was devastated and her health grew worse. As she wrote to George Combe, "dreadful spasms with loss of reason followed." Lucretia was bedridden for a month, but she told Combe that her sickness showed "the truth of phrenology." She instructed her doctors to treat her based on phrenological principles, which involved moving an ice pack to different regions of her head: "first the organs of the affections—then the moral portion—& lastly the intellectual." This attention to her psychological response to her mother's death had some effect. The *Pennsylvania Freeman* published updates on her health, noting on April 11 that Lucretia Mott is "now slowly and gradually improving."[34]

For more than a year after her mother's death, fifty-one-year-old Lucretia was depressed, unable to return to her usual routine of reading and letter writing. It took her even longer to recover her ability and inspiration to speak publicly. Anna Coffin had been her sole parent when her father was away at sea. As an adult, Lucretia had depended on her mother's assistance in running her household. She called Coffin "the life of the family circle." Coffin's grandchildren and great-grandchildren also remembered her as a vital presence, sitting in a straight-backed chair (never a rocking chair) and knitting. In 1840, when Anna Coffin was in Auburn, New York, helping Martha and David Wright move into a new house, Lucretia had confessed that her mother's "beautiful traits" made her feel inadequate. Lucretia had not devoted as much time to helping her own children—"I have so many things to take my attention"—instead depending on her mother and eldest daughter. Though Lucretia herself was often portrayed as the perfect wife and mother, she viewed Anna Coffin as a paragon of maternal virtues, albeit those associated with an independent Nantucket businesswoman. Even with her self-doubt, Lucretia had inherited some of her mother's traits. Anna Coffin passed on her love of her native island, her sharp wit, her non-conformity, and her egalitarianism to her daughter.[35]

*   *   *

In Mott's grief, the Society of Friends remained an important, if often painful, constant in her life. Though other Quakers joined abolitionist come-outers in the 1840s, Mott remained a member, narrowly avoiding disownment. Identifying organized religion as a key obstacle to their goals, abolitionists and women's rights activists questioned her ongoing affiliation with the Society of Friends. In Mott's view, her decision to stay in her spiritual and intellectual home did not lessen her heretical stance, but enabled her to attack the relationship between slavery and the church. Her Quaker garb made her an especially forceful advocate of dissent.[36]

In 1841, Lucretia wrote her Irish friends Richard and Hannah Webb that George F. White had been sowing "more discord." At this early date, he had failed to damage her Cherry Street Meeting, a situation that changed radically over the next two years. "They bear with me & my wanderings wonderfully well," she told the Webbs. However, White was causing serious problems in New York Yearly Meeting. Earlier that year, abolitionist Oliver Johnson had published his correspondence with White on the issue of Quaker participation in the American Anti-Slavery Society and the New England Non-Resistance Society. Mott commented that "I should have preferred a silent endurance of George's anathemas, not doubting it would be manifest whence his revilings came. Things begin to wear a threatening aspect." Soon afterward, New York Yearly Meeting accused two of its members, James S. Gibbons and Isaac T. Hopper, father of Mott's son-in-law Edward Hopper, of contributing to Johnson's public attack on White.[37]

Mott worried about White's threat to the Society of Friends, but his impact was felt most in her close circle of friends and relatives. She informed her former traveling companion Phebe Post Willis that White's "vagaries" had prevented her from writing: "I have not wanted to put pen to paper touching him—I ever hoping—even against hope, that he would be restored to his right mind." Her fears came true when New York Yearly Meeting disowned Hopper, Gibbons, and another abolitionist named Charles C. Marriott. Phebe's Westbury Quarterly Meeting on Long Island confirmed the first two disownments. Lucretia was furious. In her last surviving letter to Phebe, written in April 1842, Mott called the decision "bigoted & intolerant." Then she wrote "plainly" of things she had been repressing for the last three years. Lucretia criticized Phebe's brother John and James's uncle Samuel Mott for signing the disownments. She accused her friend of supporting Rachel Hicks's minute to travel to Baltimore. "I have no unity with her [Hicks] traveling about in her present censorious disposition," she argued, "quoting & perverting Scripture to suit her purpose fully as much as did the disorganizers of 1826–7." Finally, Mott threatened to sever her religious fellowship with New York Yearly Meeting. Their friendship suffered under the strain. Their regular correspondence stopped, with no extant letters between 1842 and Phebe's death in 1846. Closer to home, Edward Hopper resigned his membership in the Society of Friends in sympathy with his father.[38]

In an 1842 letter to the Webbs, Lucretia communicated her anguish over Quaker proscription. Again, she compared the current divisions to the great separation: "I told them I did not hesitate 15 years ago, to judge of the persecuting spirit of our Orthodox opposers, and I viewed the treatment of these frds. in N. York in the same light." She called the Quaker hierarchy high-handed, writing, "I doubt whether the domination of any sect is more arbitrary." Still, she remained devoted to the Society of Friends: "I know of no religious association I would prefer to it." Though she criticized the Quaker leadership, Lucretia believed in the universality of the inner light. The word "association" also helps explain her commitment. She enjoyed the community of family, friends, reformers, and even her Quaker opponents. Downplaying her own disruptive role, she urged her co-religionists to transcend their differences. Lucretia viewed the possibility of another schism as agonizing, but she also identified it as futile. She was determined to reform the Society of Friends.[39]

In the same letter, Mott also praised a "heretical" sermon by Unitarian minister Theodore Parker, titled "The Transient and Permanent in Christianity." Delivered in Boston in May 1841, Mott wrote that it had created a "great stir," causing the "old Unitarians to tremble for their reputation as Christians." As the title of the sermon suggests, Parker distinguished between the permanent "pure religion" preached by Jesus Christ and transient forms of

Christianity, including creeds, doctrines, theologies, churches, and temples. He stressed the difference between the Word of God and human "notions" of that message. Lucretia especially praised his discussion of the Bible. She appreciated Parker's criticism of the charges of heresy, infidelity, and atheism that arose when individuals dared question the infallibility of the Scriptures. Like Elias Hicks before him, Parker argued that man had made an "idol" out of the Bible, interpreting it literally despite the fact that it had been written thousands of years previously. He pointed out that, "Christian teachers themselves have differed so widely in their notion of the doctrines and meaning of those books, that it makes one weep to think of the follies deduced therefrom." Parker thus accorded the Scriptures "transient" status in Christianity. Mott noted that she and her family had never read the Bible as a "religious rite." She concluded: "Let us venerate the Good and True, while we respect not prejudice & Superstition!" Parker's sermon was one of Lucretia's favorites, to be sent to friends, relatives, and associates.[40]

Knowing Lucretia's taste for liberal religious tracts, the Webbs sent her a copy of *The Life of Joseph Blanco White*, published in London in 1845. Mott quickly made White her "*pet* author," believing his spiritual awakening offered a model for all humanity. The autobiography recounted White's journey from Seville, Spain, where he had trained to be a Catholic priest, to London, where he joined the Church of England and entered Oxford University to study for the ministry. But, according to Mott, "his views became too enlightened to remain" in the Anglican pulpit. Instead, White decided to become a Unitarian at the age of sixty. Mott described him as a "true Christian," one whose views "were the result of his own examination and reflection." She praised him for his faith in "the Divine light within us" and "conscientious Reason," and for his condemnation of "Bibleolatry," "sacerdotal religion," and "miracles." Indeed, Mott saw his story as one of "progress" "from "the darkness of Catholicism to *more* than Unitarian light." The book was unavailable in the U.S.; Mott lent her precious copy so long as it could be "soon returned."[41]

Mott's deliberate embrace of Parker and Blanco White further antagonized Philadelphia Quakers. Since 1827, Hicksites had been defending themselves against accusations of Unitarianism. Mott viewed these arbitrary sectarian boundaries as a detriment to true religion. In October 1846, in her first major speech since her mother's death two years before, Mott addressed the "Autumnal Convention" of Unitarians in Philadelphia. Invited by her friend the Rev. William Henry Furness, the leading Unitarian minister in the city, she told the assembled ministers that "I desire to see Christianity stripped of all names and things that make it technical, of the gloomy appendage of a sect." Casting aside doctrines like the Atonement, she asked, "Who is ready to hold up the purity of human nature in place of its depravity?" In place of theology, she offered "truth, love, mercy," instructing the assembly to "be not afraid of the reputation of infidelity or the opprobrium of the religious world." Yet again Lucretia found herself standing before a hostile audience, for even a liberal denomination like the Unitarians excluded women from the ministry. She criticized the use of the Bible in upholding women's subordination, which she described as "the immolation of woman at the shrine of priestcraft." The sermon aroused opposition from multiple quarters. Some criticized the "lugging in of the woman's rights question." Hicksite Quakers expressed their "uneasiness" that Lucretia had spoken before "those not of our persuasion."[42]

Mott survived this brief controversy, but the Society of Friends was in serious danger of another schism. In 1842, Green Plain Meeting in Clark County, Ohio, split from the Hicksite Indiana Yearly Meeting after being censured for criticizing George F. White's ministry. Lucretia's friends Sarah Dugdale, her son Joseph, and his wife Ruth Dugdale were abolitionists and leading members of Green Plain Meeting. By 1845, the Dugdales faced disownment for their anti-slavery activism, hindering Joseph's ability to travel as a minister. Nevertheless, Mott wrote to Sarah to report his positive reception at Philadelphia Yearly Meeting: "His ministry seem'd to carry an evidence to many, beyond *Church* authority—and all opposition—with a slight exception, was silenced." Another Friend, however, Griffith M. Cooper of Genesee Yearly Meeting in Farmington, New York, had been stripped of his ministry for speaking against the disownment of Hopper, Gibbons, and Marriott. Lucretia expected such abuse of power in the current state of the society: "But such things must needs be, while an Ecclesiastical establishment finds place among us." She called for radical change in the Discipline rather than "entire come-outerism." Another separation, she told Sarah Dugdale, would provide only a temporary solution.[43]

With this dispute simmering in the background, in the summer of 1847, James and Lucretia traveled west to attend anti-slavery gatherings and Yearly Meetings in Ohio and Indiana. James described the grueling trip of 69 days, 2,800 miles, and 71 meetings "of all kinds." After a warm reception at Ohio Yearly Meeting, Lucretia and James traveled for a week with William Lloyd Garrison and Frederick Douglass. Mott praised the "dignity of demeanor" of Garrison and the "ability & discretion" of Douglass.[44] As biographer William

McFeely notes, despite Mott's opposition to his purchase, Douglass reacted with great "patience." Though they disagreed, Douglass bore her no ill will, later describing her as "noble" and "eloquent" and defending her against those Quakers who looked at her "askance."[45]

In Richmond, Indiana, the home of Indiana Yearly Meeting, Lucretia's Quaker opponents waited for her. According to Mott, Indiana Yearly Meeting was hopeless—"they ought to have gone with the Orthodox, at the Separation"— and had voted to disown the Dugdales and Green Plain Meeting as a body "without the usual form" of calling on them individually. Rumors that Lucretia was "employed & *paid* by the A.S. Society" followed her from Ohio, leading to potential charges of violating Quaker testimony against hireling ministry. Mott's hostess Sarah Plummer, an old friend from Byberry, asked her if the rumors that she was a paid lecturer were true. Plummer told Lucretia that she had been warned to expect an "evasive" reply. Then, before the Yearly Meeting began, two female elders called on the Motts to warn them against attending without a minute (by this time, Cherry Street Meeting had withdrawn its support of Lucretia's travels). Lucretia responded that, "You know well enough we are members, & our position in Society." Undeterred, the Motts attended, and James wrote that, "Lucretia I thought spoke rather better than usual *for her*, & did not suppose any would or could say ought against it." With the conflict in Mexico pressing on her mind, Lucretia preached on nonviolence, recommending *Reflections on Peace and War* by her friend John Jackson, who described war as "legalized brutality" with "origins in depraved lusts and passions." But the elders maintained a policy of ignoring Lucretia and encouraged others to do so as well. Dr. John Plummer, Sarah's husband, entered the Women's Meeting to notify them that Lucretia's meeting was in sympathy with Green Plain due to the "*rebellious spirit*" of some of its members.[46]

Given her reception, Mott's health unsurprisingly grew worse. James reported that she suffered chills, fever, and neuralgia in her back during the last month of the trip. At the Plummers' house in Richmond, suffering from severe pain, Lucretia asked Dr. Plummer to treat her, offering to pay him more than his usual fee. He replied, "I am so deeply afflicted by thy rebellious spirit, that I do not feel I can prescribe for thee." The Motts left to find other lodgings. On the fourth day of the Indiana Yearly Meeting sessions, Lucretia stepped into the home of "widow Evans," where a number of Friends had gathered. Mott wanted to warm her feet and seek respite from her pain. A sympathetic Friend reported that Lucretia was in tears the entire time. Still, not one person in the entire room spoke to the distraught fifty-four-year-old woman. Lucretia never forgot this treatment, for her granddaughter Anna Davis Hallowell was still denouncing it decades later.[47]

Mott's continued allegiance to the Society of Friends in this period set her apart from many of her female coworkers. When Massachusetts Quaker Abby Kelley led the sexual integration of the American Anti-Slavery Society, Mott asked, "Will not the ground thou assumes, oblige thee to withdraw from the Society of Friends?" By 1841, Kelley's anti-slavery convictions caused her to break with the Quakers, "disowning" the Society before it could disown her. New England Yearly Meeting, she wrote, had contradicted "its own professed principles on the question of slavery." She told her Uxbridge Monthly Meeting that it was her duty to thus "'come out and be separate, and have no communion with the unfruitful works of darkness.'" Similarly, in 1845, Isaac and Amy Post withdrew from their meeting in Rochester, New York. Lucretia's children too were "all 'come outers,'" preferring the sermons of Unitarian William Henry Furness to Quaker preaching.[48]

The conflict between abolitionists and their churches went beyond the Society of Friends. In Seneca Falls, New York, Rhoda Bement confronted her minister, Horace P. Bogue, for failing to read her anti-slavery announcements from the pulpit of the Presbyterian church. The dispute began when Abby Kelley toured New York, calling for abolitionists to disavow ministers and churches that did not wholeheartedly condemn slavery. After their very public fight, Bogue placed Bement on trial for unchristian behavior and failing to take communion. On January 30, 1844, the church found her guilty, but she was unrepentant. She declared herself obliged to come out of this pro-slavery church.[49]

Over time, Mott's decision to stay in the Society of Friends only increased her reputation as a saint and martyr. Abby Kelley's staunch come-outerism as well as her disapproval of Mott's decision to withhold her credentials from the World's Anti-Slavery Convention prompted her to view Mott as a peacemaker.[50] Others also interpreted Mott's membership in the Society of Friends as an example of her meekness. Elizabeth Cady Stanton described Mott's sister Martha Wright, who since her disownment had disdained any church membership, as "a much stronger and more independent character than Lucretia." Nevertheless, Lucretia encouraged Stanton's own break from ecclesiastical authority. After returning from Great Britain, Lucretia wrote to her young friend to ask "art thou settled on the sure foundation, of the revealed will of God to the inner sense? Or is thy mind still perplexed with the schemes of Salvation, and plans of redemption which are taught in the schools of Theology?" Lucretia wanted "to see obedience to manifested duty—leading to practical righteousness, as the christian's standard." A wide embrace of individual moral authority, she believed, had the potential to create "large liberty" and "unbounded toleration." Mott saw herself as already liberated from "the creeds & dogmas of sects." She refused to yield her beloved Society of Friends, instead working from within to revise Quaker doctrine and structure.[51]

At the same time, Mott proved correct in the conviction that her Quaker ministry made her a potent critic of American churches. In August 1847, before her departure for the west, Mott gave a sermon at the Rev. Alonzo Hill's Second Congregational Society in Worcester, Massachusetts. According to an audience member, her topic was "Reforms of the Age," and she touched on anti-slavery, peace, anti-capital punishment, and temperance. But in a letter to the *Liberator* this correspondent expressed shock that Lucretia had emphasized the need for theological reform to achieve these other goals. She spoke against the doctrine of atonement as "paralyzing in its influence on man, and derogatory to the character of God." Furthermore, she stated that "Ecclesiastical power is always to be opposed, whether it appeared in the Pope of Rome or an Elder of a Quaker Meeting." This writer pronounced her a dangerous "infidel." Nevertheless, the church was so crowded that hundreds were turned away. Abby Kelley (now married to abolitionist Stephen S. Foster) and her daughter Alla were also in the audience. Abby declared that Mott was "decidedly more radical than when I saw her last." A month later, Abby Kelley Foster joined Mott, Garrison, and Douglass on the anti-slavery platform in Ohio.[52]

Stressed by divisions in the Society of Friends, Mott relied on the anti-slavery movement for spiritual and intellectual comfort. There, despite continued debates over strategy and ideology, she was a member of a small band of like-minded radicals, freed from the chains of sex, race, religion, and politics. After her mother's death, Lucretia grew closer to her youngest sister Martha, whom she discovered to be a political ally. In 1847, she wrote Martha that "the charge of irreligion" was a "libel" on abolitionists. She quoted extensively from the American Anti-Slavery Society's Declaration of Sentiments, pronouncing it "beautiful." "Ours," she told her sister, is "emphatically *the* religious move[men]t of the age." Now, Lucretia proclaimed, "it is our turn to cry 'Infidel' & the pseudo Church knows it too & is trembling in her shoes."[53] The following year, Mott traveled to Auburn to visit Martha, causing another crack in the foundations of church and state.

CHAPTER 8

The Year 1848

THE YEAR 1848 OFFERED THE PROSPECT of political and social transformation. In September, Lucretia reflected to George and Cecilia Combe that the past year had "seemed as though a new era was breaking in upon us." Commenting on the revolutions in Europe, the "Slavery & Peace question," "Agitation in all the Churches," and the "enlargement of Woman's Sphere," Mott observed, "we can but *hope* for some mighty overturning."[1] Though Mott only read about democratic unrest in France, Hungary, Germany, Italy, and Ireland, she helped lead the emancipatory struggle in her own nation that year, linking the anti-slavery, anti-Sabbath, and Indian reform movements, and organizing the first women's rights conventions in Seneca Falls and Rochester, New York. Seeing these reforms as "kindred in their nature," Lucretia envisioned women's rights not as a new and separate movement but rather as an extension of the universal principles of liberty and equality.[2]

After her grueling and depressing trip to Ohio and Indiana, Lucretia did not remain at home for long. She and James signed the call for an Anti-Sabbath Convention to be held in Boston in March 1848. The purpose of the convention, signers announced, was to counter "the attempt to compel the observance of any day as 'THE SABBATH' especially by penal enactments" as "unauthorized by scripture or reason." Instead, they demanded "the right to worship God according to the dictates of OUR OWN CONSCIENCES." Lucretia expected further "censure & reproach" from Philadelphia Hicksites, who were making "great efforts" to prevent the "free exercise of her individual rights." Her nemesis, George F. White, had died on October 9, 1847, but his sermons denouncing Lucretia and other abolitionists remained influential.

Lucretia reported that some of members of the Women's Meeting had objected to giving her a minute to hold meetings even within the jurisdiction of Philadelphia Yearly Meeting. Despite potential opposition, she reaffirmed her long-held belief "not to measure devotion by Sabbath observance." Lucretia recollected seeing Sabbath tracts "scattered" through the railroads cars during her western trip, appealing "to the credulity & gross superstition of the Ignorant," and she concluded that something had to be done.[3]

The Anti-Sabbath Convention, held March 23–24, drew many Garrisonian abolitionists, including Mott, William Lloyd Garrison, Charles Burleigh, and Henry Clarke Wright. Also present was Theodore Parker, the transcendentalist minister and author of Lucretia's favorite sermon, "The Transient and Permanent in Christianity." Parker continued to aggravate his fellow Unitarians while developing important connections to Boston's anti-slavery community. In 1846, Parker's friends secured him a prominent pulpit—if not a church—in the city's Melodeon hall, which Parker dubbed the "Twenty-Eighth Congregational Society of Boston."[4]

Lucretia's speech at the Anti-Sabbath Convention fully articulated her own commitment to agitation, declaring reformers' obligation "to stand out in our heresy" and rejecting any compromise with "popular views." Here, she included Theodore Parker's remarks on the first day of the convention, which proposed that the Sabbath be observed even though it was a day no different than any other. Such conciliation, she argued, only encouraged superstition. Lucretia described the Sabbath as a ritual that stood in the way of true Christianity: "The distinction has been clearly and ably drawn, between mere forms and rituals of the Church, and practical goodness; between the consecration of man, and the consecration of days, the dedication of the Church, and the dedication of our lives to God." Mott referred to the Quaker inner light, particularly as preached by Elias Hicks, to explain her opposition to the Sabbath. The time has come, she announced, "that man should judge of his own self what is right." "We are not called to follow implicitly any outward authority," she told the audience. Like other members of the convention, Mott believed that customary practices, such as the Sabbath, oppressed the individual conscience, and she denounced those who proposed to imbue custom with the force of law. But only Mott demanded that "every fetter" that bound the individual be broken.[5]

Mott had anticipated a negative reaction, but the response from Boston's mainstream clergy was especially forceful. The *Boston Recorder*, which the *Pennsylvania Freeman* derided as "the sanctimonious organ of New England

Congregationalism," portrayed her as "deranged." The reporter argued that Mott herself was proof of the doctrine of total depravity. Her outward appearance was "pleasing" and "benignant," but her remarks revealed a "soul rankling against the kingdom of God, and his Christ."[6] And indeed, Mott's vision of the "kingdom of God" differed markedly from these ministers. In Worcester the previous year, she had argued that church teachings threatened spiritual truth. Religious tradition especially hindered women by generally excluding them from the ministry. Now, in conjunction with the state, church leaders proposed to further limit the freedom of the individual. Lucretia's attack on the Sabbath was a direct attack on church power. The clerics responded in kind, attempting to dismiss Mott as insane or evil.[7]

Though Lucretia laughed at such newspaper coverage, the article in the *Boston Recorder* inspired her to greater efforts, and she wrote to Sydney and Elizabeth Neall Gay of her plans to attend the anniversary convention of the American Anti-Slavery Society in New York City. Since the dates of Philadelphia Yearly Meeting usually conflicted with the AASS annual meeting, Mott planned to attend the anniversary convention for the first time in ten years. But, she told the Gays, she had been suffering from a fever and sore throat. When she had traveled to Boston in 1847, a newspaper had reported that Mott was sixty-five years old. Though Lucretia feared the newspapers might say she was seventy-five, twenty years older than her real age, she told Elizabeth Gay she was willing to suffer these indignities for the cause.[8]

Lucretia also pressured her younger friend, "What art thou doing?"[9] Elizabeth, daughter of Mott's friend Daniel Neall, had been a member of the Philadelphia Female Anti-Slavery Society and a delegate to the World's Anti-Slavery Convention in London. After her marriage in 1845, Elizabeth and her abolitionist husband moved to Staten Island. Mott may not have known that Elizabeth was seven months pregnant, but she had little patience for anti-slavery women who did not match her intense schedule of travel to religious meetings or reform conventions. Like later women's rights activists, she bemoaned the loss of female activists to marriage and motherhood. For example, she described the career of the Grimké sisters as a "flash," and their move to New Jersey after Angelina's marriage to Theodore Weld as an "effectual extinguishment."[10] Lucretia's nagging ignored the fact that her anti-slavery career did not get underway until her youngest children were out of infancy. Not surprisingly, despite Lucretia's pressure, Lizzie Gay did not attend the American Anti-Slavery Society meeting.

On May 9, Mott delivered a speech on the "Law of Progress" to the abolitionists gathered in New York City. Offering an explicit contrast to the "go-ahead" spirit of commerce, Mott argued that "human freedom"—from war, intemperance, priestcraft, and, most importantly, slavery—was on the horizon, rapidly "engaging the attention of the nations of the earth." Scholar David Brion Davis points out that the progress of humankind through history was an "explanatory system" for reformers, who believed in a "transcendent purpose in history, a purpose gradually revealed and made manifest through human enlightenment."[11] In this speech, Mott explained her own faith in a "law" of progress working through the anti-slavery movement. Harkening back to the founding meeting of the American Anti-Slavery Society in 1833, she remembered the small band that met to declare "not merely self-evident truths—to reiterate the simplest truisms that were ever uttered": "that every man had a right to his own body, and that no man had a right to enslave or imbrute his brother." After this jab at the nation's founders, she invoked William Lloyd Garrison, instructing her listeners to "look around you over the country, and see whether he spoke in vain, when he declared that he *would be heard*." She also mentioned a recent "amalgamation" meeting in Philadelphia, called by abolitionists to cheer the Second Republic's intention to free slaves throughout France's empire. Ten years earlier, the interracial gathering at Pennsylvania Hall had sparked a riot, but now white citizens enthusiastically listened to black speakers. "These, then, are the evidences of progress," Lucretia stated. She called her allies to further action: "go on, and make advancement by our faithfulness."[12]

In different, often contradictory ways, reformers heeded Mott's call, converging on the religious, political, and commercial hotbed of central and western New York. Since their return from Indiana, she and James had been planning another trip to the "West," scheduled for June 1848, to attend Genesee Yearly Meeting, and to visit the Cattaraugus Seneca Indian reservation near Buffalo and fugitive slaves living across the border in Canada. In December 1847, Frederick Douglass had moved to Rochester to begin publication of his newspaper, the *North Star*. His enterprise was a direct challenge to Garrisonian anti-slavery newspapers like the *Liberator* and the *National Anti-Slavery Standard*. Douglass had grown disillusioned with Garrison and his ideological commitment to moral suasion and disunion. Instead, Douglass announced his willingness—like his friend, political abolitionist and free produce advocate Gerrit Smith—to view the U.S. Constitution as "hostile to the existence of slavery," and to work within the political system to end the peculiar institution.[13] As a loyal Garrisonian, Mott viewed the laws of the country as "altogether tending to rivet the chains of the oppressed." Nonetheless, she subscribed to Douglass's newspaper, viewing it as an important vehicle for the abolitionist message. Mott applauded the "diversity" of anti-slavery efforts, as long as the shared goal of abolition was not lost.[14]

Though the Second Great Awakening was largely over, the region, called the Burned Over District for its intense revivals, continued to harbor religious innovation. In March 1848, the first members of John Humphrey Noyes's utopian community arrived in Oneida, New York. The goal of the Oneida Association was spiritual perfection: to create a society free of sin. Noyes and his followers rejected the greed of modern American society in favor of communitarian living. But members of the Oneida community also scandalized Americans by practicing what critics called "free love." Abandoning the possessiveness and inequality of Victorian marriages, all members of the community were bound together in "complex marriage." And, with the approval of Noyes and a committee of elders, members of the community could have sex with as many of their "husbands" or "wives" as they chose.[15]

Anti-slavery politics drew other activists to the area surrounding the Erie Canal. Wealthy abolitionist Gerrit Smith lived just over ten miles from Oneida in Peterboro. On August 1, 1846, Smith had announced a radical plan to deed 120,000 acres of land in the Adirondacks to African Americans. His goal was to enable black settlers to meet the property requirements for voting in New York State, thus contributing to the growing political confrontation over the expansion of slavery. In April 1848, white abolitionist John Brown met with Smith to discuss moving his family to North Elba or "Timbucto" to live side by side with black residents. Brown and his family settled there the following year.[16]

Abolitionists were becoming a factor in electoral politics. Henry Stanton, husband of Elizabeth Cady Stanton, now living in the central New York town of Seneca Falls, pursued an alliance between the Liberty Party and New York's Barnburner Democrats. Two years earlier, in August 1846, President James K. Polk had proposed to resolve the conflict with Mexico by purchasing California and New Mexico for $2 million dollars. Many anti-slavery northerners already suspected that Polk's real motive was to expand the reach of slavery. Northern Democrats worried that Polk's proposal would increase the power of southern slaveholders in their party. David Wilmot, a Democratic Representative from Pennsylvania, proposed a qualification to Polk's request for funds that "neither slavery nor involuntary servitude shall ever exist in any part of said territory."[17] Wilmot's proposal divided the Democratic Party.

In New York State, so-called Barnburner Democrats endorsed Wilmot's proviso, and in a mass meeting in October 1847 announced their support for "Free Trade, Free Labor, Free Soil, Free Speech, and Free Men."[18] While Henry Stanton courted Barnburner Democrats, other political abolitionists, including Elizabeth's cousin Gerrit Smith and Frederick Douglass, viewed such alliances as compromising the goals of radical abolition: ending (rather than limiting) slavery and fighting racism and inequality. As biographer Judith Wellman notes, Elizabeth Stanton had a "ringside seat" at these debates among political abolitionists.[19]

When Mott arrived in Farmington, New York, to attend Genesee Yearly Meeting in early June, she found herself in the midst of another dispute over the morality of abolitionism. For the past decade, Hicksite Quakers had been bitterly divided over Friends' participation in the worldly American Anti-Slavery Society. Abolitionists such as Isaac and Amy Post had left their meetings to protest Quaker proscription against abolitionist activism. Others, such as Isaac Hopper, had been disowned. The conflict had also shaken Genesee Yearly Meeting. In 1839, Griffith M. Cooper reported that members of Genesee Yearly Meeting had decided not to pass judgment on Quaker abolitionists. By 1845, however, Cooper wrote to the Motts that the Meeting of Ministers and Elders (a local committee charged with overseeing ministers) had advised his monthly meeting that he was "no longer worthy to be regarded a minister among them." Lucretia wrote that Cooper "was a doomed man from the time he bore his testimony against the proceedings of New York Meeting in the case of I. T. Hopper and Charles Marriott." Following his mistreatment, the authority of elders to discipline ministers also became a matter of debate, as it had in the Hicksite schism.[20]

After delivering a sermon on the first day of Genesee Yearly Meeting, Lucretia watched as the Society of Friends verged on another split. One faction at Genesee Yearly Meeting opposed any attempt to "abandon the institutions that time and change have left us" or alter—in their view "relax"—the discipline. The dissident party advocated "the sacred rights of conscience" over institutional or ecclesiastical control. By the fourth day, approximately two hundred of the dissenting Quakers had decided to meet separately. Having been "denounced" by the conservatives, Lucretia joined these radicals, who included Isaac and Amy Post, Daniel Anthony (father of Susan B. Anthony), and Thomas and Mary Ann M'Clintock.[21] Lucretia knew Thomas M'Clintock from Philadelphia. An apothecary and member of Pine Street Meeting (where the Motts had married), M'Clintock had been one of Elias

Hicks's most important advocates in the city. In 1825, M'Clintock published a pamphlet that included extracts from William Penn's *The Sandy Foundation Shaken*. M'Clintock's goal was to show that the doctrines espoused by Elias Hicks conformed to the writings of early or "primitive" Friends. He also called Hicks's opponents a "mercenary priesthood," comparing them to the persecutors of pioneer Quakers.[22] In 1836, M'Clintock had moved to Waterloo, New York. Since then, he too had faced criticism from Genesee Yearly Meeting for, as Lucretia wrote, "uniting with their brethren in other denominations in carrying on the work of the righteous." Like Lucretia Mott and Griffith M. Cooper, Thomas M'Clintock experienced the venom of George F. White and his allies.[23]

Now Thomas M'Clintock was the spokesman for this new group of dissenting Quakers. Shortly after Genesee Yearly Meeting, M'Clintock published *An Address to Friends of the Genesee Yearly Meeting and Elsewhere*. Explaining their break with the Society of Friends, M'Clintock cited their "rights of conscience," suppressed by the "spirit of proscription and intolerance" that had overtaken their meeting. This lack of unity, M'Clintock argued, prevented Friends from fighting "War, Slavery, Intemperance, &c." By October 1848, M'Clintock and his allies had reconstituted themselves as the Congregational Friends. Thomas M'Clintock wrote their statement of principles, published as the *Basis of Religious Association*. As their name implied, these Friends entrusted individual meetings to make their own decisions. They abolished the controversial Meeting of Ministers and Elders. With twenty years of doctrinal debate behind them, the Congregational Friends decided that they would be united by "oneness of purpose" rather than theology. Finally, espousing "equality in the human family," they decided that men and women would no longer meet separately.[24]

Mott welcomed this "broader platform." As the storm gathered around Genesee Yearly Meeting, Lucretia had asked, "when will men learn that there are other & more indissoluble bonds of union than agreement in opinion in Creed or form?" Writing later that year, Mott concluded that the "Congregational form of religious association will ultimately prevail as man comes to understand Christian liberty."[25] Lucretia praised the Congregational Friends, but she did not leave her beloved Cherry Street Meeting or Philadelphia Yearly Meeting for the Congregational Friends or related groups like the Progressive Friends. Though both M'Clintock and Mott were schooled in religious schism, she declined to join M'Clintock's new organization. She saw institutional division as a limited means of addressing theological disagreements, and she probably found the idea of another division too painful. Lucretia was determined to rouse her Quaker meeting, working from within to "congregationalize" the Society of Friends.[26]

Lucretia then turned her attention to the plight of Native Americans in New York State. At Genesee Yearly Meeting, the Motts met other members of the Joint Indian Committee, established by the Genesee, New York, Philadelphia, and Baltimore Yearly Meetings to intervene in an ongoing dispute between the Seneca Indians of western New York and the predatory Ogden Land Company. Like the Cherokee in Georgia, the Seneca faced increasing pressure from white settlers and speculators to sell their land. In 1810, the Holland Land Company sold its preemption rights on Seneca reservations to the Ogden Land Company, whose shareholders included prominent businessmen and politicians. In 1826, the Ogden Land Company, with the help of some well-placed bribes, negotiated a treaty to purchase all the Seneca land along the Genesee River for $48,260, to be held in trust by the state and paid to the Seneca in the form of annuities. This treaty did not sate the Ogden Land Company's desire for Seneca land, and the shareholders encouraged the Seneca to leave their land in western New York for Indian Territory. This pressure resulted in the 1838 Treaty of Buffalo Creek, a similarly corrupt agreement gained through more bribes, misinformation, and threats.[27] That same year, Philadelphia's Hicksite Quakers formed a committee to plead the cause of the Seneca, who, they believed, had been forced to sign the removal treaty against their will. By 1839, Philadelphia Yearly Meeting was working with Genesee, New York, and Baltimore. Members of the Joint Indian Committee included its agent Griffith Cooper, pacifist John Jackson, Benjamin Ferris (a.k.a. Amicus), and James and Lucretia Mott. The committee also included some strange bedfellows, such as George F. White's ally Rachel Hicks and, before he was disowned, Charles Marriott of New York Yearly Meeting.[28]

By 1842, the Joint Committee had helped negotiate a supplemental treaty, which allowed the Seneca to remain in New York, but only at great cost. The Seneca retained control of only two reservations, the Alleghany and Cattaraugus, ceding the Buffalo Creek and Tonawanda reservations to the Ogden Land Company. In exchange, the Seneca received another payment to be paid in the form of annuities. The Seneca were deeply unhappy at the compromise, and the Tonawanda refused to leave their land. Nonetheless, the Quakers on the Joint Committee believed they had done some good: "We believe much distress has been averted from the Indians by the exertions of Friends; and although not able to arrest entirely the consequences of the treaty of 1838, yet we think Friends will feel much satisfaction in having been instrumental in restoring to the Indians a part of the land, of which they had been so unjustly deprived."[29] Following the 1842 compromise, the Quaker Joint Committee worked to secure the Indians' title to their land.

From the beginning of their involvement with the Seneca, Philadelphia Hicksites expressed concern over the "domestic arrangements" of the Indians. Quakers, including Lucretia, viewed Seneca women's labor in the fields as a visible reminder of Native American difference. Quaker women instructed their Indian "sisters" in "the duties more properly belonging to your sex." Even the Seneca realized their survival in New York State depended on this trapping of "civilization." To this end, the Indian Committee proposed to hire a female superintendent for its school on the Cattaraugus reservation. In 1845, the manual labor school had more than one hundred students, and the Indian Committee recommended that some female students live with the Quaker family who ran the farm. The experiment was a success, they reported: "ten girls at a time are constant inmates of the family; where they are taught to spin, knit, sew, cook, make bread, and other branches of domestic industry, in connexion with their school education." In 1847, the Joint Committee advised the Seneca that "history confirms the deeply interesting fact, that no people ever yet were elevated to the rank of civilization while their females were held in a servile condition, and we are also admonished by experience, that no community can be virtuous and happy, which is not chastened by the controlling example of female delicacy and refinement."[30]

Lucretia's committee handed down these Victorian decrees, but she undoubtedly viewed this domestic advice with some skepticism. In 1839, when the Indian Committee discussed the "sad state of things" among Seneca women, Lucretia suggested that Seneca women, a "council of *squaws*," be consulted. Though her use of the term "squaw" revealed condescending assumptions about Indian women, Lucretia saw the imposition of bourgeois domestic ideals on native women as heavy-handed and patriarchal. But other male and female members of the Indian Committee treated her suggestion as a joke, and one Quaker woman rebuked her. After this exchange, there is no evidence that Lucretia questioned the committee's policies toward Seneca women. She may have seen such proposals as key to Seneca survival. And, under assault from anti-abolitionist Quakers, Mott probably wanted to choose her battles. But as someone who had been criticizing women's limited sphere for more than twenty years, Lucretia's silence is striking. One explanation is that she viewed Native Americans as strange and primitive. Despite her involvement on the Indian Committee, Lucretia had not spent time with Native Americans since her childhood on Nantucket. In contrast to the free blacks and former slaves she knew in Philadelphia, she described the Seneca as "grotesque," "fantastic," and "rude." Even more telling, she did not comment on the negative impact Quaker involvement might have on Seneca women's traditional power as chiefs or clan matrons.[31]

The Motts visited the Cattaraugus reservation at what they saw as an exciting time. Not only were the Seneca "improving in their mode of living, cultivating their land, and educating their children," wrote Lucretia, "they are learning somewhat from the political agitations abroad." The Seneca chafed at the leadership of the chiefs who had negotiated the Treaty of Buffalo Creek. They were also concerned that dishonest chiefs controlled the funds from the annuities. Mott noted that the Seneca people were seeking "larger liberty—more independence," demanding changes in their form of government. Such discussions had been underway for several years. In 1845, the Indian Committee reported that the Seneca had decreed that no sale of land could be negotiated without the approval of two-thirds of an assembly of chiefs and warriors, and two-thirds of the adult male population. When the Seneca Nation approved a constitution in late 1848, it established the elected positions of president, secretary, treasurer, and an eighteen-seat council. Like the domestic reforms encouraged by the Quakers, these political changes were intended to help the Seneca coexist with their white neighbors.[32]

Religious battles on the Cattaraugus reservation also captured Lucretia's attention. The Seneca had split into two factions, those who had converted to Christianity under the aegis of the American Board of Commissions for Foreign Missions, and the so-called Pagan Party, who observed traditional religious practices. The Joint Committee of Quakers maintained a neutral position in these debates, welcoming children of both parties into their school. Their goal was not to convert the Seneca, but to advise and befriend them. The Motts met with both parties, Lucretia reported, "but we declined to decide between them, as, if attempted, we might be found equally discountenancing each form, and recommending our Quaker non-conformity." Attending the annual celebration of the Strawberry Festival, Mott revealed an open-mindedness, even relativism, toward Seneca religious practices that was not apparent in her views of Seneca gender roles. "In observing the profound veneration of the hundreds present, some twenty of whom were performers, and the respectful attention paid to the speeches of their chiefs, women as well as men," she wrote, "it was far from me to say that our silent, voiceless worship was better adapted to their condition, or that even the Missionary, Baptism, and Sabbath, and organ, are so much high evidence of a civilized, spiritual and Christian state."[33]

Writing from the Cattaraugus reservation to Philadelphia Yearly Meeting, however, James Mott expressed concern over the state of their mission. The schoolhouse was badly in need of repair, and the farm required more work than the teacher, Joseph Walton, and his family could handle. The number of students had declined. James wanted Philadelphia Yearly Meeting to send more funds, but the year after the Motts' visit, Philadelphia Yearly Meeting severed its connection to the Cattaraugus reservation and the Joint Committee. Members of the Indian Committee protested, writing that the Seneca were "yet in danger." In a letter to the Seneca Nation, however, the defeated Indian Committee explained that progress justified the break. Quakers cited "the more perfect domestication of your Women" as central to this progress. They urged the Seneca to continue withdrawing "women from the labour and drudgery of the field" and instructing their daughters in "all the useful braches of good housewifery." But members of Philadelphia Yearly Meeting also recognized their own inability to solve the problems facing the Seneca: "Those who have had to suffer the evils of a bad Government, or the mal-administration of a good one, can, generally, discern the proper remedy, with more clearness, than people at a great distance, who can neither feel the evils, nor understand their cure." Unable to envision Indians' emancipation without adoption of Anglo-American habits, the Quakers found the Seneca a source of frustration.[34]

The Motts felt more optimistic about free blacks. After leaving Cattaraugus, Lucretia and James traveled to "Canada West," the nickname for the province of Ontario, right across the border from Buffalo. Since the British abolished slavery throughout their empire in 1833, Canada had become an important destination for fugitives from the United States. By the time Mott visited, approximately 12,000 former slaves had settled there. In a letter published in the *Liberator*, Lucretia declared it "worth a journey of many miles to see 'the colored man *a man*'—in the full exercise of his energies and ingenuity." She held meetings with former slaves in Chatham, Dawn, London and Toronto. She praised their "cheerful toil," their efforts to educate their children, and their hospitality. Mott's attention to their hospitality was important. These former slaves (perhaps in contrast to the Seneca?) were "not wanting in the delicacies and refinements of social life." But Lucretia also noted the settlers' generous aid to the stream of fugitives "from the house of bondage." Such comments alerted anyone reading the *Liberator* that former slaves would receive a warm welcome in Canada. Urging fugitives onward, Lucretia wrote, "The spirit of Freedom is arousing the world."[35]

Meanwhile, Gerrit Smith and other political abolitionists gathered in Buffalo on June 14 and 15, 1848, for the National Liberty Convention. Smith's faction of the Liberty Party, called the Liberty League, asserted that slavery was unconstitutional, arguing that their rivals had betrayed pure abolitionism by acknowledging its legality in the slave states. In their founding convention the previous year, the Liberty League had staked a broad claim to radicalism, nominating Gerrit Smith for president in an election that included women. Lucretia Mott had received one vote, as had Lydia Maria Child. At the National Liberty Convention in June 1848, the interracial platform included Frederick Douglass, minister Henry Highland Garnet, and newspaper editor Samuel Ringgold Ward. At the meeting, Gerrit Smith expressed his support for "universal suffrage in its broadest sense, females as well as males being entitled to vote." This time, Mott received five votes for the league's nomination as president. If she was aware of these nominations, she did not comment. Despite her distrust of party politics, she may have appreciated this show of support from friends and allies in the fight for abolition, racial and sexual equality, and free produce.[36]

With this political ferment, Mott's family circle also influenced her path. Lucretia and James traveled east from Buffalo to Auburn to visit Lucretia's forty-two-year-old sister Martha Wright, who was six months pregnant. Lucretia intended the visit to be for business as well as pleasure. The Wrights' neighbors included former governor of New York William Seward, who, like the Hicksite Quakers, had opposed the 1838 Treaty of Buffalo Creek. In 1848, he was elected to the U.S. Senate as a Whig, where he became a vocal opponent of slavery. Seward's wife Frances Adeline Miller, an alumna of the Troy Female Seminary, also held anti-slavery sympathies. The city was home to a state prison that had adopted disciplinary methods consistent with Mott's critique of the Philadelphia penitentiary system, declaring total isolation "at variance with the human constitution." The prison administrators also encouraged education and religious conversion of inmates. On July 16, Mott spoke at Auburn State Prison and the city's Universalist Church.[37]

Just a few days before her speech to the prisoners, Lucretia and Martha had visited the home of Quakers Jane and Richard Hunt in nearby Waterloo, New York. The small gathering also included Mary Ann M'Clintock, wife of Thomas M'Clintock, and Elizabeth Cady Stanton. Their conversation ranged across recent events, including the Anti-Sabbath Convention, Genesee Yearly Meeting, the National Liberty Convention, and the passage, after twelve long years of debate, of New York's Married Women's Property Act, allowing wives to retain ownership of property that they brought into marriage. A relative newcomer to this small group of reformers, Stanton expressed her "long-accumulating discontent" as a mother, housewife, and frustrated activist. By the end of the tea party, the women made the epochal decision to place a notice in the *Seneca County Courier*, calling a convention for July 19 and 20 "to discuss the social, civil and religious condition of woman." Inviting the public to the anti-slavery Wesleyan Church in Seneca Falls, they advertised the presence of "Lucretia Mott, of Philadelphia." Lucretia sent the notice to Frederick Douglass, who published it in the *North Star*; other regional newspapers also picked up the advertisement.[38]

Though all five women embraced the plan to hold a women's rights convention, they disagreed over form and content. With Lucretia and Martha tending to a sick James in Auburn, Stanton, Mary Ann M'Clintock, and the M'Clintocks' adult daughters Elizabeth and Mary Ann met again to draft a Declaration of Sentiments. Despite the presence of three Quaker women, historians see Stanton as the principal author of the document. She based it on the Declaration of Independence, adding "women" to Thomas Jefferson's bold statement: "we hold these truths to be self-evident, that all men and women are created equal." "The history of mankind," Stanton continued, "is a history of repeated injuries and usurpations on the part of man toward woman, having in direct object the establishment of an absolute tyranny over her." If Lucretia had been present at this second meeting, the Seneca Falls declaration might have looked quite different. At the Anti-Slavery Convention, Mott had criticized Jefferson's "self-evident" truths, preferring the simple truths of liberty, justice, and humanity pronounced by the American Anti-Slavery Society. At their initial meeting, the women had proposed to discuss the "social, civil, and religious condition" of women, consistent with Quaker abolitionists' rejection of electoral politics, but Stanton listed as woman's first grievance, that man "has never permitted her to exercise her inalienable right to the elective franchise."[39] Furthermore, Stanton rejected Mott's view of women's rights as inseparable from anti-slavery, anti-clericalism, Indian reform, and prison reform. From Auburn, Mott asked Stanton, "Are you going to have any reform or other Meeting during the sittings of the Convention?" Stanton responded with stony silence. Judith Wellman suggests that the ensuing debates at the Seneca Falls convention "reflected a split not only within

the convention as a whole but, more particularly, between Stanton and Mott."
Stanton viewed women's inequality as a political and legal problem. Mott saw
women's subordination as one of many threats to individual liberty wrought
by mindless tradition and savage greed.[40]

The organizers decided to reserve the first day of the convention for
women. At 11:00 a.m. on July 19, a hot and sunny morning, the assembled
women asked Mary Ann M'Clintock, Thomas and Mary Ann's daughter, to
take notes. Mott urged the female audience "to throw aside the trammels of
education" and participate in the discussion. Stanton read the Declaration of
Sentiments.[41] The assembled women then debated the document paragraph
by paragraph. The most controversial aspect of the Declaration was Stanton's
demand for the right to vote. Coming from a family of lawyers and politicians, Stanton viewed the vote as the essence of equal citizenship. Mott allegedly replied, "Lizzie, thou wilt make the convention ridiculous."[42] Lucretia,
like the many Garrisonians and Quakers present, disdained the moral compromises involved in party politics and did not view the vote as an important
or desirable goal.

The debate spilled into the afternoon session and into the second day,
when the crowd grew even larger due to the addition of men. James Mott
chaired the meeting. Richard Hunt, Thomas M'Clintock, and Frederick
Douglass also attended. All these reformers—at Genesee Yearly Meeting or
the National Liberty Convention—had expressed previous support for wom-
en's rights. But men's participation also caused debate. While Elizabeth Stanton argued that women should lead the movement, Lucretia resolved that
"the speedy success of our cause depends upon the zealous and untiring efforts of both men and women." On this point, Mott was victorious. And, as a
political abolitionist (and a non-Quaker), Frederick Douglass provided critical support for Stanton's resolution "that it is the duty of the women of this
country to secure to themselves their sacred right to the elective franchise."
After a lively day of discussion, the convention "unanimously adopted" the
Declaration of Sentiments and passed the resolutions by a "large majority."[43]

In many ways, Mott was "the moving spirit" of the Seneca Falls Convention.[44] Her visit to central New York provided the impetus for the convention,
and she also addressed the assembly more than any other speaker. At the
same time, few of Mott's remarks were actually recorded—and the resolutions and Declaration of Sentiments revealed little of her influence. As the
only individual present at both the 1837 Anti-Slavery Convention of American Women and the Seneca Falls Convention, she probably adapted Angelina

Grimké's earlier resolution "that woman has too long rested satisfied in the circumscribed limits which corrupt customs and a perverted application of the Scriptures have marked out for her, and that it is time she should move in the enlarged sphere which her great Creator has assigned her" to the needs of the current meeting.[45] Lucretia also urged a large audience at the end of the first day to consider women's rights as one aspect of "Reforms in general," but the convention did not address the links between women's rights and other causes.[46] Instead, Stanton's insistence on women's political equality became the focus of the convention. Mott herself admitted this, telling Stanton years later, "I have never liked the undeserved praise in the Report of that Meeting's Proceedings, of being 'the moving spirit of that occasion,' when to thyself belongs the honor, aided so efficiently by the M'Clintocks."[47]

If Stanton dismissed Mott's broader reform impulse, the younger woman's Jeffersonian approach proved enormously compelling. The Declaration of Sentiments listed "the facts" of man's tyranny over women. The demand for the vote—for political power—was the most practical way for women to change the laws and customs dictating their inferiority. Many of the grievances related directly to the legal status of married women; Stanton described a married woman as "civilly dead." The clause that compared a married woman's status to that of a slave was the only indirect reference to slavery in the proceedings: "In the covenant of marriage, she is compelled to promise obedience to her husband, he becoming, to all intents and purposes, her master." The Declaration described women's exclusion from "all profitable employments," higher education, and the ministry. Furthermore, a "different code of morals" applied to women, "by which moral delinquencies which exclude women from society, are not only tolerated but deemed of little account in man." This language linked the early women's rights movement with the moral reform movement, which sought to abolish prostitution and establish a single sexual standard of premarital sexual chastity for both men and women. Finally, signers declared that man had "usurped the prerogative of Jehovah himself, claiming it as his right to assign for her a sphere of action, when that belongs to her conscience and her God."[48]

Sixty-eight women and thirty-two men signed the Declaration of Sentiments. As a practical measure, they proposed to adopt the strategies of the anti-slavery movement by hiring agents, publishing tracts, circulating petitions, and holding more conventions. They had rejected the American Anti-Slavery Society's declaration as a model, however, and they decided not to establish a national society. After witnessing divisions in the anti-slavery movement and the Society of Friends, Mott and other conventioneers wanted to avoid the factionalism engendered by institutional hierarchies. Like the dissenting Quakers at the Genesee Yearly Meeting, the women's rights movement adopted a congregational form.[49]

Energized by the meeting, activists decided to continue the conversation in Rochester on August 2. The city was a logical choice for the next women's rights convention as the home of prominent abolitionists and Congregational Friends, including Seneca Falls attendees Amy Post and Frederick Douglass, as well as Daniel Anthony and Douglass's partner William C. Nell. At first, Lucretia planned not to attend. She may have been anxious to return home to Philadelphia. But Amy Post wrote a "distressing" letter, expressing her disappointment at losing Lucretia. Writing to Thomas and Mary Ann M'Clintock, Mott told them she had reconsidered, and she hoped Stanton and the M'Clintocks would also attend "to help make the Womens [sic] Convention interesting."[50]

Historian Nancy Hewitt describes the Rochester convention as "an even more radical gathering" than the one at Seneca Falls. While the earlier convention had proposed to discuss the "condition of women," the Rochester convention considered the "Rights of women, Politically, Socially, Religiously, Industrially." The Rochester convention also appointed a woman, Abigail Bush, to serve as the meeting's president. And, unlike the Seneca Falls convention, feminists in Rochester faced open opposition to their platform. For this reason, Mott's presence was invaluable. An experienced speaker and debater, she countered every argument against women's equal rights.[51]

Lucretia's first sparring partner was an ally, William C. Nell, a black Garrisonian from Boston. He gave a speech offering "grateful homage" to women's "energies and rare devotion" to the anti-slavery movement. Mott objected to his "language of flattering compliment," which she associated with the "sickly sentimentality of the Ladies Department." Mott viewed his praise, however innocent, as circumscribing women's activities. Though other female reformers used their role as mothers and wives to argue for political influence, Lucretia opposed any attempt to assign women moral superiority. Nell had referred to "man" as a "tyrant;" she reminded the audience that "woman is equally so when she has irresponsible power."[52]

Other men present raised outright objections to women's rights. Mr. Coulter argued that women's "proper sphere" was the home. Lucretia suggested he reread his Bible, observing, "it was not strange that he had imbibed such views, coming as he did from New Haven, Conn. [home of

Congregationalist Yale University]; said we had derived our views too much from the clergy instead of the Bible." Mr. Sully invoked the writings of St. Paul, arguing that, "man shall be the head of woman." He also believed that egalitarian marriages would lead to unnecessary political disagreements between husband and wife. Mott pointed out that Quakers did not promise obedience. Furthermore, stated the eminently rational Lucretia, "she had never known any other mode of decision except a resort to argument, an appeal to reason."[53]

Though the second convention adopted the Seneca Falls Declaration of Sentiments with over one hundred signatures, Mott had a greater impact on the proceedings of the Rochester convention. As she had at Seneca Falls, Lucretia reminded the convention that there was more at stake than women's rights. "Our aim," she stated, "should be to elevate the lowly and aid the weak." But, rather than arguing for middle-class women's condescension to the needy, she stressed that the "oppressed"—including women—should "*feel* and *act*." She advised women to demand their rights. Mott described "this as the beginning of the day when woman shall rise, when she shall occupy her appropriate position in society."[54]

Writing of her summer travels for the readers of the *Liberator*, Lucretia described her journey to Cattaraugus, Canada West, Seneca Falls, and Rochester. She was "encouraged" that "this long neglected subject," women's rights, was finally receiving attention. Remembering the 1840 split in the American Anti-Slavery Society, she knew that some abolitionists might oppose the new movement. Lucretia reminded readers that, "he will not love the slave less, in loving universal humanity more." Repeating the message she delivered to the women's rights conventions, Mott argued "all these subjects of reform are kindred in their nature; and giving to each its proper consideration, will tend to strengthen and nerve the mind for all."[55]

The events of the year had strengthened and rejuvenated Lucretia. She was "now as well as ever," she told George Combe. "My James & self are both grow[in]g more fleshy." They also had nine grandchildren. The previous year, Anna Mott Hopper had given birth to her third living child, a son named George. Maria Davis had three children, Anna, Henry, and Charles. Elizabeth Cavender, pregnant with her son Henry, had a toddler named Fanny. And Thomas and Marianna Pelham Mott had two young daughters, Isabella and Emily.[56]

Despite her advancing age, Lucretia showed no signs of slowing down. In October, she and Sarah Pugh walked through "pouring rain" to attend a "Convention of the Colored People" in Philadelphia. The purpose of the meeting was to raise support for Douglass's newspaper. In addition to the editor of the *North Star*, delegates to the convention included Charles Lenox Remond, who had refused his seat at the World's Anti-Slavery Convention in support of the American women, and Henry Highland Garnet, who had attended the National Liberty Convention. African American women, including Philadelphia Female Anti-Slavery Society members Harriet Purvis and Hetty Reckless, participated as equals. Mott told Elizabeth Cady Stanton that, "as they include women & *white* women too, I can do no less, with the interest I feel in the cause of the Slave, as well as of Woman, than be present & take a little part." Following close on the heels of the Seneca Falls and Rochester conventions, this meeting placed African Americans at the center of the struggle for racial and sexual equality. Though she recognized that she was an outsider, this "colored" convention affirmed Lucretia's sense that women's rights and anti-slavery were inseparable and interrelated.[57]

*   *   *

The Seneca Falls and Rochester conventions had not resolved the political differences between veteran activist Mott and her younger colleague Stanton. Almost immediately, Stanton began to challenge her role model. Stuck at home with three small boys, she decided to "pilot" young women willing to explore new careers. Both conventions had considered women's economic dependence. Excluded from most forms of employment, working women struggled to support themselves through low-paying and undesirable jobs such as domestic service or sewing. In one of the few professional occupations open to women, female teachers received lower salaries than their male counterparts. With Stanton's encouragement, two young women, Elizabeth M'Clintock and Anna Southwick, decided to break into the lucrative and glamorous business of silk importing. In a September 1849 letter to Mott, Stanton suggested that her son-in-law, Edward M. Davis, aid these women on their "new path to wealth and distinction."[58]

A successful silk importer, Edward M. Davis seemed well suited to helping these entrepreneurs. He was the lead partner in the firm of E.M. Davis and Company, located at 27 Church Alley, near James Mott's wool business. But Davis faced the financial challenges endemic to business in the early republic. According to Mott, in 1844, when he was "out of business," Davis's reform commitments led him to consider adopting the "Association principle" upon his return to "mercantile life." He proposed not only sharing his profits with his employees, but hiring female clerks as well. Davis discussed the idea with Elizabeth Neall and Elizabeth M'Clintock, but nothing came of it. In 1848, E.M. Davis and Company lost $40,000, forcing Davis into partnership with Charles Wharton. Thus, when Lucretia approached Edward with Stanton's letter in the fall of 1849, he was "bound with others" and not in "a situation to decide independently of the judgment of those he consulted."[59] The answer from Davis was no.

Mott was sympathetic to her son-in-law's financial situation, but she did not want to discourage Elizabeth or Anna. She advised them that "there must be a beginning to every thing." Citing the number of women employed in Philadelphia's retail and wholesale stores, Mott wrote, "all agree that for a beginning, a retail store would be preferable." Lucretia invited the two Elizabeths and Anna to stay with the Motts and "try, try again!" She also forwarded the results of Davis's discussion with his partner and employees, and Maria Mott Davis's dramatization and "caricatures" of the meeting.[60]

Elizabeth Cady Stanton was shocked by the tone of these "Philadelphia documents," which she perceived as ridiculing women. Stanton returned her own "combative" response, a drama written with Elizabeth M'Clintock. "Excuse us," Stanton wrote Mott, "for making our first attack on those of thine own household." The script describes Edward Davis as a "Merchant Prince," sitting in a "luxurious arm-chair" in a "handsomely furnished apartment." After he instructs his employee Rush Plumly on women's oppression, Lucretia Mott enters with Stanton's letter. Davis brushes off the suggestion that he employ female clerks: "It would not do. What can have induced these girls to step so far beyond their accustomed limits[?]" Mott answers that *she* had "labored to awaken / In the heart of woman, the strong desire / The earnest wish for freedom." At Mott's urging, Davis consults his partner, who objects to "the whole proposition." Then Davis consults his employees. Some of these "dramatis personae" are Mott relatives. Henry Earle, son of Lucretia's cousin Mary Hussey Earle, responds, "My mother thinks women are inferior." Tallman Wright, son of Martha, is the only character who expresses support for women's elevation, adding, "it is not for me to say which thine honor shall hold most dear, 'the interests of the House' or those of woman."[61]

Stanton's play showed her commitment to women's rights, which bowed not at all to friendship or practicality. Davis's abolitionist activities already threatened his credit rating, and female employees might further damage his reputation. In the coming years, financial necessity forced Davis to take on more partners before finally declaring bankruptcy in 1857.[62] But it is worth noting that Lucretia, herself something of an ideologue, greatly enjoyed the play. She read it at a meeting of the executive committee of the Pennsylvania Anti-Slavery Society, reporting that "Edwd. & Rush were present" and took "the flagellation" with "ill grace." They faced even more humiliation as the drama elicited "discussion up & down Market St." Mott viewed this discussion as an encouraging sign. Echoing her comments at the Rochester convention, Lucretia praised the two Elizabeths for their "determination to *act*."[63]

Though Stanton may have unfairly maligned Edward Davis, many men— even liberal men—viewed the idea of women's rights as absurd. Less than a month after the exchange between Stanton and Mott, Richard Henry Dana Sr. came to Philadelphia to deliver one of his famous lectures on Shakespeare. One of the founders of the literary magazine *North American Review*, Dana was a poet and critic. In Philadelphia, he included a lecture on "Woman and Her Influence on Society," in which he warned that the women's rights movement threatened to "unsex" women. Instead, this "resolute, chivalric" speaker praised women's "innocence, tenderness and confiding love of man." The *Pennsylvania Freeman* reported that Dana's lecture "excited disapprobation on the part of the audience."[64]

Mott listened to Dana "with great regret." The next week, she offered her response in a two-hour lecture in the large saloon of the Assembly Building. The room was so full that many who came to hear her were unable to get in.[65] Mott believed that Dana's lecture was "fraught with sentiments calculated to retard the progress of woman to the highest elevation destined by her Creator." As she had at the Anti-Sabbath Convention, Mott argued that woman must judge for herself what is right. In a time when works of "mercy and benevolence" proliferated, Mott asked, "why should not woman seek to be a reformer?"[66] Dana had mocked women who served as presidents or secretaries of benevolent societies, but Mott defended women's ability to conduct their own business. Emphasizing action, she argued that women "will never make much progress in any moral movement, while they depend upon men to act for them." In addition, Mott denied "that the present position of woman is her true sphere of usefulness; nor will she attain to this sphere, until the disabilities and disadvantages, religious, civil, and social, which impede her progress, are removed out of her way."[67]

Though Mott did not mention the political obstacles blocking women's "true sphere of usefulness," her speech, later published as the "Discourse on Woman," reconciled Stanton's electoral goals with her own. Mott pointed out that woman's exclusion from citizenship made her "a cipher in the nation." "It is with reluctance," she told her audience, "that I make the demand for the political rights of woman." As this Garrisonian Quaker explained, "Far be it from me to encourage woman to vote, or to take an active part in politics, in the present state of our government." But Mott's commitment to women's right to vote was firm: "Her right to the elective franchise however, is the same, and should be yielded to her, whether she exercises that right or not." She concluded by calling upon women to lay claim to their rights.[68]

Mott's "Discourse on Woman" was printed and widely circulated. When women's rights activists in Ohio invited Mott to a convention in Salem in April 1850, Lucretia sent them a copy of the "Discourse." Jane Elizabeth Jones read the essay to the convention, as well as a letter from Mott advising women to "not ask *as favor*, but demand *as right*, that every civil and ecclesiastical obstacle be removed out of the way." Mott did not mention the right to vote, but she applauded the Salem convention for recognizing "the bearing which the circumscribed sphere of woman has on the great political and social evils that curse and desolate the land."[69]

In the coming decade, women's rights activists across the country asserted women's "co-equality" with men. In 1853, Mott declared the great principle of women's rights was "the co-equality of woman with man, and her right to practice those arts of life for which she is fitted by nature." The term recognized the fundamental equality of men and women while also acknowledging their differences. At the same time, however, feminists debated the shape and strategy of their movement.[70]

CHAPTER 9

Conventions

In December 1851, Hungarian author Madame Terezia Walder Pulszky called on Mott at her new home at 338 Arch Street. During the winter months, Edward and Maria Davis, Thomas and Marianna Mott, and their children lived with Lucretia and James in the large brick townhouse. Lucretia's new dining room was 30 feet long, perfect for hosting weekly Folger family gatherings. Lucretia treasured these reunions, especially after her brother Thomas Coffin died in 1849. One month before Thomas's sudden death from cholera, Mott observed his fifty-first birthday, writing "we wish he had allotted the day to us here. We are growg. quite romantic 'as the years draw nigh.'"[1] In addition to her family, Lucretia entertained out-of-town Quakers for Yearly Meeting as well as distinguished guests such as "Madame P" and her entourage.

Pulszky was touring the United States with Hungarian revolutionary Louis Kossuth. In 1848, American abolitionists cheered as Kossuth fought for Hungary's independence from Austria, but their applause had gone silent by 1851. Fearful of alienating Hungary's potential allies, Kossuth refused to condemn slavery. His wife declined an invitation to tea at the Motts for the same "Anti Slavery reasons." Only Madame Pulszky braved an audience with the "dangerous" Lucretia Mott.[2] When debating the subject of slavery, Madame P. described Mott's eyes flashing "with indignation and her lips quiver[ing] with a hasty impatience, displacing the placid harmony of her countenance and conversation." Though Pulszky and Mott disagreed about American slavery, Madame P. admitted falling "beneath the charm of her moral superiority."[3]

Excerpted in the *Pennsylvania Freeman*, Madame P.'s reminiscence contributed to the ongoing public debate about Mott and other female activists. After the first women's rights conventions, multiple and conflicting images of female reformers filled the nation's newspapers. Some, like James Gordon Bennett's popular *New York Herald*, painted them as masculine shrews; others allowed abolitionists and feminists to shape their public image as symbols of female virtue and examples of equality. Mott's allies depicted her as a devout matron and a representative woman. Lucretia never worried about femininity or propriety; with her friends' paeans, she probably felt no need.[4]

Despite her wishes, Mott was a leader of the new women's rights movement. Lucretia's passion was fighting slavery. Feeling that "the Slave" had the "first claim" on her time and energy, she urged Elizabeth Cady Stanton and other young reformers to take the platform at the annual, and sometimes semi-annual, women's right meetings.[5] At these conventions, Mott and other activists analyzed the obstacles to women's equal citizenship. With her long history of confronting religious authorities, Mott contributed an incisive critique of the way church and state cooperated to limit women's sphere.[6] Yet as firmly as she believed in women's rights, the women's movement did not inspire her with the same sense of urgency, righteousness, or moral intensity as abolition. Committed to a universal conception of liberty, Mott questioned the tactical conservatism and narrow vision of some early women's rights activists.

Women's rights activists inaugurated their national movement at a convention in Worcester, Massachusetts, on October 23 and 24, 1850. Previous conventions had been explicitly regional, garnering local participants and attention. In Worcester, 500–1,000 reformers attended from across the northeast, attracting the notice of newspapers in Massachusetts, New York, and Pennsylvania. Lucretia signed the call for the convention, which invited men and women to "harmonize in opinion and cooperate in effort, for the reason that they must unite in the ultimate achievement of the desired reformation."[7] This statement recalled her resolution on participation of male allies at the Seneca Falls Convention. The goal that activists "harmonize in opinion" proved more elusive. Female and male delegates at the Worcester convention discussed the strategy to be adopted by the young movement, revealing early divisions over respectability and race that hardened after the Civil War.

Mott's perspective, as always, was that of a radical purist. The debate began when Paulina Wright Davis, president of the convention, advised feminists to abide by society's prejudices and customs. Though she acknowledged that men might be responsible for depriving women of their rights, Davis proposed that "harsh judgments and harsh words will neither weaken the opposition, nor strengthen our hands. Our address is to the highest sentiment of the times; and the tone and spirit due to it and becoming in ourselves, are courtesy and respectfulness."[8] Lucretia immediately responded, suggesting that women's rights activists, like abolitionists, "speak with the earnestness and severity of truth." And they must not be too polite to assign blame. After Garrisonian abolitionist Wendell Phillips argued that women too must be held responsible for their inferiority, Mott shot back that "He did not reason thus when he spoke of the wrongs of the Slave." Mott advised women not to plead for their rights, but to demand them. In this scene—often replayed at other reform conventions—Mott's uncompromising stance served as a necessary balance to the pretty diplomacy of Davis's speech.[9]

Mott's comments drew on the philosophical and personal ties between the anti-slavery and women's rights movements. Given the abolitionist sympathies of most women's rights activists, slavery often provided a metaphor for women's oppression. Sarah Grimké, for example, described the "very being" of a married woman as "like that of a slave, absorbed in her master." Mott rarely adopted this comparison, as it inevitably raised questions about the severity of women's condition and the difficulty of tracing the origins of women's subjugation. Though Mott agreed with Phillips that white middle-class women were among the most ardent defenders and beneficiaries of domesticity, she attributed women's love of sentiment to their inferior education. Like her heroine Wollstonecraft, Mott believed that equal intellectual and professional opportunities would prompt women to reject the shelter of the private sphere.[10]

However inapt the comparison between slavery and patriarchy, race and gender, the two movements overlapped. As British writer Harriet Taylor Mill, wife of John Stuart Mill, pointed out, abolitionists were the "originators" of this "first collective protest against the aristocracy of sex." Abolitionists served as the principal organizers of the Worcester convention, and the meeting was integrated. Frederick Douglass, present at the first two women's rights conventions, attended. Sojourner Truth, a former slave from Ulster County, New York, who had been speaking to anti-slavery audiences since 1844, addressed the convention, agreeing with Mott that man was to blame for woman's oppression. In the spirit of these abolitionist connections, the convention resolved that, "every party which claims to represent the humanity, civilization, and progress of the age, is bound to inscribe on its banners, Equality before the law, *without distinction of sex or color*" (emphasis added).[11]

Yet the links between women's rights and anti-slavery posed potential problems for feminists. Jane Gray Swisshelm, editor of the Pittsburgh *Saturday Visiter*, challenged the strategic benefits of the relationship, declaring, "in a woman's rights convention the question of color had no right to a hearing." A supporter of anti-slavery efforts, she believed that abolitionists were already making their case to the public. Women's rights activists must do the same, independent of the anti-slavery movement, Swisshelm instructed: "One thing at a time!"[12] Furthermore, the abolitionists' radical social vision undermined feminists' struggle for respectability. James Gordon Bennett of the *New York Herald* complained that the "old grannies" and "fugitive slaves and fugitive lunatics" at the Worcester convention had advocated "socialism, abolition, amalgamation, and infidelity."[13]

Swisshelm's response to Bennett's negative portrayal of the activists reconciled feminists' demands for sexual equality with the important differences between men and women. The *New York Herald* described Mott as a "General" or "Caesar": "all bone, gristle, and resolution," accurately capturing Mott's status, while stripping her of all feminine characteristics. Swisshelm portrayed Mott as the ideal woman: "A wife, a mother and a grandmother—a lady who moves in the first circles of the aristocratic city of brotherly love. She has ever been a pattern of the domestic virtues—her children have arisen to call her blessed, and her husband also he doth praise her, as well as the poor and needy, the trodden and oppressed to whom she has ever been an active and steadfast friend." Swisshelm reclaimed the mantle of womanhood from opponents who considered female reformers—especially women's rights activists—unsexed. She highlighted Mott as an example of a woman who successfully balanced her private and public life.[14] Though Mott did not protest Swisshelm's tribute or other flowery descriptions of her domesticity at the time, she later complained, writing, "I *will not* be lionized when I can avoid it."[15]

United in challenging their evisceration in the press, feminists continued their internal debates in two rival accounts of the Worcester convention. Paulina Wright Davis edited the official proceedings to exclude all dissenting voices, promoting her desire for high sentiment and harmony of opinion. Mott obliged her colleague by selling copies of the *Proceedings*, but privately she disapproved of Davis's account.[16] In a letter to thirty-two-year-old Oberlin College graduate Lucy Stone, who emerged from the Worcester convention as a leader of the women's rights movement, Mott noted that Davis's *Proceedings* had "disappointed many, & met with a slow sale."[17]

Lucretia preferred Harriet Taylor Mill's account of the convention, published as "The Enfranchisement of Women" in the *Westminster Review* in July 1851. As the title of her article indicates, Mill focused on women's political and civil rights. She also shared Mott's view that "custom" was one of the principal obstacles to women's equality. Mill argued that the fact "that an institution or a practice is customary is no presumption of its goodness, when any other sufficient cause can be assigned for its existence." She embraced the universal message of the early women's rights conventions that "we deny the right of any portion of the species to decide for another portion, or any individual for another individual, what is and what is not their 'proper sphere.'" Mott sent a copy to William Lloyd Garrison asking him to publish the whole article in the *Liberator*.[18]

In these early years, Lucretia saw evidence of progress for women all around her. In 1849, Elizabeth Blackwell graduated from Geneva Medical College, the first woman in the country to receive a medical degree. In 1853, Blackwell's future sister-in-law Antoinette Brown became the first woman ordained a Congregationalist minister. Closer to home, Mott noted the establishment of the Philadelphia School of Design for Women (1848) and the Female Medical College of Pennsylvania (1850). Mott herself used female physicians when possible, especially her fellow women's rights activist Dr. Ann Preston. Though Lucretia had not (and would not) read *Uncle Tom's Cabin* because she viewed novels as frivolous, she called the success of Harriet Beecher Stowe's book, published in 1852, "gratifying": "50,000 copies printed & nearly all sold, yielding her $10,000." As she had at anti-slavery meetings, Mott listed these items to encourage and inspire her women's rights audiences.[19]

Meanwhile, Mott regularly attended the proliferating series of women's rights conventions. Following another gathering in Worcester in 1851, feminists held meetings in West Chester, Pennsylvania, Syracuse, Cleveland, Philadelphia, Cincinnati, and New York City. At the Syracuse Convention in September 1852, they again discussed establishing a national organization, but decided against it. Lucretia wrote to Lucy Stone, their "congregational independence" prevented the "seeds of dissolution" from undermining the movement.[20]

Somewhat reluctantly, Lucretia assumed a leadership role. She wrote to Stone of her intention to attend the Syracuse Woman's Rights Convention and "to do & say all that I can, & that I am qualified for." But, she added, "as to presiding, that is something I *cannot do*, with any sort of ability." Typically self-effacing, even to the point of false modesty, Lucretia argued that as a "born & bred Quaker" she lacked the necessary qualifications, including the "graces & manner of polished Society."[21] Instead, she recommended Mary Ann Johnson, a lecturer on physiology and wife of abolitionist Oliver Johnson, who had presided at the West Chester Woman's Rights Convention earlier that year. The couple had lived in Philadelphia since 1851, when Oliver became editor of the *Pennsylvania Freeman*.[22] Notwithstanding her demurral, Lucretia was elected president, and the *Pennsylvania Freeman* reported that she "was prompt at every emergency, rigid in her sense of propriety, arresting every digression not pertinent to the subject before them; and she presided with more efficiency than we have often witnessed."[23]

Lucretia enjoyed the intellectual combat these meetings occasioned, informing the assembled reformers that she believed "in agitation—in the wisdom of not keeping still."[24] Two "emergencies" disrupted the Syracuse convention. Many male women's rights supporters attended, including the Rev. Samuel J. May and Gerrit Smith, but several men came for the express purpose of haranguing the women. One minister criticized women's rights activists for modeling themselves on the attention-seeking sunflower rather than the modest violet. After several admonitions against these sexual metaphors, Mott stopped him from speaking.[25]

Mott eagerly resumed a longstanding debate over the utility of the Bible. Still a year away from ordination, Antoinette Brown proposed a resolution "that the Bible recognizes the rights, duties and privileges of Woman as a public teacher, as every way equal with those of man; that it enjoins upon her no subjection that is not enjoined upon him; and that it truly and practically recognizes neither male nor female in Christ Jesus." Though many of members of the convention agreed with her interpretation of Scripture, the Congregational Friends, Hicksite Quakers, and free thinkers in the audience recoiled from using the book as an authority. Thomas M'Clintock opposed the resolution because the Bible was a historical document open to differing interpretations. Ernestine Rose, a Polish American atheist raised a Jew, also opposed the resolution, stating, "I can have no objection whatever to Miss Brown's expression of her opinion on the Bible, provided only, I am not required to acquiesce in it, if I do not agree with it; and I do not." Finally, Lucretia stepped down from the chair to speak against the resolution. Noting that pro-slavery advocates relied on the Bible to justify their position, she argued that "It is not to be supposed that all the advice given by the Apostles, to the women of their day, is applicable to our more intelligent age; nor is there any passage in Scripture, making those texts binding on us." On Lucretia's motion, Brown's resolution was tabled.[26]

The following year, internal disputes gave way to more familiar public clashes when Lucretia and other activists confronted an unruly mob in New York City. In 1853, women's rights activists held an eastern convention in New York and a western convention in Cleveland. Despite the anniversary meetings held every spring in Manhattan, reformers viewed the city as unfriendly territory. While New York had a tradition of egalitarian working-class politics and anti-slavery activism, it was better known for its Democratic political machine, Tammany Hall, whose bosses relied on mob violence to intimidate reluctant voters and political opponents alike. Chief among Tammany's enforcers was Captain Isaiah Rynders, founder of the influential Empire Club in 1844.

Rynders was very nearly Mott's antithesis. He was a pure partisan, glorying in the violent political contests of the two-party system. As a Democrat loyal to the southern wing of the party, he harassed African Americans, abolitionists, and Whigs. In May 1850, Rynders and his gang had disrupted the annual meeting of the American Anti-Slavery Society with cries of "The Constitution," "The Church," "South Carolina," "Mississippi," "James Gordon Bennett," and "Bennett's Herald!" Abolitionists dismissed the mob as "pliant tools" of scheming politicians and traders, "who have used them to speculate profitably upon Southern prejudices and interests."[27] Lucretia herself viewed party politics as an oppressive force in American life, another form of enslavement. She was a pure or ultra reformer, seeking to liberate humanity from racism, slavery, war, intemperance, sexual inequality, and corrupt human government. Rynders, in agreement with the biting comments in Bennett's *New York Herald*, viewed Mott and her allies as anarchists and fanatics who threatened his political interests as well as the very fabric of the nation. He was ready for the arrival of the women's rights activists.

Women's rights activists proposed a three-pronged assault on this bastion of the national Democratic Party. First, Antoinette Brown planned to offer her credentials as a delegate to the "World's Temperance Convention" scheduled for September 1853. Despite the thirteen years that had passed since the World's Anti-Slavery Convention, that slight was fresh in the minds of female reformers. And, as expected, the white male delegates rejected Brown. They also rejected an African American delegate, James McCune Smith. Then Brown and other "black and white, orthodox and heretic" reformers proceeded to hold their own convention, which they named the "Whole World's Temperance Convention." Mott addressed this "Whole World's Convention," declaring that "all these great reformatory movements are in accordance with each other." She advised reformers not to be afraid of uniting the causes of

"Peace, Temperance, Liberty" and "Women's Rights" as they were already united in the individual.[28]

After the Whole World's Temperance Convention adjourned, feminists proceeded to the Broadway Tabernacle for the Woman's Rights Convention. Elected president again, Mott presided over a rowdy convention of 2,500 people. In addition to the usual male hecklers, the delegates had to deal with Captain Rynders. On the first day of the convention, Rynders and his men repeatedly interrupted a speech by Ernestine Rose. Against violence of any sort, even to suppress a mob, Mott stepped aside to let Rose call for the police. The next morning, Lucretia praised the women for their "calm moral courage" in the face of danger; she observed that "not a scream was heard from any woman." But the police did not scare off Rynders and his men, who returned that evening. The published *Proceedings* described the "terrific uproar, shouting, yelling, screaming, bellowing, laughing, stamping." As they had at the American Anti-Slavery Society meeting, Rynders and his men yelled names and phrases designed to aggravate, including "Burleigh" (Mott's friend Charles C. Burleigh, whose hirsute appearance always excited comment), "Truth" (Sojourner Truth), "shut up," "take a drink," "go to bed," and "go it, Lucy." None of the speakers could be heard over the chaos. At the suggestion of Ernestine Rose, Mott closed the convention.[29]

As the activists walked out of the church, they were pushed and shoved by the mob. Mott told her children and grandchildren what happened next. When she noticed that some of the more "timid" women were being jostled, she asked her escort to take care of those women. "But who will take care of you?" he asked. Mott answered, "this man," placing her hand on the arm of "one of the roughest of the mob." After he recovered from his initial shock, the man led her out of the building "to a place of safety."[30] Biographer Margaret Hope Bacon speculates that the man was Captain Rynders, but more than likely he was not, as Rynders was a dapper sporting man. Nevertheless, after talking to Lucretia, the ruffian concluded that she was a "good, sensible woman."[31]

In October, women's rights activists met a better reception at the western Woman's Rights Convention. In Cleveland, Mott gave a passionate speech denouncing the union of "Church and State," blaming "priestcraft" for women's oppression and giving examples of ministers who opposed the women's rights movement. Quoting her favorite poet William Cowper, Mott told the audience, "such dupes are men to custom," advising her listeners to eschew the Bible, which she blamed for "the existing abuses of society." She observed, "we too often bind ourselves by authorities rather than by truth." This simple statement articulated one of Mott's most biting critiques of the power of "Church and State" to dictate the lives of women and African Americans. One of her most oft-repeated phrases was, "Truth for Authority, not Authority for Truth."[32] Lucretia continued this theme when she and Lucy Stone addressed an overflowing crowd at Smith and Nixon's Concert Hall in Cincinnati on October 14. The *Cincinnati Daily Commercial* praised Mott's "genuine wit," reporting that Mott called the Bible "a giant scarecrow, across the pathway of human progression." In Ohio, Lucretia and James also visited the family of her late uncle Mayhew Folger and her "orthodox cousin" Levi Coffin, famous for his work on the Underground Railroad.[33]

Combining her interest in women's rights with her devotion to the slave, Mott then took a steamboat to Maysville, Kentucky, to visit her sister Martha Wright's Pelham relatives. Their journey down the Ohio River brought them to the slave state of Kentucky—the reverse of the dramatic escape by the fictional slave Eliza in Stowe's *Uncle Tom's Cabin*. Lucretia wrote that the "banks of the river afforded constant & varying scene, & we enjoyed the day—tho' no passengers were attractive." In her first trip this far west, the diverse and somewhat unsavory throng aboard the boat may have startled Mott. Herman Melville's description of those on board a Mississippi River steamer may give some indication of her fellow passengers: "Natives of all sorts, and foreigners; men of business and men of pleasure; parlour men and backwoodsmen; farm-hunters and fame-hunters; heiress-hunters, gold-hunters, buffalo-hunters, bee-hunters, happiness-hunters, truth-hunters, and still keener hunters after all these hunters." In the midst of all these men on the make, Mott complained of the slowness of the boat, asking herself, "Can I write amid such perpetual jarring?"[34]

The Pelhams, like their neighbors, were slaveholders. Mott reported that "a real slave-lookg. girl" (perhaps referring to her color or her clothing) came into their bedroom "sans ceremony" to light the fire in the morning. A "world-renowned Quaker," Mott was scheduled to hold a "religious meeting" in Maysville. John Pelham told his former sister-in-law Martha that he hoped "Mrs. Mott wd. not allude to slavery." But when Lucretia addressed the large crowd in front of the Maysville County Courthouse, she spoke "freely of the effects of slavery, not only upon the slaves, but upon the masters," denouncing "the system for its inherent wickedness and inhumanity." Mott spoke in her usual direct but pleasant style. Though "she said some things that were far from palatable," the audience received her warmly, inviting her to give another speech "on Woman" that evening. Mott wrote her children that it was, "a great gathering & [gave] apparent satisfaction."[35]

As the anti-slavery fight became more intense, Mott grew bored and frustrated with the women's rights movement. She attended the annual meetings in Philadelphia in 1854 and Cincinnati in 1855, but the following year she criticized "the surfeit of conventions." As Lucy Stone planned the 1856 annual convention in New York City, Mott wrote, "I rather hoped the year would be suffered to pass, before another Call was issued. I did not like to say so to thee, lest it appear a waning of interest in the great Cause." But, she reassured Lucy, she and Martha fully intended to be there.[36] Addressing the convention that November, Mott gave some indication why she thought the women's rights movement needed a break. She told the audience, "You have heard all, it seems to me, that can be said upon the subject." After rehearsing the encouraging signs of progress, Mott offered a resolution that echoed her earlier debate with Wendell Phillips: "That as the poor slave's alleged contentment with his servile and cruel bondage, only proves the depth of his degradation; so the assertion of woman that she has all the rights she wants, only proves how far the restrictions and disabilities to which she has been subjected have rendered her insensible to the blessings of true liberty." Six years after the Worcester convention, the resolution articulated Lucretia's irritation with her sex and the slow progress of the women's rights movement. The convention unanimously passed her resolution.[37]

In 1857, Mott expressed the same desire to let the convention "slide." This time, Lucy Stone agreed. Stone had married Henry Blackwell (brother of Elizabeth Blackwell) in 1855. The following year, she made the scandalous decision to keep using her maiden name. Lucretia suggested, "Why not add the name of Blackwell—Lucy Blackwell Stone as the French wives do?" Twenty-five years older than Stone, Mott had not even considered using the name "Coffin" after her marriage. Her Nantucket background was well known. Now, decades later, she had an established reputation as a Mott. Lucretia's reference to the "French" practice may also indicate that she viewed multiple names as pretentious. But, she told Lucy, "Its yr. business not mine." After Stone gave birth to a daughter, Alice Stone Blackwell, in September 1857, women's rights activists did not organize another convention until May 1858.[38]

Lucretia's reluctance to hold more women's rights conventions reflected her frustration with the timidity of her fellow activists and her competing obligations to anti-slavery. Offering an implicit comparison to abolitionist anniversaries, Lucretia told Lucy Stone that she feared the repetition of meetings and speakers was depleting the movement's strength. To her sister Martha, Lucretia was more blunt. She ranted, "We are not petitiong—we are holdg no mgs—we are doing nothg. save that two medical schools for women are in operatn." Such complaints contradicted her earlier advice to Lucy Stone to adopt a "congregational" structure. But they also expressed her sense that merely reiterating the wrongs of woman accomplished little. Using the same language she had used to describe female citizenship, Lucretia wrote Martha, "I can but feel a very cipher in this movet." Furthermore, the women's rights movement also required reformers' time, and Mott was fully committed to the Philadelphia Female Anti-Slavery Society and the Pennsylvania Anti-Slavery Society. She informed Lucy Stone that she had not responded to a letter sooner due to "Anti-Slavery Mgs" and "Fair Circles." The cause of abolition still held Mott's "first claim."[39]

Mott was also uninterested in the issues of sexual respectability that consumed the women's rights movement by the end of the decade. Lucretia did not attend the Women's Rights Convention held in 1858 in New York City, but her sister Martha served as secretary. Susan B. Anthony, who attended her first women's rights convention in 1852, was elected president. Anthony allowed anyone who wished to speak to do so, causing a minor scandal when Stephen Pearl Andrews, a free love advocate, addressed what he called the "vital point" of women's "unwilling maternity." Some reformers, including Andrews and Mott's friend Henry Clarke Wright, believed that women's control over their bodies was essential to their liberation. Rather than advocating the use of contraception, Clarke Wright advised women—rather than men—to control and limit sexual relations in marriage.[40]

Most women's rights activists were reluctant to discuss sexuality on their platform. Martha Wright wrote to Susan B. Anthony that she was "sorry for all that was said" because "it is a subject that no Conventional or Legislative action can ever reach." The more conservative women in the audience probably shared the "shocked" response of Lucretia's friend Elizabeth Neall Gay. Even Miller McKim was eager to distance abolitionists from the "ultra free love people," asking Lucretia to use her influence against them. She declined his suggestion as "ungracious." Having experienced personal attacks for her beliefs for years, she argued, "Let each & all expound their own creed, & then let us judge."[41] Mott may have found the subject of free love distasteful, but she also hated "prudery." She viewed sexual and scientific knowledge as key to women's intellectual advancement. As a sixty-five-year-old grandmother, Mott had little concern for her own virtue. She tried to assuage Lizzie Gay's "wrath over Pearl Andrews," writing "Never fear for our cause. We can 'live down' all the harm that 'free-love' or the 'Maternity-question' can do us, only let not our faith fail us."[42]

Mott attended the annual convention the following year in New York

City, but vowed never to do so again. She found the "fixed speeches" a poor substitute for spontaneous and passionate discussion. Lucretia too faced criticism from the newspapers and other reformers that her speech was "neither very fresh nor very forcible." Her short address on the progress of the cause was followed by cries for "Phillips," "Lucy Stone," and "Garrison." Unfortunately, Lucretia agreed. She wrote Martha that "To be stuck up, to speak ½ an hour, with nothg. special to inspire you at the time, is an inflictn. and a bore on the audience—I have great faith in the Quaker creed, 'to speak, as the Spirit giveth utterance.'"[43]

As a result, she watched from the sidelines as the topic of marriage divided women's rights activists. As president of the 1860 convention, Martha Wright directly addressed Lucretia's concerns in her opening remarks. She referred to those in the movement "who ask, 'What is the use of these continual Conventions? What is the use of this constant iteration of the same things?'" Wright sounded an optimistic note in response, "When we see what has been already achieved, we learn the use of this 'foolishness of preaching'"[44] But it was Elizabeth Cady Stanton's long-awaited speech on divorce that caused the most excitement. Stanton argued that marriage was "a mere legal contract." Accordingly, she resolved that, "any constitution, compact or covenant between human beings, that failed to produce or promote human happiness, could not, in the nature of things, be of any force or authority;—and it would be not only a right, but a duty, to abolish it." Stanton proposed to transform marriage from an untouchable sacred relationship to an ordinary legal arrangement, to be entered, altered, and exited at the will of the parties.[45]

The Rev. Antoinette Brown Blackwell responded that marriage was "as permanent as the life of the parties." In the place of the current model of marriage, she proposed a "perfect union" of equals. Blackwell concluded, "Give [woman], then, some earnest purpose in life, hold up to her the true ideal of marriage, and it is enough—I am content!" Some reformers present, including Wendell Phillips, objected to the topic being raised at all. He declared, "This convention is no marriage convention." But other activists viewed it as "vital." Ernestine Rose responded that women, men, and marriage were not yet as they "ought to be": "it is to be hoped that through the Woman's Rights movement—the equalizing of the laws, making them more just, and making woman more independent—we will hasten the coming of the millennium, when marriage shall indeed be a bond of union and affection. But, alas! it is not yet so." At the end of the debate, Mary Grew rose to invoke the absent Lucretia Mott as "the embodiment of all domestic beauty and wifely care and motherly fidelity."[46]

Grew's reminder that women's rights activists exemplified female virtues did nothing to stop newspapers from questioning the modesty and femininity of the women present. "No true woman could listen to [these resolutions] without turning scarlet," cried the *New York Observer*. Stanton, in this editor's view, proposed to "turn the world into one vast brothel." Even women's rights advocate Horace Greeley criticized Stanton for defining "Marriage as a Business" in his *New York Tribune*.[47] Lucretia, "the embodiment of all domestic beauty," however, was difficult to shock. She called Stanton's resolutions "extravagant," but she also noted her "great faith in Elizabeth Stanton's quick instincts & clear insight in all appertaining to women's rights." And, like Ernestine Rose, Lucretia recognized that women lived in the real world.[48]

Mott also had a personal interest in liberalizing divorce law. In 1847, she had witnessed the dissolution of the marriage of actress Fanny Kemble, a relative of Cecilia Combe, and wealthy South Carolinian Pierce Butler. Butler had close friends in Philadelphia, and the couple visited frequently. Fanny hated slavery, and she clashed with her slaveholding husband, who complained of her insubordination. Lucretia commented, "What an illustratn. it furnishes of the evil of the church law—requirg. obedience of the wife."[49] In 1855, Caroline Chase Stratton, daughter of Lucretia's Mount Holly cousin Ruth Bunker Chase, had married her second husband, Charles Wood, an Auburn businessman. By 1859, Caroline was back in Mount Holly, and, following a year's separation, she divorced Wood in November 1860. Lucretia fully supported her decision. After a last meeting in which Wood "arraigned" Caroline and Martha Wright with "railg. accusations," Mott commented, "you are lucky such an intimacy should be at an end."[50]

Through these controversies, Mott advised women's rights activists to be uncompromising, a lesson she learned in the anti-slavery movement. She was not the only activist to divide her time between the women's rights and abolitionist platforms. Sojourner Truth, Lucy Stone, Susan B. Anthony, and Ernestine Rose also raised their voices on behalf of women and slaves. Even in this illustrious company, Mott was notable for her continued emphasis on "Woman's Rights" as part of a larger struggle for "Human Rights." The Fugitive Slave Act of 1850 raised the stakes between anti-slavery and pro-slavery advocates. As abolitionists tried new tactics to resist slavery, Mott and the Philadelphia Female Anti-Slavery Society stayed true to their non-resistant principles. But they were unyielding in their opposition to the new law. Just as she had urged women's rights activists to agitate, Mott instructed abolitionists to be "disturbers of the peace."[51]

CHAPTER 10

Fugitives

ROBERT PURVIS ONCE CALLED LUCRETIA MOTT "the most belligerent Non-Resistant he ever saw." She liked the characterization, telling an audience of abolitionists, "I am no advocate of passivity": "I have no idea, because I am a Non-Resistant, of submitting tamely to injustice inflicted either on me or on the slave."[1] Her refusal to link pacifism to inaction informed her response to the Fugitive Slave Act of 1850. After the failure of Wilmot's Proviso, Congress spent two years debating how to incorporate lands gained from Mexico. The resulting Compromise of 1850 abolished the slave trade (but not slavery) in the District of Columbia, instituted the doctrine of popular sovereignty in the New Mexico territory, allowing these new states to decide whether to legalize slavery, and implemented a drastic fugitive slave law. The law gave slave catchers the power to force any individual—regardless of political or religious beliefs—to participate in the capture of a fugitive. It also established harsh fines and jail terms for anyone who aided an escaped slave. Finally, the law placed the onus on the alleged fugitive to prove he or she was a free person. In other words, Fugitive Slave Act presumed any African American claimed by a southerner was a slave. Though all abolitionists shared Mott's vehement opposition to the law, they disagreed over the best way to resist its enforcement.

Ongoing divisions in the anti-slavery movement did not affect Mott's close friendship with Robert and his wife Harriet Forten Purvis. In July 1850, Lucretia and Harriet traveled to New York Central College in McGrawsville. The college was one of the few institutions in the country to accept women and African Americans. Harriet's sons, Joseph and Robert, were students at the college, and Lucretia was invited to deliver the commencement address. On the way, Mott delighted in shocking her fellow rail passengers by sitting with Harriet Purvis as an equal. Mott's speech also upset the trustees by "denying the doctrine of human depravity," but Charles Reason, an African American professor of Greek, Latin, and French, defended her to the anti-slavery Baptists and Methodists in the audience. Lucretia's comments did not offend Harriet, who with her husband later joined the Progressive Friends, an offshoot of the Congregational Friends. The Progressive Friends welcomed "all persons who recognize the Equal Brotherhood of the Human Family, without regard to sex, color, or condition."[2]

Shortly after Lucretia and Harriet left central New York, the state's abolitionists offered a public response to the impending passage of the Fugitive Slave Act. Gerrit Smith, the political abolitionist and benefactor of New York Central College, sponsored a "Fugitive Slave Convention" in Cazenovia. The convention drew two thousand people, including black and white abolitionists, female reformers, and escaped slaves. Frederick Douglass, Samuel J. May, and other members of the convention endorsed Smith's "A Letter to the American Slaves," which advocated violent resistance to the Fugitive Slave Law. Like Elias Hicks in 1811, the letter described American slaves as "prisoners of war," but Smith deviated from the Quaker minister in his willingness to encourage rebellion: "Therefore, by all the rules of war, you have the fullest liberty to plunder, burn, and kill, as you may have occasion to do to promote your escape." The letter also informed slaves that they would find allies in the north, members of the American Anti-Slavery Society, Liberty Party, and "the great mass of the colored men of the North." "It is not to be disguised," the letter continued, "that the colored man is as much disposed, as a white man, to resist, even unto death those who oppress him."[3]

Though Gerrit Smith wanted to unite abolitionists against the new law, his language disturbed many white Garrisonians, who opposed any deviation from their non-resistant principles. After printing excerpts from Smith's letter, the *Pennsylvania Freeman* applauded "most" of his sentiments, but judged "some" as inexpedient and immoral. "Though cautiously avoiding to commit the members of the Convention to an advocacy of violent insurrections," the editor noted, "we are by no means sure of the pacific tendency of some portions of its advice."[4] The editorial voice was probably that of Cyrus M. Burleigh, brother of Lucretia's friend Charles. He offered the same perspective in October, when former slave Samuel Ringgold Ward, a delegate at the Cazenovia convention, gave a series of lectures in Philadelphia. The *Pennsylvania*

Freeman observed that Ward's meetings were well attended, but judged some of his remarks to be "too belligerent," including "encouragements to violence, on the part of the people of color, in resisting kidnappers."[5]

Unsurprisingly, black abolitionists were quicker to judge the new reality created by the Fugitive Slave Act. Shortly after Ward's visit to Philadelphia, African American activists met in the Brick Wesley Church. Robert Purvis, William Still, and others resolved "to resist the law at any cost and at all hazards," and to pledge their "lives" and "fortunes" against it. These members of the Pennsylvania Anti-Slavery Society reaffirmed their commitment to the "moral means of truth," but they found the law so atrocious that they vowed to "resist to the death any attempt to enforce it upon our persons."[6]

Lucretia bridged the radical resistance of Purvis and the pacifism of the *Pennsylvania Freeman*. Modeling "belligerent non-resistance," Mott and her coworkers in the Philadelphia Female Anti-Slavery Society vowed to disobey the law. The society repudiated "all allegiance to such constitutional provisions, and to all laws *which have been or may be enacted* to sustain the system of American Slavery." Promising civil disobedience, Mott proposed an active—even aggressive—form of moral suasion. She wrote to William Lloyd Garrison that it was an "important time to seize the public mind"; she believed the "moral sense" of the country was ready for change. Mott and other abolitionists rightly sensed that the Fugitive Slave Act would provoke new opposition to slavery.[7]

As a result of their proximity to slave states, Philadelphia abolitionists had been on the front lines of the Underground Railroad for decades. Just three years earlier, in 1847, abolitionists had won two hard-fought victories. The Pennsylvania legislature passed a law prohibiting "the use the of our jails . . . of our magistrates, justices, aldermen, jailors, &c., in the recapture and return of runaway slaves." At the same time, the legislature repealed a law that had required slaves to live in the state for six months before claiming freedom. Now, Pennsylvania law declared fugitives free from the moment they set foot in the state.[8] These laws encouraged more slaves to pass through Philadelphia on the way to freedom. In March 1849, a Virginia man named Henry Brown traveled from Richmond to Philadelphia in a box via the Adams' Express. After a twenty-four hour journey, he was delivered to the offices of the Pennsylvania Anti-Slavery Society. Miller McKim brought "Box" Brown to the Motts' house to tell his story. Lucretia reported that Brown's wife and three children had been sold from him a year ago, and "from that time he resolved on obtaining his own freedom."[9] Such success stories were threatened by the 1850 Fugitive Slave Act, which overruled Pennsylvania's personal liberty laws. Pennsylvania citizens, even those otherwise unsympathetic to abolitionists, grew outraged at this federal intrusion into their state.

Battles over fugitives erupted across the north, testing abolitionists' abstract commitment to resisting the Fugitive Slave Act. On September 11, 1851, a Maryland slave owner named Edward Gorsuch and a party that included his son, nephew, three friends, and a deputy marshal, traveled to Christiana, in Lancaster County, Pennsylvania, in search of four runaways. They encircled the home of a fugitive named William Parker, who had gathered the runaways together for protection. Local blacks and Quakers rushed to the aid of the former slaves, and some armed African Americans attacked the slave catchers, killing Gorsuch. Parker and the other fugitives escaped, but three white men and more than thirty black men were arrested and charged not with murder, but with treason. Reporting on the Christiana Riot, the *Pennsylvania Freeman* leaped to the defense of the fugitives: "What right has the American nation to expect any thing else from its own teachings, and its own actions? Have they not proclaimed 'Liberty or Death'? . . . Would it not be well for those who denounce them as murderers and traitors, to ask themselves whether they would not have defended their own liberty, and that of their wives and children, by similar means?" Ironically, by placing the Christiana fugitives in the same political tradition as the revolutionary founders, they affirmed the government's assertion that the defense of the fugitives amounted to insurrection.[10]

Even as they struggled with the moral implications of armed self-defense, Philadelphia abolitionists mobilized to support the arrested men. At the October 1851 annual meeting of the Pennsylvania Anti-Slavery Society, members debated a resolution on the Fugitive Slave Act. Oliver Johnson objected to any language that might encourage violence, but Mary Grew asserted that the PASS was not a peace society. Robert Purvis argued, "The colored man, in defending himself and his liberty, had only been true to himself, true to his family, true to liberty, and true to God." Mott, who had just visited the Christiana activists in jail, argued that, "the opposition and violence we have to encounter only show the necessity of more active and extended anti-slavery effort. We must expect to suffer for our principles, and be prepared to endure calmly and unflinchingly whatever may come to us."[11] As these debates continued, the Philadelphia Vigilance Committee raised over $600 to aid the fugitives and prisoners. And, after the trial began on November 24, Mott and other members of the Philadelphia Female Anti-Slavery Society attended, cheering the verdict of not guilty on December 11. Though he dismissed the treason charges, Judge Robert C. Grier, a Pennsylvania Democrat appointed by former President Polk to the U.S. Supreme Court, condemned the violence at Christiana, blaming the Philadelphia Female Anti-Slavery Society for the "foul murder": "the blood taints with even deeper dye the skirts of those who promulgated doctrines subversive of all morality and all government."[12]

The following year, the publication of *Uncle Tom's Cabin* also raised national awareness of the plight of fugitives. Harriet Beecher Stowe urged her readers to "*feel right*" and "*pray*" for the "distressed Christians" in slavery.[13] But Philadelphia abolitionists did not fully endorse the book. Robert Purvis experienced the final chapter, in which some of the black characters emigrate to Africa, as a physical "blow," and he attributed Stowe's reliance on colonization to racial prejudice. At the Pennsylvania Anti-Slavery Society annual meeting, Mott ascribed Stowe's sympathetic portrayal of slaves to the decades of moral labor by abolitionists. Miller McKim complained that Mott's theory was "unsustained supposition," in conflict with Stowe's own statement that she was moved by the harshness of the Fugitive Slave Act.[14] Though Mott was reluctant to credit the novel for transforming the nation's conscience, abolitionists were invigorated by its success. The Pennsylvania Anti-Slavery Society offered a copy to every new subscriber to the *Pennsylvania Freeman*. At the end of the year, the city's abolitionists created a revitalized General Vigilance Committee, chaired by Robert Purvis. William Still, the PASS office clerk, served as the agent for the committee and thus became the primary link between the committee and fugitive slaves. James Miller McKim and Quaker Passmore Williamson attended the founding meeting, but African Americans, including Charles Reason, the new head of the Institute for Colored Youth in Philadelphia, comprised the majority of members.[15]

Members of the General Vigilance Committee not only aided fugitives but proactively encouraged slaves to leave their masters. Since the 1847 repeal of the state's six-month requirement, abolitionists considered any slaves arriving in Pennsylvania—even in the company of their owner—to be free. In 1855, Passmore Williamson informed Jane Johnson, an enslaved woman traveling with John Wheeler, a North Carolina Democrat and the U.S. minister to Nicaragua, that she and her two children were free. He and William Still then helped Johnson and her children escape from Wheeler, who grabbed Johnson to prevent her from leaving. In an effort to retrieve his slave, Wheeler secured a writ of habeas corpus for Passmore Williamson. After making sure that Still had escorted Johnson and her two children to safety, Williamson appeared in court. With Lucretia's son-in-law Edward Hopper as one of his lawyers, Williamson was convicted of contempt of court for not "producing" Jane Johnson. He also denied knowledge of her whereabouts. Judge John Kane sentenced Williamson to Moyamensing prison, where he spent more than three months while lawyers argued his case.[16]

At trial, Williamson's lawyers produced a surprise witness: Jane Johnson. Johnson risked capture by U.S. marshals in order to testify that Williamson had not "abducted" her. Instead, in front of a furious Wheeler, Johnson stated her intention to run away. A veiled Jane Johnson had entered the court in the company of Mott, Sarah McKim, and Sarah Pugh, but her departure was more dramatic. With federal marshals in pursuit, Jane Johnson, Mott, Miller McKim, and an armed guard jumped into a carriage. They were followed by another carriage containing four additional officers "for protection." Mott commented, "We didn't drive slow comg. home." The two carriages drove to Mott's house on Arch Street, but Johnson quickly exited through the back door onto Cuthbert Street and reentered the carriage. Mott managed to place a small meal of crackers and peaches in Johnson's hands before she drove off. After helping to secure Passmore Williamson's freedom, Jane Johnson successfully evaded capture.[17]

Mott's carriage ride with armed men contradicted her commitment to moral suasion, but it also expressed her belligerent non-resistance. As a woman with a national reputation, Mott believed that her presence provided necessary comfort and protection to Jane Johnson. Moreover, Mott offered a very public display of the alternatives to violence. As discovered in the Civil Rights Movement over a century later, nonviolence was more effective when joined with disciplined self-defense against outright murder. Mott also understood that slaveholders and mobbers might show her deference they would not grant a former slave or free black. She resolved to face "calmly" and "unflinchingly" the hostility of pro-slavery advocates, but it was an entirely different matter for Robert Purvis or Jane Johnson, who might be killed with relative impunity.[18]

Despite these dramas, the Philadelphia Female Anti-Slavery Society maintained its official reluctance to buy the freedom of fugitives. At the 1852 annual meeting of the Pennsylvania Anti-Slavery Society, Esther Moore, who had resigned from the Philadelphia Female Anti-Slavery Society to work with the Vigilance Committee, spoke passionately about a recent case in which two free women had been kidnapped from Chester County and taken to Baltimore. While Mott acknowledged the interest and passion aroused by the Fugitive Slave Act, she reminded abolitionists that their principal purpose was to end slavery. Mott proposed a resolution opposing the purchase of runaways as "an unwise appropriation of funds" meant for the "overthrow of the slave system and the emancipation of every slave."[19] Under pressure from Mott, the convention unanimously adopted the resolution. In 1856, Mott repeated these sentiments after the Philadelphia Female Anti-Slavery Society received a letter from Samuel Janney, a Virginia Quaker, suggesting that abolitionists start a fund to purchase runaways with "peculiar hardships."[20]

Mott's hard-line stance on purchasing fugitives reflected her continued intellectual allegiance to the founding principles of the American Anti-Slavery Society. At anti-slavery meetings, she frequently quoted the AASS Declaration of Sentiments to justify an argument in favor of moral versus physical power. Her inflexible devotion to the document frustrated some of her fellow abolitionists in the Pennsylvania Anti-Slavery Society, a Garrisonian organization that nonetheless tolerated more disagreement than the Philadelphia Female Anti-Slavery Society. At another meeting, after Mott spoke in favor of a free produce resolution, Oliver Johnson objected to her use of the Declaration of Sentiments as an official constitution. The Declaration, he argued, "was not an *authority*." Johnson argued that even Garrison's views had evolved. Mott disagreed, but pointed out that she had only used the Declaration to support her own views.[21]

Mott grew more rigid as she aged and the conflict over slavery intensified. Her absolutism also made her a harsh opponent. After the death of Judge John Kane, who had issued the writ of habeas corpus in the Jane Johnson case, for example, Mott expressed "satisfaction that the flying bondsman had no longer cause to fear the power of this officer." Long focused on changing minds, Mott also became content to see her enemies die out.[22]

In 1854, the Kansas-Nebraska Act further transformed the political landscape, expanding the reach of slavery and outraging abolitionists. The law established the two territories named in the act, setting them on the path to statehood. But in an effort to appease both northern and southern interests, Illinois Senator Stephen Douglas applied the doctrine of popular sovereignty, developed to resolve the debate over land acquired from Mexico. As a result, this measure effectively repealed the Missouri Compromise, which established the old Louisiana Territory above the 36° 30' latitude as free land. Mott's circle was incensed. The *Pennsylvania Freeman* called the Kansas-Nebraska Act a "conspiracy" and a "plot." The Philadelphia Female Anti-Slavery Society petitioned the state and national legislature against the bill. James McCrummell, who chaired the first Philadelphia Female Anti-Slavery Society meeting, presided over an "Anti-Nebraska" meeting among the city's blacks.[23] Outside this diehard group, former Whig, Liberty, Free Soil, and Democratic loyalists launched the Republican Party. A truly sectional party, the Republicans vowed to limit slavery to the areas where it currently existed. Finally, pro- and anti-slavery factions headed to Kansas in an attempt to sway the vote.

Again, abolitionists debated the morality of using violence. The following year, Harriet Beecher Stowe's brother Henry Ward Beecher, pastor of Plymouth Church of the Pilgrims in Brooklyn, New York, and the most powerful minister in the country, advocated sending Sharp's rifles to free-state settlers in Kansas. He argued, "there was more moral power in one of those instruments, so far as the slaveholders of Kansas were concerned, than in a hundred Bibles." Beecher led the movement to ship these so-called "Beecher's Bibles" to Kansas. When pro-slavery forces attacked the free-state capital of Lawrence in May 1856, Beecher's status as the most popular spokesman for Bleeding Kansas was secured.[24]

Bleeding Kansas provoked contradictory feelings in Mott and other Garrisonians. Martha Wright expressed her desire for "those who *don't* think it wrong to fight" to join the anti-slavery settlers, but she commented, "no one can be truly a *Christian*, unless he adopts the non-resistant doctrine." In her reply to Martha, Lucretia pointed out that the battles in Kansas led to intellectual "inconsistency," giving Beecher and her friend Miller McKim as examples. According to Lucretia, McKim, who was "not quite a Peace man," praised an article by Beecher on self-defense. At the same time, he criticized Lucy Stone for suggesting that suicide was better than slavery. Lucretia noted the hypocrisy of advocating self-defense for white male settlers but not for enslaved men and women.[25]

As Kansas erupted, the Philadelphia Female Anti-Slavery Society rallied their members to the standard of disunion. Adopting military metaphors, they described the struggle between slavery and freedom as a "war of extermination." After fighting broke out in Kansas, the Philadelphia Female Anti-Slavery Society proclaimed, "God be thanked that it is come to this!" Noting the "moral revolution" in public opinion, the Philadelphia women rejoiced that the American people were ready to take sides in the "open war" between "liberty and slavery." Their hope for abolition, however, rested not on military victory but "on our faith that the people of the North will, one day, dissolve their guilty and most impolitic union with slaveholders, and, establishing a government, under which slavery shall not exist . . . shall set themselves free from the temptation to support an institution from which their better nature revolts."[26]

Lucretia described the moral and political transformation of the country for her Scottish correspondents George and Cecilia Combe. As signs of the "progress of the Anti-Slavery movement," she noted that "our largest Halls may now be had for lectures on the subject" that "draw large audiences, who listen with applause to the most radical sentiments." When Senator Charles Sumner of Massachusetts spoke to the anniversary meeting of the American Anti-Slavery Society in 1855, Lucretia described the convention as "the best ever held in that City." Sumner had inspired antislavery audiences with his speech "The Necessity, Practicability, and Dignity of the Anti-Slavery Enterprise, with Glimpses at the Special Duties of the North."[27] The following year, Sumner delivered a speech called "The Crime Against Kansas," on the floor of the Senate. He impugned Southern morals by comparing slavery to prostitution. He charged Senator Andrew Butler of South Carolina with sparing "no extravagance of manner or hardihood of assertion" in defense of slavery's "wantonness." When Butler's relative Representative Preston Brooks avenged his honor by viciously beating Sumner with a gutta-percha cane, the Philadelphia Female Anti-Slavery Society vowed to "renew our warfare" against slavery.[28]

For many years, the Philadelphia Female Anti-Slavery Society's primary means of warfare against slavery was the anti-slavery fair. The members described it as their most "arduous" work, involving an extensive subcommittee (in 1853, the committee included 44 white and black members) and months of planning.[29] This popular week-long event, held every year during the Christmas season, sold anti-slavery and free produce goods—sewed by members of the Philadelphia Female Anti-Slavery Society and donated by anti-slavery women in the U.S. and England—to raise money to fund abolitionist efforts. Celebrating their twentieth anniversary in 1853, the Philadelphia Female Anti-Slavery Society noted that since the first fair in 1835, it had donated more than $13,000, worth almost $320,000 today, to the Pennsylvania Anti-Slavery Society. In the 1850s, the fair raised an average of $1500.47 per year, or $32,945.88.[30] In addition to the Pennsylvania Anti-Slavery Society, the regular beneficiaries of the fair funds were anti-slavery newspapers, including the *Pennsylvania Freeman* (until it ceased publication in 1854), the *National Anti-Slavery Standard*, the *Liberator*, and the *North Star*, and the Vigilance Committee.

Despite the fundraising success of anti-slavery fairs in cities like Philadelphia, Boston, and New York, not all abolitionist women were initially enthusiastic. These critics worried that fair organizers violated women's appropriate role by engaging in business and financial matters. Others thought the fairs crass, commercial, and morally suspect. Though certainly open to women in business, Mott too had her doubts. In 1841, she wrote that, "On being repeatedly called on to give my reasons against them—I was constrained to admit that it was the abuse of them that was objectionable." Mott overcame her reservations, becoming an unabashed supporter. In 1852, she told an anti-slavery audience, "I love these Fairs, and am never weary with them, and never ready for the lights to be put out. To those whose hearts are in this work of Anti-Slavery truth it is never tiresome or old." Like her anti-slavery sisters in Boston, Mott viewed the fairs as a way of awakening moral sensibilities. She described the fairs, and the funds they raised, as "a means of spreading the truth, which is our only reliance and hope, and in which we have full confidence to bring in the millennial day of liberty and brotherhood."[31]

In 1858, Lucretia described the bustle of the Philadelphia anti-slavery fair for her sister Martha. She attended the fair every day with another sister, Eliza Yarnall. Mott's granddaughters Anna Davis and Lue Hopper (both twenty years old), along with Sarah McKim, Mary Grew, and Sarah Hallowell, staffed tables selling goods such as quilted skirts and books. The crowd included "colored & white promenadg. & childn. without number, makg. such a noise." Mott concluded, "our price of admissn. must be raised next year." Former slave William Wells Brown read his play *The Escape; or, A Leap for Freedom*. Mott observed that it "took very well." Anna Hopper, chair of the fair committee, appeared every evening to collect the money raised (that year, $1461.37). Still, the success of the fair was bittersweet. Miller McKim observed that "we had grown grey in the Cause . . . & our childn. & childn.'s childn. were takg. the lead." Referring to deceased allies and friends, including Esther Moore, Isaac Hopper, and Cyrus Burleigh, Mott noted "how many vacant places there were."[32]

The movement was changing. While Mott and most Garrisonians attributed anti-slavery progress to the "Moral Principle," other abolitionists observed that bloodshed had changed the national consciousness.[33] After settling on Gerrit Smith's land in the Adirondacks, John Brown joined several of his sons in Kansas in 1855. In retaliation for a pro-slavery attack on Lawrence, Brown and his men murdered five settlers at Pottawatomie Creek. Thereafter, violent clashes between pro- and anti-slavery settlers increased. Obscuring his role in the Pottawatomie massacre, Brown emerged from the fighting in

Kansas as an anti-slavery hero. And he convinced powerful allies, including Gerrit Smith, Frederick Douglass, Theodore Parker, and women's rights activist Thomas Wentworth Higginson, of the need for "righteous violence."[34]

Confronted with legal victories for pro-slavery interests, these abolitionists had grown disillusioned with the potential for political change. In 1857, the Supreme Court ruled against an enslaved man named Dred Scott, a Missouri resident who had lived with his owner for several years in Illinois and Wisconsin. Scott sued his owner, John Sandford, arguing that his time in the north had rendered him legally free. Seeking to resolve the conflict between the free and slave states once and for all, Chief Justice Roger Taney, a Maryland Democrat, declared that African Americans (slave or free) were not citizens and thus had no right to plead their case in the American courts:

> They are not included, and were not intended to be included, under the word "citizens" in the Constitution, and can therefore claim none of the rights and privileges which that instrument provides for and secures to citizens of the United States. On the contrary, they were at that time considered as a subordinate and inferior class of beings, who had been subjugated by the dominant race, and, whether emancipated or not, yet remained subject to their authority, and had no rights or privileges but such as those who held the power and the Government might choose to grant them.[35]

Taney's decision, supported by a majority that included Justice Grier from Pennsylvania, not only invalidated all prior compromises, it eradicated the very notion of a free state. The ruling appalled black and white abolitionists, and shocked more moderate northerners. Abraham Lincoln worried that "we shall *lie down* pleasantly dreaming that the people of *Missouri* are on the verge of making their State *free*, and we shall *awake* to the *reality* instead, that the *Supreme* Court has made *Illinois a slave* State."[36]

Mott's associates saw such revulsion as a sign of national moral regeneration. When Martha Wright's neighbor Senator William Seward declared, "that the United States must and will, sooner or later, become either entirely a slaveholding nation, or entirely a free- labor nation," the Philadelphia Female Anti-Slavery Society rejoiced that politicians had finally awakened to the doctrine of disunion. They viewed the Dred Scott decision as a sign that slaveholders were "terror-stricken" and desperate.[37]

But John Brown and his allies saw the decision as a sign of the deepening strength of the slave power. In a doomed effort to take the war against slavery into the south, John Brown planned an attack on Harper's Ferry, Virginia. Not only did the town contain a federal arsenal, the surrounding area included a large population of free and enslaved blacks. Brown spent several months in a farmhouse outside the town making contact with neighboring African Americans. He also met secretly with Frederick Douglass in Chambersburg, Pennsylvania, and asked him to join his small army of sixteen whites and five blacks. Douglass declined, fearing Brown was "going into a perfect steel trap, and that once in he would never get out alive." Douglass's predictions proved true. On October 16, 1859, Brown and his men seized the federal arsenal, but, two days later Colonel Robert E. Lee and the U.S. marines captured a wounded Brown and the surviving men. Two of Brown's sons died in the battle. On trial in Virginia for treason, conspiracy, and murder, John Brown told the court, "Now, if it is deemed necessary that I should forfeit my life for the furtherance of the ends of justice, and mingle my blood further with the blood of my children and with the blood of millions in this slave country whose rights are disregarded by wicked, cruel, and unjust enactments,—I submit; so let it be done!" John Brown was executed on December 2, 1859.[38]

Though Mott and the Philadelphia Female Anti-Slavery Society disapproved of John Brown's methods, they nevertheless considered him a "moral hero," a martyr to the "glorious cause of human liberty." On November 16, 1859, the Philadelphia Female Anti-Slavery Society passed four resolutions on the Harper's Ferry "insurrection." These activists considered the violence to be "the natural fruits of the system of American slavery," "which inevitably arouses resistance to itself in the hearts of all true lovers of freedom, which resistance must be manifested in accordance with their various characters and principles." After acknowledging Brown's different "principles," they focused on their shared "hatred of slavery and ardent love of liberty." They praised Brown for his "heroic self-sacrifice" in giving his life for abolition. The Philadelphia Female Anti-Slavery Society described the insurrection as a "warning" that the nation should abolish slavery peacefully, "lest that system should be overthrown in blood." But the Philadelphia Female Anti-Slavery Society ended by reiterating their belief that "moral reforms are accomplished only by moral power." Wholeheartedly concurring with Brown's motives, the PFASS rejected his methods. The immoral "weapons of physical warfare" only lead to inconsistency, hypocrisy, and corruption.[39]

Joining Brown's sympathizers across the north, Philadelphia abolitionists rallied to his aid. Lucretia's niece Anna Temple Brown helped raise money to pay for lawyers for Brown's associates. Lucretia opened her home to Brown's wife Mary Ann, as she traveled to Virginia to visit her husband. After Brown's execution, Miller McKim escorted Mary Ann and her husband's body back to North Elba.[40]

Brown's raid also heightened tensions in the city of Philadelphia and across the nation. For the first time in its history, the Philadelphia Female Anti-Slavery Society's fair was threatened by "pro-slavery influences." To avert violence, the mayor ordered the society to take down its banner, with a picture of the Liberty Bell and the phrase "Proclaim Liberty throughout all the land." Though the women removed the banner, the trustees of the Concert Hall proceeded to call the sheriff to evict them. As a result, the Philadelphia Female Anti-Slavery Society moved the fair to the Assembly Buildings, which had hosted the event for many years. Despite the disruption, the fair raised $1683.23. This success contrasted sharply with the outrage and panic of white southerners. After John Brown's capture, slaveholders embarked on a "reign of terror" to suppress any possibility of further rebellion. The Philadelphia Female Anti-Slavery Society identified this as a sign of their "weakness." As Mary Grew commented in the society's annual report, "perhaps Southern chivalry never before demanded the suppression of a Ladies' Bazaar."[41]

*   *   *

In 1857, when James was sixty-nine and Lucretia sixty-five, they moved to a farm in Chelten Hills, eight miles north of Philadelphia. Their house, called Roadside, was across Old York Road from a farm owned by Thomas Mott and Edward M. Davis. The Motts added a kitchen and living area to the old stone farmhouse, but it retained its original character. Surrounded by cherry, apple, pear, maple, and oak trees, granddaughter Anna Davis Hallowell remembered, "it had the charm of oddly shaped rooms and queer passages, with unexpected turnings and steps up in one place, and down in another." Hallowell fondly described the library as the family's "sanctum," with pictures of William Lloyd Garrison, George Thompson, Elias Hicks, Miller McKim, and Robert Purvis decorating the walls. The Motts also hung a map of Nantucket and a Coffin genealogy. Warmed by a Franklin stove, the room contained Mott's worktable, where she read the newspaper, wrote letters, settled accounts, or sewed carpet rags.[42]

As the nation roiled, Lucretia enjoyed the pleasures of country life. During the summer, she picked peas and shelled them for dinner. She loved to make old Nantucket recipes, such as blackberry pudding, calf's head, or corn soup.[43] But she especially loved the company of her family and friends. In 1853, Lucretia's youngest daughter Martha, known as Pattie, married businessman George Lord. Two years later, Pattie gave birth to her first child Ellen, or Nelly. After James and Lucretia moved to Roadside, the Lords moved in with them. In 1859, the Motts celebrated the marriage of their granddaughter Anna Davis to twenty-four-year-old Hicksite Quaker Richard Price Hallowell. Lucretia's inner circle also included a new member, Unitarian minister Robert Collyer. From a working-class background in England, Collyer started his career as a Methodist preacher. After his immigration to the U.S., he found employment in a Pennsylvania hammer factory, but lost his job in the panic of 1857. To support himself, he broke stones on the highway for $1 a day. Then, after the Methodists fired him for his anti-slavery sermons, he converted to Unitarianism in 1859. In 1862, he was offered the pulpit of Theodore Parker's Twentieth-Eighth Congregational Society (Parker had died in Italy in 1860). He declined in order to continue a "kind of Circuit revival," preaching to Unitarians in the western United States.[44]

Lucretia encouraged Collyer's spiritual journey. She described reading Henry Buckle's *History of Civilization in England* with Collyer and her son-in-law Edward. Buckle's goal was to chart the laws of human progress. To Mott's approval, he targeted "superstition and false Theology," dismissing the doctrine of predestination as a "Theological hypothesis or dogma." Lucretia and Collyer also went to see Ralph Waldo Emerson lecture on "The Law of Success." Emerson described America's success as "the way of the world; 'tis the law of youth, and of unfolding strength." He disapproved of the "shallow Americanism" of get rich quick schemes, and encouraged his fellow citizens to follow their "aptitude." But Mott disagreed with Emerson's statement that "Nature knows how to convert evil to good: Nature utilizes misers, fanatics, show-men, egotists, to accomplish her ends; but we must not think better of the foible for that." Just as she had objected to Stowe's crediting the Fugitive Slave Law for her inspiration, Mott told him "wickedness works only evil & that continually." Nevertheless, Collyer was "carried away with delight," and Mott thanked Emerson for the lecture. Emerson replied, "I got some leaves out of yr. book."[45]

Though James Mott had retired from business, the Motts continued their devotion to anti-slavery, women's rights, liberal religion, social welfare, non-resistance, and Indian reform. They drove their carriage into Philadelphia to attend reform conventions, anti-slavery and Quaker meetings, and lectures, and, after a railroad line was built, they took the train. In April 1859, Lucretia attended the trial of the alleged fugitive Daniel Dangerfield, also known as Daniel Webster. She took a seat near Dangerfield, but her presence so "disturbed the equanimity of the chief counsel" that he demanded she move. The U.S. Commissioner in this case was John Cooke Longstreth, a Quaker. Mott approached him and quietly "expressed to him the earnest hope that his conscience would not allow him to send this poor man into slavery." She and other members of the Philadelphia Female Anti-Slavery Society stayed in the courtroom all night until Longstreth released Dangerfield. The society reported that a "shout of joy" went out into street at his acquittal, a "favorable sign of the times." Still, a pro-slavery mob waited for Dangerfield, so some Quaker men confounded the crowd by escorting one African American man to a waiting carriage while Dangerfield "quietly walked out and away."[46]

Mott cheered Dangerfield's release and the changing tide of public opinion it represented. But the family harmony that prevailed at Roadside was to be short lived. Geographical distance, illness, and death strained the close emotional and political ties in Lucretia's family. And, after the first shots of the American Civil War were fired at Fort Sumter, family members disagreed about the morality of war, even a war for emancipation. The Civil War also fractured their larger community of abolitionists and women's rights activists.

CHAPTER 11

Civil War

In March 1860, Lucretia helped her daughter Elizabeth Cavender
pack "sundry boxes & trunks" for her move from nearby Chelton Corner to
a farm called Eddington. Lucretia wanted to have "as frequent intercourse as
possible, while they are within reach." Her worries about losing touch with
Elizabeth were well founded. The Cavenders were so busy managing the
farm and taking care of Thomas's elderly mother that Lucretia and Elizabeth
didn't see each other for months. In addition, Lucretia was concerned about
her daughter's marriage. Always skeptical about Thomas Cavender's interest
in electoral politics, she also questioned his abilities as a husband and father.
Once, mother and daughter arranged to meet at Edward Hopper's home in
the city to discuss Elizabeth's marital "*troubles*."[1]

Even as Lucretia fretted about Elizabeth, current events dominated conversations in her parlor. In the aftermath of John Brown's insurrection, the nation had become even more polarized. A rising Republican Party was attacking
pro-slavery interests, but not fully embracing Mott's egalitarian principles. In
February 1860, Senator William Seward gave a speech calling for the admission
of Kansas as a free state. Miller McKim, a pragmatist, praised the senator and
recommended the speech. Mott was disappointed. Though she had agreed with
Seward that the clash between slavery and freedom was an "Irrepressible Conflict," she criticized him for disparaging blacks. She also chastised Seward for
seeking to "*allay*, rather than *foment* the National excitement." Mott repeated her
criticism at the next monthly meeting of the Philadelphia Female Anti-Slavery
Society, condemning the Senator for rejecting racial equality and suggesting that
preserving the "union" was more important than abolishing slavery.[2]

Mott's response to Seward's speech reflected her ongoing commitment to moral power and racial equality, convictions that increasingly distinguished her from her relatives, friends, and peers. During the Civil War and Reconstruction, reformers faced a series of political choices and shifting alliances. As many of her colleagues rallied to the Republican Party, the Union army, and the ballot box, Lucretia remained critical of the compromises involved in waging war and defining equal citizenship. She attributed emancipation not to guns or politicians, but to "the higher heroism, which had, unflinchingly, carried on, during thirty years, a *moral* war against the great system of American slavery."[3] Mott's devotion to abolitionists' moral war, particularly racial justice, shaped her political decisions during and after the South's rebellion.

For Mott and other abolitionists, President Abraham Lincoln's first test was his inaugural speech. In December 1860, following the presidential election, South Carolina seceded. By the time of Lincoln's inauguration on March 4, five additional states had left the Union. In his speech, Lincoln declared "that in contemplation of universal law, and of the Constitution, the Union of these states is perpetual." But, in the hope of a quick resolution, he promised to protect the property and security of the people of the South, downplaying the divisiveness of slavery.[4] Discussing the address with one relative, Lucretia concluded it was "infernal & diabolical." The *National Anti-Slavery Standard* shared her opinion that "The speech was made with the face turned toward the South and with both knees bowed down before the idol it worships, as have been all those delivered from the same place for half a century." But Miller McKim, James Mott, and Martha Wright viewed Lincoln's inaugural more favorably, observing that "it reflects on our judg[ment] to speak so harshly of it."[5] A disunionist who distrusted party politics and condemned political compromise, Lucretia was only too happy to bid farewell to slave states. While Lincoln debated whether or not to provoke Confederate forces by resupplying the Union soldiers stationed at Fort Sumter, South Carolina, Mott commented, "wise judgment may recall [Major Robert] Anderson, without sacrifice of principle—indeed, all the Slave States might go—without fightg. about it."[6] The fact that Mott was willing to leave slaves at the mercy of their masters suggested that perhaps she privileged her own purity over the welfare of those in bondage. But she also believed that disunion would lead to the disintegration of the South's peculiar institution.

Despite a rare disagreement over the first inaugural, Lucretia and James were as happy and politically attuned as ever. On April 10, 1861, two days before Confederates bombarded the recently provisioned Fort Sumter, Lucretia and James celebrated their golden wedding anniversary with a family party at Roadside. At sixty-eight, Mott continued to complain of dyspepsia and sometimes dizziness. Seventy-three-year-old James was losing his vision. Lucretia wrote "it is really affectg. to see him choose the strongest light, & after awhile, even then, lay down his book or Paper & say I cant see to read." She and Maria Davis took turns reading to James. Lucretia kept her good humor, telling Martha that "He hears well however, and is not lame, or bald, or toothless."[7]

Once the fighting began, younger abolitionists enlisted, hoping to turn the Union army into an army of liberation. Martha's son Lieutenant William Wright and his First New York Independent Battery were part of the Army of the Potomac. In December 1861, Willie traveled through Philadelphia on his way to Washington. He later fought in the battles of Antietam, Fredericksburg, and Gettysburg. At Gettysburg, Willie received a severe bullet wound in his chest that only narrowly missed his lungs.[8] Edward and Norwood Hallowell, brothers of Mott's grandson-in-law Richard Hallowell, served as colonels in two famous African American regiments, the Fifty-Fourth and Fifty-Fifth Massachusetts Volunteers.[9] In December 1863, Caroline Stratton Wood's daughter Laura Stratton married her childhood sweetheart Colonel Fitzhugh Birney, son of political abolitionist and delegate to the World's Anti-Slavery Convention James G. Birney, in William Henry Furness's church in Philadelphia. The pacifist Mott described Col. Birney's uniform as "awful" and "imposing." Six months later, "Fitz" died in Washington, D.C., after contracting pneumonia in the army.[10]

While many of these younger abolitionists had never proclaimed nonviolent principles, even former non-resistants joined the war effort. Lucretia's son-in-law Edward M. Davis served as a quartermaster in Republican hero General John C. Fremont's Army of the West in Missouri. Confident in Edward's abolitionism, Lucretia expressed her disappointment in his betrayal of peace for expediency. She wrote to Martha, "He flatters himself that the abolitn. of slavery—end, justifies the means."[11] After Davis's service led to his disownment from Cherry Street Meeting, Maria resigned in sympathy. But Davis's hopes were fulfilled when Fremont declared martial law and freed slaves in Missouri. Unwilling to alienate slaveholding Unionists, however, President Lincoln removed Fremont from his command in November 1861. This action solidified Lucretia's view of the president as a "miserable compromiser." Even worse, she accused Lincoln of drumming up "false charges" against Fremont and Edward Davis for supplying "rotten and condemned" blankets to Union soldiers to justify his actions. After testifying before Congress, Davis was exonerated and resigned from the army.[12]

Unlike Davis and other reformers, Mott was not led by the possibility that the war might abolish slavery to change her attitude toward violence or party politics. She viewed the Civil War as "the natural result of our wrong doings, and our atrocious cruelties." In a July 1861 letter to the *National Anti-Slavery Standard*, she corrected a newspaper article that quoted her as saying the war should be "prosecuted with energy and faith." She did not endorse the war. Rather, Mott told readers, she had argued that the war should not be "*stayed* by any compromises which shall continue the unequal, cruel war on the rights and liberties of our unoffending fellow-beings, a war waged from generation to generation, with all the physical force of our government, the President himself Commander-in-Chief."[13] Lucretia criticized any conciliation on the issue of slavery, complaining to Martha that "There has seemed rather a stolid determination of late among a class of politicians, that this War shall have nothing to do with Slavery." She wrote, "I feel almost to despair of any good result from the present commotion—We know full well that the battle field is a precarious resort, to obtain the right—that sorrows multiply there."[14]

Lucretia continued to advocate moral means as "more effectual." Writing early in the war, when the Union Army sustained consecutive losses at Bull Run and Ball's Bluff, she argued that the "moral protest & demand of the people" were "likely to do more, than any of the armies have yet accomplished." She returned to the old strategy of the anti-slavery petition, advising that "Petitions should now be poured in from all quarters—so that poor Abe, M'Clellan & the others may see how unavailing all their proslavery conservatism is."[15]

Mott's coworkers in the Philadelphia Female Anti-Slavery Society concurred. In the 1862 *Annual Report*, corresponding secretary Mary Grew noted that the goal of abolitionists had been to "redeem the nation from its sin, without this baptism of blood." But, she wrote, "they have never doubted that, failing in this, there was no other alternative for the nation than disruption and the horrors of war."[16] The women of the Philadelphia Female Anti-Slavery Society did not view the Republican Party, President Lincoln, or the Union army as agents of emancipation. Like Mott, they attributed the national transformation to moral suasion: "The heart of the Northern *people* is slowly and irrevocably decreeing the doom of slavery."[17]

This conviction only faltered with the Emancipation Proclamations of

1862 and 1863. After the bloody battle of Antietam in September 1862, Lincoln issued a preliminary order freeing all slaves in the Confederacy. Lucretia cautiously admitted, "we must acknowledge an increase of hope for the Slave." When Lincoln issued the official proclamation on January 1, 1863, the Philadelphia Female Anti-Slavery Society applauded: "The day of America's jubilee has dawned at last; and we who have watched and striven through the dark night of her despotism, now hail that dawning with joy and gratitude unutterable." While rejoicing, the society was firm about the document's limitations. Since the Emancipation Proclamation only freed slaves in the rebel states, the society urged abolitionists to continue fighting for the complete abolition of slavery. In addition, they worried about the persistence of racial prejudice. "We should keep on our armour," the belligerent non-resistant Lucretia advised.[18]

Most northern women did not share Mott's skepticism over the war or emancipation. The Civil War presented northern women with new opportunities for public activism. They formed soldiers' aid societies and worked under the auspices of the U.S. Sanitary Commission, founded to help supply the Union army with necessary items such as socks and bandages. In 1861, the Philadelphia Female Anti-Slavery Society worried that so many women were sewing for the soldiers they would be unable to hold their annual fair. Though the fair raised $1608.68, it was the last one held for the rest of the conflict.[19]

Northern women also forged new careers in politics and nursing. Young Philadelphia Quaker Anna Dickinson became a stump speaker for the Republican Party, drawing throngs of people carried away by her "eloquence" and "pathos." James Mott had advised the young woman at the beginning of her career, Lucretia reported, "& he is now much gratified with her success." But Lucretia noted her ideological differences from the young Quaker, writing that Dickinson "has more *fight* than I can go with."[20] In 1863, Lucretia read *Hospital Sketches* by Louisa May Alcott, daughter of Abba Alcott, one of the original members of the Philadelphia Female Anti-Slavery Society. Mott admired the fictionalized account of Louisa's service in a Washington, D.C., army hospital. "I want something to do," the heroine, Tribulation Periwinkle, declares at the beginning of the story. The following year, Lucretia's granddaughter Maria Hopper and her aunt Abby Hopper Gibbons worked in a field hospital near General Ulysses Grant's headquarters at City Point, Virginia.[21]

Women's rights activists hoped the Civil War might bring not only emancipation, but also an expanded definition of female citizenship. Though they suspended their annual conventions for the duration of the war, on May 14,

1863, Elizabeth Cady Stanton and Susan B. Anthony organized a meeting of the "Loyal Women of the Republic" in New York City. Their goal was to consider "woman's legitimate work" in the "defense and preservation" of republican self-government. This meeting launched the Women's National Loyal League, a patriotic organization dedicated to support the government, but only "in so far as it makes the war for freedom." The women praised Lincoln's Emancipation Proclamation, and sought further confirmation that the war was being waged for "justice and humanity."[22]

The Women's National Loyal League organized a massive campaign of pamphlets and petitions calling for emancipation. Their original petition to Congress read, "The undersigned, women of the United States above the age of eighteen years, earnestly pray that your honorable body will pass at the earliest practicable day an act emancipating all persons of African descent held to involuntary service or labor in the United States." Susan B. Anthony enlisted the help of the Philadelphia Female Anti-Slavery Society in gaining signatures for their petition, forwarding 100 copies in October 1863. An interracial committee including Abby Kimber, Margaretta Forten, and Sarah D. Purvis circulated the petitions. By the end of the war, the Women's National Loyal League had obtained an impressive 400,000 signatures.[23]

Yet two other issues captured the wartime attention of Mott and her colleagues in the Philadelphia Female Anti-Slavery Society. The first was the poor treatment of black soldiers. At its monthly meeting in September 1862, the Philadelphia Female Anti-Slavery Society hosted two soldiers fighting with the First South Carolina Volunteers, the first African American regiment commanded by abolitionist and women's rights activist Thomas Wentworth Higginson. Prince Rivers and Brian White both detailed their escape from slavery to the Union army. The society praised Sergeant Rivers's "true nobility of soul," and they were awestruck by White's six-day journey in manacles to reach Union lines. But the abolitionists were outraged when, after leaving the meeting, Rivers was "insulted and assaulted" on the streets of Philadelphia.[24]

After the Emancipation Proclamation called for the further enlistment of African American men, the army established Camp William Penn on land leased from Edward M. Davis and Mott's neighbor, Radical Republican financier Jay Cooke. Lucretia could watch black soldiers drill from her front porch. She wrote that the camp was "the absorbing interest just now." She asked, "Is not the change in feeling, & conduct toward this oppressed class, beyond all we could have anticipated—&marvelous in our eyes?"[25] However remarkable the transformation, much work remained. Her friend Robert Purvis spoke passionately of the "injustice to the colored soldier," paid $10 per month to the white soldier's $13 per month. The Philadelphia Female Anti-Slavery Society also observed that the city's railway cars banned black passengers, forcing the families of soldiers stationed at Camp William Penn to walk "back and forth from the city to visit their relatives." The society made fighting this discrimination a priority.[26]

Members of the Philadelphia Female Anti-Slavery Society also devoted themselves to aiding former slaves. The advance of the Union army prompted an exodus from slavery even before Lincoln issued the Emancipation Proclamation. The army was ill-equipped to take care of the men, women, and children who fled to their lines. Northern reformers organized to send missionaries, teachers, and supplies to Union-occupied areas like the Sea Islands of South Carolina. Maintaining the distinction between anti-slavery and other forms of activism, the society believed its duty was to "watch and warn and urge universal emancipation."[27] But individual members sewed clothes and raised funds for freedmen's aid societies or traveled south as teachers. Lucretia joined the Friends Association for the Aid and Elevation of the Freedmen. In December 1862, she reported to Martha Wright that at one of their first meetings she "found some 30 or 40 sewing away 2 or 3 machines going—Several boxes have been sent." By 1864, the Philadelphia Female Anti-Slavery Society estimated that Philadelphia citizens had donated over $100,000 to freedmen's relief. Lucretia expressed amusement that prominent Quakers—previously antagonistic to abolitionism—were "all alive to the subject."[28]

Younger members of the Philadelphia Female Anti-Slavery Society enlisted in the "Port Royal Experiment" in the Sea Islands. Matilda Thompson traveled to South Carolina planning to work as a teacher, and ended up marrying Brigadier General Rufus Saxton, military commander of the Department of the South. She corresponded regularly with the society. Charlotte Forten, granddaughter of James Forten, taught on St. Helena Island from October 1862 to May 1864. The society praised her efforts, describing her as one "whose early youth was consecrated to the Anti-Slavery cause."[29] Quaker sisters Anne and Jane Heacock taught at Port Royal from 1863 to 1869. Before they left Philadelphia, Lucretia offered her "best wishes": "We shall be very glad to hear from you—and shall think of you often in your new occupation."[30]

Abolitionists expressed anxious enthusiasm for this "new field of labor," signaling as it did the eventual end of their movement. Some reformers, assuming that emancipation was now inevitable, abandoned anti-slavery societies in favor of freedmen's aid societies. Miller McKim left the Pennsylvania Anti-Slavery Society in December 1863 to form the American Freedmen's Aid Commission. Former social and political outcasts, McKim and his allies sought new legitimacy from the Republican Party and the federal government. The rather practical goal of McKim's new organization was "to aid, more efficiently, in supplying the immediate and pressing physical wants of the Freed people."[31] Less than a year later, the Pennsylvania Anti-Slavery Society closed its office (where Henry "Box" Brown had been mailed) in Philadelphia. As Lucretia explained, "for 'tis only an expense since Miller left us." Unlike her friend, Lucretia continued to distinguish between the goals of the anti-slavery and freedmen's aid movements, but she worked tirelessly for both. As she described to her sister and daughter-in-law, "I go in @ 8 oclk in the Cars—stay all day and all night by reason of Freedmen's Mgs. & Fem. A.S. Society." Yet Lucretia's disappointment with Miller's decision was one sign of ever more bitter divisions over the future of the anti-slavery movement.[32]

In the summer of 1864, the presidential election split abolitionists. With emancipation in reach, William Lloyd Garrison, Miller McKim, and Frederick Douglass endorsed Lincoln's reelection. But prominent lecturer and Garrison ally Wendell Phillips supported John C. Fremont as the Republican Party candidate. Phillips savaged what he saw as Lincoln's moral failures. In October, he denounced those "who have stood with me on a disunion platform for twenty years submit, and support Mr. Lincoln as 'the less of two evils.'"[33] Lucretia had little interest in the election, aside from its divisive impact upon the anti-slavery community, but she sympathized with Phillips's purism. Miller McKim was so frustrated with her that he suggested they avoid political discussions in the future. Lucretia commented—prematurely—that "I cant believe all this wide diff[erence] will lead to any serious 'split.'" Her judgment of national politics was similarly naive. The Republican Party nominated Lincoln instead of Fremont, and General William T. Sherman's victory in Atlanta secured Lincoln's reelection. Northerners rallied to finish their war on the slaveholding Confederacy.[34]

Lucretia observed the "wonderful excitement" following General Robert E. Lee's surrender at Appomattox Courthouse on April 9, 1865, but the mood at Roadside was one of deep sadness. Lucretia wrote Martha that the news of Union victory reached Philadelphia at 10 p.m. and the Motts' farm at midnight. The ringing of church bells, however, kept Elizabeth Cavender awake until 3 a.m. Lucretia told Martha that two doses of morphine finally helped her daughter sleep. Since Elizabeth's move to Eddington, Lucretia had worried about her lonely daughter. Her concern grew after Elizabeth's fourteen-year-old son Henry, known as Harry, died suddenly in September 1863. Elizabeth was overwhelmed with grief. She was not the first of Mott's children to suffer such a loss. Most recently, Anna Hopper's oldest daughter Lucretia, known as Lue, had died of tuberculosis in December 1861. But Elizabeth received little emotional succor from her husband, who was consumed by financial troubles and ignored his wife's deteriorating mental and physical condition. By early 1865, Lucretia wrote of her "anxiety" for the "dangerous state" of Elizabeth's health. And by April, Elizabeth, ill with some form of cancer, had moved into her parents' house.[35]

Her daughter's decline shaped Lucretia's response to the end of a bloody war she had never supported. Thomas Cavender seldom visited, and when he did he criticized the doctors, including Mott's friend Ann Preston. Lucretia, who had been critical of the match from the beginning, now called Thomas a "wretch." Worried about Elizabeth's mental state, Lucretia broke the news of Lincoln's assassination gradually. The "dear invalid" burst into tears at the news. Later that month, the local sheriff put Eddington up for sale, presumably for Thomas's failure to pay taxes. Thomas planned to rent a room for himself and his son Charley from the new owners while Elizabeth's daughters stayed with her at Roadside. This emotional upheaval was tempered by moments of quiet optimism. Though Elizabeth was weak from hemorrhaging, she and Lucretia sat by the window watching the departure of black soldiers from Camp William Penn. As Lucretia described in a letter to her daughter Pattie Lord, now living with her family in Brooklyn, New York, "the last Regiment went off from Camp W.P. & marched thro' our grounds—with the band, & such hurrahg., & takg. off caps & biddg. goodbye!"[36]

When forty-year-old Elizabeth Cavender died on September 4, 1865, Lucretia derived some comfort from knowing "our precious sufferer is removed from it all!" As they mourned for their daughter, the Motts' relationship with Thomas Cavender worsened. Cavender had borrowed a large sum of money from James Mott. On October 31, he gave the $5,000 he owed his frugal father-in-law to Edward Hopper. Lucretia described the tense meeting in one of her typical "family" letters, intended for multiple recipients, to Pattie in Brooklyn and Martha in Auburn. According to Lucretia, "not a word" passed between the former brothers-in-law. Understandably, the next time ten-year-old Charley Cavender visited his grandparents, "his mind [was] greatly stirred ag[ains]t his Grandfr., for 'trying to get money out of his father—he didn't *want* to stay here anyhow.'" Mott rightly worried that Thomas was trying to alienate Charley from Elizabeth's family. Elizabeth's eldest daughter Fanny remained with her grandparents.[37]

*   *   *

The cessation of military conflict did not end political infighting among Mott's fellow reformers. Many abolitionists, Mott included, viewed the ballot as a crucial protection for African American men. But other feminists saw the postwar period as an opportunity to win voting rights for women. The ensuing debate over the ideological and strategic relationship between freedmen's political rights and women's suffrage severed the already tenuous connection between the anti-slavery and women's rights movements. Amid this rancor, Mott unsuccessfully promoted her understanding of these causes as inseparable, refusing to see blacks and women as competitors.

For Mott, the first and most painful break occurred when her friend Miller McKim reorganized the freedmen's aid movement. "Heterodox" Mott and "Conservative" McKim had always enjoyed debating religion, politics, and anti-slavery strategy. In 1865 and 1866, these lively discussions became more personal. McKim had recently helped found a new national freedmen's aid organization, the American Freedmen's Union Commission, to direct all aid going to the South. Led by prominent male abolitionists and ministers, the organization worked in close partnership with the federal government's newly established Freedmen's Bureau. McKim appealed to Mott and the Friends Association for the Aid and Elevation of the Freedmen to join his "Reconstructive Union." Mott's sharp response took McKim by surprise. She wrote to Martha that "I told him it was objected, that Woman was ignored in their new organizatn., & if really a reconstructn. for the Nation she ought not so to be—and it wd. be rather 'a come down' for our Anti Slavery and Quaker women to consent to be thus overlooked." Mott also opposed the expansive focus of the American Freedmen's Union Commission on "the people of the south, without distinction of race or color." She informed McKim, "the Freedmen's interests are very near & dear to me—and I rather dread mixing them with the offspring of Rebels unrepentant." In response, McKim accused her of becoming "more heretical" in her views. Mott was hurt that their "warm" friendship could be so easily broken. After Sarah and Miller McKim moved to Llewellyn Park, New Jersey, in the spring of 1866, the relationship grew colder.[38]

Mott's exchange with McKim was an indication of larger troubles in the factionalized anti-slavery community. With the Thirteenth Amendment on its way to ratification, abolitionists debated their duty to former slaves. In May 1865, William Lloyd Garrison resigned from the American Anti-Slavery Society, declaring that the work of abolitionists was done. His old friend Wendell Phillips disagreed. At the annual meeting of the Pennsylvania Anti-Slavery Society in October 1865, Phillips condemned the administration of President Andrew Johnson, in the process of pardoning former Confederates. He argued that anti-slavery societies must continue until slavery and racial prejudice were finally defeated. "How I wish you cd. have heard Wendell P. on the state of the country," Lucretia wrote Martha and Pattie.[39]

Viewing the "spirit of slavery" as alive and well, Mott and the Philadelphia Female Anti-Slavery Society vowed to continue. At a lively meeting of the society in January 1866, Margaret Burleigh, widow of Cyrus Burleigh, proposed disbanding. In response, Lucretia argued that "to dissolve now would be to desert the Slave's cause, as human beings are still virtually held as Slaves in defiance of law." Robert Purvis agreed. He told the society, "The colored man's danger is greater than ever. Without the ballot he will be in danger of extermination."[40] Mary Grew wrote of the existence of southern black codes and other efforts to retain slavery. Siding with Phillips and the remaining members of the American Anti-Slavery Society, the Philadelphia Female Anti-Slavery Society concluded to work for the enfranchisement of African American men, asserting, "the ballot in the hand of the freedmen is essential to this liberty."[41]

Personal and familial ties sustained some friendships through these hard times. In 1864, Lucretia's niece Ellen Wright had married William Lloyd Garrison, Jr. After the war, Garrison stayed in touch with Lucretia through Ellen and Willie. After learning that she had been sick, Garrison wrote, "I feel a strong desire that you should remain in the body until the time for my departure has also come, that I may go hand in hand with you to the spirit world."[42] In December 1865, Miller's daughter Lucy McKim married Wendell Phillips Garrison, named for his father's old friend and ally.

Still, the bitterness of these years strained many relationships. At the Yearly Meeting of Progressive Friends at Longwood in June 1866, Oliver Johnson, former editor of the *Pennsylvania Freeman* and the *National Anti-Slavery Standard*, denounced Wendell Phillips and argued that it was too soon to press for black male suffrage. Robert Purvis's daughter Hattie was so upset that she could hardly bear to be in the same room as Johnson. Mott wrote, "Had her father been there, as was expected, he [couldn't] have stood it, but she felt too young to contradict or oppose him."[43]

Susan B. Anthony was also present at Longwood, urging reformers to demand not only black suffrage but also women's suffrage. She represented a new organization called the American Equal Rights Association (AERA), founded the previous month at the first women's rights convention since the end of the war. With national attention on the political and civil rights of African Americans, women's rights activists sharpened their focus on suffrage. A controversial demand at the Seneca Falls Convention now became the main goal of the movement. Incorporating African American and women's rights into one organization, the American Equal Rights Association advocated "universal" suffrage. As Mott explained to Wendell Phillips, Anthony and Elizabeth Cady Stanton believed that, "the negro's hour was decidedly the time for woman to slip in." Mott had her reservations. She wrote that in "this perilous hour for Liberty" it was "unwise" to renew the struggle for women's rights. But, she added, "what can we now do, but go to the meeting."[44]

Mott's loyalty to Anthony and Stanton overcame many of her doubts, and she agreed to be president of the American Equal Rights Association. As she wrote to Stanton, "even admitting that this is decidedly the freedmen's hour, we may do what we can among ourselves and make what stir we can."[45] In a memorial signed by Mott, Stanton, Anthony, and Frederick Douglass, they asserted that "Woman and the colored man are loyal, patriotic, property-holding, tax paying, liberty-loving citizens; and we cannot believe that our sex or complexion should be any ground for civil or political degradation." The association urged Congress to live up to the ideal of a "GOVERNMENT BY THE PEOPLE, AND THE WHOLE PEOPLE; FOR THE PEOPLE, AND THE WHOLE PEOPLE." But Mott's own statements on equal suffrage were relatively weak. She told one convention that the right to vote "cannot be consistently withheld from women."[46]

Mott's age was beginning to affect her tolerance for meetings and other organizational work. One of the first items on the agenda of the American Equal Rights Association was the upcoming constitutional convention in New York State. Stanton and Anthony, native New Yorkers, wanted to excise the word "male" from the state constitution and include voting rights for African Americans. While visiting Pattie in November 1866, Mott met Anthony at Stanton's New York City apartment to strategize. Lucretia complained to her family that "This Equal Rights movet. is no play—but I cant enter into it—Just hearg. their talk & the readg.—made me ache all over." Lucretia was happy to get away, but the next day she found Anthony waiting for her at the Lords' house. She commented, "You see how little rest, this side Jordan there is for the aged."[47]

Mott was also weary of mediating ongoing political tensions among activists. Prompted by the American Equal Rights Association, abolitionists debated whether or not to fight for women's suffrage and black suffrage at the same time. At a May 1867 meeting of the New England Anti-Slavery Society, Stephen S. Foster and Parker Pillsbury urged abolitionists to take up both issues. Mott, who was visiting her granddaughter Anna Davis Hallowell in Medford, lamented "anything like a feeling of division or opposition among us." Recalling her message at the Whole World's Temperance Convention, Mott pleaded, "We cannot separate these great reformatory movements— and let us feel that we are still united together." Though she had her own concerns about the American Equal Rights Association, she did not like to see one side attack the other. And attack they did. Wendell Phillips, Abby Kelley Foster, and Henry Clarke Wright opposed the introduction of women's suffrage in the meeting. As Lucretia reported back to her family, "the eve[nin]g was too much occupied with antagonistic speeches on the wom. question."[48]

These disagreements made the American Equal Rights Association, in Lucretia's view, "dreadful up-hill work." The organization struggled to raise money. As activists turned their attention to two state suffrage referenda in Kansas, Lucretia signed a desperate appeal to the "friends of equal rights" for funds to "send Tracts and Speakers into the State."[49]

The Kansas campaign caused irreparable damage to the American Equal Rights Association. Lucy Stone, Henry Blackwell, Stanton, and Anthony headed to the state to urge voters to pass both the women's suffrage and black suffrage measures. Initially welcomed by enthusiastic audiences, the eastern speakers were optimistic. But everything changed after the New York constitutional convention rejected women's suffrage in June 1867. Stanton was outraged, writing in the *New York Tribune* that "the higher orders of womanhood" deserved priority over the "lower orders of . . . washed and unwashed, lettered and unlettered manhood," a deliberate slight on African American men.[50] Following New York's lead, the Republican Party in Kansas dropped its support of the women's suffrage referendum. To the dismay of Stone and Blackwell, Stanton and Anthony sought help from the Democratic Party and an eccentric, bigoted financier named George Francis Train. Garrison wrote to Anthony to condemn Train as a "crack-brained harlequin and semilunatic" and an "abusive assailant" of African Americans.[51] After Kansas's voters defeated the women's suffrage and black suffrage proposals, Stanton and Anthony ignored these friends to win Train's financial support for their newspaper, *The Revolution*, started in January 1868.[52]

Lucretia was horrified at her allies' cooperation with Train. In a January 21, 1868, letter to Martha, Lucretia wrote, "The Revolution is not satisfactory & I have not the littlest notion of being a subscriber . . . I only wait for the May Mg. to withdraw from every office." She was also concerned that Train amplified Stanton's worst tendencies. As early as December 1865, Stanton had debated if women should step back and let "Sambo" walk into the voting booth first. Now, Lucretia commented, "Elizh. Stanton's sympathy for 'Sambo' is very questionable."[53]

The fierceness of the dispute also caused Lucretia to question her core belief in the fundamental link between the anti-slavery and women's rights movements. She concluded that "it was a great mistake to unite" "these great reformatory movements." She also regretted the organization of the American Equal Rights Association or any "Socy. for Wom. Rig." Despite her criticism of women's rights conventions in the 1850s, she described the congregational format as "far more effective, & all that we ought to have attempted." True to her word, Mott resigned from the American Equal Rights Association in May 1868. In her letter, she recommended that the association be discontinued.[54]

As Lucretia penned her political concerns to Martha in the Lords' parlor in Brooklyn, her mind wandered to her feverish husband, who lay sleeping upstairs. James had been sick with a cough and fever since their arrival at Pattie's. The doctor had visited the previous day, Lucretia wrote, and "he thot. him better yestery. but his fever came on after he left—& he has not yet been down this morng." Lucretia also complained of her health: "I too have cold hands & feet followed by fever & night sweats—so that we are rather a forlorn old pair."[55] In the coming days, Lucretia became increasingly anxious for her husband. She sent for Anna Hopper on January 24, 1868. On January 26, at age seventy-nine, James died of pneumonia.[56]

The family brought James's body back to Philadelphia. They held a large funeral at Anna and Edward Hopper's house before burying him in Fair Hill Cemetery. Speaking to the assembled crowd, Robert Purvis proclaimed, "I thank God for such a life!" Mourning his sudden loss, Mary Grew published a biographical sketch celebrating James's anti-slavery career. She described him as a person of "quiet power" who did not "falter or shrink" in the face of danger. When James signed the American Anti-Slavery Society's Declaration of Sentiments in 1833, Grew recalled, he enlisted in the "defense of the most unpopular moral reform of this age and country." As a fellow advocate of free produce, she paid close attention to James's decision to abandon the cotton business and abstain from the products of slavery. She declared that "his domestic and business life was the illustration of his religion." Grew also reprinted tributes from other abolitionists. James's colleagues on the executive committee of the Pennsylvania Anti-Slavery Society described him as "firm, gentle and just, refusing all compromise with wrong, claiming all human rights for the colored man, and illustrating in his daily life the religion taught in the Sermon on the Mount." William Lloyd Garrison wrote, "My respect, esteem, affection, and veneration for him were as strong and exalted as it is lawful to cherish for any human being. He was gentle, and yet had great strength of purpose and will."[57]

Philanthropic and business endeavors had made James Mott a household name. His obituary in the *New York Evening Post* described his success in creating a "permanent foundation" for the wool trade in Philadelphia. The *Post* also heralded his sound financial practices: "As a merchant, no man was more highly esteemed for upright dealing, punctuality of engagements, and liberal treatment of debtors."[58] James's last will and testament, written with Lucretia's approval in November 1865, attests to his careful accounting and, after years of struggle, his wealth. It is also a testament to his regard for his wife and their shared commitment to women's rights. Under English common law, widows were entitled to one-third of their husband's estate for life. Most states adopted this common law practice, but Pennsylvania placed restrictions on the widow's dower, narrowly defining the husband's estate and privileging his creditors. In providing for Lucretia, James went beyond both Pennsylvania law and the traditional widow's dower. He left Lucretia $10,000 outright and placed the rest of his estate in trust, with Lucretia as the sole beneficiary of all rents, profits, and interest. Upon Lucretia's death, he bequeathed $10,000 to his son Thomas. He also entrusted Thomas to invest $15,000 to provide for Elizabeth Cavender's children (no other provisions were made for grandchildren). The rest of his estate was to be divided evenly among his three remaining daughters. By 1880, James Mott's estate was worth $117,669.33, today equivalent to over $2.3 million.[59]

After her grandfather's death, Anna Davis Hallowell remembered her grandmother's "sense of desolation." Lucretia had lost her true love and companion of more than fifty-six years. She moved out of the bedroom she had shared with James at Roadside to a small room called the "middle room."

Lucretia stopped her regular attendance at First-day (Sunday) Quaker meeting, which she and James had always attended together. Two months after his death, she wrote to her son-in-law George Lord observing the sad anniversary. "Every day since has been counted by me," she noted. Lucretia talked about James to anyone who would listen, remembering "the blessing of his long life with me."[60] And she did not return to her regular routine for months. Her friends and allies in the Philadelphia Female Anti-Slavery Society marked her absence from their monthly meetings. At the March meeting, the minutes recorded that "a feeling of quiet sadness seemed to pervade the meeting." Finally, in June 1868, Lucretia returned to the Philadelphia Female Anti-Slavery Society seeking comfort, continuity, and a sense of purpose.[61]

In keeping with their original intent to end slavery and racial prejudice, the Philadelphia Female Anti-Slavery Society pursued two main goals after the Civil War: universal male suffrage and integration of Philadelphia's railway lines. Of course, many members were strong proponents of women's rights. Mott, now president of the society, had been president of the American Equal Rights Association. Former president Sarah Pugh had suggested closing the Philadelphia Female Anti-Slavery Society in order to form a state auxiliary to the AERA.[62] But the society decided to remain an anti-slavery society. And as such, they were quite clear that their duty was to secure freed-*men* the right to vote.

In advocating enfranchisement, the society adopted gender-specific language. In 1866, when Congress passed the Fourteenth Amendment defining citizens as "all persons born or naturalized in the United States" and guaranteeing them equal protection and due process, the Philadelphia Female Anti-Slavery Society criticized the law for not going far enough in establishing the political rights of African Americans. While their women's rights colleagues in the American Equal Rights Association protested the inclusion of the word "male" in the second clause specifying voters, the society did not comment on the limitation. Instead, they complained that by not explicitly granting black men the right to vote, Congress "practically declared that the country and the Government belong to the white man; and that the colored man is to be legislated for, and otherwise disposed of, in such manner as may best serve the fancied interests of the white race."[63] In 1868, the organization declared that their work would not be complete until a former slave stands up as a "MAN, full panoplied with all the defenses of an American citizen." This language was deliberate. The members of the Philadelphia Female Anti-Slavery Society supported the goals of the American Anti-Slavery Society and petitioned for black male suffrage.[64]

The Philadelphia Female Anti-Slavery Society relied on familiar weapons in the struggle for African American equality. Replacing the old anti-slavery fairs, they sponsored Festivals of the Friends of Freedom to raise money. In December 1868, the festival raised $700, a respectable amount, if less than in the antebellum heyday. Members continued to petition the state and national legislature on African American suffrage. Viewing the Fourteenth Amendment as inadequate, they pressed Congress to enact universal (male) suffrage. One petition sent just weeks before Congress passed the Fifteenth Amendment in February 1869 stated, "We earnestly ask for this, in order that their personal freedom, recently declared by the Constitution, shall be completed and secured."[65] And they remained moral suasionists. As Mary Grew described, "We seek to promote a correct public sentiment, and inspire zeal for righteousness in the hearts of the people, by publishing and proclaiming the truth, and the just demands of the colored man."[66]

While the Philadelphia Female Anti-Slavery Society ignored the status of white and black women in their discussions of suffrage, their campaign for the integration of streetcars emphasized the dignity and respectability of black women and children. During the Civil War, the society had noted that the families of African American soldiers at Camp William Penn were forced to walk eight miles from Philadelphia to visit their husbands, brothers, and sons. In response to this injustice, the society prepared a long formal appeal to the Passenger Railroad Company.[67] At the end of the war, discrimination persisted with a profound impact on Philadelphia's black families. As Mary Grew reported, "A father, carrying his sick child, in haste to reach his home; mothers with their infants in their arms; weary-footed men and women returning from the business and labors of the day, in the heat of the summer, and the storms of the winter, have been refused admission to the cars, or compelled to stand on platforms, and have, also, in some instances, been violently ejected from them." In cooperation with other organizations, members of the Philadelphia Female Anti-Slavery Society personally visited presidents and directors of the railways, forcing them to hold a public meeting on the subject. Still, only one company, the Philadelphia and Darby Railroad Company, had abandoned its discriminatory policies. In October 1865, when famous Underground Railroad conductor and Union spy Harriet Tubman visited Roadside, she was "badly used" by the railroad. Lucretia described Tubman, who now lived in Auburn, New York, as a "wonderful woman" and urged Martha to "talk with her about the Freedmen & their right to vote."[68]

With their male relatives leading the fight in the legislature and in the streets, African American women spearheaded the Philadelphia Female Anti-Slavery Society's campaign against railroad operators. William Still, husband of member Letitia Still, had founded the Social, Civil, and Statistical Association in 1860; the organization made streetcar integration one of its principal goals. In 1864, Philadelphia blacks, including Harriet Purvis's younger brother William Forten, founded the Pennsylvania State Equal Rights League. The League, led by Octavius Catto, urged blacks to force the issue by riding the cars. Catto specifically called upon black men to assert their rights and to "vindicate their manhood, and no longer suffer defenseless women and children to be assaulted or insulted."[69] But independently of the Equal Rights League, African American women defined this issue as one of particular personal and political importance. In September 1866, Harriet Purvis told the Philadelphia Female Anti-Slavery Society that any optimism about Reconstruction was useless "when she could not be allowed, weary as she was, to take a seat in the cars." She lambasted the Republican Party for not doing enough to advocate the rights of northern blacks, and she urged more public discussions of racism. Other African American women avidly pursued justice in the courts. Indeed, women of color filed the majority of lawsuits challenging racial segregation on railroads.[70]

As historian Barbara Welke shows, female litigants tended to come from relatively elite backgrounds. The daughter and wife of wealthy men, Harriet Purvis may have felt especially aggrieved by the indignity of her treatment. She faced insults and possibly violence from rough conductors. And her status as a "lady," entitled to respectful treatment from men, was at stake. Philadelphia Mayor Alexander Henry inserted himself in the controversy by declaring he would not want his wife and daughters to ride the cars with African Americans. Like his counterparts in the south, then, Mayor Henry justified racial exclusion by invoking the protection of white womanhood. This argument made the alliance of white and black women in the Philadelphia Female Anti-Slavery Society all the more important. As Mary Grew commented, "Possibly he was not fully conscious that he was thus condemning the ladies of other families to be pushed with brutal violence from the cars to the street pavement."[71] Yet Purvis's reference to her weariness also purposefully transcended class lines. African American women, regardless of their class, marital status, or occupation, were treated as inferior.

Though activists achieved a victory in March 1867 when Governor Geary signed an act forcing railroad companies to accept black passengers, the Philadelphia Female Anti-Slavery Society recognized that this law was not enough. Some legislators were actively working to repeal it. And, later that year, the Pennsylvania Supreme Court upheld the legality of railroad segregation. The case involved an African American woman named Mary E. Miles, who filed suit after a conductor of the West Chester and Philadelphia Railroad Company forcibly ejected her for refusing to move to a seat in the back of the car. Like other African American women, she risked violence to challenge segregation, but she was also more likely than a male litigant to win her suit. After Miles won $5 in damages in the lower courts, the railroad company appealed. The state Supreme Court reversed the lower court's decision, holding that "the railroad had a right to promulgate regulations in order to ensure the safety and comfort of passengers and that a policy of separating races was permissible because the railroad was entitled to avoid potential disruptions due to other passengers' anger over being seated near a passenger of a different race."[72] Miles was probably Mary Ann (nee London) Miles, a twenty-six-year-old domestic servant whose husband, Alfred, worked in a hotel. The *North American and U.S. Gazette* described her as an "intelligent and respectable looking colored woman." The Philadelphia Female Anti-Slavery Society was well aware of her case. Miles's lawyer was George H. Earle, son of Lucretia's cousin Mary Hussey Earle. After the Pennsylvania Supreme Court's decision, Mary Grew argued that the decision "cruelly taunts colored citizens with their exclusion from civil and political office."[73]

While Mott's Philadelphia Female Anti-Slavery survived the infighting among abolitionists by remaining true to its founding principles, the American Equal Rights Association collapsed under the weight of its political divisions. Tensions had been building in the association since the Kansas campaign. After the insertion of the word "male" in the Fourteenth Amendment, some activists, including Mott's friend Elizabeth Cady Stanton, staunchly opposed the Fifteenth Amendment for neglecting women. Historians have attacked, lamented, and defended Stanton's racist strategies in this period. Michele Mitchell identifies Stanton's use of racial epithets as "intriguing, surprising, regrettable, contradictory, and predictable." By contrast, Ann Gordon argues that the focus on Stanton's racism ignores "Stanton's core convictions" and oversimplifies "complex problems in her thinking." Gordon asserts that, "it is difficult but necessary to comprehend that she pursued this tactic in defense of universal suffrage."[74]

Mott's perspective at that time suggests the validity of all these views. She objected to Stanton's seemingly reckless pursuit of women's suffrage and fully supported the enfranchisement of African American men, resigning from the American Equal Rights Association after Stanton's reactionary turn. Nevertheless, Mott loved both Stanton and Anthony, and declined to see them as enemies. After her departure from the American Equal Rights Association, Mott endorsed the idea of independent conventions devoted to women's suffrage. In January 1869, she presided over the first women's suffrage (as opposed to women's rights) convention in Washington, D.C., organized by Josephine Griffing and the Universal Franchise Association. But the divisions in the American Equal Rights Association were on full display in Washington. The *History of Woman Suffrage,* edited by Stanton and Anthony, described this convention as "the first public occasion when the women opposed to the XIV Amendment, measuring their logic with Republicans, Abolitionists, and colored men, ably maintained their position." Mott's son-in-law Edward M. Davis, Frederick Douglass, and Robert Purvis's son Dr. Charles Burleigh Purvis argued that women should "hold their claims in abeyance" until African American men gained the right to vote. Robert Purvis was the only African American man to oppose them, demanding "for his daughter all he asked for his son or himself."[75] Mott's remarks at this convention were not recorded, but both sides saw her as a peacemaker. Grace Greenwood, writing for the *Philadelphia Press,* described her as the "dear, revered Lucretia Mott," who "sanctioned" and "sanctified" the meeting with her presence. Kansas Republican Sam Wood was more blunt: "Mrs. Mott is a splendid old lady. She has more sense than a hundred Susan B's."[76]

Four months later, Mott's "sanctifying" presence was missing at the explosive final meeting of the American Equal Rights Association. Desiring her sanction, and in denial over her resignation, the conference organizers listed Mott as president. And, despite Mott's notable absence, Stanton used her name in order to advocate for a Sixteenth Amendment enfranchising women: "Think of Patrick and Sambo and Hans and Yung Tung, who do not know the difference between a monarchy and a republic, who cannot read the Declaration of Independence or Webster's Spelling book, making laws for Lucretia Mott, Ernestine L. Rose, Susan B. Anthony, or Anna E. Dickinson." Mott did not comment on Stanton's reference to the "lower orders" of manhood. She undoubtedly sympathized with Frederick Douglass's retort that "When women, because they are women, are hunted down through the cities of New York and New Orleans; when they are dragged from their houses and hung upon lamp-posts . . . when their children are not allowed to enter schools; then they will have an urgency to obtain the ballot equal to our own." Lucy Stone also saw the value of the Fifteenth Amendment.

Though she understood Stanton's devotion to the female sex, Stone stated, "I thank God for that XV amendment, and I hope that it will be adopted in every state."[77]

Mott was present the next day when women's rights activists met to consider forming a national women's suffrage organization. The personal and political wounds of the previous years were evident in the "whisperg. and unsettlemt." on the platform. Witnessing this discord, Lucretia expressed nostalgia for the early women's rights conventions. As she described to Martha: "I didn't like Susan B.A. and E.C.S. sittg. there on the back ground like—a side box on the platform—Altho' they make some mistakes—and perhaps mis statements . . . yet I cant bear to have them ignored in any way." Two opposing factions had formed, one around Stanton and Anthony, the other around Lucy Stone and Henry Blackwell. Mott ascribed the "wide separatn." to "personal dissension" following Stanton and Anthony's alliance with Train. "No chance of reunion," Mott commented.[78]

Instead, by the end of the year, two rival women's suffrage organizations existed. Stanton and Anthony formed the National Woman Suffrage Association in May 1869, and Stone organized the American Woman Suffrage Association in November 1869. In the beginning, Mott remained neutral, attending events organized by both groups. A supporter of the Fifteenth Amendment and an advocate of black civil rights, Mott gravitated toward Stone's American Woman Suffrage Association. Even after their disastrous association with George Francis Train, however, Mott referred to Stanton and Anthony as her "loved co-adjutors."[79]

After the political strain of the immediate postwar years, Lucretia's heart and mind were not in the women's suffrage movement. Anticipating the Washington, D.C., women's suffrage convention, she had told Martha, "The ball is well in motion, & numbers of new names appear, entering in to the toilsome service of rolling sd. ball—glad my day is over."[80] But her day was not yet over. Women's rights activists continued to pursue her favor. Lucretia also supported a new organization named the Free Religious Association. And, after the violence of the Civil War, she devoted herself to peace.

CHAPTER 12

Peace

ON MARCH 10, 1870, THE WOMEN of the Philadelphia Female Anti-Slavery Society held their final monthly meeting. Four of the original members, Mott, Sarah Pugh, Margaretta Forten, and Sidney Ann Lewis, were present. For thirty-six years, they had circulated and signed petitions, sponsored lectures, published their resolutions and annual reports, and sewed in fair circles. From 1836 to 1861, their anti-slavery fairs had raised a total of $36,205.23, or $884,000 today. This interracial group had also endured scorn and violence from without, as well as ideological divisions within. All other female anti-slavery societies had collapsed under the pressure. During their long history, many of their coworkers had died, including Esther Moore and Grace Douglass. The previous month, Lucretia's sister Eliza Yarnall had died of pneumonia at age seventy-five. Lucretia remembered that "We were like twin sisters 10 months the longest time we were ever separated." Though Eliza was not a member, the Philadelphia Female Anti-Slavery Society acknowledged her death. After reminiscing, the women dispensed with business, voting to donate their remaining funds to the *National Anti-Slavery Standard*. This quiet meeting laid the groundwork for a concluding celebration to be held on March 24. They invited scattered former members, like Elizabeth Neall Gay and Sarah McKim, to the gathering.[1]

When Mott opened the meeting at the Assembly Building, which had long welcomed abolitionists, she was overcome with emotion. She told the crowd that, "her heart was so full that there was room only for a feeling of thankfulness." She remembered their lowly origins in 1833, when members risked having their names "cast out as evil." This small band of women never imagined living to see their work completed. She told her allies, "The Lord had triumphed gloriously." Other speakers included Edward M. Davis, Robert Purvis, and Aaron Powell, editor of the *National Anti-Slavery Standard*. The Philadelphia Female Anti-Slavery Society displayed its minute books on tables, and at the end of the meeting donated them to the Historical Society of Pennsylvania. Margaretta Forten offered the society's final resolution, "that the Philadelphia Female Anti-Slavery Society, grateful for the part allotted to it in this great work, and rejoicing in the victory which has concluded the long conflict between Slavery and Freedom in America, does now and hereby disband."[2]

Mary Grew, for many years the society's corresponding secretary and the author of its annual reports, agreed. Her last annual report, however, reflects members' ongoing concern with the problem of racism in American society. Grew commented on the continuing strength of racial prejudice, evident in "negro pews," segregated schools, and exclusion of blacks from labor unions and organizations like the American Medical Association. She wrote, "Neither State nor Church is yet really converted to Christianity." For most members, the end of the Philadelphia Female Anti-Slavery Society did not mean retirement. Though their work as an anti-slavery society was accomplished, Grew suggested, "the debt which we owe [the anti-slavery cause] can be redeemed only by faithful service in other fields of labor."[3]

Only slightly slowed by age, Mott's commitment to racial equality was undiminished. She complained of her poor health, lack of appetite, bad digestion, and faulty memory. In an 1872 letter to her sister Martha, Lucretia admitted that she weighed only 76 ½ pounds. Still, with James' generous bequest, Mott continued to donate funds to educate and aid former slaves. And her interest in Philadelphia's African American population continued. With sixty-eight year old Dillwyn Parrish, son of Dr. Joseph Parrish, as her companion, she spoke at every black church in greater Philadelphia. She was also a regular donor and visitor to the Aged Colored Home in West Philadelphia, twenty miles from Roadside. And her interest in a broad range of reforms, including peace, free religion, and women's rights, continued to take her across the northeast.[4]

After the carnage of the Civil War, Mott deepened her commitment to pacifism. As a Quaker, she had always borne testimony against war. As an abolitionist, she adhered to the strategies of moral suasion and nonresistance, moral weapons used to attack the bulwark of institutions upholding slavery, including the church, state, and military. Though she supported the black troops stationed at Camp William Penn, she opposed their deployment.

These beliefs linked her to the most radical group of pacifists in the United States. In 1866, these activists founded the Universal Peace Union. The same year, Mott and her friend and fellow Quaker Alfred Love began its Pennsylvania branch, the Pennsylvania Peace Society. Mott regularly served as president or officer of both organizations.[5]

The primary goal of the Universal Peace Union was to "remove the causes and abolish the customs of war."[6] And, like the anti-slavery movement, its effort was necessarily international. In 1870, as war between France and Germany raged in Europe, Lucretia's old friend Richard D. Webb wrote asking for contributions to ameliorate its "awful ravages and sufferg." Lucretia responded that there was "more life and interest in Peace meetings now than ever before." "Even the woman question, as far as voting goes," she told him, "does not take hold of my every feeling as does War." Lucretia hoped the Franco-Prussian war had opened "eyes & consciences to the unchristian— the wicked—the barbarous resort to murderous weapons."[7]

To change the *"will of the people,"* the Universal Peace Union and its branches bombarded the American public with pamphlets.[8] Even Lucretia admitted, "they print too much"; her granddaughter vowed to enlist if she received another letter on the back of a peace pamphlet. The Universal Peace Union also advocated arbitration, disarmament, and an international court. As a model, Mott and her coworkers endorsed the successful Treaty of Washington in 1871, which called for an international tribunal to meet in Geneva, Switzerland, to settle U.S. grievances against Great Britain for supplying the Confederate Navy in violation of its stated neutrality.[9]

Mott and her fellow pacifists also attacked customs that they believed inculcated a thirst for violence in Americans. At a November 1869 meeting of the Pennsylvania Peace Society, Mott applauded the abolition of corporal punishment in schools, "a specie of barbarism that our intellects had outgrown." But, at another meeting she decried schools "in which war is taught as a system." Describing the martial fervor of post-Civil War America, she told fellow activists, "To-day there is so much effort made to educate men in the principles of war, that they . . . learn to murder one another." She also criticized "the toys that are given to children, that in many instances are calculated to awaken a love of military trappings." After attending a Decoration (Memorial) Day ceremony, Mott bemoaned "such playg. soldier as there was!—'tis awful." Finally, Mott and her allies opposed capital punishment, the continued existence of which caused Lucretia to "blush" and "hang down" her head.[10]

Importantly, Mott held women accountable for their violent society. In

1846, as hostility between the U.S. and Great Britain simmered, she had written that war was the harvest of "seed sown by the mother's hand."[11] Three decades later, she told a women's peace festival that, "I have often resisted the impression that woman differs so widely from man, and I think we have not the facts to substantiate it." She observed that men had been the leading voices for peace in the U.S., while "women have very generally encouraged war, and in the late strife in our country the women on both sides took an active part and encouraged the men." Following their outburst of patriotic support for Union or Confederate forces, women had only recently embraced the cause of peace, and Mott doubted their enfranchisement would end "these evils."[12] Though she did not mention her by name, Mott referred to Julia Ward Howe, author of the Civil War anthem "Battle Hymn of the Republic" and a member of Lucy Stone's American Woman Suffrage Association. An officer of the Universal Peace Union, Howe also organized women's peace congresses, arguing that mothers were innately opposed to war. "You say that women should not vote because they cannot fight," Howe told a Boston audience, "and I say that women should vote because they cannot fight." Publicly, Mott welcomed new reformers like Howe. In private, however, Lucretia contrasted "these 11th hour J. W. Howes" to longtime activists like Stanton.[13]

Mott's involvement in the Universal Peace Union also led her back to the "claims" of Native Americans.[14] Thirty years earlier, the proposed removal of Seneca Indians from western New York engaged her attention. Native Americans in the west now faced a similar combination of greedy settlers and hostile governments. In November 1872, the U.S. army tried to force Chief Captain Jack and Modoc Indians onto a reservation in northern California. The Modocs resisted, but they had no chance of victory against the U.S. army. On April 11, 1873, they resorted to murder, killing two peace commissioners and Brigadier General Edward Canby. Captain Jack and five other Modocs were sentenced to death. The Universal Peace Union sent a delegation to Washington to ask President Ulysses Grant for clemency. Upon learning that Grant was visiting her neighbor Jay Cooke, Mott hurried over to confront the president in person. As she had in the anti-slavery movement, Mott advocated a combative pacifism, waging war with her voice. President Grant listened as the tiny eighty-year-old woman argued against capital punishment. Before she left, he whispered in her ear, "Madam, they will not all be executed." He spared two men, hanging Captain Jack and three others.[15]

The Modoc War forced Mott to consider whether she, or any other Quaker, had done enough for Indians. In a speech to pacifists, she reflected on

Friends' successful intervention after the Treaty of Buffalo Creek. She praised a handful of Quakers like Griffith Cooper and Joseph Walton, "willing to sacrifice their time and leave their families," as "truly alive" to the plight of Native Americans. In contrast to the anti-slavery movement, however, Indian reform fell short. Mott criticized Quakers, and by extension, herself: "we have never considered the wrongs of the Indian as our own. We have aided in driving them further and further west, until as the poor Indian has said, 'You will drive us away, until we go beyond the setting sun.'"[16] Apart from her tolerance of their traditional religious practices, Mott had not identified with Native American men and women. She may have finally realized the inadequacies of her old Indian Committee, whose attempts to remake the Seneca in the political and domestic image of whites now seemed condescending.

Mott also maintained an active interest in liberal religion. In 1867, she attended the founding meeting of the Free Religious Association, organized by radical Unitarians who felt stifled by their conservative denomination. Though she initially balked at the invitation—she told Unitarian minister Octavius B. Frothingham that she was "old, and feeble, and nearly worn out"—she later rejoiced at the existence of this small organization of likeminded religious radicals.[17] The Free Religious Association embraced many of Mott's core beliefs: nonsectarianism, religious freedom, practical religion, and rationalism. Furthermore, the organization required no "test of speculative or religious belief" for membership.[18] As a result, the association welcomed liberals of all religions, including Quakers, Jews, and Spiritualists. Rabbi Isaac Wise was one of the founding directors; Felix Adler, who later founded the Society for Ethical Culture, also joined. In addition to Mott, other female members included Hannah Stevenson, a friend of the late Theodore Parker, and Ednah Dow Cheney, founder of the New England Woman's Club. Both women were active in the New England Freedmen's Aid Society.[19]

Mott's speech to the Free Religionists in Boston justified the new organization by reference to her own troubled relationship to the Society of Friends. Mott objected to being introduced as a representative of the Quakers. After years of criticism from both Orthodox and Hicksite Friends, Mott emphasized, "I am here, as some say, 'on my own hook.'" She admitted, however, to being "much attached to the organization to which I belong." Despite her own devotion to the Society of Friends, she recommended that the Free Religious Association recognize "the come-outer element," encouraging "dissent from organization." Accordingly, she defined herself as a "kind of outlaw in my own society." Mott concluded with her hope that the convention produce "so enlarged a charity and so enlarged an idea of religion, and of the proper cultivation of the religious nature and element in man, as to be able to bear all things."[20]

Between 1867 and 1875, Mott made six trips to Boston, staying with Anna Davis Hallowell in Medford, to attend meetings of the Free Religious Association. She spoke to the organization on many now familiar topics. Mott opposed the use of the Bible as an authority, stating, "I cannot accept its inspiration as a whole, and cannot see why it should be read as a book of worship in the schools or in the churches." Instead, she advised, "let us recognize revelation and truth wherever we find it." She referred to Sabbath observance as superstitious and to Jesus as a non-conformist. Her definition of free religion invoked the Quaker inner light. Lucretia believed that "love, and justice, and mercy, and right" are "innate, self-defined." She told her audience, still largely composed of Harvard-educated ministers, "divine power will be ours, if we seek it; and when these principles are stated they are self-evident, they need no learned oratory."[21]

Mott's lasting contribution to the association came in the form of a constitutional amendment in 1874. One object of the Free Religious Association was "to promote the scientific study of theology." Mott suggested this phrase be changed to read, "to encourage the scientific study of the religious nature or element in man—the ever-present Divine inspiration." She opposed any effort to "define God." Mott quoted her old friend George Combe that "it is greatly to be regretted that theology has ever been connected with religion; and religion so much injured by the conjunction." Finally, she wondered whether a scientific study of theology was even possible: "Is not the basis of all science, fact, demonstration, or self-evident truth? Can we create a science on our speculations?"[22]

When in Boston, Mott also attended meetings of Unitarian minister John Turner Sargent's Radical Club. The gatherings attracted a vibrant group of Free Religionists, reformers, and intellectuals, including John Weiss, Octavius Frothingham, Thomas Wentworth Higginson, Elizabeth Peabody, Hannah Stevenson, Ednah Dow Cheney, and Wendell Phillips. Mott heard presentations by Dr. Frederick Henry Hedge of Harvard Divinity School on pantheism (Mott described it as "hifluton" in some parts and "scientific & metaphysical" in others) and Harvard scientist Dr. Nathaniel Southgate Shaler on Darwin's theory of evolution. Bolstering as it did her faith in scientific knowledge and human progress, Mott pronounced Shaler's talk excellent.[23]

Mott's intellectual engagement provided an important distraction during a period of profound grief. Her daughter-in-law and niece, Marianna Pelham Mott, had escorted Mott to the first meeting of the Free Religious Association. In 1872, Marianna died of a stroke in Europe. Two years later, Mott's old friend Miller McKim died at age sixty-four at his home in New Jersey. In August of that year, Mott's oldest daughter Anna Hopper died after a five-month battle with throat cancer. Lucretia wrote Pattie, "It is all inexpressibly sad, & I have no life for anythg."[24] Lucretia had lost not only a daughter but a longtime coworker in the Philadelphia Female Anti-Slavery Society. Anna was also a member of the Board of Managers for Swarthmore College, founded in 1869. The coeducational Quaker institution was another family project. James Mott had also served on the Board of Managers. At the opening ceremony, Lucretia had planted two oak trees. She told Pattie and George Lord it was a "perfect Establishmt."[25] Then, only a month after Anna's death, her eighteen-year-old son Isaac Hopper died of typhoid fever.

Perhaps most shocking was the death of Lucretia's youngest sister and only surviving sibling, Martha Wright. After a brief struggle with typhoid pneumonia, Martha died at her daughter Ellen Wright Garrison's home in Boston on January 4, 1875.[26] Since their mother's death in 1844, Lucretia and Martha had formed a close bond, exchanging regular letters and visits between Philadelphia and Auburn. Together, they had attended the Seneca Falls women's rights convention. Though Lucretia tried to remain neutral after the breakup of the American Equal Rights Association, Martha joined Stanton's National Woman's Suffrage Association, serving as president of its New York branch. In 1870, after the *Nation*, founded by Miller McKim and his son-in-law Wendell Phillips Garrison, repeatedly attacked the women's rights movement as "gross folly," Martha wrote short, scathing letters to the magazine. Lucretia cheered her sister and bemoaned McKim's conservatism. She described the magazine as "hateful": "Some of the comments on our movet are base—out-Heraldg. the old Herald in Anti Slav[er]y days." Of McKim, Lucretia only commented, "He is a strange talker now a days."[27]

In a letter to Martha's daughter, Eliza Wright Osborne, Lucretia repeated the anguished language she had used after learning of Anna Hopper's diagnosis: "How sad it all is!" Lucretia also thanked Eliza for the keepsake of Martha's red shawl. The rest of her letter was filled with concern for Martha's husband, "poor, dear, stricken brother David," and her adult children. Lucretia imagined Martha's home in Auburn as "desolate" without her, and she wondered how David would manage everything on his own. Martha's death was a "severe blow."[28]

Martha Wright's biographers argue that she was a more "ardent" suffragist than her sister; Lucretia would have agreed.[29] Especially after bitter fights between abolitionists and feminists in Kansas, Lucretia withdrew herself from the women's rights movement, frequently invoking her age as an excuse. But her reluctance also reflected deep-seated reservations. Requests for her help, such as gathering signatures for petitions, literally made Lucretia sick. She had "ached" after meeting with Stanton and Anthony in 1866. An 1871 visit from Paulina Wright Davis, Mott wrote, brought on "water brash— I excused myself & retired—had a great 'frowg. [throwing] up' time."[30] Mott had always suffered from bad digestion, and water brash (or acid reflux) was one of her symptoms. Her intense physical reaction to Davis's visit also suggests anxiety and even revulsion. Personal tensions among her friends and fellow activists undoubtedly contributed to her stress. After the struggles in the Society of Friends and the American Anti-Slavery Society, Mott had no stomach for organizational schism or movement infighting. And, given the criticism of her speech to the 1859 women's rights convention, she may have dreaded more uninspired speeches on women's suffrage.

Furthermore, Mott's illness may have been an unconscious rebellion against the goals of the women's movement, which now privileged suffrage, particularly for white women, above other issues. Mott had always insisted on equality, but she blanched at fighting so openly for her own interests over those of African Americans. Also, as someone who valued purity over politics, she viewed the women's rights movement as hopelessly compromised. In 1872, Lucretia insisted to Elizabeth Cady Stanton that, "I must be allowed to be a cypher."[31] Still, her desire to hide did not mean she lost all interest in women's rights. Mott relied on Martha and her son-in-law Edward M. Davis to lend their time, energy, money, and voices to the cause. And a conflicted Mott attended lectures and conventions, read newspapers including the new *Woman's Journal*, published by the American Woman Suffrage Association, and lent her famous name to the movement.

The deep divide between the two newly formed suffrage associations forced Mott to juggle her friendships and her ideals. In March 1870, she received a letter from Theodore Tilton, editor of the *Independent*, who hoped to reconcile the American Woman Suffrage Association and the National Woman Suffrage Association. Mott agreed "willingly" to have her name attached to his letter. She recalled that she had pleaded with "active workers on both sides in Boston [AWSA] & New York [NWSA]" to "have one universal society." Mott wrote, "I hope it is not too late for this proposed union to take place."[32] On April 6, with Pattie Lord as her escort, Mott attended Tilton's arbitration in New York City. Representing the American Woman Suffrage Association were Lucy Stone, Thomas Wentworth Higginson, and George Curtis. Josephine Griffing, Parker Pillsbury and Charlotte Wilbour attended on behalf of the National Woman Suffrage Association. Mott described the meeting in a letter to her sister Martha: "Quite a free talk, & several proposals made—none of wh[ich] acceded to, by the 3 from Boston. . . . I went 'not expectg. great things, & I didn't get 'em.'" Lucretia's account shows her own (and Martha's) bias toward Stanton, Anthony, and the National Association. Pattie, probably the only truly neutral person in the room, thought Tilton "too much a partizan on their side ["the Stanton-Anthony side"] to be an impartial outsider—ditto her mother." Lucretia concluded she was "glad to be out of it all, & never mean to join another Organizatn."[33]

Pattie had accurately assessed her mother's sympathies. Though she repeatedly denied any partisanship, Mott clearly—and to her great discomfort—favored the National Woman Suffrage Association. In October 1870, Paulina Wright Davis organized a "Second Decade Convention" to celebrate the twentieth anniversary of the first national women's rights convention at Worcester. Mott agreed to have her name placed on the call, but only if the Boston party were invited.[34] When it met in New York City, however, the Second Decade Convention was decidedly a National Association affair. Convention attendees included Mott, Martha Wright, Stanton, Anthony, and Paulina Wright Davis. Aside from Mott, only two women, Sarah Pugh and Caroline Stratton, represented Philadelphia. According to Mott, the sympathies of most Philadelphia activists lay with the American Woman Suffrage Association. Since the women of the Philadelphia Female Anti-Slavery Society had endorsed the Fifteenth Amendment, this is not surprising. The presence of Pugh and Stratton probably resulted more from Mott's influence than any spirit of bipartisanship. In addition to listing the delegates, newspaper reports commented on the "saintly beauty" of the "good, motherly-looking Quakeress," Lucretia Mott.[35]

At the convention, Davis read a short "History of the Woman's Rights Movement." Though she attempted neutrality, Davis's account favored the Stanton-Anthony faction, especially in her portrayal of the post-Civil War period. Davis traced women's rights in the United States from the early bravery of Frances Wright to "new workers" like Anna Dickinson, Charlotte Wilbour, and (in acknowledgement of the American Association) Julia Ward Howe. She mentioned important events leading up to the Worcester

Convention, such as Mary S. Gove's physiology lectures, the Anti-Slavery Conventions of American Women, and the World Anti-Slavery Convention. Despite this nod to anti-slavery, she also included the recent Kansas campaign and George Francis Train, leaving for history to decide if his participation was "for good or ill." And she described the "injustice" of enfranchising black men over white women. The convention proceedings, published by Davis with her "History," describe the apparently effusive response of Stanton and Mott. Stanton, who planned to write her own history of the women's rights movement, noted its "historical accuracy and completeness." When approached by Stanton in 1855, Mott had offered a brief history of Quaker and Nantucket women. At the Second Decade convention, she suggested Davis include some of this information, pointing out that, "Among Quakers there had never been any talk of woman's rights—it was simply human rights; and in Nantucket, which was founded by the Quakers, the women had always transacted business."[36] Davis did not follow her advice, and she also ignored Mott's use of the term *human* rights, which pointed to even more glaring omissions. Davis's "History" failed to mention any African American women or men. And Sojourner Truth and Frederick Douglass, both present at the Worcester Convention, did not attend the Second Decade Convention. The leaders of the National Woman Suffrage Association had not only heeded Jane Swisshelm's early advice to separate the issues of race and sex, they had purged African Americans themselves from the history and leadership of the movement.[37]

Though her commitment to the Fifteenth Amendment should have inclined her toward the American Woman Suffrage Association, Mott objected to the Boston party's emphasis on respectability. Most members of the American Association disapproved of a talented new activist affiliated with the New Yorkers: Victoria Woodhull, a divorcée and clairvoyant from a family of itinerant hucksters. In 1868, Woodhull and her sister Tennessee Claflin had developed an intimate friendship with the exemplar of American economic progress "Commodore" Cornelius Vanderbilt. With Vanderbilt's backing, the sisters opened the first female brokerage firm on Wall Street. Woodhull began attending women's rights conventions, and by January 1871 she represented the women's suffrage movement in a speech before the House Judiciary Committee. Woodhull argued that the Fourteenth Amendment had included women in its definition of citizenship. As a result, women's continued exclusion from the right to vote was a violation of the Fourteenth and Fifteenth Amendments. Woodhull told suffragists, "We *will have* our rights.

We say no longer by your leave. We have besought, argued, and convinced, but we have failed; *and we will not* fail."[38]

Based in part on Woodhull's legal argument, the National Woman Suffrage Association adopted an aggressive strategy, encouraging women around the country to assert their right to vote by registering and going to the polls. In Philadelphia, Edward M. Davis organized the Citizen's Suffrage Association on this principle. In November 1872, Susan B. Anthony was arrested at her home in Rochester, New York, for voting in the presidential election. As she told Stanton, she "had gone and done it!!—positively voted the Republican ticket—strait."[39]

For members of the American Woman Suffrage Association, Woodhull's political genius was undermined by her willingness to flaunt social conventions. Woodhull collaborated with Stephen Pearl Andrews, the free love advocate who scandalized the 1858 women's rights convention in New York City. And, in her speeches and writings, Woodhull attacked the institution of marriage as "sexual slavery." In an 1871 speech, she advocated "one sexual standard for all": "Women must rise from their position as *ministers* to the passions of men to be their equals. . . . They must be trained to be *like* men, permanent and independent individualities, and not their mere appendages or adjuncts, with them forming but one member of society. They must be companions of men from *choice, never* from necessity."[40] At an American Woman Suffrage Association meeting in May 1871, Mott was one of the few reformers present to oppose a resolution directed at Woodhull and complaining of "recent attempts in this city [New York] and elsewhere to associate the Woman Suffrage cause with the doctrine of Free Love."[41]

Mott also jumped to Woodhull's defense the following year. In the November 2, 1872 issue of her newspaper, *Woodhull & Claflin's Weekly*, Woodhull exposed the Rev. Henry Ward Beecher's affair with a parishioner, Elizabeth Tilton, wife of newspaper editor Theodore Tilton. Woodhull revealed the relationship in an attempt to challenge what she saw as the hypocrisy of religious leaders who preached morality but practiced free love. After Woodhull's arrest for violating obscenity laws, most of her friends and allies ran from any association with her name, including, according to Mott, Elizabeth Cady Stanton and Edward Davis. Before she knew of the truth of Woodhull's charges, Mott speculated that she was insane. Still, she thought, "It is a great outrage to imprison her on such a charge." Later, Mott described Woodhull's treatment as "hateful."[42]

Mott's support for Woodhull grew from her dislike of prudery. Mott detested efforts to suppress frank discussions of sex or biology in the name of modesty. She believed modesty was another social custom confining women to a state of ignorance and inferiority. In 1873, Congress passed the broad "Act for the Suppression of Trade in, and Circulation of, Obscene Literature and Articles for Immoral Use," also known as the Comstock Act for its originator Anthony Comstock, a religious New York businessman and Union Army veteran concerned about the pervasiveness of sex in American culture. Under the new law, Comstock had the power to police everything from pornography to contraception to prostitution. Mott commented, "Comstock's power ought to be limited or taken away." In late 1877, Comstock arrested Ezra Heywood, a free love advocate and author of *Cupid's Yoke*, a pamphlet discussing methods of limiting conception. The following year, President Rutherford B. Hayes, concluding that the book should not be classified as obscene, pardoned Heywood. Mott wrote Gerrit Smith's daughter, Elizabeth Smith Miller, "glad Heywood is at liberty."[43]

After her 1875 trip to the Free Religious Association meeting in Boston, Mott seldom traveled far from home. When she did attend local and national reform conventions, her old friends and allies seized upon the opportunity to bid her farewell. In 1876, the National Woman Suffrage Association temporarily moved its operations to Philadelphia for the celebration of the nation's centennial. Suffragists hoped to be included in the ceremonies, with official sanction given their "Declaration of the Rights of the Women of the United States," written by Stanton, Anthony, Matilda Joslyn Gage, and Sara Spencer. The new Declaration reflected activists' years of struggle. They protested the insertion of the word "male" into the federal and state constitutions. And they described universal male suffrage as creating an "aristocracy of sex." They concluded, "we ask of our rulers, at this hour, no special favors, no special privileges, no special legislation. We ask justice, we ask equality, we ask that all civil and political rights that belong to citizens of the United States, be guaranteed to us and our daughters forever."[44] Stanton wanted the new Declaration "lithographed, framed, & signed by those who inaugurated the movement for women's enfranchisement." After Mott called at their Philadelphia headquarters, Susan B. Anthony wrote in her diary, "*her name must go* first into the Centennial Autograph Book."[45]

The suffragists' plans were thwarted when organizers refused to give them a place on the platform. On July 4, 1876, after Richard Lee, a former Confederate general and descendent of a delegate to the Continental Congress, read the Declaration of Independence, Susan B. Anthony and three other suffragists walked onto the stage. Stanton described what happened next: "Susan walked up to Mr Ferry the presiding officer . . . & presented ours of 1876. It was nicely rolled up, & tied with red, white, & blue ribbons[.] Mr Ferry rose up made a graceful bow & received it, although he & Gen Hawley had forbidden us even to present it, a ceremony that would not occupy *a single minute*."

The suffragists then held their own meeting in William Henry Furness's Unitarian Church on Pine Street. Mott presided over the meeting, and she was "so full of the subject, its memories & promises that she made half a dozen speeches of wit & wisdom." After one of her short speeches, the Hutchinsons, a family of anti-slavery singers, began the hymn "Nearer, My God, to Thee." The whole congregation joined in to honor Mott. In appreciation for Anthony's months of labor organizing the event, Mott gave her ten dollars "for thy own *personal* use." Acknowledging the difficulties of self-supporting female activists, she wrote, "It is too hard for our widely extended National Socy. to suffer thee to labor so unceasingly without a consideratn."[46]

Mott's last national appearance occurred in July 1878 at the thirtieth anniversary celebration of the Seneca Falls and Rochester women's rights conventions. This "Third Decade" celebration occurred only eight years after Davis's "Second Decade" event, revealing a simmering internal debate over which conventions deserved recognition. Though Mott had an uneasy relationship to the contemporary women's suffrage movement, she and Sarah Pugh made the long journey from Philadelphia to Rochester. Other original signers of the Seneca Falls Declaration of Sentiments also attended, including Amy Post, Elizabeth Cady Stanton, and Frederick Douglass, still a strong supporter of women's rights.

Two newspapers, each representing a different faction of the women's rights movement, printed Mott's speech at the convention. The American Woman Suffrage Association's newspaper, the *Woman's Journal*, garbled Mott's words to suggest that, if granted the right to vote, women would "elect into office only those who are pure in intention and honest in sentiment." While many women's rights activists espoused the idea that women's enfranchisement would purify and reform government, Mott did not. She believed women were no different from men. It is more likely that her message mixed her condemnation of political corruption with a statement of simple equality and capability: "Place women in equal power, and you will find her capable of not abusing it. . . . Forbid her not, and she will use moderation."[47] Matilda Joslyn Gage, a Stanton-Anthony ally and the editor of *National Citizen and*

Ballot Box, did not report Mott's remarks on suffrage. Instead, Gage recorded her participation in discussion of two resolutions on the right of "individual conscience" and the insidious influence of "priestcraft and superstition." Gage believed organized religion was a fundamental source of women's oppression. Since this topic had always been central to Mott's ministry, it was fitting that she spoke in favor of these resolutions in Rochester. Mott distinguished between "true Christianity and theological creed." Significantly, neither she nor Frederick Douglass mentioned women's subjugation in their remarks. Instead, they both spoke on morality and self-sacrifice. Perhaps thinking of some suffragists' unwillingness to sacrifice for black men's voting rights, Mott told the audience that, "true righteousness and goodness were the only right for the correction of a wrong." The two competing newspapers agreed on one thing. After Mott finished, the entire convention rose to its feet. Speaking for the convention, a sixty-year-old Frederick Douglass said "Good-bye."[48]

Mott surely appreciated these tributes, but she also found them embarrassing. "I'm a very much overrated woman," she told her family, "it is humiliating." And she was understandably reluctant to be eulogized before her time. After reading a biographical article in the *Index*, published by the Free Religious Association, Lucretia commented, "It's better not to be in a hurry with obituaries.[49] She claimed not to fear death, however, viewing it as "the order of nature . . . natural and right." As always, she abhorred superstitions about "the dissolution of the body, the passage of the spirit, the exchange of worlds." Death, she argued, had been turned into a "bugbear" by "old and severe theologies." It has been "held over the human soul like a rod of terror." Though she mourned her own relatives even to the point of depression, Lucretia described death as "an occasion of much joyfulness—the inward peace of the soul."[50]

In several of her final speeches, Mott mentioned remarks made by poet and newspaper editor William Cullen Bryant that emphasized their shared belief in progress. Bryant was one year younger than Mott, but the two famous figures had little in common aside from their age. A critic of slavery, Bryant was very much a figure of American politics. An ardent Jacksonian Democrat, he later supported the Free Soil and Republican parties. At his eightieth birthday party, Cullen gave an "interesting review of this century." Mott enjoyed reading Bryant's account of the many and marvelous changes they had witnessed. Byrant, somewhat anachronistically, called the Gilded Age an "age of charity." He argued that, "The people of civilized countries have become more enlightened, and enjoy a greater degree of freedom. They have become especially more humane and sympathetic, more disposed to alleviate each others' sufferings." Bryant described the end of slavery as one example of new attention to the "the liberties and rights of the humbler classes." Most important, Bryant and Mott agreed that "universal peace" should be "one of the next great changes." He called for armies to be disbanded and soldiers returned to their "fields and workshops."[51] Their last common goal also proved to be the most elusive.

In May 1880, Mott made her final public appearance at Philadelphia Yearly Meeting. Maria Davis, who lived with her husband at Roadside, escorted her "festive young mother of 87." As she commented to her sister Pattie, "she always did thrive on a spree." Maria described the amazing scene: "It was an ovation every day in the multitudes who came 'just to take her by the hand'—and the only way to escape this, for it was very exhausting, was to leave the meeting just before the closing minute read." Someone sitting directly behind Maria and her mother whispered, "Well, Lucretia has outlived her persecutors."[52] Once an outcast for her participation in the anti-slavery movement, Hicksite Quakers now revered Mott as a minister and elder. Her dedication to the Society of Friends had also made an impact. As Mott wrote five years earlier, Philadelphia Yearly Meeting was "much more liberal than formerly." They had even taken steps to equalize and join men's and women's separate meetings.[53]

Mott's frailty now confined her to Roadside. Her family gathered around her. Lucretia received letters and visits from old friends and admirers, including Mary Grew, Robert Collyer, Oliver Johnson, and Lucy Stone. Mary Grew, her long-time coworker in the Philadelphia Female Anti-Slavery Society, wrote, "I want to thank you, before you go, for all that you have been to me; for all the blessedness which has flowed from your soul into my soul, from your life into my life."[54] In a November 1 letter, Lucy Stone described the thirtieth anniversary of the Worcester women's rights convention. Ednah Dow Cheney, Mott's fellow free religionist, had proposed a resolution, "That this convention presents its greetings to its venerable early leader and friend Lucretia Mott, whose life in its rounded perfection as wife, mother, preacher, and reformer is the prophecy of the future of woman." Stone also thanked her for "help given so freely to our inexperience." Through the struggles and tensions of the post-Civil War women's movement, both sides loved Mott as one of their own.[55]

Lucretia fell ill in early November. She was in severe pain and at times incoherent. Two days before her death, she entered a period of "mortal struggle." This once vital woman, whose "go-ahead-ativeness" amused and frustrated her family, was ready to die. According to her granddaughter, she repeated the same phrases over and over again: "Let me go!" "Oh, let me die!" On November 11, at 4:00 p.m., Lucretia cried out, "O my! my! my!" Afterward, she fell asleep, never to awake again. At 7:30 p.m., surrounded by her remaining children, Maria, Thomas, and Pattie, Lucretia took her last breath.[56]

Lucretia was buried next to James in a simple Quaker grave in Fair Hill cemetery. Thousands of people attended her internment. As her granddaughter remembered, everyone was quiet. Someone asked, "Will no one say anything?" Another replied, "Who can speak? The preacher is dead."[57]

Epilogue

LUCRETIA MOTT—OR RATHER HER PUBLIC IMAGE—had a curious afterlife. She was eulogized and memorialized across the country. Her papers at the Friends Historical Library of Swarthmore College contain almost two boxes of sympathy letters, newspaper clippings, and a volume full of obituaries. Paeans to her benevolence and goodness abounded. The *Unitarian Review and Religious Magazine* described her "essential womanliness" as well as her "indescribable mingling of saintliness and sense." Her friend William Henry Furness adapted the beatitudes to remember her "long and saintly life": "Blessed was her spirit, lowly, in self-forgetfulness, for hers was the kingdom of heaven." He remembered that, "she dwelt in the world while she dwelt above it, diffusing happiness all around her." Mary Grew wrote in the *Philadelphia Ledger* that "The name of Lucretia Mott is a synonym for a rare combination of Christian graces." The *Phrenological Journal and Science of Health* paid tribute to her humanitarianism as well as her "unusually large head" and "high quality" brain.[1]

African Americans also mourned her loss. On November 14, 1880, the Rev. Henry Highland Garnet led a memorial service at his Shiloh Presbyterian Church in New York City. The ceremony was planned to coincide with similar events in Boston, Washington, and Baltimore. The *New York Times* reported that the audience "consisted mainly of well-to do colored people." One activist noted that it was a fitting place to remember one "whose life work in behalf of human freedom had been spent so largely in aid of the colored race."[2] African Americans in the District of Columbia donated a floral arrangement in her honor to the National Woman Suffrage Association annual convention. In gratitude, Edward M. Davis delegated Elizabeth Cady Stanton and Susan B. Anthony to present a photograph of Mott to Howard

University, opened in 1866 to students "without regard to color, sex, or previous condition." Mary Clemmer, who wrote about the ceremony for the *Independent*, noted that Mott had fought for "great principles" "when to do so was to bring her womanliness into bitter question." "And yet," she wrote, "in wifehood, in motherhood, in every attribute of affection this woman was as true as any other."[3]

One homage recognized Mott's interest in women's health and her support for female physicians. The year after her death, Anna Forest Rowe, a graduate of Elizabeth Blackwell's Women's Medical College of the New York Infirmary for Woman and Children, opened the Lucretia Mott Dispensary in Brooklyn, New York. Though some Quaker physicians were affiliated with the institution, there is no evidence that Rowe knew Mott. The clinic served poor women and children, and, during its short life, Dr. Rowe treated 15,000 patients and performed almost 350 operations. By 1892, however, Rowe had "wore herself out by service" and had to be forcibly removed. Due to the considerable influence of Rowe's husband, a lawyer, the Lucretia Mott Dispensary was dissolved by an act of the New York State Legislature, which also prohibited the use of the name "Lucretia Mott" in any hospital, infirmary, or dispensary. Since the clinic had engaged in extensive fundraising, and had past experience with attempted fraud, they probably wanted to limit the possibility that a scam artist might try to raise funds in the clinic's name.[4]

Phebe Ann Coffin Hanaford, a suffragist and relative, captured the tone of most memorials in a poem published in the *Christian Recorder*, the newspaper of the African Methodist Episcopal Church. One stanza declared:

> She was a standard-bearer firm and true,
> Though small in stature, yet a giant soul,
> Frail as a lily, yet as spotless, too,
> And mighty in a moral self-control.[5]

Such assessments of Mott's "stainless purity" began during her lifetime. In 1853, Hanaford had published a novel loosely based on Mott called *Lucretia, The Quakeress, or Principle Triumphant*. The story veers wildly from Mott's life when the character Lucretia, a Quaker abolitionist from Nantucket, falls in love with a slaveholder named Morton Fitzroy. She refuses his proposal and dedicates her life to preaching and helping others. After many years, her moral example sways him and, in an unlikely twist, the couple marries, living on Fitzroy's plantation with his happy former slaves. Like many of Mott's obituaries, Hanaford's story and, more importantly, her poem, describe a person, who, frankly, was too good to be true. As women's rights activist Elizabeth Oakes Smith wrote of Lucretia, "she was herself a poem."[6]

These portrayals served an important purpose for the activists who penned them. In the midst of a struggle for leadership in the women's suffrage movement, members of the National Woman Suffrage Association took the lead in memorializing Mott. In January 1881, at the NWSA annual convention in Washington, D.C., Elizabeth Cady Stanton eulogized her mentor as "the sum of all womanly virtues": "As wife, mother, friend, she was marked for her delicate sentiments, warm affections, and steadfast loyalty; as housekeeper, for her rigid economy, cleanliness, order, and exhaustless patience." In a sharp appraisal of the public consciousness, Stanton also observed that many of the writers now praising Mott had vilified her as "an infidel, a fanatic, [and] an unsexed woman" only twenty years earlier. Then Stanton revealed her partisan agenda. Despite evidence to the contrary, she described Mott as "steadfast" and "loyal" to the goals of the National Woman Suffrage Association. And Stanton used Mott's death to make an argument for women's suffrage: "Why are the press and the pulpit, with all their eulogiums of her virtues, so oblivious to the humiliating fact of her disfranchisement?"[7]

This rewriting of Mott's conflicted relationship to the women's rights movement, and particularly the issue of suffrage, gave legitimacy to the National Woman Suffrage Association. In a published reminiscence, lawyer and NWSA lecturer Phebe Couzins wrote that "While Lucretia Mott's character was gentle, sweet, and lovely, let her record also be 'a fearless rebuker of evil and error in both high and low places.'" Here Couzins was not as concerned with evil as with error, because the purpose of Couzins' remembrance was to promote the National Woman Suffrage Association. Like Stanton, Couzins argued that Mott's "devotion to the National Association never swerved from its allegiance from the hour of its formation—in the spring of '69—because she recognized its broad and liberal spirit from the beginning. The American Association, which had seceded, forming a conservative organization with a limited outlook, refused to join with Mrs. Mott."[8]

Couzins' identification of the National Association with broadness and liberality points to the most important reason for invoking Mott's sainted memory. Not only did these commentators tout her as an exemplary woman, Lucretia lent anti-slavery credibility to an organization—and a movement—that faced accusations of racism throughout its history. When the Nineteenth Amendment declared that, "The right of the citizens of the United States to vote shall not be denied or abridged by the United States or by any State on account of sex," black women confronted Jim Crow laws designed to keep them disfranchised. White suffragists ignored these troubles to celebrate their victory. In 1921, Alice Paul's National Woman's Party, an organization instrumental in passing the Nineteenth Amendment, donated a statue of Stanton, Anthony, and Mott to the United States Capitol. African American woman were not invited to the ceremony. Mary White Ovington, a white founder of the National Association for the Advancement of Colored People, wrote, "I think when your statue of Lucretia Mott, Susan B. Anthony and Elizabeth Cady Stanton is unveiled and it is realized that no colored woman has been given any part in your great session, the omission will be keenly felt by thousands of people throughout the country." Adelaide Johnson's sculpture reflected this strange disconnect between Mott's life, especially her critical relationship to the suffrage movement, and the segregated suffrage celebration. Mott's bust sits in front of—and slightly removed from—the busts of Stanton and Anthony.[9]

Despite the adoration of suffragists, Mott does not fit easily into histories of nineteenth-century feminism. In most recent scholarship, she appears only in her relationship to Elizabeth Cady Stanton.[10] But Mott's life suggests a more complicated, racially egalitarian history of early feminism. An early advocate of sexual equality, Mott read Wollstonecraft and defended Fanny Wright when both were extremely unpopular. She believed in liberating women from the social customs, laws, and biblical interpretations that dictated their shallow, confined existence. Her discomfort with the organized women's rights movement began with her opposition to Stanton's suffrage resolution at the Seneca Falls convention. Though Mott attended and presided over women's rights conventions, and devoted speeches and sermons to the topic, she maintained a critical distance. As activists turned their attention to white women's voting rights after the Civil War, her estrangement became even more pronounced. Mott continued to emphasize the relationship of women's rights to other social issues. And, in her impossible role as peacemaker, she criticized the women's suffrage movement without rejecting it.

As feminists celebrated Mott, her former colleagues in the anti-slavery movement forgot her. Abolitionists began to write the history of their movement during Mott's lifetime. These mostly male authors hailed from Massachusetts, New York, and some western states, and their accounts reflected this gender and regional bias. As Julie Roy Jeffrey observes, the first of these books, Samuel J. May's *Some Recollections of our Antislavery Conflict*, devoted significant attention to the actions of male abolitionists. And, though he did acknowledge the labors of notable women, including Mott, he emphasized their beauty, morality, and sentimentality.[11] After William Lloyd Garrison sent her a copy, Lucretia noted it was not a "thorough history" and she suggested that Garrison and Miller McKim unite to publish such a book.[12] Another account, Oliver Johnson's *William Lloyd Garrison and His Times*, similarly glorified and minimized Mott's contributions. He described her as "a shining example of all the virtues that exalt womanhood." Johnson also argued that Mott was among those who had "done the most to break the fetters of the American slaves." After this praise, however, he devoted only one paragraph to her career.[13]

One exception was William Still's *The Underground Rail Road*, published in 1872. As the title suggests, Still focused on the dramatic escapes of fugitive slaves. As a former member of the Pennsylvania Anti-Slavery Society, he also included short biographies of abolitionists from his state. Still did not neglect women, offering sketches of Esther Moore, Lucretia Mott, and others. Though Mott had objected to some aspects of the Underground Railroad, specifically the diversion of funds from abolition and the purchase of fugitives, she aided many escaped slaves. As a result, Still asserted that "this book would be incomplete" without an account of her life. Though his minibiography suffers from the familiar flowery tributes to her noble and pure womanhood, Still effectively captures Mott's radicalism. In contrast to Stanton, Still refers to her as an "enfranchised spirit." He described her as "free from all control, save that of conscience and God." Still wrote, "We cannot think of the partial triumph of freedom in this country, without rejoicing in the great part she took in the victory."[14]

Historians of the anti-slavery movement have continued the tradition of dismissing Mott's contributions. Even after decades of scholarship on female abolitionists, recent histories emphasize the achievements of political and violent abolitionists, most all of whom were men.[15] Yet among white abolitionists, Mott was perhaps the earliest and most consistent proponent of immediate abolition and racial equality. Her commitment to moral suasion, to personal and ideological purity, helped sustain the Philadelphia Female Anti-Slavery Society, one of the longest-lived and most effective abolitionist organizations. For Mott and the Philadelphia Female Anti-Slavery Society, moral suasion represented not only a strategy to end slavery, but a means to achieve racial equality. While they may not have secured the abolition of chattel slavery, they certainly contributed to its demise by raising the nation's consciousness of its evils. And in their own circle, Mott and her allies lived anti-racism to an extent rarely seen in the anti-slavery movement.

Mott repeatedly expressed her desire to be a "cipher" in the women's rights movement. Instead, idealized by her followers, she became a cipher in American history. Her beatification began during her lifetime, and indicated her success in changing American ideas about race, sex, and religion. In a review of Anna Davis Hallowell's *James and Lucretia Mott, Life and Letters*, the *Philadelphia Ledger and Transcript* noted that "there could not be a greater contrast in any century than between the harsh unfriendliness, social and religious, the almost excommunication for conscience sake through which this husband and wife lived their youth and middle age, and the jubilee of acquiescence and triumph which their life's evening knew."[16] Mott should be remembered, not in this evening's haze, but in the midst of heated religious and political struggle. In a period dominated by evangelicalism, Mott's rejection of scriptural and ecclesiastical authority was deeply unsettling to many Americans. Her racial egalitarianism made her unusual even among fellow abolitionists. And her commitment to abolition and racial equality over women's suffrage was unique among feminists. In her time, Lucretia Mott was a true follower of "the way called heresy."[17]

Introduction: Heretic and Saint

1. Daniel Kilbride, "Southern Medical Students in Philadelphia, 1800–1861: Science and Sociability in the 'Republic of Medicine,'" *Journal of Southern History* 65, 4 (1999): 697–732.

2. "Sermon to the Medical Students," in Dana Greene, ed., *Lucretia Mott: Her Complete Speeches and Sermons* (New York: Edwin Mellen, 1980), 82–83, 84, 88–89.

3. "Remarks, Delivered to the Anti-Sabbath Convention," in Greene, 62; "Remarks, Delivered at the Twenty-Fourth Annual Meeting of the Pennsylvania Anti-Slavery Society," in Greene, 262.

4. Declaration of the Anti-Slavery Convention," *Liberator*, Jan. 4, 1834.

5. Jean H. Baker, *Sisters: The Lives of America's Suffragists* (New York: Hill and Wang, 2005), 6. Recent exceptions include Kathryn Kish Sklar, "'Women Who Speak for an Entire Nation': American and British Women at the World Anti-Slavery Convention, London, 1840," in Jean Fagan Yellin and John C. Van Horne, eds., *The Abolitionist Sisterhood: Women's Political Culture in Antebellum America* (Ithaca, N.Y.: Cornell University Press, 1994), 301–33; Nancy Isenberg, "'To Stand Out in Heresy': Lucretia Mott, Liberty, and the Hysterical Woman," *Pennsylvania Magazine of History and Biography* 127, 1 (Jan. 2003): 7–23; Judith Wellman, *The Road to Seneca Falls: Elizabeth Cady Stanton and the First Woman's Rights Convention* (Urbana: University of Illinois Press, 2004); Sally G. McMillen, *Seneca Falls and the Origins of the Women's Rights Movement* (New York: Oxford University Press, 2008).

6. Elizabeth Cady Stanton, Susan B. Anthony, and Matilda Joslyn Gage, *History of Woman Suffrage* (Rochester, N.Y.: Susan B. Anthony, 1887), 1: 420, 424.

7. Margaret Hope Bacon, *Valiant Friend: The Life of Lucretia Mott* (New York: Walker, 1980), cover, 6; Otelia Cromwell, *Lucretia Mott: The Story of One of America's Greatest Women* (Cambridge, Mass.: Harvard University Press, 1958). Other female activists have received significant scholarly attention, for example, Dorothy Sterling, *Ahead of Her Time: Abby Kelley and the Politics of Anti-Slavery* (New York: Norton, 1991); Carolyn L. Karcher, *The First Woman in the Republic: A Cultural Biography of*

Lydia Maria Child (Durham, N.C.: Duke University Press, 1994); Nell Irvin Painter, *Sojourner Truth: A Life, a Symbol* (New York: Norton, 1996); Jean Fagan Yellin, *Harriet Jacobs: A Life* (New York: Basic Books, 2004); Catherine Clinton, *Harriet Tubman: The Road to Freedom* (Boston: Little, Brown, 2004); and Lori D. Ginzberg, *Elizabeth Cady Stanton: An American Life* (New York: Hill and Wang, 2009).

8. Anna Davis Hallowell, *James and Lucretia Mott: Life and Letters* (Boston: Houghton Mifflin, 1884), v, vi.

9. Rebecca Larson, *Daughters of Light: Quaker Women Preaching and Prophesying in the Colonies and Abroad, 1700–1775* (New York: Knopf, 1999), chap. 4; Lisa Tetrault, "The Incorporation of American Feminism: Suffragists and the Postbellum Lyceum," *Journal of American History* 96, 4 (March 2010): 1027–56.

10. Hallowell, 252–54, 353.

11. "Discourse on Woman," in Greene, 154.

12. Beverly Wilson Palmer, Holly Byers Ochoa, and Carol Faulkner, eds., *Selected Letters of Lucretia Coffin Mott* (Urbana: University of Illinois Press, 2002), xvii, xx. For these activists, see especially Louis Ruchames and Walter Merrill, eds., *Letters of William Lloyd Garrison*, 5 vols. (Cambridge, Mass.: Harvard University Press, 1971–81); Henry Mayer, *All on Fire: William Lloyd Garrison and the Abolition of Slavery* (New York: St. Martin's, 1998); Gerda Lerner, *The Grimké Sisters of South Carolina: Rebels Against Slavery* (Boston: Houghton Mifflin, 1967); Larry Ceplair, ed., *The Public Years of Sarah and Angelina Grimké, 1835–1839* (New York: Columbia University Press, 1989); Kathryn Kish Sklar, "'The Throne of My Heart': Religion, Oratory, and Transatlantic Community in Angelina Grimké's Launching of Women's Rights, 1828–1838," in Kathryn Kish Sklar and James Brewer Stewart, eds., *Women's Rights and Transatlantic Antislavery in the Era of Emancipation* (New Haven, Conn.: Yale University Press, 2007), 211–41.

13. Some scholars see the origins of the women's rights movement in the anti-slavery movement, including Ellen Carol Dubois, *Feminism and Suffrage: The Emergence of an Independent Women's Movement in America, 1848–1869* (Ithaca, N.Y.: Cornell University Press, 1978); Yellin and Van Horne, eds., *The Abolitionist Sisterhood*; Kathryn Kish Sklar, *Women's Rights Emerges Within the Antislavery Movement, 1830–1870* (New York: Bedford/St. Martin's, 2000). Others question this connection, including Painter, *Sojourner Truth*; Nancy Isenberg, *Sex and Citizenship in Antebellum America* (Chapel Hill: University of North Carolina Press, 1998); and Julie Roy Jeffrey, *The Great Silent Army of Abolitionism: Ordinary Women in the Antislavery Movement* (Chapel Hill: University of North Carolina Press, 1998).

14. John Stauffer, *The Black Hearts of Men: Radical Abolitionists and the Transformation of Race* (Cambridge, Mass.: Harvard University Press, 2002), 2–3. Other recent examples include Jonathan H. Earle, *Jacksonian Anti-Slavery and the Politics of Free Soil, 1824–1854* (Chapel Hill: University of North Carolina Press, 2003); and Stanley Harrold, *The Rise of Aggressive Abolitionism: Addresses to the Slaves* (Lexington: University Press of Kentucky, 2004). These studies ignore female abolitionists, whose activism has been well documented. See also Michael D. Pierson, *Free Hearts and Free*

Homes: *Gender and American Antislavery Politics* (Chapel Hill: University of North Carolina Press, 2003); Beth Salerno, *Sister Societies: Women's Anti-Slavery Organizations in Antebellum America* (DeKalb: Northern Illinois University Press, 2005).

15. On the mythical nature of the meeting between Stanton and Mott, see Isenberg, *Sex and Citizenship*, 2–6. For the transatlantic dimensions of women's rights see Bonnie S. Anderson, *Joyous Greetings: The First International Women's Movement, 1830–1860* (New York: Oxford University Press, 2000). For analysis of racism in the women's rights movement, see especially Louise Michele Newman, *White Women's Rights: The Racial Origins of Feminism in the United States* (New York: Oxford University Press, 1999); Kathi Kern, *Mrs. Stanton's Bible* (Ithaca, N.Y.: Cornell University Press, 2002), 6, 8, 109–16; Ellen Carol DuBois and Richard Candida Smith, eds., *Elizabeth Cady Stanton, Feminist as Thinker: A Reader in Documents and Essays* (New York: New York University Press, 2007); Ginzberg, *Elizabeth Cady Stanton*.

16. "Sermon to Medical Students," in Greene, 85.

17. H. Larry Ingle, *Quakers in Conflict: The Hicksite Reformation* (Wallingford, Pa.: Pendle Hill, 1986, 1998).

18. *Pennsylvania Freeman*, March 18, 1847.

19. Some versions of her sermons are more reliable than others. Her close friend James Miller McKim published her "Sermon to the Medical Students," *Pennsylvania Freeman*, March 8, 1849. David Brion Davis, *Slavery and Human Progress* (New York: Oxford University Press, 1984), 156, 11.

Chapter 1. Nantucket

1. LCM to Anna Davis Hallowell, Sept. 13, 1876 and LCM to Mary Hussey Earle, Feb. 20, 1863, in Beverly Wilson Palmer, Holly Byers Ochoa, and Carol Faulkner, eds., *Selected Letters of Lucretia Coffin Mott* (Urbana: University of Illinois Press, 2002), 494, 331; Anna Davis Hallowell, *James and Lucretia Mott: Life and Letters* (Boston: Houghton Mifflin, 1884), 18, 20.

2. LCM to Elizabeth Cady Stanton, March 16, 1855, in Palmer, 234; Lisa Norling, *Captain Ahab Had a Wife: New England Women and the Whalefishery* (Chapel Hill: University of North Carolina Press, 2000), 51–53.

3. Hallowell, 19; Robert J. Leach and Peter Gow, *Quaker Nantucket: The Religious Community Behind the Whaling Empire* (Nantucket: Mill Hill Press, 1997), 9; Nathaniel Philbrick, "'Every Wave Is a Fortune': Nantucket Island and the Making of an American Icon," *New England Quarterly* 66, 3 (Sept. 1993): 434–47.

4. Leach and Gow, 9, 23–26.

5. Margaret Hope Bacon, *The Quiet Rebels: The Story of Quakers in America* (Wallingford, Pa.: Pendle Hill, 1999), 9–16.

6. Bacon, *The Quiet Rebels*, 21–22; Elizabeth Pease, *Society of Friends in the United States: Their Views of the Anti-Slavery Questions, and Treatment of the People of Colour.*

Compiled from Original Correspondence (Darlington: John Wilson, 1840), 17–18, 22, 23; Ryan P. Jordan, *Slavery and the Meetinghouse: The Quakers and the Abolitionist Dilemma, 1820–1865* (Bloomington: Indiana University Press, 2007), 72–74.

7. Bacon, *The Quiet Rebels*, 17.

8. Bacon, *The Quiet Rebels*, 30–31, 36–41, 55.

9. Nathaniel Philbrick, *In the Heart of the Sea: The Tragedy of the Whaleship Essex* (New York: Penguin, 2000), 5–6, 53–57.

10. Quoted in Hallowell, 23.

11. Leach and Gow, 74, 75; Thomas P. Slaughter, *The Beautiful Soul of John Woolman, Apostle of Abolition* (New York: Hill and Wang, 2008), 236–37.

12. Philbrick, "'Every Wave Is a Fortune," 442; Leach and Gow, 117; Benjamin Coffin, "Manumission of a Slave," Dec. 15, 1775, Edouard A. Stackpole Collection 335, Folder 51, Nantucket Historical Association (NHA). There were at least two prominent Benjamin Coffins on Nantucket at the time. Leach and Gow attribute this manumission to Benjamin Coffin the schoolteacher (and seemingly conflate all Benjamin Coffins). I attribute the manumission to Mott's grandfather as he seeks to free his slaves before his "decease"; he died in 1780. See Eliza Starbuck Barney Genealogy, Collection 186, NHA; Jean R. Soderlund, *Quakers and Slavery: A Divided Spirit* (Princeton, N.J.: Princeton University Press, 1985).

13. Hallowell, 20–22.

14. Daniel Vickers, "Nantucket Whalemen in the Deep-Sea Fishery: The Changing Anatomy of an Early American Labor Force," *Journal of American History* 72, 2 (Sept. 1985): 277–96; David J. Silverman, "The Impact of Indentured Servitude on the Society and Culture of Southern New England Indians, 1680–1810," *New England Quarterly* 74, 4 (Dec. 2001): 622–66; Leach and Gow, 74, 102; Norling, *Captain Ahab*, 19, 96; Philbrick, *In the Heart of the Sea*, 5, 6, 8, 26–27.

15. LCM to Elizabeth Cady Stanton, March 16, 1855, in Palmer, 234.

16. Quoted in Hallowell, 23. Lisa Norling sees Nantucket women as similar to their counterparts on the mainland, rather than as exceptions; see Norling, *Captain Ahab*, 16–17, and Lisa Norling, "Judith Macy and Her Daybook; or, Crevecoeur and the Wives of Sherborn," *Historic Nantucket* 40, 4 (Winter 1992): 68–71, http://www.nha.org/history/hn/HNnorling-judith.htm.

17. Norling, *Captain Ahab*, 94; Leach and Gow, 125.

18. Hallowell, 25–26; Norling, *Captain Ahab*, 90–94.

19. Philbrick, "'Every Wave Is a Fortune," 435; Leach and Gow, 124, 134–35.

20. Estate of William Folger, Account Books Collection, AB 137, NHA.

21. Michael A. Jehle, *From Brant Point to the Boca Tigris: Nantucket and the China Trade* (Nantucket: Nantucket Historical Association, 1994), 53–54; Norling, 91; Leach and Gow, 133.

22. Thomas Coffin to Micajah Coffin, May 1, May 29, June 2, 1790, Coffin Family Papers, Collection 150, Folder 52, NHA; Partnership Agreement, July 7, 1790, Charles Congdon Collection 36, Folder 12, NHA; Micajah Coffin to Thomas Coffin, May 29,

June 2, 1790, Micajah Coffin Letterbooks, Charles Congdon Collection 36, Folder 4, NHA. For Thomas's voyage on the Lucy see Judith Navas Lund, *Whaling Masters and Whaling Voyages Sailing from American Ports: A Compilation of Sources* (New Bedford, Mass.: New Bedford Whaling Museum, 2001). Alexander Starbuck, *History of the American Whale Fishery* (New York: Arogsy-Antiquarian, 1964) 2: 660; www.measuringworth.com using Consumer Price Index.

23. Leach and Gow, 99–100; Norling, 94–95.

24. Leach and Gow, 85; Norling, 89–90.

25. Leach and Gow, 82–83, 85, 104–7, 116. See also Jack D. Marietta, *The Reformation of American Quakerism, 1748–1783* (Philadelphia: University of Pennsylvania Press, 1984).

26. Norling, *Captain Ahab*, 101–10.

27. LCM to Richard and Hannah Webb, Feb. 25, 1842, in Palmer, 106; see also LCM to James Mott, Sr., June 29, 1822, in Palmer, 12 and LCM to Nathaniel Barney, March 19, 1852, in Palmer, 213. On Martha Coffin Pelham Wright's first marriage see Sherry H. Penney and James D. Livingston, *A Very Dangerous Woman: Martha Wright and Women's Rights* (Amherst: University of Massachusetts Press, 2004), 19–24. For more on Woolman, see Slaughter.

28. LCM to David and Martha Wright, Aug. 28, 1840, Mott Manuscripts, Friends Historical Library, Swarthmore College (FHL); Margaret Hope Bacon, *Valiant Friend: The Life of Lucretia Mott* (New York: Walker, 1980), 12.

29. LCM to David and Martha Wright, August 28, 1840, Mott Manuscripts, FHL.

30. Alexander Starbuck, *History of the American Whale Fishery, from Its Earliest Inception to the Year 1876* (1878; New York: Argosy-Antiquarian, 1964), 1: 188, 196; Micajah Coffin to Thomas Coffin, Aug. 6, 1793, Micajah Coffin to Isaac Coffin, Aug. 26, 1797, Congdon Papers 36, Folder 4 Micajah Coffin letterbooks, NHA. Thomas Coffin also helped found the Nantucket Bank, which was robbed in 1795; see Thomas Coffin, Jr., and George Fogler, Jr., to "Gentlemen of the Nantucket Bank Committee, New Bedford, Feb. 3, Folder 11, Banks of Nantucket, 91, NHA. The *Lydia* was home to an interesting assortment of people. In 1800, the captain discovered that one of his crew was a woman, who had been undetected through two voyages. On two voyages, the first in 1809 and the next in 1812, the ship's captains (both named Swain) were killed by whales. The Lydia finally ended her career in a wreck off Nantucket in 1818. See Starbuck, 196, 208, 210, 222.

31. Philbrick, *In the Heart of the Sea*, 11. On Sarah Coffin, see Bacon, *Valiant Friend*, 12.

32. Hallowell, 26–30.

33. Hallowell, 31.

34. Hallowell, 478–79; Memorial of the Monthly Meeting of New York concerning Elizabeth Coggeshall (New York: James Egbert, 1852), 7–8; Hugh Barbour, Christopher Densmore, Elizabeth H. Moger, Nancy C. Sorel, Alson D. Van Wagner, and Arthur J. Worrall, *Quaker Crosscurrents: Three Hundred Years of Friends in the New York Yearly Meetings* (Syracuse, N.Y.: Syracuse University Press, 1995), 102–3; H. Larry Ingle, *Quakers in Conflict: The Hicksite Reformation* (Wallingford, Pa.: Pendle Hill, 1986, 1998), 9–10, 75; "Hannah Barnard," *Friends' Intelligencer*, Aug. 2, 1884; Bacon, *Valiant Friend*,

16, Otelia Cromwell, *Lucretia Mott* (Cambridge, Mass.: Harvard University Press, 1958), 1. For more on Barnard see Jennifer Rycenga, "A Greater Awakening: Women's Intellect as a Factor in Early Abolitionist Movements, 1824–1834," *Journal of Feminist Studies in Religion* 21, 2 (Fall 2005): 31–59.

35. Hallowell, 478–79; Barbour et al., *Quaker Crosscurrents*, 102.

36. On the *Brookes* diagram and British sugar boycotts see Adam Hochschild, *Bury the Chains: Prophets and Rebels in the Fight to Free an Empire's Slaves* (New York: Houghton Mifflin, 2005), 155–56, 192–96.

37. Priscilla Wakefield, *Mental Improvement, or the Beauties and Wonders of Nature and Art in a Series of Instructive Conversations* (New Bedford, Mass.: Caleb Greene & Son, 1799), 11–15; Jon-Paul C. Dyson, "From Sermons in Stone to Studies in Science: The Transformation of 19th-Century Juvenile Natural History," Ph.D. dissertation, State University of New York at Buffalo, 2002; Camilla Leach, "Religion and Rationality: Quaker Women and Science Education, 1790–1850," *History of Education* 35, 1 (Jan. 2006): 69–90. On Mott's education see Hallowell, 31–32; Bacon, *Valiant Friend*, 13; Cromwell, 7–8.

38. Wakefield, *Mental Improvement*, 75–84.

39. Micajah Coffin to John Coggeshall, August 13, 1801, Micajah Coffin letterbooks, Folder 4, Congdon Papers 36, NHA. Anna Coffin's sayings can be found in Maria Mott Davis's handwritten booklet of quotations, Folger Family Papers 118, Folder 13, NHA For the implications of racial hierarchy in whaling see Philbrick, *In the Heart of the Sea*, 24–27; W. Jeffrey Bolster, *Black Jacks: African American Seamen in the Age of Sail* (Cambridge, Mass.: Harvard University Press, 1997), 177–80.

40. *Pennsylvania Mercury and Universal Advertiser*, March 29, 1788; Thomas Coffin to Micajah Coffin, May 29, 1790, Folder 52, Coffin Family Papers, Collection 150, NHA.

41. Jehle, 55–61; Hallowell, 32; Walter Hayes, *The Captain from Nantucket and the Mutiny on the Bounty: A Recollection of Mayhew Folger, Mariner, who Discovered the last Mutineer & his Family on Pitcairn's Island: together with Letters & Documents never previously published* (Ann Arbor, Mich.: William L. Clements Library, 1996), 30, 36, 43.

42. Hallowell, 25, 32–33; Jehle, 60; Starbuck, 1: 196–97.

43. Hallowell, 32–33; Jehle, 61. Swain and his crew denied the charges; see *Boston Gazette*, Jan. 24, 1803, 2. For Spanish colonial policy in this era see Vera Lee Brown, "Anglo-Spanish Relations in the Closing Years of the Colonial Era," *Hispanic American Historical Review* 5, 3 (Aug. 1922): 329–483, and "Contraband Trade: A Factor in the Decline of Spain's Empire in America," *Hispanic American Historical Review* 8, 2 (May 1928): 178–89; Jerry W. Cooney, "'Doing Business in the Smuggling Way': Yankee Contraband in the Rio de la Plata," *American Neptune* 47, 3 (1987): 162–68.

44. Hallowell, 33.

45. *Boston Gazette*, Jan. 24, 1803, 2; Hallowell, 33.

46. *North Star*, May 19, 1848.

47. *Hall v. Gardner*, 1 Mass. 172 (1804).

48. On fraudulent trade, which would become especially relevant in debates over Quaker complicity in slavery, see discussion of the 6th Query, Philadelphia Quarterly Meeting (women's), Feb. 6, 1838, Microfilm MR-Ph 452, FHL. See David Brion Davis,

"The Quaker Ethic and the Antislavery International" and "The Preservation of English Liberty I," in Thomas Bender, ed., *The Antislavery Debate, Capitalism and Abolitionism as a Problem in Historical Interpretation* (Berkeley: University of California Press, 1992), 45–49, 69–71.

49. *Hall v. Gardner.*

50. *Hall v. Gardner*; James D. Schmidt, "'Restless Movements Characteristic of Childhood': The Legal Construction of Child Labor in Nineteenth-Century Massachusetts," *Law and History Review* 23, 2 (Summer 2005): 315–50. Joanne Pope Melish argues that such apprenticeships were part of an effort to extend slavery in the North; see Melish, *Disowning Slavery: Gradual Emancipation and Race in New England, 1780–1860* (Ithaca, N.Y.: Cornell University Press, 1998), 100–101. Mark A. Nicholas argues that the guardianship system protected Indians, as guardians often fought for fair treatment for their charges; see Nicholas, "Mashpee Wampanoags of Cape Cod, the Whalefishery, and Seafaring's Impact on Community Development," *American Indian Quarterly* 26, 2 (Spring 2002): 165–97, and Micajah Coffin to Asa Fish, July 14, 1794, Folder 52, Collection 150, Coffin Family Papers, NHA. Mye's father was an African American named Newport Mye and his mother was Sarah Soncansin, a Wampanoag with proprietary rights. See Nicholas, 184; Vickers, 290.

51. Davis, "The Quaker Ethic and the Antislavery International," 45, 61–63

52. For African Americans on whaling crews see Philbrick, *In the Heart of the Sea*, 18, 25–27; Bolster.

53. John Milton Earle, Mass. Senate Report #96 of 1861, or *Report to the Governor and Council Concerning the Indians of the Commonwealth Under the Act of April 6, 1859* (Boston: William White, 1861); James F. Mye household, 1870 U.S. census, Plymouth County, Massachusetts, population schedule, city of Plymouth, dwelling 431, family 453, National Archives micropublication M593, roll 639; page 643.

54. Micajah Coffin to Thomas Coffin, July 5, July 10, Oct. 5, 1804; March 20, March 29, 1805, Micajah Coffin Letterbooks, Folder 4, Congdon Family Papers, Collection 36, NHA.

55. Hallowell, 34.

Chapter 2. Nine Partners

1. *Boston Directory* (Boston: Edward Cotton, 1805, 1806, 1807); Micajah Coffin to Thomas Coffin, July 5, July 10, Oct. 5, 1804, Micajah Coffin Letterbooks, Congdon Papers 36, Folder 4, NHS; Otelia Cromwell, *Lucretia Mott* (Cambridge, Mass.: Harvard University Press, 1958), 12.

2. Minutes of the Committee to Establish Nine Partners Boarding School, vol. 1, May 1805, FHL; Margaret Hope Bacon, *Valiant Friend: The Life of Lucretia Mott* (New York: Walker and Company, 1980), 21.

3. Bacon, 20–21.

4. Anna Davis Hallowell's husband Richard P. Hallowell wrote *The Quaker Invasion of Massachusetts* (Boston: Houghton Mifflin, 1883) to remind readers of the role of

Quaker missionaries in the rise of religious tolerance in Massachusetts. The education offered at Westtown School was almost identical to that at Nine Partners; see Joan M. Jensen, "Not Only Ours But Others: The Quaker Teaching Daughters of the Mid-Atlantic, 1790–1850," *History of Education Quarterly* 24, 1 (Spring 1984): 9–11.

5. "Sketch of a Plan for the Establishment of a Boarding School in the Nine Partners," Minutes of the Committee to Establish Nine Partners Boarding School, vol. 1; Barry Levy, *Quakers and the American Family: British Settlement in the Delaware Valley* (New York: Oxford University Press, 1988), 260–61.

6. "Sketch of a Plan"; James Mott to Joseph Tallcott, Oct. 17, 1813, in Joseph Tallcot, *Memoirs of Joseph Tallcot* (Auburn, N.Y.: Miller, Orton, and Mulligan, 1855), 107; Levy, *Quakers and the American Family*, 236.

7. Quoted in Linda K. Kerber, *Women of the Republic: Intellect and Ideology in Revolutionary America* (New York: Norton, 1986), 229, chap. 7, passim; Mary Kelley, *Learning to Stand and Speak: Women, Education, and Public Life in America's Republic* (Chapel Hill: University of North Carolina Press, 2006), 25–30, 67–68, passim; "Sketch of a Plan"; Rosemarie Zagarri, *Revolutionary Backlash: Women and Politics in the Early American Republic* (Philadelphia: University of Pennsylvania Press, 2008). See also Abigail Mott, *Observations on the Importance of Female Education and Maternal Instruction, with their Beneficial Influence on Society* (New York: Mahlon Day, 1827).

8. "Sketch of a Plan."

9. Minutes of the Committee to Establish Nine Partners Boarding School, vol. 1; Bacon, 23–24; Tallcot, *Memoirs*.

10. James Mott, *Observations on the Education of Children; and Hints to Young People on the Duties of Civil Life* (New York: Samuel Wood, 1816), 4, 6, 9, 16; Steven Mintz, *Huck's Raft: A History of American Childhood* (Cambridge, Mass.: Belknap Press of Harvard University Press, 2004), 80.

11. Mintz, 58–59; Maria Edgeworth and Richard Lovell Edgeworth, *Practical Education*, 2 vols., 1st American ed. (New York: Hopkins, Brown & Stanbury, 1801), 1: 158. For Mott on Edgeworth see "Remarks, Delivered at the Seventh National Women's Rights Convention," in Dana Greene, ed., *Lucretia Mott: Her Complete Speeches and Sermons* (New York: Edwin Mellen, 1980), 228.

12. LCM to James Mott, Sr., June 29, 1822, in Beverly Wilson Palmer, Holly Byers Ochoa, and Carol Faulkner, eds., *Selected Letters of Lucretia Coffin Mott* (Urbana: University of Illinois Press, 2002), 11.

13. "Information for Parents and other inclining to send Children for Education at the Boarding School at Nine Partners," March 1800, Minutes of the Committee, FHL; Anna Davis Hallowell, *James and Lucretia Mott, Life and Letters* (Boston: Houghton Mifflin, 1884), 36; Levy, *Quakers and the American Family*, 256–57.

14. William Cowper, *The Task*, Book V, "The Winter Morning Walk," ll. 299–304; LCM to Richard and Hannah Webb, April 2, 1841, in Palmer, 92. On Susanna Marriott see Judith Colucci Breault, *The World of Emily Howland: Odyssey of a Humanitarian* (Milbrae, Calif.: Les Femmes, 1975), 9–11; Hallowell, 37.

15. "The Following Questions were offered by the Teachers in the Nine-Partners'

Boarding-School, to their Pupils, and the Answers given in by them. The Scholars had the Liberty of Recurring to Books for Aid, when they found themselves unable to give proper answers without such assistance" (Danville, Vt.: Daniel Lowell, 1818), 5, 7.

16. "The Following Questions," 21, 22, 23; Hallowell, 13.

17. Hugh Barbour, Christopher Densmore, Elizabeth H. Moger, Nancy C. Sorel, Alson D. Van Wagner, and Arthur J. Worrall, *Quaker Crosscurrents: Three Hundred Years of Friends in the New York Yearly Meetings* (Syracuse, N.Y.: Syracuse University Press, 1995), 153; A. Mott, *Observations*, 23.

18. Hallowell, 37; on female subjectivity and education, see Kelley, 17.

19. Michel Foucault, *Discipline and Punish: The Birth of the Prison* (New York: Vintage, 1979), 195–228; David Rothman, *The Discovery of the Asylum: Social Order and Disorder in the New Republic* (Boston: Little Brown, 1971), 79–88; Mintz, *Huck's Raft*, 81.

20. Foucault, 206; A. Mott, *Observations*, 5; Hallowell, 36; LCM to George and Cecilia Combe, March 24, 1853, in Palmer, 127, 131.

21. "Mutiny of the Bounty," *Northern Whig* (Hudson, N.Y.), Nov. 14, 1809, 2.

22. Walter Hayes, *The Captain from Nantucket and the Mutiny on the Bounty: A Recollection of Mayhew Folger, Mariner, who Discovered the last Mutineer & his Family on Pitcairn's Island: together with Letters & Documents never previously published* (Ann Arbor, Mich.: William L. Clements Library, 1996), 28, 37–45, 41, 79; Hallowell, 33. See also LCM to Adam and Anne Mott, Nov. 8, 1813, in Palmer, 5.

23. Hayes, 62.

24. Minutes for May 25, 1807 and July 1808, Minutes of the Committee Relative to the Establishment of a Boarding School at the Nine Partners; Jensen, "Not Only Ours But Others," 8; Kathryn Kish Sklar, *Catharine Beecher: A Study in American Domesticity* (New York: Norton, 1976), 96–97.

25. Sarah Mott to Phebe Post Willis, Sept. 3, 1808, Feb. 13, 1814, Gertrude Burleigh to ?, undated, Phebe Post Willis Papers, University of Rochester; Jensen, 10, 11.

26. Hallowell, 37–38.

27. Lisa Norling, *Captain Ahab Had a Wife: New England Women & the Whalefishery, 1720–1870* (Chapel Hill: University of North Carolina Press, 2000), 66, 175–76; Ellen K. Rothman, "Sex and Self-Control: Middle-Class Courtship in America, 1770–1870," *Journal of Social History* 15, 3 (Spring 1982): 410.

28. Levy, 73–74, 132–34; Hallowell, 40–42.

29. Minutes for May 6, 1805, May 3, 1808, July 1808, May 9, 1809, Minutes of the Committee Relative to the Establishment of a Boarding School at the Nine Partners; Hallowell, 37–38, 40; Notes on the Life of Lucretia Mott, as given in an interview to Sarah J. Hale, Box 6, Mott Manuscripts, FHL.

30. Hallowell, 6, 9–10.

31. Hallowell, 4–5; Graham Russell Gao Hodges, "Liberty and Constraint: The Limits of Revolution," in Ira Berlin and Leslie M. Harris, eds., *Slavery in New York* (New York: Norton, 2005), 94–96

32. Nell Irvin Painter, *Sojourner Truth: A Life, A Symbol* (New York: Norton, 1996), 22; Jean R. Soderlund, *Quakers and Slavery: A Divided Spirit* (Princeton, N.J.: Princeton

University Press, 1985), 4, 22; David N. Gellman, *Emancipating New York: The Politics of Slavery and Freedom, 1777–1827* (Baton Rouge: Louisiana State University Press, 2006), 27–29.

33. Hallowell, 11.

34. Hallowell, 11–12, 15.

35. LCM to Adam and Anne Mott, Nov. 8, 1813 in Palmer, 5; LCM to Martha Coffin Wright, Feb. 4, 1870, photocopy in Mott Manuscripts, FHL; Notes from an interview with Thomas Cornell, 1879, Box 6, Mott Manuscripts, FHL; J. Leander Bishop, *A History of American Manufactures from 1608 to 1860* (Philadelphia: Edward Young, 1866), 1: 571; 2: 131.

36. Gary Nash, *Forging Freedom: The Formation of Philadelphia's Black Community, 1720–1840* (Cambridge, Mass.: Harvard University Press, 1988), 4, 134, 143; Bacon, 41. On the Pennsylvania Abolition Society, see Richard S. Newman, *The Transformation of American Abolitionism: Fighting Slavery in the Early Republic* (Chapel Hill: University of North Carolina Press, 2002), chaps. 1–3, passim.

37. Hallowell, 41–43. On the importance of personal relationships in a credit economy, see Scott A. Sandage, *Born Losers: A History of Failure in America* (Cambridge, Mass.: Harvard University Press, 2005), 30.

38. LCM to Josephine Butler, April 20, 1869, in Palmer, 415.

39. On married women's legal status and its implications see Sandra F. Van Burkleo, *Belonging to the World: Women's Rights and American Constitutional Culture* (New York: Oxford University Press, 2001); Hendrik Hartog, *Man and Wife in America: A History* (Cambridge, Mass.: Harvard University Press, 2002).

40. To James Mott and Children, June 19, 1849, in Palmer, 188; Hallowell, 440; Bacon, 30. On premarital pregnancy see Rothman, "Sex and Self-Control," 413–15; Daniel Smith and Michael S. Hindus, "Premarital Pregnancy in America, 1640–1971: An Overview and Interpretation," *Journal of Interdisciplinary History* 5 (Spring 1975): 537–70.

41. Hallowell, 42–43.

42. Hallowell, 45–47.

43. Hallowell, 49–50; Nash, *Forging Freedom*, 142, 213.

44. LCM to Martha Coffin Wright, Feb. 4, 1870, Mott Manuscripts, FHL, in Palmer, 455; Hallowell, 47, 48, 50, 52, 55; Bacon, 33–34; Sandage, *Born Losers*, 30.

45. Hallowell, 54–55; LCM to William and Mary Johnson, Jan. 17, 1842, Mott Manuscripts, FHL; LCM to Sydney Howard Gay April 13, 1850, in Palmer, 201; Bacon, 36.

Chapter 3. Schism

1. Anna Davis Hallowell, *James and Lucretia Mott, Life and Letters* (Boston: Houghton Mifflin, 1884), 62. On Lucretia's speaking voice, see Samuel J. May, *Some Recollections of our Antislavery Conflict* (Boston: Fields, Osgood, 1869), 91; Louise Hall Tharp, *Until Victory: Horace Mann and Mary Peabody Mann* (Boston: Little, Brown, 1953), 253.

2. Memorial of Lucretia Mott, Philadelphia Monthly Meeting of Women Friends, 112–13, MR-PH Reel 375, FHL.

3. LCM to Unidentified Recipient, Dec. 15, 1819, in Beverly Wilson Palmer, Holly Byers Ochoa, and Carol Faulkner, *Selected Letters of Lucretia Coffin Mott* (Urbana: University of Illinois Press, 2002), 8; H. Larry Ingle, *Quakers in Conflict: The Hicksite Reformation* (Wallingford, Pa.: Pendle Hill, 1986, 1998), 226; Otelia Cromwell, *Lucretia Mott* (Cambridge, Mass.: Harvard University Press, 1958), 30.

4. *Memorial of the Monthly Meeting of New York concerning Elizabeth Coggeshall* (New York: James Egbert, 1852), 3–5; Rebecca Larson, *Daughters of Light: Quaker Women Preaching and Prophesying in the Colonies and Abroad, 1700–1775* (New York: Knopf, 1999), 80; Margaret Hope Bacon, *Valiant Friend: The Life of Lucretia Mott* (New York: Walker 1980), 37; Cromwell, 32.

5. W. H. J. [William H. Johnson], "Lucretia Mott," *The Lily*, Feb. 1, 1854, 19.

6. For the place of Hicksites in this larger context see Daniel Walker Howe, *What Hath God Wrought: The Transformation of America, 1815–1848* (New York: Oxford University Press, 2007), 4–5, 195–97.

7. Ingle, 98; Hallowell, 91–92, 81–82, 99. Cromwell, 34–35.

8. LCM to Adam and Anne Mott, Dec. 29, 1822, in Palmer, 13; Ingle, 39.

9. Mark G. Schmeller, "Bates, Barnabas," http://www.anb.org.libezproxy2.syr.edu/articles/15/15-00045.html; *American National Biography Online*, Feb. 2000, accessed May 23, 2008; Elias Hicks to Barnabas Bates, March 6, 1826, Folder 248, MS044, Elias Hicks Manuscript Collection, FHL; Jonathan H. Earle, *Jacksonian Anti-Slavery and the Politics of Free Soil, 1824–1854* (Chapel Hill: University of North Carolina Press, 2004), 5,10–11; Ryan P. Jordan, *Slavery and the Meetinghouse: The Quakers and the Abolitionist Dilemma, 1820–1865* (Bloomington: Indiana University Press, 2007), 11–12, 82–84.

10. Barnabas Bates, *Remarks on the Character and Exertions of Elias Hicks, in the Abolition of Slavery, being An Address delivered before the African Benevolent Societies, in Zion's Chapel, New York, March 15, 1830. By Barnabas Bates* (New York: Mitchell and Davis, 1830), 9, 12.

11. Elias Hicks, *Observations on the Slavery of the Africans and their Descendants* (New York: Samuel Wood, 1811), 3, 7, 19.

12. Bates, 11.

13. *Letters of Elias Hicks* (New York: Isaac T. Hopper, 1834), 44, 45, 61; Ingle, 82.

14. Ingle, 12; Bruce Dorsey, "Friends Becoming Enemies: Philadelphia Benevolence and the Neglected Era of American Quaker History," *Journal of the Early Republic* 18, 3 (Fall 1998): 395–428; On the impact of disestablishment on American female reformers, see Kathryn Kish Sklar, "'The Throne of My Heart': Religion, Oratory, and Transatlantic Community in Angelina Grimké's Launching of Women's Rights, 1828–1838," in *Women's Rights and Transatlantic Antislavery in the Era of Emancipation*, ed. Kathryn Kish Sklar and James Brewer Stewart (New Haven, Conn.: Yale University Press, 2007), 213–16.

15. Ingle, 17–20, 84–86; *An Authentic Report of the Testimony in a Cause at Issue in the Court of Chancery of the State of New Jersey, between Thomas L. Shotwell, Complainant, and Joseph Hendrickson and Stacey Decow, Defendants. Taken Pursuant to the rules of the Court by Jeremiah J. Foster. In Two Volumes* (Philadelphia: J. Harding, 1831), 2: 39–40, 376.

16. LCM to James Mott, St., Jan. 24, 1819, in Palmer, 7; LCM to Richard and Hannah Webb, Feb. 25, 1842, in Palmer, 113.

17. LCM to James Mott, Sr., June 29, 1822, in Palmer, 12.

18. Sherry H. Penney and James D. Livingston, *A Very Dangerous Woman: Martha Wright and Women's Rights* (Amherst: University of Massachusetts Press, 2004), 18–19.

19. *Letters of Paul and Amicus: Originally Published in The Christian Repository; A Weekly Paper, printed at Wilmington, Delaware* (Philadelphia: Joseph Rakestraw, 1828), advertisement to the reader, 7, 22–23; LCM to Richard and Hannah Webb, Feb. 25, 1842, in Palmer, 112–13; Ingle, 98–102.

20. LCM to Richard and Hannah Webb, Feb. 25, 1842, in Palmer, 113; *Letters of Paul and Amicus*, 184, 403–4, 415.

21. *Letters of Paul and Amicus*, 189, 389, 291.

22. *Letters of Paul and Amicus*, 147; *Letters of Elias Hicks* (New York: Isaac T. Hopper, 1834), 43.

23. *Letters of Paul and Amicus*, 25, 268, 33.

24. *Letters of Paul and Amicus*, 314; LCM to Richard and Hannah Webb, Feb. 25, 1842, in Palmer, 113; Ingle, 119.

25. *The Misrepresentations of Anna Braithwait, in Relation to the Doctrines Preached by Elias Hicks, Together with The Refutation of the Same, in a letter from Elias Hicks, to Dr. Atlee of Philadelphia* (Philadelphia: 1824), 5; *Calumny Refuted, Or, Plain facts versus Misrepresentations: Being a Reply to a Pamphlets, Entitled "The Misrepresentations of Anna Braithwaite"* (Philadelphia: 1824), 5; Ingle, 33, 126–29.

26. *The Misrepresentations of Anna Braithwait*, 7, 8, 10, 11, 12.

27. *Letter of Elias Hicks to Edwin A. Atlee.* (Philadelphia: 1824), 5, 6–7, 8, 1.

28. *Misrepresentations of Ann Braithwait*, 3–4.

29. Ingle, 50–51; *The Cabinet, or Works of Darkness brought to Light. Being a Retrospect of the Anti-Christian conduct of some of the leading characters in the Society called Friends, towards that eminent and devoted Servant of the Lord, ELIAS HICKS, when on his last visit of Gospel Love to the inhabitants of the city of Philadelphia. Also, A brief statement of facts, illustrative of the treatment of that faithful Messenger of the Gospel, PRISCILLA HUNT, at a meeting for worship, held in Pine-street Meeting House,—together, with part of a discourse, delivered by her, at Green-street Meeting House* (Philadelphia: printed for the Compiler, 1824), 36. See also Thomas D. Hamm, "Quakerism, Ministry, Marriage, and Divorce: The Ordeal of Priscilla Hunt Cadwalader" *Journal of the Early Republic* 27 (Fall 2008): 407–31.

30. *The Cabinet, or Works of Darkness brought to Light*, 34.

31. *An Authentic Report*, 2: 38; 1: 421; LCM to Elizabeth Cady Stanton, March 16, 1855, in Palmer, 234.

32. Thomas Eddy to John Warder dated 10/18/1822 in *The Cabinet, or Works of Darkness brought to Light*, 7. See also *An Authentic Report*, 1: 171, 426.

33. *Letters of Paul and Amicus*, 399, 410.

34. *A Letter, on the Dispute of Statements of Anna Braithwaite and Elias Hicks. Said to have been Written by Ann Shipley. Reprinted from the New York Edition. With a Review of the Same* (Philadelphia: 1824), 4, 10–11.

35. *An Examination of a Pamphlet, Entitled The Misrepresentations of Anna Braithewaite, in Relation to the Doctrines Preached by Elias Hicks* (New York: 1824), 13.

36. *An Examination of an Epistle issued by a Meeting of the Followers of Elias Hicks At Green Street Monthly Meeting-house, in Philadelphia, the 4th and 5th of the 6th Month, 1827, being a Statement of Facts relative to the Separation from the Society of Friends* (Philadelphia: 1827), 28, 21.

37. *The Cabinet, or Works of Darkness brought to Light*, 33.

38. LCM to Adam and Ann Mott, April 23, 1826, in Palmer, 15; Ingle, 163

39. Ingle, 186–87.

40. Ingle 197, 207–8; *An Authentic Report*, 1: 456; Minutes for April 16–21, 1827, Women's Yearly Meeting, Arch Street, Microfilm MR Ph 515, FHL.

41. *An Authentic Report*, 1:459.

42. [Catharine Beecher], "Circular Addressed to Benevolent Ladies of the U. States," Dec. 1, 1829, printed in *Christian Advocate and Journal*, Dec. 25, 1829, 65–66 (*American Periodical Series, 1800–1850*, Microfilm, Reel 1749), reprinted online as document 35 in "How did the Removal of the Cherokee Nation from Georgia Shape Women's Activism in the North, 1817–1838?" in Kathryn Kish Sklar and Thomas Dublin, eds., *Women and Social Movements in the United States, 1600–2000* (2004), http://asp6new.alexanderstreet.com.libezproxy2.syr.edu/wasm/wasmrestricted/DP52/doc35.htm. See also Alisse Portnoy, *Their Right to Speak: Women's Activism in the Indian and Slave Debates* (Cambridge, Mass.: Harvard University Press, 2005). For other models of evangelical womanhood, see Catherine A. Brekus, *Strangers and Pilgrims: Female Preaching in America, 1740–1845* (Chapel Hill: University of North Carolina Press, 1998).

43. *An Examination of an Epistle*, 6, 8, 9; Ingle, 218.

44. *An Address to Friends within the Compass of the Yearly Meeting held in Philadelphia* (Philadelphia: D. & S. Neall, 1827), 6, 7; *An Epistle to Friends of the Quarterly and Monthly Meetings within the Compass of the Yearly Meeting held in Philadelphia, Adopted at a General Meeting of Friends at Green Street Meeting House* (Philadelphia: D. & S. Neall, 1827), 10.

45. Ingle, 212–13; Bacon, 46.

46. Bacon, 39, 46; LCM to Adam and Anne Mott, April 23, 1826, in Palmer, 15; Cromwell, 34. For the demographic transition and the strategy of spacing, see Susan Klepp, *Revolutionary Conceptions: Women, Fertility, and Family Limitation in America, 1760–1820* (Chapel Hill: University of North Carolina Press, 2009), 47–49.

47. Bacon, 45; LCM to Anne Mott, February 26, 1827, in Palmer, 16.

48. LCM to Adam and Anne Mott, April 23, 1826, in Palmer, 15; Ingle, xiv. See also Mary Grew, *James Mott: A Biographical Sketch* (New York: William P. Tomlinson, 1868), 8.

49. Elizabeth Heyrick, *Immediate, Not Gradual Abolition; Or, An Inquiry into the*

Shortest, Safest, and Most Effectual Means of Getting Rid of West Indian Slavery (Philadelphia: Philadelphia Ladies' Anti-Slavery Society, 1836), 3, 16, 23–24; Carol Faulkner, "The Root of the Evil: Free Produce and Radical Antislavery, 1820–1860," *Journal of the Early Republic* 27, 3 (Fall 2007): 377–405. For the British boycott see Seymour Drescher, *Capitalism and Antislavery: British Mobilization in Comparative Perspective* (New York: Oxford University Press, 1987), 78–79; Adam Hochschild, *Bury the Chains: Prophets and Rebels in the Fight to Free an Empire's Slaves* (New York: Houghton Mifflin, 2005), 193.

50. Heyrick, 3, 5, 24; Clare Midgley, "Slave Sugar Boycotts, Female Activism and the Domestic Base of British Anti-Slavery Culture," *Slavery and Abolition* 17, 3 (Dec. 1996): 137–62; T. H. Breen, *The Marketplace of Revolution: How Consumer Politics Shaped American Independence* (New York: Oxford University Press, 2004). For Orthodox participation, see Ruth Ketring Nuermberger, *The Free Produce Movement: A Quaker Protest Against Slavery* (1942; New York: AMS Press, 1970); Emma J. Lapsansky-Werner and Margaret Hope Bacon, eds., *Benjamin Coates and the Colonization Movement in America, 1848–1880* (University Park: Pennsylvania State University Press, 2005); Jordan, *Slavery and the Meetinghouse*, 36–40.

51. "Free Dry Goods' Store," *Genius of Universal Emancipation*, May 1830; "Lydia White," *Friends' Intelligencer*, May 13, 1871; Nuermberger, 119.

52. Hallowell, 88.

53. W. P. Garrison, "Free Produce Among the Quakers" *Atlantic Monthly* (Oct. 1868): 487; Nuermberger, *The Free Produce Movement*, 59, 113; Faulkner, "Root of the Evil," 379–80, 403–5.

54. Hallowell, 49; Bacon, 41, 217.

55. Quoted in Julie Winch, *A Gentleman of Color: The Life of James Forten* (New York: Oxford University Press, 2002), 191; Richard S. Newman, *The Transformation of American Abolitionism: Fighting Slavery in the Early Republic* (Chapel Hill: University of North Carolina Press, 2002), 4–5, 98–99.

56. "Circular from the Free Produce Society of Pennsylvania," *Genius*, July 14, 1827.

57. "Colored People in Philadelphia," *Genius*, Feb. 1831; "Colored Free Produce Society," *Genius*, May 1831; "Colored Females' Free Produce Society" *Genius*, May 1831; "Coloured Female Free Produce Society," *Genius*, Aug. 1831; Margaret Hope Bacon, *But One Race: The Life of Robert Purvis* (Albany: State University of New York Press, 2007), chap. 1, 30.

58. Hallowell, 87.

59. Lori D. Ginzberg, "'The Hearts of Your Readers Will Shudder': Fanny Wright, Infidelity, and American Freethought," *American Quarterly* 46, 2 (June 1994): 195–26; Celia Morris, *Fanny Wright: Rebel in America* (Urbana: University of Illinois Press, 1992). For women and politics in the early republic, see especially Rosemarie Zagarri, *Revolutionary Backlash: Women and Politics in the Early American Republic* (Philadelphia: University of Pennsylvania Press, 2007).

60. LCM to Richard and Hannah Webb, Feb. 25, 1842, in Palmer, 113; Ginzberg,

"The Hearts of Your Readers Will Shudder," 195, 200–201, 203, 208, 210; Morris, *Fanny Wright*, 174–75, 182, 184, 199; Abner Kneeland, "Elias Hicks," *The Olive Branch and Christian Inquirer* (New York: Charles Nichols Printer, 1828), 1: 235–36.

61. LCM to Richard and Hannah Webb, Feb. 25, 1842, in Palmer, 113; Ingle, 61. See also LCM to Martha Coffin Wright, Sept. 5, 1855, in Palmer, 244.

62. LCM to Caroline Healy Dall, Aug. 9, 1867, in Palmer, 392; Mary Wollstonecraft, *Vindication of the Rights of Woman* (Mineola, N.Y.: Dover., 1996), 8–9. Eilenne Hunt Botting and Christine Carrey, "Wollstonecraft's Philosophical Impact on Nineteenth Century American Women's Rights Advocates," *American Journal of Political Science* 48, 4 (October 2004): 707–22.

63. LCM to Caroline Healy Dall, Aug. 9, 1867, in Palmer, 392; LCM to Martha Coffin Wright, Sept. 5, 1855, in Palmer, 244; LCM to Elizabeth Neall Gay, May 7,1858, in Palmer, 272. Ginzberg, "'The Hearts of Your Readers Will Shudder,'" 196.

64. William Ellery Channing, "Unitarian Christianity; Delivered at the Ordination of Jared Sparks in the First Independent Church of Baltimore on May 5, 1819," http://www.transcendentalists.com/unitarian_christianity.htm, accessed May 23, 2008.

65. "Honor Due All Men," in *The Works of William E. Channing, D.D.* (Boston: Crosby, Nichols, 1853), 3: 306, 305; Hallowell, 109. Daniel Walker Howe, *The Unitarian Conscience: Harvard Moral Philosophy, 1805–1861* (Middletown, Conn.: Wesleyan University Press, 1970, 1988).

66. Megan Marshall, *The Peabody Sisters: Three Women Who Ignited American Romanticism* (New York: Houghton Mifflin, 2005), 161, 159–65, passim.

67. To the London Yearly Meeting of Friends, c. April 14, 1830, in Palmer, 17–19; Hallowell, 107; Bacon, 48–49; Cromwell, 36–37.

68. Hallowell, 107.

Chapter 4. Immediate Abolition

1. Maria to Edward M. Davis, May 7, 1838, Mott Manuscripts, FHL. For one example of an interracial gathering, see LCM to David and Martha Wright, June 4–6, 1838, Mott Manuscripts, FHL.

2. Quoted in Henry Mayer, *All on Fire: William Lloyd Garrison and the Abolition of Slavery* (New York: St. Martin's, 1998), 87, 84–94.

3. David Walker, *Walker's Appeal, in Four Articles; Together with a Preamble to the Coloured Citizens of the World, Third Edition* (Boston: David Walker, 1830); *Documenting the American South*, University Library, University of North Carolina at Chapel Hill, 2001, http://docsouth.unc.edu/nc/walker/walker.html; Mayer, 84.

4. Merton L. Dillon, "Lundy, Benjamin," http://www.anb.org.libezproxy2.syr.edu/articles/15/15-00430.html; *American National Biography Online*, Feb. 2000, accessed June 2, 2008; "Ladies Repository," *Genius of Universal Emancipation*, Jan. 1, 1830; see also *Genius*, Nov. 27, 1829, May 1830.

5. "The Dark River," *Chicago Tribune*, Nov. 12, 1880, 8; Mary Grew, *James Mott: A Biographical Sketch* (New York: William P. Tomlinson, 1868), 8.

6. "The Dark River," 8. See also Margaret Hope Bacon, *Valiant Friend: The Life of Lucretia Mott* (New York: Walker, 1980), 54.

7. Lucretia Mott to Phebe Post Willis, Feb. 2, 1838, Phebe Post Willis Papers, Rare Books and Special Collections, University of Rochester; William Lloyd Garrison to Helen E. Garrison, March 19, 1835, in Walter M. Merrill, ed., *The Letters of William Lloyd Garrison*, vol. 1, *I Will be Heard! 1822–1835* (Cambridge, Mass.: Belknap Press of Harvard University Press, 1971), 468; Anna Davis Hallowell, *James and Lucretia Mott, Life and Letters* (Boston: Houghton Mifflin, 1884), 296.

8. Mayer, 120–21.

9. "To the Senate and House of Representatives of the United States of America, in Congress Assembled," *Liberator*, Feb. 18, 1832, reprinted online as document 7 in Beth Salerno, "How Did Local Antislavery Women Form National Networks in the Antebellum United States," in Kathryn Sklar and Thomas Dublin, eds., *Women and Social Movements in the United States, 1600–2000* (2007), http://asp6new.alexanderstreet. com.libezproxy2.syr.edu/wasm/wasmrestricted/DP80/doclist.htm; Susan Zaeske, *Signatures of Citizenship: Petitioning, Antislavery, and Women's Political Identity* (Chapel Hill: University of North Carolina Press, 2003), 36–37; Beth Salerno, *Sister Societies: Women's Anti-Slavery Organizations in Antebellum America* (DeKalb: Northern Illinois University Press, 2005), 22.

10. See Richard S. Newman, *The Transformation of American Abolitionism: Fighting Slavery in the Early Republic* (Chapel Hill: University of North Carolina Press, 2002).

11. "Declaration of the Anti-Slavery Convention," *Liberator*, Jan. 4, 1834; Bacon, *Valiant Friend*, 56; Sherry H. Penny and James D. Livingston, *A Very Dangerous Woman: Martha Wright and Women's Rights* (Amherst: University of Massachusetts Press, 2004), 41; H. Larry Ingle, *Quakers in Conflict: The Hicksite Reformation* (Wallingford, Pa.: Pendle Hill, 1986, 1998), 97; Hallowell, 114.

12. "Declaration of the Anti-Slavery Convention," *Liberator*, Jan. 4, 1834; Hallowell, 113–15; Bacon, *Valiant Friend*, 56–57.

13. Margaret Hope Bacon, *But One Race: The Life of Robert Purvis* (Albany: State University of New York Press, 2007), 40; Hallowell, 115–16.

14. Declaration of the Anti-Slavery Convention," *Liberator*, Jan. 4, 1834.

15. Hallowell, 121. Bruce Dorsey, *Reforming Men and Women: Gender in the Antebellum City* (Ithaca, N.Y.: Cornell University Press, 2002), 168–69.

16. Philadelphia Female Anti-Slavery Society (PFASS) Minutes, Dec. 14, 1833, Papers of the Pennsylvania Abolition Society (PAS Papers), Reel 30, HSP.

17. PFASS Minutes, Dec. 14, 1833, PAS Papers, Reel 30, HSP.

18. Jean R. Soderlund, "Priorities and Power: The Philadelphia Female Anti-Slavery Society," in Jean Fagan Yellin and John C. Van Horne, eds., *The Abolitionist Sisterhood: Women's Political Culture in Antebellum America* (Ithaca, N.Y.: Cornell University Press, 1994), 72–73 passim. See also Carolyn Williams, "The Female Anti-Slavery

Movement: Fighting Against Racial Prejudice and Promoting Women's Rights in Antebellum America," in Yellin and Van Horne, 159–77; Erica Armstrong Dunbar, *A Fragile Freedom: African American Women and Emancipation in the Antebellum City* (New Haven, Conn.: Yale University Press, 2008), chap. 4; Otelia Cromwell, *Lucretia Mott* (Cambridge, Mass.: Harvard University Press, 1958), 51.

19. On female antislavery societies, see Salerno, *Sister Societies*; Julie Winch, ed., *The Elite of Our People: Joseph Willson's Sketches of Black Upper-Class Life in Antebellum Philadelphia* (University Park: Pennsylvania State University Press, 2000), 23, 26–27, 29–30; Bacon, *But One Race*, 48; LCM to Phebe Post Willis, Sept. 13, 1834, in Beverly Wilson Palmer, Holly Byers Ochoa, and Carol Faulkner, eds., *Selected Letters of Lucretia Coffin Mott* (Urbana: University of Illinois Press, 2002), 29, 32; *Pennsylvania Freeman*, March 29, 1838.

20. *National Enquirer*, Oct. 15, 1836; PFASS Minutes, Oct. 13, 1834, March 12, April 9, Aug. 11, 1835, March 10, 1836, March 8, 1838, PAS Papers, Reel 30, HSP; *Third Annual Report of the Philadelphia Female Anti-Slavery Society* (Philadelphia: Merrihew and Gunn, 1837), 4–5.

21. Lucy Williams to LCM, June 25, 1834, PFASS Correspondence, PAS Papers, Reel 31, HSP; Salerno, 34–36.

22. *National Enquirer*, Oct. 15, 1836.

23. PFASS to the Anti-Slavery Societies and Friends of the Oppressed Generally, Nov. 10, 1836, in Palmer, 36; PFASS Minutes, Nov. 11, 1836, PAS Papers, Reel 30, HSP.

24. See Kathryn Kish Sklar, *Women's Rights Emerges Within the Antislavery Movement, 1830–1870* (New York: Bedford, 2000), 107–10, 119–21.

25. *National Enquirer*, June 17, June 24, July 20, 1837. L's response supports scholar Alisse Portnoy's recent contention that the exchange between Beecher and Grimké was not only about female behavior but also a conflict between the conservative views of colonization advocates and the confrontational tactics of radical abolitionists. Alisse Portnoy, *Their Right to Speak: Women's Activism in the Indian and Slave Debates* (Cambridge, Mass.: Harvard University Press, 2005), 4, 14; Dorsey, *Reforming Men and Women*, 141–46.

26. Angelina Grimké, Letter to Catharine Beecher, Aug. 2, 1837, reprinted in Sklar, *Women's Rights Emerges*, 142–43.

27. LCM to Phebe Post Willis, March 16, 1831, March 26, 1836, Phebe Post Willis Papers, University of Rochester; *The Friend*, July 13, 1833; LCM to Phebe Post Willis, July 26, 1833, Phebe Post Willis Papers, University of Rochester; Bacon, *Valiant Friend*, 50.

28. James Mott to PPW, May 23, 1834, LCM to PPW, March 10, 1835, LCM to PPW, May 19, 1836, Phebe Post Willis Papers.

29. *National Enquirer*, Aug. 24, 1836; PFASS Minutes, Aug.11, Sept. 8, 1836, PAS Papers, Reel 30, HSP; Salerno, 52–54.

30. LCM to Elizabeth Cady Stanton, March 16, 1855, in Palmer 233; *Proceedings of the Anti-Slavery Convention of American Women, Held in the City of New York, May 9th, 10th, 11th, 12th, 1837* (New York: William S. Dorr, 1837), 3.

31. *Proceedings*, 9.

32. John Greenleaf Whittier to Angelina and Sarah Grimké, Aug. 14, 1837, in Sklar, 129–30; Palmer, 234.

33. Quoted in the *National Enquirer*, May 27, 1837.

34. *Proceedings*, 8.

35. PFASS Minutes, May 18, June 8, 1837, PAS Papers, Reel 30, HSP; *Third Annual Report*, 5.

36. PFASS Minutes, Sept. 14, 1837, PAS Papers, Reel 30, HSP; *Third Annual Report*, 7–8.

Chapter 5. Pennsylvania Hall

1. *National Enquirer*, Dec. 21, 1837; Merton L. Dillon, "Lovejoy, Elijah Parish," http://www.anb.org.libezproxy2.syr.edu/articles/15/15-00423.html, *American National Biography* Online, Feb. 2000, accessed May 28, 2010.

2. *National Enquirer*, Nov. 23, 30, 1837.

3. PFASS Minutes, Jan. 12, 1837, PAS Papers, Reel 30, HSP; *History of Pennsylvania Hall, which was Destroyed by a Mob, On the 17th of May, 1838* (Philadelphia: Merrihew and Gunn, 1838), 6.

4. *History of Pennsylvania Hall*, 3, 8.

5. *History of Pennsylvania Hall*, 70.

6. *History of Pennsylvania Hall*, 116, 120.

7. *History of Pennyslvania Hall*, 117, 167–69.

8. Sarah Grimké to Elizabeth Pease, May 20 (?), 1838, in Gilbert H. Barnes and Dwight L. Dumond, *Letters of Theodore Dwight Weld, Angelina Grimké Weld, and Sarah Grimké* (New York: Appleton, 1934), 2: 678–79. See also Robert Abzug, *Passionate Liberator: Theodore Dwight Weld and the Dilemma of Reform* (New York: Oxford University Press, 1980), 199–200; Gerda Lerner, *The Grimké Sisters from South Carolina* (Chapel Hill: University of North Carolina Press, 1967, 2004), 179–72.

9. Barnes and Dumond, 2:679.

10. Lucretia Mott to Edward M. Davis, June 18, 1838, in Beverly Wilson Palmer, Holly Byers Ochoa, and Carol Faulkner, eds., *Selected Letters of Lucretia Coffin Mott* (Urbana: University of Illinois Press, 2002), 44.

11. *History of Pennsylvania Hall*, 136, 123, 168.

12. *History of Pennsylvania Hall*, 154; LCM to EMD, June 18, 1838, in Palmer, 43 and Hallowell, 130; *Proceedings of the Anti-Slavery Convention of American Women, held in Philadelphia, May 15th, 16th, 17th, and 18th, 1838* (Philadelphia: Merrihew and Gunn, 1838), 8.

13. *Proceedings* (1838), 5; *History of Pennsylvania Hall*, 127.

14. "Report of a Delegate to the Anti-Slavery Convention of American Women, held in Philadelphia, May 1838," *Liberator*, Sept. 28, 1838; *History of Pennsylvania Hall*, 130, 135.

15. *History of Pennsylvania Hall*, 137; "Report of a Delegate to the Anti-Slavery Convention of American Women."

16. *History of Pennsylvania Hall*, 139–40.

17. Maria to Edward M. Davis, May 7, 1838, Mott Manuscripts, FHL; Hallowell, 128–29; Bacon, *Valiant Friend*, 75.

18. LCM to Anne Warren Weston, June 7, 1838, in Palmer, 42–43.

19. *Pennsylvania Freeman*, Feb. 14, 1839. See also Sept. 13, Oct. 4, 1838, April 2, 1840.

20. PFASS Minutes, June 14, Nov. 8, 1938, Jan. 17, 1839, PAS Papers, Reel 30, HSP; LCM to Abby Kelley, March 18, 1839, in Palmer, 48.

21. PFASS Minutes, March 14, 1839, PAS Papers, Reel 30, HSP. See also *Sixth Annual Report of the Philadelphia Female Anti-Slavery Society* (Philadelphia: Merrihew and Thompson, 1840), 13. Dunbar, *Fragile Freedom*, 94, Jean R. Soderlund, "Priorities and Power: The Philadelphia Female Anti-Slavery Society," in Jean Fagin Yellin and John C. Van Horne, eds., *The Abolitionist Sisterhood: Women's Political Culture in Antebellum America* (Ithaca, N.Y.: Cornell University Press, 1994), 71.

22. *Proceedings of the Third Anti-Slavery Convention of American Women, held in Philadelphia, May 1st, 2nd, 3rd, 1839* (Philadelphia: Merrihew and Thompson, 1839), 6.

23. *Sixth Annual Report*, 11.

24. Hallowell, 136; LCM to Abby Kelley, March 18, 1839, in Palmer 47; *Pennsylvania Freeman*, May 23, 30, 1839, May 21, 1840.

25. *Pennsylvania Freeman*, May 30, 1839, Oct. 24, 1844. On PFASS influence see Soderlund, "Priorities and Power," 80–84.

26. Sarah Forten to Angelina Grimké, April 15, 1837, quoted in Kathryn Kish Sklar, *Women's Rights Emerges Within the Antislavery Movement, 1830–1870* (New York: Bedford/St. Martin's, 2000), 99; for racial prejudice among American Quakers see Elizabeth Pease, *Society of Friends in the United States: Their Views of the Anti-Slavery Questions, and Treatment of the People of Colour. Compiled from Original Correspondence* (Darlington: John Wilson, 1840).

27. PFASS Minutes, Nov. 10, 1853, PAS Papers, Reel 30, HSP.

28. *Pennsylvania Freeman*, April 11, 1839, May 22, 1845, June 25, 1840.

29. LCM to James Miller McKim, Dec. 29, 1839, in Palmer, 69. On nonresistance, see Valarie H. Ziegler, *The Advocates of Peace in Antebellum America* (Macon, Ga.: Mercer University Press, 2001).

30. LCM to Richard D. and Hannah Webb, April 2, 1841, in Palmer, 91; LCM to Nathaniel and Elisa Barney, Nov. 8, 1839, in Palmer, 59–61. Charles C. Burleigh reported that one Friend commented: "if he [White] had only spoken out the name of Lucretia Mott, he would have deserved full credit for honesty telling just what he meant." CCB to J. Miller McKim, Oct. 16, 1839, Mott Manuscripts, FHL; Bacon, 50. On Quaker opposition to Garrisonian abolitionism, see Ryan P. Jordan, *Slavery and the Meetinghouse: The Quakers and the Abolitionist Dilemma, 1820–1865* (Bloomington: Indiana University Press, 2007).

31. "Diary of William Adams" (transcribed by Christopher Densmore, FHL), Nov. 9, 1841, reprinted in *The Friend*, Sept. 1874; diary entry April 20, 1843, reprinted in *The Journal*, March 31, 1875; diary entry April 11, 1841, reprinted in *The Journal*, June 17, 1874; diary entry Nov. 8, 1841, reprinted in *The Friend*, Sept. 1874.

32. Women's Yearly Meeting, May 10–15, 1841, Microfilm MR Ph 515, FHL; see also May 12–14, 1845, May 10–14, 1847, May 15–19, 1848, for example; LCM to Phebe Post Willis, Jan. 6, 1842, in Palmer, 104; Bacon, 107.

33. Charles C. Burleigh to J. Miller McKim, Oct. 16, 1839, Mott Manuscripts, FHL; Charles C. Burleigh, Resolution at the American Anti-Slavery Society Convention, quoted in *Pennsylvania Freeman*, May 19, 1841; LCM to Phebe Post Willis, Feb. 12, 1838, Phebe Post Willis Papers, University of Rochester.

34. *Pennsylvania Freeman*, March 5, 1840; LCM to Maria Weston Chapman, May 13, 1840, in Palmer, 75–76.

35. LCM to Maria Weston Chapman, May 13, 1840, in Palmer, 75; James Mott, *Three Months in Great Britain* (Philadelphia: J. Miller M'Kim, 1841), 17.

Chapter 6. Abroad

1. Frederick B. Tolles, *Slavery and "The Woman Question": Lucretia Mott's Diary of Her Visit to Great Britain to Attend the World's Anti-Slavery Convention of 1840* (Haverford, Pa.: Friends Historical Association, 1952), 49.

2. Charles C. Burleigh to James Miller McKim, Sept. 13, 1838, Mott Manuscripts, FHL (thanks to Helene Quanquin for her transcription); LCM to McKim, Dec. 29, 1839, in Beverly Wilson Palmer, Holly Byers Ochoa, and Carol Faulkner, eds., *Selected Letters of Lucretia Coffin Mott* (Urbana: University of Illinois Press, 2002), 68; LCM to Edward M. Davis, June 18, 1838, in Palmer, 43.

3. Burleigh to McKim, September 13, 1838.

4. Anna Davis Hallowell, *James and Lucretia Mott, Life and Letters* (Boston: Houghton Mifflin, 1884), 118, 120. LCM to James Miller McKim, March 15, 1838, in Palmer, 40; LCM to Phebe Post Willis, Feb. 12, 1838, Aug. 28, 1836, Phebe Post Willis Papers, University of Rochester.

5. LCM to Phebe Post, Aug. 28, 1836; LCM to James Miller McKim, March 15, 1838, in Palmer, 38.

6. William Cohen, "Burleigh, Charles Calistus," http://www.anb.org.libezproxy2.syr.edu/articles/15/15–00102.html; *American National Biography Online*, Feb. 2000, accessed June 18, 2008; "Funeral of C. C. Burleigh," *New York Times*, June 17, 1878; LCM to Maria Weston Chapman, May 29, 1839, in Palmer, 49.

7. William Wells Brown, *Three Years in Europe* (London: Charles Gilpin, 1852), 264–65; LCM to Joseph and Ruth Dugdale, March 28, 1849, in Palmer, 179.

8. LCM to James Miller McKim, Dec. 29, 1839, in Palmer, 68. On Kimberton, see Joan M. Jensen, "Not Only Ours But Others: The Quaker Teaching Daughters of the Mid-Atlantic, 1790–1850," *History of Education Quarterly* 24, 1 (Spring 1984): 11–13.

9. LCM to Phebe Post Willis, Nov. 1, 1838, Phebe Post Willis Papers, University of Rochester; Hallowell, 143; Henry Mayer, *All on Fire: William Lloyd Garrison and the Abolition of Slavery* (New York: St. Martin's, 1998), 290; *Liberator*, June 5, 1840. On

wool manufacturing, see L.G. Connor, "A Brief History of the Sheep Industry in the United States," in *Annual Report of the American Historical Association for the Year 1918* (Washington, D.C.: Government Printing Office, 1921), 1: 109–10.

10. Maria Mott Davis to Edward M. Davis, May 3, 1838, Mott Manuscripts, FHL; Hallowell, 142.

11. Dio Lewis, *Talks About People's Stomachs* (Boston: Fields, Osgood, 1870), 282.

12. Margaret Hope Bacon, *Valiant Friend: The Life of Lucretia Mott* (New York: Walker, 1980), 6; Lewis, *Talks About People's Stomachs*, 78.

13. Hallowell, 142; James Mott to Nathaniel Barney, Nov. 9, 1843, Mott Family Papers, Nantucket Historical Association (NHA); John Russell Bartlett, *Dictionary of Americanisms* (Boston: Little, Brown, 1877), 248; T. J. Stiles, *The First Tycoon: The Epic Life of Cornelius Vanderbilt* (New York: Knopf, 2009), 78.

14. James Mott to Nathaniel Barney, Nov. 9, 1843, Mott Family Papers, NHA; LCM to James Miller McKim, April 18, 1834 [?], Mott Mansucripts, FHL. See also James Mott to Nathaniel Barney, Oct. 26, 1847, Mott Family Papers, NHA.

15. LCM to James Miller McKim, Dec. 29, 1839, in Palmer 69.

16. *Proceedings of the General Anti-Slavery Convention, Called by the Committee of the British and Foreign Anti-Slavery Society, and held in London from Friday June 12th, to Tuesday, June 23rd, 1840* (London: British and Foreign Anti-Slavery Society, 1841), iii. On the WASC see Kathryn Kish Sklar, "'Women Who Speak for an Entire Nation': American and British Women at the World Anti-Slavery Convention, London, 1840," in Jean Fagan Yellin and John C. Van Horne, eds., *The Abolitionist Sisterhood: Women's Political Culture in Antebellum America* (Ithaca, N.Y.: Cornell University Press, 1994), 301–33; Clare Midgley, *Women Against Slavery: The British Campaigns, 1780–1870* (London: Routledge, 1992), 131–32, 158–63.

17. Hallowell, 144.

18. *Pennsylvania Freeman*, Aug. 6, 1840; Donald R. Kennon, "'An Apple of Discord': The Woman Question at the World's Anti-Slavery Convention of 1840," *Slavery and Abolition* 5, 3 (1984): 248. On Abby Kimber at Kimberton, see Jensen, "Not Only Ours But Others," 13.

19. Tolles, *Slavery and the "Woman Question"*, 13–14; James Mott, *Three Months in Great Britain* (Philadelphia: J. Miller M'Kim. 1841), 4; Ira V. Brown, *Mary Grew: Abolitionist and Feminist (1813–1896)* (Selinsgrove, Pa.: Susquehanna University Press, 1991).

20. Tolles, 19, 21.

21. Tolles, 17; Mott, *Three Months*, 5, 11.

22. Elizabeth Cady Stanton, Susan B. Anthony, and Matilda Joslyn Gage, *History of Woman Suffrage*, vol. 1, *1848–1861* (New York: Fowler and Wells, 1881), 420–22.

23. LCM to Richard and Hannah Webb, April 2, 1841, in Palmer, 93; LCM to James Miller McKim, May 8, 1834, in Palmer, 25.

24. Mott, *Three Months*, 15–16; Tolles, 25.

25. Sklar, "Women Who Speak for an Entire Nation," 321.

26. Tolles, 23, 26, 32, 49 40.

27. LCM to Daniel O'Connell, June 17, 1840, in Palmer, 77–78; Hallowell, 471–72.

28. Mott, *Three Months*, 18; Tolles, 28; *Memorial of Sarah Pugh: A Tribute of Respect from her Cousins* (Philadelphia: J.B. Lippincott, 1888), 11, 26.

29. *Proceedings of the General Anti-Slavery Convention*, 26, 27; Tolles, 31, 58.

30. Stanton, Anthony, and Gage, *History of Woman Suffrage*, 1: 61–62; Lori D. Ginzberg, *Elizabeth Cady Stanton: An American Life* (New York: Hill and Wang, 2009), 41.

31. On Stanton as historian, see especially Nancy Isenberg, *Sex and Citizenship in Antebellum America* (Chapel Hill: University of North Carolina Press, 1998), 1–6; Kathi Kern, *Mrs. Stanton's Bible* (Ithaca, N.Y.: Cornell University Press, 2001), 20–21.

32. Tolles, 36.

33. LCM to Maria Weston Chapman, July 29, 1840, in Palmer 79; *Proceedings*, 32–33; Tolles, 27.

34. *Proceedings of the General Anti-Slavery Convention*, passim.

35. *Proceedings of the General Anti-Slavery Convention*, 437, 445–46; Tolles, *Slavery and the "Woman Question"*, 40.

36. Tolles, 29; LCM to Richard and Hannah Webb, Feb. 25, 1842, in Palmer, 110.

37. Stanton, Anthony, and Gage, *History of Woman Suffrage*, 1: 62.

38. *Proceedings of the General Anti-Slavery Convention*, 431; Tolles, 39, 57.

39. Tolles, 42–44; "The Rejected Protest," *Liberator*, July 31, 1840.

40. Tolles, 58, 46–67; Mott, *Three Months*, 28–29.

41. Tolles, 30, Mott, *Three Months*, 43.

42. Tolles, 32.

43. Tolles, 48, 56, 60.

44. Mott, *Three Months*, 52–54; Tolles, 63–65; Mayer, 294.

45. LCM to George Combe, April 26, 1847, in Palmer, 148.

46. George Combe, *Notes on the United States of North America: During a Phrenological Visit 1838–9–40*, 3 vols. (Edinburgh: Maclachlan, Stewart, 1841), 2: 28; LCM to George and Cecilia Combe, Nov. 10, 1848, in Palmer, 168.

47. LCM to Phebe Post Willis, Nov. 1, 1838, Phebe Post Willis Papers, University of Rochester.

48. "Lucretia Mott," *Liberator*, July 30, 1841; Tolles, 68.

49. "Lucretia Mott," *Liberator*, July 30, 1841.

50. James Mott, *Three Months*, 65–66, 68.

51. Tolles, 72.

52. LCM to Phebe Post Willis, Aug. 28, 1836, Phebe Post Willis Papers, University of Rochester.

53. Tolles, 73–74, 75.

54. Tolles, 75, 49.

55. Tolles, 77; James Mott, *Three Months*, 84; Francis B. Whitlock, *Two New Yorkers: Editor and Sea Captain 1833* (New York: Newcomen Society, 1945), http://www.delanoye.org/Primary/Newcomen.html.

56. "Report of the Delegates to the London Convention," *Pennsylvania Freeman*, Oct. 15, 1840.

57. *Pennsylvania Freeman*, Oct. 22, Nov. 26, 1840.

58. *Pennsylvania Freeman*, Nov. 26, Dec. 10, 1840.

59. *Pennsylvania Freeman*, July 9, 1840.

60. *Pennsylvania Freeman*, Nov. 19, 1840.

61. *Pennsylvania Freeman*, Dec. 3, 1840.

62. Lucretia Mott, "Address, delivered at the Whole World's Temperance Convention, New York City, September 1–2, 1853," in Dana Greene, ed., *Lucretia Mott: Her Complete Speeches and Sermons* (New York: Edwin Mellen, 1980), 200.

63. Isenberg, *Sex and Citizenship*, 5.

Chapter 7. Crisis

1. *Pennsylvania Freeman*, Nov. 5, 1840, July 5, 1838, Dec. 20, 1838; Margaret Hope Bacon, *But One Race: The Life of Robert Purvis* (Albany: State University of New York Press, 2007), 78–81; Graham Russell Gao Hodges, *David Ruggles: A Radical Black Abolitionist and the Underground Railroad in New York City* (Chapel Hill: University of North Carolina Press, 2010).

2. Julie Roy Jeffrey, *The Great Silent Army of Abolitionism: Ordinary Women in the Antislavery Movement* (Chapel Hill: University of North Carolina Press, 1998), 139–62; Nancy Isenberg, *Sex and Citizenship in Antebellum America* (Chapel Hill: University of North Carolina Press, 1998), chap. 4.

3. LCM to Elizabeth Pease, Feb. 18, 1841, in Beverly Wilson Palmer, Holly Byers Ochoa, and Carol Faulkner, eds., *Selected Letters of Lucretia Coffin Mott* (Urbana: University of Illinois Press, 2002), 87; Margaret Hope Bacon, *Valiant Friend: The Life of Lucretia Mott* (New York: Walker, 1980), 100.

4. James Mott to Nathaniel Barney, March 6, 1841, Mott Family Papers, NHA; Lucretia Mott, "Sermon, delivered in the Unitarian Church, Washington, D.C., January 15, 1843," in Dana Greene, ed., *Lucretia Mott: Her Complete Speeches and Sermons* (New York: Edwin Mellen, 1980), 38.

5. Mott's sermon can be found in the *Liberator*, Oct. 15, 1841 and in Greene, 25–34.

6. *Pennsylvania Freeman*, Feb. 1, 1844; *Liberator*, Feb. 10, 1843; *New-York Evangelist*, March 16, 1843.

7. "Lucretia Mott at the Capitol," *Philanthropist*, Feb. 1, 1843; LCM to Nathaniel Barney Feb. 14, 1843 in Palmer, 121.

8. Mott's sermon can be found in Greene, 35–51.

9. In Bacon, *Valiant Friend*, 105.

10. LCM to Nathaniel Barney, Feb. 14, 1843, in Palmer, 121.

11. Seventh Annual Report of the PFASS printed in the *Pennsylvania Freeman*, March 17, 1841. See also Bacon, *But One Race*, 50–54; Julie Winch, *Philadelphia's Black Elite: Activism, Accommodation, and the Struggle for Autonomy, 1787–1848* (Philadelphia: Temple University Press, 1988), chap. 6.

12. PFASS Minutes, Feb. 8, March 8, April 12, 1849, PAS Papers, Reel 30, HSP; Sixteenth

Annual Report of the PFASS, printed in *Pennsylvania Freeman*, Feb. 7, 1850. See also Jean R. Soderlund, "Priorities and Power: The Philadelphia Female Anti-Slavery Society," in Jean Fagan Yellin and John C. Van Horne, eds., *The Abolitionist Sisterhood: Women's Political Culture in Antebellum America* (Ithaca, N.Y.: Cornell University Press, 1994), 76–77; Erica Armstrong Dunbar, *Fragile Freedom: African American Women and Emancipation in the Antebellum City* (New Haven, Conn.: Yale University Press, 2008), 95.

13. PFASS Minutes, March 3, Sept. 9, 1841, Nov. 10, Dec. 8, 1842, PAS Papers, Reel 30, HSP.

14. PFASS Minutes, Oct. 8, 1846, PAS Papers, Reel 30, HSP. Beth Salerno and Erica Armstrong Dunbar see this debate as disagreement between white and black abolitionists, but there is no evidence that the divisions were racial. Margaretta Forten, Harriet Purvis, Sarah Douglass and other lifelong members remained in the society. Beth A. Salerno, *Sister Societies: Women's Antislavery Organizations in Antebellum America* (Dekalb: Northern Illinois University Press, 2005), 140–41; Dunbar, 95.

15. PFASS Minutes, April 10, 1856, PAS Papers, Reel 30, HSP.

16. Lucretia Mott, "Diversities," *Liberty Bell. By Friends of Freedom*, Jan. 1, 1844. See also Mott's remarks in PFASS Minutes, June 10, 1847, PAS Papers, Reel 30, HSP.

17. Soderlund, "Priorities and Power," 72–73; PFASS Minutes, Dec. 11, 1845, PAS Papers, Reel 30, HSP.

18. "Free Produce Question," *Liberator*, Mar. 1, 1850; "Correspondence between the Buckingham Female A.S. Society and the Female A.S. Society of Philadelphia," *Genius of Universal Emancipation*, Oct. 1837; PFASS Minutes, Oct. 13, Dec. 8, 1842, Apr. 11, 1848, PAS Papers, Reel 30, HSP; Bacon, *But One Race*, 96, 97. On free produce as a divisive issue in the PFASS see Carol Faulkner, "The Root of the Evil: Free Produce and Radical Antislavery, 1820–1860," *Journal of the Early Republic* 27 (Fall 2007): 377–405.

19. PFASS Minutes, May 19, 1842, June 12, 1845, March 12, 1847, PAS Papers, Reel 30, HSP. For resignations over disunionism, see PFASS Minutes, Feb. 13, 1848, PAS Papers, Reel 30, HSP.

20. *Pennsylvania Freeman*, Jan. 14, 1847.

21. *Pennsylvania Freeman*, March 18, 1847.

22. Lucretia Mott, "What Is Anti-Slavery Work?" *Liberty Bell. By Friends of Freedom*, Jan. 1, 1846.

23. *Pennsylvania Freeman*, Dec. 24, 1846

24. LCM to Nathaniel Barney, March 6, 1841, in Palmer, 88–89. On Mary Gove (later Nichols), see Ellen Carol DuBois, "Feminism and Free Love," http://www.h-net.org/~women/papers/freeloveintro.html.

25. *Pennsylvania Freeman*, Aug. 14, 1845, March 18, 1847; PFASS Minutes, June 23, 1842, PAS Papers, Reel 30, HSP; see also Bacon, *But One Race*, 98; PFASS Minutes April 11, 1844, Jan. 14, June 10, 1847, PAS Papers, Reel 30, HSP.

26. *Pennsylvania Freeman*, June 18, 25, July 2, 1846; Bacon, *Valiant Friend*, 114. Also available in *Niles' National Register*, July 4, 1846; Margaret Hope Bacon, *Lucretia Mott Speaking: Excerpts from the Sermons & Speeches of a Famous Nineteenth Century Quaker Minister & Reformer* (Wallingford, Pa.: Pendle Hill, 1980), 21.

27. LCM to George Combe, April 26, 1847, in Palmer, 150–51.

28. *Report of the Association for the Relief and Employment of Poor Women* (Philadelphia: Ellwood, Chapman, 1845, 1847, 1848); *Fifth Annual Report of the Northern Association for the Relief and Employment of Poor Women* (Philadelphia: North American, 1849); *Reports and Realities from a Sketch-Book of a Manager of the Rosine Association* (Philadelphia: J. Duross, 1855), 12.

29. *Eleventh Annual Report* (Philadelphia: Deacon and Peterson, 1855), 4; "Rules for the Government of the Women," Box 1, Northern Association of the City and County of Philadelphia for the Relief and Employment of Poor Women, FHL.

30. *Seventh Annual Report* (Philadelphia: Saturday Post Book and Job Printing Office, 1851), 5; Northern Association Constitution 1849, Box 1, Northern Association of the City and County of Philadelphia for the Relief and Employment of Poor Women, FHL. On the Rosine Association, see Isenberg, *Sex and Citizenshi*, 130–31; Diana Pearce, "The Feminization of Poverty: Women, Work, and Welfare," *Urban and Social Change Review* 2 (1978), 28–36.

31. For example, Amended Constitution 1856, Box 1, Northern Association of the City and County of Philadelphia for the Relief and Employment of Poor Women, FHL; *Ninth Annual Report* (Philadelphia: Saturday Post Book and Job Printing Office, 1853); *Report of the Association for the Relief and Employment of Poor Women* (Philadelphia: Ellwood, Chapman, 1845).

32. LCM to Martha Coffin Wright, Jan. 12, 1844, in Palmer, 132. On Thomas Cavender and the PASS, see *Pennsylvania Freeman*, May 28, 1840, May 12, 1841, Aug. 22, 1844. Cavender also had a run-in with the PFASS, see PFASS Minutes, Dec. 12, 1844, PAS Papers, Reel 30, HSP.

33. Bacon, *Valiant Friend*, 109; LCM to George and Cecilia Combe, March 24, 1843, in Palmer, 129.

34. LCM to George and Cecilia Combe, March 2, 1846, in Palmer, 137–38; *Pennsylvania Freeman*, April 11, 1844.

35. LCM to George and Cecilia Combe, March 2, 1846, in Palmer, 138; LCM to Martha and David Wright, Aug. 28, 1840, Mott Manuscripts, FHL; Anna Davis Hallowell, *James and Lucretia Mott, Life and Letters* (Boston: Houghton Mifflin, 1884), 266–67.

36. Ellen DuBois, "Women's Rights and Abolition: The Nature of the Connection," in Lewis Perry and Michael Fellman, *Antislavery Reconsidered: New Perspectives on the Abolitionists* (Baton Rouge: Louisiana State University Press, 1979), 244; Isenberg, *Sex and Citizenship*, 88, 89, chap. 4, passim; Judith Wellman, *The Road to Seneca Falls: Elizabeth Cady Stanton and the First Women's Rights Convention* (Urbana: University of Illinois Press, 2004), chaps. 4, 5; Ryan P. Jordan, *Slavery and the Meetinghouse: The Quakers and the Abolitionist Dilemma, 1820–1860* (Bloomington: Indiana University Press, 2007), 57, 82, passim. On Mott as a liberal force among the Hicksites, see Chuck Fager, "Lucretia Mott: Liberal Quaker Theologian," *Quaker Theology* (Spring–Summer 2004), http://www.quaker.org/quest/issue-10-mott-CEF-01.htm.

37. LCM to Richard and Hannah Webb, April 3, 1841, in Palmer, 93–94; LCM to

Nathaniel Barney, March 6, 1841, in Palmer, 88. On Mott's relationship to Cherry Street Meeting, see also Isaac T. Hopper to Joseph A. Dugdale, Sept. 3, 1841, Dugdale Manuscripts, FHL.

38. LCM to Phebe Post Willis, Jan. 6, 1842, in Palmer, 102; LCM to Phebe Post Willis, April 28, 1842, Phebe Post Willis Papers, University of Rochester; Bacon, *Valiant Friend*, 103. Willis's position may have been closer to Mott's than she originally thought; see Wellman, 119.

39. LCM to Richard and Hannah Webb, Feb. 25, 1842, in Palmer, 106, 108, 112.

40. LCM to Richard and Hannah Webb, Feb. 25, 1842, 107; Theodore Parker, "A Discourse on the Transient and the Permanent in Christianity; Preached at the Ordination of Mr. Charles S. Shackleford, in the Hawes Place Church in Boston, May 19, 1841," *Electronic Texts in American Studies*, University of Nebraska-Lincoln Libraries, 2007, http://digitalcommons.unl.edu/cgi/viewcontent.cgi?article=1013&context=etas; LCM to George Julian, Nov. 11, 1848, in Palmer, 177.

41. Hallowell, 284; LCM to George Julian, Nov. 14, 1848, in Palmer, 176; LCM to George Combe, April 26, 1847, in Palmer, 148–49. See also Nancy Isenberg, "'To Stand Out in Heresy': Lucretia Mott, Liberty, and Hysterical Woman," *Pennsylvania Magazine of History and Biography* 127, 1 (2003): 7–24.

42. Mott's speech can be found in Greene, 53–57, Hallowell, 284–87, and *Liberator*, April 30, 1847; Bacon, *Valiant Friend*, 114.

43. LCM to Sarah Dugdale, Oct.7, 1845 in Palmer, 135–37.

44. LCM to Nathaniel Barney, Oct. 30–31, 1847, in Palmer, 155–57; James Mott to Nathaniel Barney, Oct. 26, 1847, NHA.

45. *North Star*, May 19, 1848, Jan. 26, June 29, 1849; William S. McFeely, *Frederick Douglass* (New York: Norton, 1991), 144–45.

46. LCM to Nathaniel Barney, Oct. 30–31, 1847, in Palmer, 155–57; James Mott to Nathaniel Barney, Oct. 26, 1847, NHA; John Jackson, *Reflections on Peace and War* (Philadelphia: T.E. Chapman, 1846), 9, 2.

47. Hallowell, 292, 294; James Mott to Nathaniel Barney, Oct. 26, 1847, NHA.

48. LCM to Abby Kelley, March 18, 1839, in Palmer, 47; Wellman, 111, 119; Dorothy Sterling, *Ahead of Her Time: Abby Kelley and the Politics of Antislavery* (New York: Norton, 1991), 123; LCM to George and Cecelia Combe, Sept. 10, 1848, in Palmer, 171.

49. Wellman, 130–33. Julie Roy Jeffrey, *Great Silent Army of Abolitionism: Ordinary Women in the Antislavery Movement* (Chapel Hill: University of North Carolina Press, 1998), 145–50.

50. Isenberg, *Sex and Citizenship*, 62–63.

51. Sherry H. Penney and James D. Livingston, *A Very Dangerous Woman: Martha Wright and Women's Rights* (Amherst: University of Massachusetts Press, 2004), 114, 230; LCM to Elizabeth Cady Stanton, March 23, 1841, in Palmer, 90; Wellman, 100.

52. "Lucretia Mott at Worcester," *Liberator*, Sept. 17, 1847; LCM to Nathaniel and Elisa Barney, Oct.30 and 31, 1847, in Palmer, 157, 159; *Pennsylvania Freeman*, Sept. 23, 1847; Bacon, *Valiant Friend*, 117, Sterling, 243. Mott's theological views were controversial

even in the anti-slavery movement. See Edmund Quincy's introduction to the *Liberator* report and Valentine Nicholson's reply in the *Liberator*, Oct. 22, 1847.

53. LCM to Martha Coffin Wright [?], c. May 22, 1847, in Palmer, 153.

Chapter 8. The Year 1848

1. LCM to George and Cecilia Combe, Sept. 10, 1848, in Beverly Wilson Palmer, Holly Byers Ochoa, and Carol Faulkner, eds., *Selected Letters of Lucretia Coffin Mott* (Urbana: University of Illinois Press, 2002), 168–69.

2. Judith Wellman, *The Road to Seneca Falls: Elizabeth Cady Stanton and the First Woman's Rights Convention* (Urbana: University of Illinois Press, 2004), 172; LCM to Edmund Quincy, Aug. 24, 1848, in Palmer, 167.

3. Palmer, 161 n2; LCM to Nathaniel Barney, March 14, 1848, in Palmer, 160. See also Dana Greene, ed., *Lucretia Mott: Her Complete Speeches and Sermons* (New York: Edwin Mellen, 1980), 69.

4. Dean Grodzins, *American Heretic: Theodore Parker and Transcendentalism* (Chapel Hill: University of North Carolina Press, 2002), 473–77.

5. LCM, "Remarks, delivered to the Anti-Sabbath Convention," in Greene, 59–79; Nancy Isenberg, *Sex and Citizenship in Antebellum America* (Chapel Hill: University of North Carolina Press, 1998), 85.

6. Quoted in *Pennsylvania Freeman*, April 20, 1848.

7. Isenberg, *Sex and Citizenship*, 87.

8. LCM to Sydney Gay and Elizabeth Neall Gay, May 1, 1848, in Palmer, 162; Margaret Hope Bacon, *Valiant Friend: The Life of Lucretia Mott* (New York: Walker, 1980), 119.

9. LCM to Sydney Gay and Elizabeth Neall Gay, May 1, 1848, in Palmer, 162; Bacon, 119.

10. LCM to Elizabeth Cady Stanton, Oct. 3, 1848, in Palmer, 173; LCM to Thomas and Mary Ann M'Clintock, July 29, 1848, in Palmer, 164.

11. LCM, "Law of Progress," in Greene, 75; David Brion Davis, *Slavery and Human Progress* (New York: Oxford University Press, 1984), 156, 11.

12. LCM, "Law of Progress," in Greene, 71–79; Davis, *Slavery and Human Progress*, 159; Otelia Cromwell, *Lucretia Mott* (Cambridge, Mass.: Harvard University Press, 1958), 127.

13. William S. McFeely, *Frederick Douglass* (New York: Norton, 1991), 149–52; Frederick Douglass, "What to the Slave Is the Fourth of July," in David Blight, ed., *Narrative of the Life of Frederick Douglass, an American Slave, Written by Himself, with Related Documents* (New York: Bedford Books, 2003), 168–69.

14. LCM, "Law of Progress," in Greene, 77; Mott, "Diversities," *Liberty Bell: By Friends of Freedom*, Jan. 1, 1844; LCM to George and Cecilia Combe, Sept. 10, 1848, in Palmer, 170.

15. LCM to Nathaniel Barney, March 14, 1848, in Palmer, 160; Spencer Klaw, *Without Sin: The Life and Death of the Oneida Community* (New York: Allen Lane, 1993), 72.

16. John Stauffer, *The Black Hearts of Men: Radical Abolitionists and the Transformation of Race* (Cambridge, Mass.: Harvard University Press, 2001), 138–39, 169. For Smith's support for free produce see *Pennsylvania Freeman*, Oct. 11, 1838, Oct. 17, 1839, Oct. 24, 1844, Jan. 1, 1846.

17. Quoted in Jonathan H. Earle, *Jacksonian Anti-Slavery and the Politics of Free Soil, 1824–1854* (Chapel Hill: University of North Carolina Press, 2004), 3, 1–2.

18. Earle, 51, 68, 72.

19. Earle, 73, 76; Wellman, 173–77; Stauffer, 24.

20. LCM to Nathaniel and Elisa Barney, November 8, 1839, in Palmer, 61; LCM to Sarah Dugdale, October 7, 1845, in Palmer, 136; Wellman, 178.

21. Wellman, 178–80; Lucretia Mott to George and Cecilia Combe, Sept. 10, 1848, in Palmer, 169; LCM to George Julian, Nov. 14, 1848, in Palmer, 177.

22. William Penn, *The Sandy Foundation Shaken: Or, Those so Generally Believed and Applauded Doctrines, of One God, subsisting in three distinct and separate persons, The impossibility of God's pardoning Sinners, without a plenary satisfaction, The Justification of Impure Persons, by an Imputative Righteousness, Refuted, from the authority of Scripture Testimonies and Right Reason* (Philadelphia: 1825), v, 78; H. Larry Ingle, *Quakers in Conflict: The Hicksite Reformation* (Wallingford, Pa.: Pendle Hill 1986, 1998), 53, 144.

23. LCM to Nathaniel and Elisa Barney, November 8, 1839, in Palmer, 61; LCM to Phebe Post Willis, Jan. 6, 1842, in Palmer, 103.

24. Wellman, 178–79, 181; Palmer, 178 n 13.

25. LCM to Nathaniel Barney, March 14, 1848, in Palmer, 161; LCM to George Julian, Nov. 4, 1848, in Palmer, 177.

26. LCM to Elizabeth Cady Stanton, Oct. 25, 1849, in Palmer, 190.

27. Michael Leroy Oberg, *Native America: A History* (Malden, Mass.: Blackwell, 2010), 181–85, 195; Anthony F. C. Wallace, *The Death and Rebirth of the Seneca* (New York: Knopf, 1970); 323–24; "The Treaty Upheld," *New York Times*, April 24, 1891.

28. Minutes of the Indian Committee, Dec. 4, 1838, May 13, 1839, May 14, 1841, Philadelphia Yearly Meeting (Hicksite) Indian Committee, RG 2/Phy/780, FHL.

29. Report of the Indian Committee, May 16, 1843, Indian Committee, FHL; Oberg, 195; Laurence M. Hauptman, *Conspiracy of Interests: Iroquois Dispossession and the Rise of New York State* (Syracuse, N.Y.: Syracuse University Press, 1999), 191–96.

30. Minutes, June 7, 1843, Reports, May 13, 1845, Indian Committee, FHL; *Proceedings of the Joint Committee of the Society of Friends for Promoting the Civilization and Improving the Condition of the Seneca Nation of Indians* (Baltimore: William Wooddy, 1847), 145, 147. See also Report from a Meeting with the Seneca Chiefs, May 14, 1840, Indian Committee, FHL.

31. LCM to James Miller McKim, July 19, 1839, in Palmer, 56; LCM to Edmund Quincy, Aug. 24, 1848, in Palmer, 166; Bacon, 124–25. Louise Michele Newman, *White Women's Rights: The Racial Origins of Feminism in the United States* (New York: Oxford University Press, 1999), 117, 119; Sally Roesch Wagner, *Sisters in Spirit: Haudenosaunee*

(Iroquois) Influence on Early American Feminists (Summerton, Tenn.: Native Voices, 2001), 32, 44.

32. LCM to Edmund Quincy, Aug. 24, 1848, in Palmer, 166; Indian Committee Report, May 13, 1845, FHL; Oberg, *Native America*, 212–13.

33. LCM to Edmund Quincy, Aug. 24, 1848, in Palmer 166; Wallace, 13, 17, 324; William Fenton, "Toward the Gradual Civilization of the Indian Natives: The Missionary and Linguistic Work of Asher Wright," *Proceedings of the American Philosophical Society* 100, 6 (Dec. 1956): 567–81.

34. James Mott to Joseph Warner, June 23, 1848, Report, Jan. 25, 1849, Indian Committee, FHL.

35. LCM to Edmund Quincy, Aug. 24, 1848, in Palmer, 165–66 (see also *Liberator*, Oct. 6, 1848); Fergus M. Bordewich, *Bound for Canaan: The Epic Story of the Underground Railroad, America's First Civil Rights Movement* (New York: Amistad/Harper-Collins, 2005), 246, 260. For more on Canada West, see "The Black Canadian Experience in Ontario 1834–1914," Archives of Ontario, http://www.archives.gov.on.ca/english/on-line-exhibits/black-history/index.aspx; Sharon Roger Hepburn, *Crossing the Border: A Free Black Community in Canada* (Urbana: University of Illinois Press, 2007).

36. Michael D. Pierson, *Free Hearts and Free Homes: Gender and American Antislavery Politics* (Chapel Hill: University of North Carolina Press, 2003), 49–52; "Liberty League and Its Nominees," *Liberator*, July 2, 1847; Earle, 158; Wellman, 176; Carol Faulkner, "The Root of the Evil: Free Produce and Radical Antislavery, 1820–1860," *Journal of the Early Republic* 27 (Fall 2007): 377–405.

37. David J. Rothman, *The Discovery of the Asylum: Social Order and Disorder in the New Republic* (New York: Little, Brown, 1970, 1991), 87; Sherry H. Penney and James D. Livingston, *A Very Dangerous Woman: Martha Wright and Women's Rights* (Amherst: University of Massachusetts Press, 2004), 55; Ann D. Gordon, *The Selected Papers of Elizabeth Cady Stanton and Susan B. Anthony*, vol. 1, *In the School of Anti-Slavery, 1840–1866* (New Brunswick, N.J.: Rutgers University Press, 1998), 433; LCM to Elizabeth Cady Stanton, July 16, 1848, in Palmer, 163. On Seward's opposition to the Treaty of Buffalo Creek, see Stephen J. Valone, "William Seward, Whig Politics, and the Compromised Indian Removal Policy in New York State, 1838–1843," *New York History* 82, 2 (2001): 106–34.

38. Lori D. Ginzberg, *Elizabeth Cady Stanton: An American Life* (New York: Hill and Wang, 2009), 54–55; Wellman, 189, 188, 152–54.

39. Wellman, 192–93; Declaration of Sentiments, Women's Rights Historical Park, National Park Service, http://www.nps.gov/wori/historyculture/declaration-of-sentiments.htm.

40. LCM to Elizabeth Cady Stanton, July 16, 1848, in Palmer, 163; Wellman, 204.

41. *Report of the Woman's Rights Convention, Held at Seneca Falls, N.Y., July 19th and 20th, 1848* (Rochester, N.Y., 1848), in Gordon, 76; Wellman, 194–95.

42. Quoted in Wellman, 195; Ginzberg, 61–62.

43. Gordon, 78, 82, 83; Wellman, 197–98, 203; Martha S. Jones, *All Bound Up*

Together: The Woman Question in African American Public Culture, 1830–1900 (Chapel Hill: University of North Carolina Press, 2007), 71.

44. *Report of the Woman's Rights Convention*, 76.

45. *Report of the Woman's Rights Convention*, 77.

46. Gordon, 78; Wellman, 196.

47. LCM to Elizabeth Cady Stanton, March 16, 1855, in Palmer, 236.

48. Gordon, 79–81.

49. Gordon, 79–81.

50. LCM to Thomas and Mary Ann M'Clintock, July 29, 1848, in Palmer, 164; Nancy A. Hewitt, "Feminist Friends: Agrarian Quakers and the Emergence of Woman's Rights in America," *Feminist Studies* 12, 1 (Spring 1986): 33.

51. Hewitt, 29; "Report of the Woman's Rights Convention Rochester, 1848," *Rochester University Library Bulletin* 4, 11 (Aug. 1948), http://www.lib.rochester.edu/index.cfm?PAGE=2448.

52. "Report of the Woman's Rights Convention Rochester"; Jones, *All Bound Up Together*, 72.

53. Report of the Woman's Rights Convention Rochester."

54. "Report of the Woman's Rights Convention Rochester"; Cromwell, 135.

55. LCM to Edmund Quincy, Aug. 24, 1848, in Palmer, 166–67.

56. LCM to George and Cecilia Combe, Sept. 10, 1848, in Palmer, 171.

57. LCM to Elizabeth Cady Stanton, Oct. 3, 1848, in Palmer, 173; Jones, 76–77.

58. Elizabeth Cady Stanton to LCM, Sept., 26, 1849, in Gordon, 147; Stanton's resolution, "Report of the Woman's Rights Convention Rochester"; LCM to Elizabeth Cady Stanton, Oct. 25, 1848, in Palmer, 190; Bacon, 128.

59. LCM to Elizabeth McClintock and Elizabeth Cady Stanton, Nov. 27, 1849, in Palmer, 192–93; Sylvia D. Hoffert, "Female Self-Making in Mid-Nineteenth-Century America," *Journal of Women's History* 20, 3 (Fall 2008): 39.

60. LCM to Elizabeth Cady Stanton, Oct. 25, 1849, in Palmer, 189; LCM to Elizabeth McClintock and Elizabeth Cady Stanton, Nov. 27, 1849, in Palmer 193.

61. Elizabeth Cady Stanton to LCM, Nov. 12, 1849, in Gordon, 149; "Drama by E.C.S. and Elizabeth W. McClintock," in Gordon, 152–60.

62. Hoffert, 41, 52.

63. LCM to Elizabeth McClintock and Elizabeth Cady Stanton, Nov. 27, 1849, in Palmer, 194.

64. *Pennsylvania Freeman*, Dec. 13, 1849, Nancy Isenberg, " 'To Stand Out in Heresy': Lucretia Mott, Liberty, and Hysterical Woman," *Pennsylvania Magazine of History and Biography* 127, 1 (2003): 16–17; Cromwell, 148–49; Joseph Flibbert, "Dana, Richard Henry," http://www.anb.org.libezproxy2.syr.edu/articles/16/16-00413.html, *American National Biography Online*, Feb. 2000, accessed May 21, 2009.

65. Mott, "Discourse on Woman," in Greene, 143; *Pennsylvania Freeman*, Dec. 20, 1849.

66. "Discourse on Woman," 147.

67. "Discourse on Woman," 147, 153.

68. "Discourse on Woman," 154, 156, 161.

69. LCM to the Salem, Ohio, Woman's Convention, in Palmer, 203–4.

70. "Remarks, at the Woman's Rights Convention, New York City," in Greene, 203; Isenberg, *Sex and Citizenship*, xviii.

Chapter 9. Conventions

1. LCM to James Mott and Children, June 19, 1849, in Beverly Wilson Palmer, Holly Byers Ochoa, and Carol Faulkner, eds., *Selected Letters of Lucretia Coffin Mott* (Urbana: University of Illinois Press, 2002), 188; Anna Davis Hallowell, *James and Lucretia Mott, Life and Letters* (Boston: Houghton Mifflin, 1884), 269–70, 326–29.

2. LCM to George Combe, May 21, 1852, in Palmer, 216.

3. *Pennsylvania Freeman*, March 10, 1853.

4. Nancy Isenberg, *Sex and Citizenship in Antebellum America* (Chapel Hill: University of North Carolina Press, 1998), 96–97, xviii, 70–74; Sylvia D. Hoffert, *When Hens Crow: The Woman's Rights Movement in Antebellum America* (Bloomington: Indiana University Press, 1995), 11–12.

5. LCM to Elizabeth Cady Stanton, Oct. 25, 1849, in Palmer, 190.

6. Kathryn Kish Sklar, *Women's Rights Emerges Within the Antislavery Movement, 1830–1870* (New York: Bedford Books, 2000), 60; Isenberg, xiii.

7. Call to the Convention as reprinted in *The Proceedings of the Woman's Rights Convention, Held at Worcester, October 23d & 24th, 1850* (Boston: Prentiss & Sawyer, 1851), 3–5. See also John McClymer, "Introduction," "How Do Contemporary Newspaper Accounts of the 1850 Worcester Woman's Rights Convention Enhance Our Understanding of the Issues Debated at That Meeting?" in Kathryn Kish Sklar and Thomas Dublin, *Women and Social Movements in the United States, 1600–2000* (Binghamton: State University of New York at Binghamton, 2006), http://asp6new.alexanderstreet.com.libezproxy2.syr.edu/wasm/wasmrestricted/DP67/intro.htm.

8. Paulina W. Davis, "Address by Paulina W. Davis," *Proceedings of the Woman's Rights Convention 1850*, 6–14.

9. "Woman's Rights Convention," *New York Daily Tribune*, Oct. 25, 1850, 5–6; "Woman's Rights Convention," *New York Herald*, Oct. 25, 1.

10. "Letter XII: Legal Disabilities of Women," in Sarah Grimké, *Letters of the Equality of the Sexes and the Condition of Women* (Boston: Knapp, 1838).

11. Harriet Taylor, "Enfranchisement of Women," *Westminster and Foreign Quarterly Review* (July 1851): 289–311; Evening Session, Oct. 23, 1850, in *Proceedings of the Woman's Rights Convention, 1850*, 14–15; "Grand Demonstration of Petticoatdom at Worcester," *Boston Daily Mail*, Evening Edition, Oct. 25, 1850, 1; Nell Irvin Painter, *Sojourner Truth: A Life, a Symbol* (New York: Norton, 1996), 114–15.

12. "The Worcester Convention," *Saturday Visiter*, Nov. 2, 1850: 166; Sylvia D.

Hoffert, *Jane Grey Swisshlem: An Unconventional Life, 1815–1884* (Chapel Hill: University of North Carolina Press, 2004), 143.

13. "Woman's Rights Convention," *New York Herald*, Oct. 28, 1850, 4.

14. "Woman's Rights Convention," *New York Herald*, Oct. 25, 1850, 1; "The Worcester Convention," 166; Isenberg, 96.

15. LCM to Philadelphia Family, Feb. 1, 1869, in Palmer, 411.

16. Hoffert, 13; John McClymer, "Introduction."

17. LCM to Lucy Stone, Aug. 6, 1851, in Palmer, 207.

18. Harriet Taylor, "Enfranchisement of Women," *Westminster and Foreign Quarterly Review* (July 1851): 289–311; LCM to William Lloyd Garrison and Helen Benson Garrison, Sept. 11, 1851, in Palmer, 209.

19. LCM to George Combe, May 21, 1852, in Palmer, 215–16; "Speech, to the Woman's Rights Meeting, West Chester, Pennsylvania, June 2, 1852," in Dana Greene, ed., *Lucretia Mott: Her Complete Speeches and Sermons* (New York: Edwin Mellen, 1980), 193; Margaret Hope Bacon, *Valiant Friend: The Life of Lucretia Mott* (New York: Walker, 1980), 136–37.

20. LCM to Lucy Stone, Aug. 16, 1852, in Palmer, 219.

21. LCM to Lucy Stone, Aug. 16, 1852, in Palmer, 220.

22. President's Address to the Women's Rights Convention, in *The Proceedings of the Woman's Rights Convention Held at West Chester, PA., June 2d and 3d, 1852* (Philadelphia: Merrihew and Thompson, 1852), 7–10.

23. *Pennsylvania Freeman*, Sept. 25, 1852.

24. "Remarks, delivered at the Woman's Rights Convention, Syracuse," in Greene, 195.

25. *Proceedings*, Thursday, Sept. 9, 1852, Evening Session; Friday, Sept. 10, 1852, Afternoon Session; National Woman's Rights Convention, 3rd: 1852, Sept. 8–10: Syracuse, New York (Syracuse, N.Y.: J.E. Masters, 1852).

26. *Proceedings*, National Woman's Rights Convention, 3rd.

27. *Pennsylvania Freeman*, May 16, 1850. For more on Rynders, see Tyler Anbinder, *Five Points: The 19th-Century New York Neighborhood That Invented Tap Dance, Rigged a Presidential Election, and Became the World's Most Notorious Slum* (New York: Plume, 2001), 141–44, 166.

28. Elizabeth Cady Stanton, Susan B. Anthony, and Matilda Joslyn Gage, *History of Woman Suffrage*, vol. 1, *1848–1861* (New York: Fowler and Wells, 1881), 506; "Address delivered at the Whole World's Temperance Convention" in Greene, 199, 201. For more on the Whole World's Temperance convention, see Isenberg, 99–100; Susan B. Anthony to Lucy Stone, May 1, 1853, Antoinette L. Brown to Susan B. Anthony, Aug. 2, 1853, Lucy Stone to Elizabeth Cady Stanton, Aug. 14, 1853, in Ann Gordon, ed., *The Selected Papers of Elizabeth Cady Stanton and Susan B. Anthony*, vol. 1, *In the School of Anti-Slavery, 1840–1866* (New Brunswick, N.J.: Rutgers University Press, 1997), 219–26.

29. "Remarks to the Woman's Rights Convention, New York City," in Greene, 206–7; Second Day: Evening Session, *Proceedings of the Woman's Rights Convention, Held at the Broadway Tabernacle, in the City of New York, on Tuesday and Wednesday, Sept. 6th*

and 7th, 1853 (New York: Fowler and Wells, 1853), 86–96; *History of Woman Suffrage*, 1: 506, 571; Gordon, 226.

30. Hallowell, 133–34.

31. Bacon, 5–6; Hallowell, 134. "The Empire Club Chief," *New York Times*, Jan. 14, 1885.

32. "Remarks, Delivered at the National Women's Rights Convention," Greene, 215, 217; Hallowell, 460.

33. LCM to Philadelphia Family, Oct. 17, 1853, in Palmer, 227; Palmer, 228 n3.

34. LCM to Philadelphia Family, Oct. 17, 1853, in Palmer, 227; Herman Melville, *The Confidence Man* (London: Longman, 1857), 9.

35. LCM to Philadelphia Family, Oct. 17, 1853, in Palmer, 228; Hallowell, 339–40; Sherry H. Penney and James D. Livingston, *A Very Dangerous Woman: Martha Wright and Women's Rights* (Amherst: University of Massachusetts Press, 2004), 104; *Pennsylvania Freeman*, Nov. 4, 1853. See also Thomas B. Stevenson to LCM, Oct. 13, 1853, Mott Manuscripts, FHL.

36. LCM to Lucy Stone, Oct. 31, 1856, in Palmer, 254.

37. "Remarks, Delivered at the Seventh National Woman's Rights Convention," in Greene, 227, 233.

38. LCM to Lucy Stone, July 1, 1857, in Palmer, 259; LCM to Lucy Stone, Oct. 31, 1856, in Palmer, 255.

39. LCM to Lucy Stone, July 1, 1857, in Palmer, 259; LCM to Lucy Stone, Oct. 31, 1856, in Palmer, 254; LCM to Martha Wright, Dec. 31, 1855, Mott Manuscripts, FHL.

40. Martha Coffin Wright to Susan B. Anthony, June 8, 1858, in Gordon, 372–73; Penney and Livingston, 127; Henry Clarke Wright, *The Unwelcome Child, or, The Crime of an Undesigned and Undesired Maternity* (Boston: Bela Marsh, 1860).

41. Martha Coffin Wright to Susan B. Anthony, June 8, 1858, in Gordon, 372–73; LCM to Martha Coffin Wright, July 6, 1858, in Palmer, 274, 277, nn 2, 3.

42. LCM to Elizabeth Neall Gay, Dec. 9, 1858, in Palmer, 280.

43. LCM to Martha Coffin Wright and Anna Temple Brown, May 31, 1859, in Palmer, 288, 289n3; *National Woman's Rights Convention, 9th: 1859 May 12: New York, NY* (Rochester, N.Y.: Steam Press of A. Strong and Co., 1859). Sally G. McMillen, *Seneca Falls and the Origins of the Women's Rights Movement* (New York: Oxford University Press, 2008), 140. See also LCM to Martha Coffin Wright, May 22, 1859, Mott Manuscripts, FHL.

44. *Proceedings of the Tenth National Woman's Rights Convention, Held at the Cooper Institute, New York City, May 10th and 11th, 1860* (Boston: Yerrinton and Garrison, 1860), 4.

45. "Tenth National Woman's Rights Convention," in Gordon, 421, 418–19; Amy Dru Stanley, *From Bondage to Contract: Wage Labor, Marriage, and the Market in the Age of Slave Emancipation* (New York: Cambridge University Press, 1998), 184–85. See also Susan B. Anthony to Lucy Stone, May 1, 1853, in Gordon, 220.

46. "Second Day," *Proceedings of the Tenth National Woman's Rights Convention*.

47. Quoted in Gordon, 431.

48. LCM to Anna Temple Brown, May 28, 1860, Mott Manuscripts, FHL; LCM to Martha Coffin Wright(?), July 5, 1860, in Palmer, 299.

49. LCM to Martha Coffin Wright, Anna Temple Brown, and Martha Mott Lord, Jan. 21, 1864, in Palmer 337; Daniel Kilbride, *An American Aristocracy: Southern Planters in Antebellum Philadelphia* (Columbia: University of South Carolina Press, 2006), 39–40.

50. LCM to Martha Coffin Wright and Eliza Wright Osbourne, March 19, 1861, in Palmer, 309; Bacon, 174.

51. "Remarks, to the Woman's Rights Convention, New York City, September 6–7, 1853," in Greene, 205; "Remarks, to the Twenty-Fourth Annual Meeting of the Pennsylvania Anti-Slavery Society," in Greene, 262.

Chapter 10. Fugitives

1. "Remarks, delivered at the Twenty-Fourth Annual Meeting of the Pennsylvania Anti-Slavery Society, Oct. 25–26, 1860," in Dana Greene, ed., *Lucretia Mott: Her Complete Speeches and Sermons* (New York: Edwin Mellen, 1980), 262.

2. LCM to Joseph and Ruth Dugdale, July 12, 1850, in Beverly Wilson Palmer, Holly Byers Ochoa, and Carol Faulkner, eds., *Selected Letters of Lucretia Coffin Mott* (Urbana: University of Illinois Press, 2002), 204, 206. Joining the Purvises at the first meeting of the Progressive Friends in Kennett Square, Pennsylvania, were Thomas M'Clintock, Joseph Dugdale, Ernestine Rose, Oliver Johnson, and James and Lucretia Mott. Wanting to support the new group, the Motts defied Philadelphia Yearly Meeting to attend. *Pennsylvania Freeman*, Oct. 16, 1852; Joseph Dugdale to John and Rebecca Ketcham, March 6, 1853, Dugdale Manuscripts, FHL; *Pennsylvania Freeman*, June 2, 1853; Margaret Hope Bacon, *But One Race: The Life of Robert Purvis* (Albany: State University of New York Press, 2007), 105–6.

3. Stanley Harrold, *The Rise of Aggressive Abolitionism: Addresses to the Slaves* (Lexington: University Press of Kentucky, 2004), 123–35, 191–92.

4. *Pennsylvania Freeman*, Sept. 12, 1850.

5. *Pennsylvania Freeman*, Oct. 10, 1850; LCM to Richard D. and Hannah Webb, May 14, 1849, in Palmer, 186.

6. *Pennsylvania Freeman*, Oct. 31, 1850.

7. PFASS Minutes, June 13, 1850, PAS Papers, Reel 30, HSP (emphasis added); LCM to William Lloyd and Helen Garrison, Sept. 11, 1851, in Palmer, 208. See also *Seventeenth Annual Report of the Philadelphia Female Anti-Slavery Society* (Philadelphia: Merrihew and Thompson, 1851), 3, 7.

8. *Pennsylvania Freeman*, March 11, 1847.

9. LCM to Joseph and Ruth Dugdale, March 28, 1849, in Palmer, 180.

10. *Pennsylvania Freeman*, Sept. 18, 1851; Thomas Slaughter, *Bloody Dawn: The Christiana Riot and Racial Violence in the Antebellum North* (New York: Oxford University Press, 1991).

11. *Pennsylvania Freeman*, Oct. 16, 1851.

12. *Pennsylvania Freeman*, Dec. 18, 1851, Feb. 12, 1852; Nat Brandt and Yanna Koy

Brandt, *In the Shadow of the Civil War: Passmore Williamson and the Rescue of Jane Johnson* (Columbia: University of South Carolina Press, 2007), 71.

13. Harriet Beecher Stowe, *Uncle Tom's Cabin* (Philadelphia: Henry Altemus, 1894), 628.

14. *Pennsylvania Freeman*, April 29, Nov. 6, 1852.

15. LCM to Hannah Darlington, Jan. 11, 1853, in Palmer, 226; *Pennsylvania Freeman*, December 2, 1852, Dec. 9, 1852; Brandt and Brandt, 27.

16. Brandt and Brandt, 35–36, 83, 140, 141.

17. Brandt and Brandt, 122–23; LCM to Martha Coffin Wright, Sept. 4, 1855, Mott Manuscripts, FHL; Anna Davis Hallowell, *James and Lucretia Mott, Life and Letters* (Boston: Houghton Mifflin, 1884), 356–57. See also Philadelphia Female Anti-Slavery Society, *Twenty-Second Annual Report* (Philadelphia: Merrihew and Thompson, 1856).

18. Lance Hill, *The Deacons for Defense: Armed Resistance and the Civil Rights Movement* (Chapel Hill: University of North Carolina Press, 2006).

19. *Pennsylvania Freeman*, Dec. 23, 1852.

20. PFASS minutes, March 13, 1856; see also Oct. 12, 1854, PAS Papers, Reel 30, HSP.

21. *Pennsylvania Freeman*, Nov. 4, 1853.

22. PFASS Minutes, April 5, 1858, PAS Papers, Reel 30, HSP.

23. *Pennsylvania Freeman*, Feb. 23, March 30, 1854; PFASS Minutes, Feb. 9, 1854, PAS Papers, Reel 30, HSP.

24. Debby Applegate, *The Most Famous Man in America: The Biography of Henry Ward Beecher* (New York: Doubleday, 2006), 281–82.

25. LCM to Martha Coffin Wright, February 26, 1856, in Palmer, 247; Martha Coffin Wright to Lucretia Mott, Feb. 14, 1856, Garrison Family Papers, Smith College, quoted in Penney and Livingston, 123.

26. *Twentieth Annual Report of the Philadelphia Female Anti-Slavery Society* (Philadelphia: Merrihew and Thompson, 1854), 7; *Twenty-First Annual Report* (Philadelphia: Merrihew and Thompson, 1855), 3; *Twenty-Second Annual Report*, 4.

27. LCM to George and Cecilia Combe, May 25, 1855, LCM to Elizabeth Pease Nichol, May 28, 1855, in Palmer, 238, 240 n4.

28. Charles Sumner, *The Crime Against Kansas* (Boston: John P. Jewett, 1856), 9; PFASS Minutes, June 12, 1856, PAS Papers, Reel 30, HSP.

29. *Twenty-First Annual Report*, 12; *Pennsylvania Freeman*, Sept. 15, 1853.

30. *Twentieth Annual Report*, 6. See also Jean R. Soderlund, "Priorities and Power: The Philadelphia Female Anti-Slavery Society," in Jean Fagan Yellin and John C. Van Horne, eds., *The Abolitionist Sisterhood: Women's Political Culture in Antebellum America* (Ithaca, N.Y.: Cornell University Press, 1994), 82–84.

31. *Pennsylvania Freeman*, Dec. 23, 1852, Jan. 2, 1851; Lee Chambers-Schiller, "'A Good Work Among the People': The Political Culture of the Boston Anti-Slavery Fair," in Yellin and Van Horne, 253, 262; Julie Roy Jeffrey, *The Great Silent Army of Abolitionism: Ordinary Women in the Antislavery Movement* (Chapel Hill: University of North Carolina Press, 1998), 108–9, 120–21, 122–23.

32. LCM to Martha Coffin Wright, Dec. 27, 1858, in Palmer, 283–84.

33. *Pennsylvania Freeman*, Dec. 8, 1853.

34. John Stauffer, *The Black Hearts of Men: Radical Abolitionists and the Transformation of Race* (Cambridge, Mass.: Harvard University Press, 2001), 2; David S. Reynolds, *John Brown, Abolitionist* (New York: Vintage, 2005), 152, 158, 206.

35. *Dred Scott v. Sandford*, 60 U.S. 393 (1856).

36. Abraham Lincoln, "A House Divided," June 16, 1858, in William E. Gienapp, ed., *This Fiery Trial: The Speeches and Writings of Abraham Lincoln* (New York: Oxford University Press, 2002), 50.

37. William H. Seward, "The Irrepressible Conflict," Oct. 25, 1858, in George E. Baker, ed., *The Works of William H. Seward* (New York: Houghton Mifflin, 1884), 4: 292; *Report of the Twenty-Fourth and Twenty-Fifth Years of the Philadelphia Female Anti-Slavery Society* (Philadelphia: Merrihew and Thompson, 1859), 10.

38. Stauffer, *Black Hearts of Men*, 237, 248; Zoe Trodd and John Stauffer, eds., *Meteor of War: The John Brown Story* (Maplecrest, N.Y.: Brandywine Press, 2004), 132; Hannah Geffert (with Jean Libby), "Regional Black Involvement in John Brown's Raid on Harper's Ferry," in Timothy Patrick McCarthy and John Stauffer, eds., *Prophets of Protest: Reconsidering the History of American Abolitionism* (New York: New Press, 2006), 165–79.

39. "Remarks, delivered at the Twenty-Fourth Annual Meeting," in Greene, 261; Philadelphia Female Anti-Slavery Society Resolution on John Brown, Passed November 16, 1859, Reel 30, Pennsylvania Abolition Society, HSP.

40. Palmer, 292–93 n 5; Hallowell, 391.

41. *Twenty-Sixth Annual Report* (Philadelphia: Merrihew and Thompson, 1860), 15, 17; Minutes of the Annual Meeting of the PFASS, Feb. 9, 1860, PAS Papers, Reel 30, HSP.

42. Hallowell, 371–73; Margaret Hope Bacon, *Valiant Friend: The Life of Lucretia Mott* (New York: Walker, 1980), 165–67.

43. Hallowell, 376.

44. For more on Collyer, see also LCM to Martha Coffin Wright, July 27, 1860, in Palmer, 303; LCM to Martha Coffin Wright, Dec. 27, 1862, in Palmer 325–26.

45. LCM to Martha Coffin Wright, Dec. 27, 1858, in Palmer, 282–83. Ralph Waldo Emerson, "Success," in *The Works of Ralph Waldo Emerson*, Ralph Waldo Emerson Institute, http://www.rwe.org/?option=com_content&task=view&id=41&Itemid=42.

46. Hallowell, 387–89; *Twenty-Sixth Annual Report*, 9–10; Otelia Cromwell, *Lucretia Mott* (Cambridge, Mass.: Harvard University Press, 1958), 168.

Chapter 11. Civil War

1. LCM to Martha Coffin Wright, March 12, 1860, Dec. 27, 1862, in Beverly Wilson Palmer, Holly Byers Ochoa, and Carol Faulkner, eds., *Selected Letters of Lucretia Coffin*

Mott (Urbana: University of Illinois Press, 2002), 295, 323; LCM to Mary Hussey Earle, Feb. 20, 1863, in Palmer, 332.

2. LCM to Martha Coffin Wright, March 12, 1860, in Palmer, 294–95; PFASS Minutes, March 8, 1860, PAS Papers, Reel 30, HSP.

3. PFASS Minutes, Dec. 12, 1863, PAS Papers, Reel 30, HSP.

4. Abraham Lincoln, First Inaugural Address, March 4, 1861, in William E. Gienapp, *This Fiery Trial: The Speeches and Writings of Abraham Lincoln* (New York: Oxford University Press, 2002), 88, 90.

5. LCM to Martha Coffin Wright and Eliza Wright Osborne, March 19, 1861, in Palmer 308; *National Anti-Slavery Standard*, March 9, 1861, quoted in Palmer, 311 n 2.

6. LCM to Martha Coffin Wright and Eliza Wright Osborne, March 19, 1861, in Palmer, 310.

7. LCM to Martha Coffin Wright, Anna Temple Brown, and Martha Mott Lord, Jan. 21, 1864, in Palmer, 339; LCM to Martha Coffin Wright and Anna Temple Brown, April 10, 1865, in Palmer, 356.

8. LCM to Martha Coffin Wright, Dec. 5, 1861, in Palmer 317; Sherry H. Penny and James D. Livingston, *A Very Dangerous Woman: Martha Wright and Women's Rights* (Amherst: University of Massachusetts Press, 2004), 156–57, 163–64.

9. Palmer, 334 n 10.

10. LCM to Martha Coffin Wright, Anna Temple Brown, and Martha Mott Lord, Jan. 21, 1864, in Palmer, 339, 341 n 11; "Fitzhugh Birney," in Thomas Wentworth Higginson, ed., *Harvard Memorial Biographies* (Cambridge, Mass.: Sever and Francis, 1866), 1: 415–24.

11. Palmer, 321 n 3; LCM to Martha Coffin Wright, Aug. 18, 1861, Mott Manuscripts, FHL.

12. LCM to Martha Coffin Wright, Nov. 6, 1861, in Palmer, 313; LCM to Philadelphia Family, July 17, 1862 in Palmer, 320, 321 n 3.

13. LCM to the Editor, *National Anti-Slavery Standard*, July 13, 1861, in Palmer, 312.

14. LCM to Martha Wright, Nov. 6, 1861, in Palmer, 315–16. See also LCM to Martha Wright, Nov. 4, 1861, Mott Manuscripts, FHL.

15. LCM to Martha Coffin Wright, Dec. 5, 1861, in Palmer, 318.

16. *Twenty-Eighth Annual Report* (Philadelphia: Merrihew and Thompson, 1862), 15.

17. *Twenty-Seventh Annual Report* (Philadelphia: Merrihew and Thompson, 1861), 19.

18. LCM to Martha Coffin Wright, Dec. 27, 1862, in Palmer, 323; *Twenty-Ninth Annual Report* (Philadelphia: Merrihew and Thompson, 1863), 4; "Speech, Delivered to the American Anti-Slavery Society at Its Third Decade Meeting, Philadelphia, December 3–4, 1863," in Dana Greene, ed., *Lucretia Mott: Her Complete Speeches and Sermons* (New York: Edwin Mellen, 1980), 265.

19. PFASS Minutes, November 14, 1861, PAS Papers, Reel 30, HSP; *Twenty-Eighth Annual Report*, 22. On the U.S. Sanitary Commission see Jeannie Attie, *Patriotic Toil: Northern Women and the American Civil War* (Ithaca, N.Y.: Cornell University Press, 1998); Judith Ann Geisberg, *Civil War Sisterhood: The U.S. Sanitary Commission and Women's Politics in Transition* (Boston: Northeastern University Press, 2000).

20. LCM to Mary Hussey Earle, Feb. 20, 1863, in Palmer, 332–33; J. Matthew Gallman, *America's Joan of Arc: The Life of Anna Elizabeth Dickinson* (New York: Oxford University Press, 2006). See Elizabeth Leonard, *Yankee Women: Gender Battles in the Civil War* (New York: Norton, 1994); Lyde Cullen Sizer, *The Political Work of Northern Women Writers and the Civil War, 1850–1872* (Chapel Hill: University of North Carolina Press, 2000); Carol Faulkner, *Women's Radical Reconstruction: The Freedmen's Aid Movement* (Philadelphia: University of Pennsylvania Press, 2003).

21. LCM to MCW, June 2, 1863, Mott Manuscripts, FHL; Margaret Hope Bacon, *Abby Hopper Gibbons: Prison Reformer and Social Activist* (Albany: State University of New York Press, 2000), 123. For Civil War nursing see Leonard, chap. 1; Jane E. Schultz, *Women at the Front: Hospital Workers in Civil War America* (Chapel Hill: University of North Carolina Press, 2007).

22. *Proceedings of the Meeting of the Loyal Women of the Republic, held in New York, May 14, 1863* (New York: Phai, 1863), 1, 2, 32–35, 48–51; Wendy Hamand Venet, *Neither Ballots Nor Bullets: Women Abolitionists and the Civil War* (Charlottesville: University of Virginia Press, 1991). On northern women's patriotism, see Nina Silber, *Gender and the Sectional Conflict* (Chapel Hill: University of North Carolina Press, 2009), chap. 2.

23. Elizabeth Cady Stanton, Susan B. Anthony, and Matilda Joslyn Gage, *History of Woman Suffrage*, vol. 2, *1861–1876* (Rochester, N.Y.: Susan B. Anthony, 1881), 79; PFASS Minutes, Sept. 10, Oct. 8, Dec. 12, 1863, PAS Papers, Reel 30, HSP; Venet, *Neither Ballots Nor Bullets*, 148.

24. PFASS Minutes, Sept. 11, 1892, PAS Papers, Reel 30, HSP; *Twenty-Ninth Annual Report*, 17. See also Stephen V. Ash, *Firebrand of Liberty: The Story of Two Black Regiments That Changed the Course of the Civil War* (New York: Norton, 2008), 37, 209.

25. LCM to Anne and Jane Heacock, July 23, 1863, in Palmer, 335.

26. LCM to Marianna Pelham Mott and Martha Coffin Wright, Sept. 7, 1864; *Thirtieth Annual Report* (Philadelphia: Merrihew and Thompson, 1864), 24; Margaret Hope Bacon, *But One Race: The Life of Robert Purvis* (Albany: State University of New York Press, 2007), 148–50.

27. *Twenty-Ninth Annual Report*, 21; see also LCM to Martha Coffin Wright, Anna Temple Brown, and Martha Mott Lord, Jan. 21, 1864, in Palmer, 338.

28. LCM to Martha Coffin Wright, Dec. 27, 1862, in Palmer, 325; *Thirtieth Annual Report*, 10; LCM to Martha Coffin Wright, Anna Temple Brown, and Martha Mott Lord, January 21, 1864, in Palmer, 338. See also Faulkner, *Women's Radical Reconstruction*.

29. *Twenty-Ninth Annual Report*, 21; Forten quoted in Faulkner, *Women's Radical Reconstruction*, 74. See also PFASS minutes, June 11, Dec.12, 1863, March 8, 1866, PAS Papers, Reel 30, HSP; Willie Lee Rose, *Rehearsal for Reconstruction: The Port Royal Experiment* (New York: Oxford University Press, 1964), 78, 211; Faulkner, 73–74.

30. LCM to Anne and Jane Heacock, Jan. 2, 1863, in Palmer, 326, 327 n 9.

31. Quoted in Faulkner, *Women's Radical Reconstruction*, 16, 33; PFASS Minutes, Dec. 10, 1863, PAS Papers, Reel 30, HSP.

32. LCM to Marianna Pelham Mott and Martha Coffin Wright, Sept. 7, 1864, in Palmer, 344.

33. *Liberator*, Oct. 28, 1864, in Palmer 351 n 6.

34. LCM to July 3, 1864, Mott Manuscripts, FHL. See also LCM to Martha Coffin Wright, Sept. 25, 1864, in Palmer, 346; LCM to Martha Coffin Wright and Eliza Wright Osborne, Oct. 31, 1864, in Palmer, 346, 349.

35. LCM to Martha Wright and Anna Temple Brown, April 10, 1865, in Palmer, 356; LCM to Marianna Pelham Mott and Martha Coffin Wright, Sept. 1864, in Palmer, 344; LCM to Mary Robbins Post, March 14, 1865, in Palmer, 354. See LCM to Martha Coffin Wright, Maria Mott Davis, and Anna Temple Brown, Jan. 17, 1865, in Palmer, 352; LCM to Martha Coffin Wright, Sept. 12, 1863, Mott Manuscripts, FHL.

36. LCM to Martha Mott Lord, July 22, 1865, Mott Manuscripts, FHL; Anna Davis Hallowell, *James and Lucretia Mott, Life and Letters* (Boston: Houghton Mifflin, 1884), 416; LCM to Martha Mott Lord, May 2, 1865, in Palmer, 359–60.

37. LCM to Martha Coffin Wright and Martha Mott Lord, Nov. 2, 1865, in Palmer, 365–66.

38. LCM to Martha Coffin Wright and Anna Temple Brown, April 10, 1865, in Palmer, 357; LCM to James Miller McKim, c. April 15, 1866, in Palmer, 370; Faulkner, *Women's Radical Reconstruction*, 34. See also LCM to Pattie, April 22, 1866, Mott Manuscripts, FHL.

39. LCM to Martha Coffin Wright and Martha Mott Lord, December 2, 1865, in Palmer 365, 368.

40. *Thirty-Second Annual Report* (Philadelphia: Merrihew & Son, 1866), 12; PFASS Minutes, January 25, 1866, PAS Papers, Reel 30, HSP.

41. *Thirty-Second Annual Report*, 16.

42. William Lloyd Garrison to Lucretia Mott, April 8, 1867, Mott Manuscripts, FHL.

43. LCM to Martha Wright, June 11, 1866, in Palmer, 373–74.

44. LCM to Wendell Phillips April 17, 1866, in Palmer 371.

45. LCM to Elizabeth Cady Stanton, April 22, 1866, in Palmer, 372.

46. Memorial of the American Equal Rights Association to the Congress of the United States, in Palmer, 383, 384; LCM to Equal Rights Convention in Albany, Nov. 18, 1866, in Palmer, 379.

47. LCM to Philadelphia Family, Nov. 15, 1866, in Palmer, 377; Ellen Carol DuBois, *Feminism and Suffrage: The Emergence of an Independent Women's Movement in America, 1848–1869* (Ithaca, N.Y.: Cornell University Press, 1978), 66–67.

48. Quoted in Palmer, 390 n 1; LCM to Anna Mott Hopper and Roadside and Suffern Families, May 30, 1866, in Palmer, 389.

49. LCM to Martha Coffin Wright, Sept. 3, 1867, in Palmer, 394; "To the Public," c. July 1867, in Palmer, 391.

50. Quoted in Michele Mitchell, " 'Lower Orders,' Racial Hierarchies, and Rights Rhetoric: Evolutionary Echoes in Elizabeth Cady Stanton's Thought During the late

1860s," in Ellen Carol DuBois and Richard Candida Smith, eds., *Elizabeth Cady Stanton: Feminist as Thinker* (New York: New York University Press, 2007), 135.

51. William Lloyd Garrison to Susan B. Anthony, Jan. 4, 1868, in Ann Gordon, ed., *The Selected Papers of Elizabeth Cady Stanton and Susan B. Anthony*, vol. 1, *Against an Aristocracy of Sex, 1866–1873* (New Brunswick, N.J.: Rutgers University Press, 2000), 124.

52. For the history of the AERA in Kansas see DuBois, *Feminism and Suffrage*, chap. 3.

53. LCM to Martha Coffin Wright, Jan. 21, 1868, in Palmer, 398–99; *National Anti-Slavery Standard*, Dec. 20, 1865, in Gordon, 564.

54. LCM to Martha Coffin Wright, Jan. 21, 1868, in Palmer, 399; LCM to the AERA, c. May 14, 1868, in Palmer, 407.

55. LCM to Martha Coffin Wright, Jan. 21, 1868, in Palmer, 398, 399.

56. Palmer, 401 n 13; Hallowell, 433.

57. Hallowell, 434, 436; Mary Grew, *James Mott: A Biographical Sketch* (New York: William P. Tomlinson, 1868), 7–8, 9, 15, 18–19, 28, 31, 39.

58. Grew, 32.

59. Will and Account Book, Box 6, Mott Manuscripts, FHL; Marylynn Salmon, *Women and the Law of Property in Early America* (Chapel Hill: University of North Carolina Press, 1986), 163–65, 186; Carole Shammas, Marylynn Salmon, and Michel Dahlin, *Inheritance in America from Colonial Times to the Present* (New Brunswick, N.J.: Rutgers University Press, 1987), 100–101.

60. LCM to George Lord, March 26, 1868, Mott Manuscripts, FHL; Hallowell, 440.

61. PFASS Minutes, Feb. 13, March 12, April 9, June 11, 1868, PAS Papers, Reel 30, HSP.

62. LCM to Martha Coffin Wright, Jan. 21, 1868, in Palmer, 399.

63. *Thirty-Third Annual Report* (Philadelphia: Merrihew & Son, 1867), 8.

64. *Thirty-Fourth Annual Report* (Philadelphia: Merrihew & Son, 1868), 28. For Mott's use of this language, see "Speech, Delivered at the Meeting of the Pennsylvania Anti-Slavery Society, November 22, 1866," in Greene, 284.

65. To the U.S. Senate, c. Feb. 3, 1869, in Palmer, 414; *Thirty-Fifth Annual Report* (Philadelphia: Merrihew & Son, 1869), 22; PFASS Minutes, Jan. 14, 1869, PAS Papers, Reel 30, HSP.

66. *Thirty-Fourth Annual Report*, 29.

67. PFASS Minutes, Nov. 10, 1864, PAS Papers, Reel 30, HSP.

68. LCM to Martha Coffin Wright, Oct. 2, 1865, LCM to Martha Coffin Wright and Martha Mott Lord, Nov. 2, 1865, in Palmer, 364, 268; *Thirty-First Annual Report*, 17–18, 20.

69. Roger Lane, *Roots of Violence in Black Philadelphia, 1860–1900* (Cambridge, Mass.: Harvard University Press, 1986), 50; Bacon, *But One Race*, 152–53; *Thirty-First Annual Report*, 18.

70. PFASS minutes, Sept. 13, 1866, PAS Papers, Reel 30, HSP; Bacon, *But One Race*, 153; Barbara Welke, "When All the Women Were White, and All the Blacks Were Men:

Gender, Class, Race, and the Road to Plessy, 1855-1914," *Law and History Review* 13, 2 (Autumn 1995): 278. See also Hugh Davis, "The Pennsylvania Sate Equal Rights League and the Northern Black Struggle for Legal Equality, 1864-1877," *Pennsylvania Magazine of History and Biography* 126, 4 (Oct. 2002): 614, 626.

71. *Thirty-Third Annual Report*, 26; Lane, 50; Welke, 275, 284-86.

72. *The West Chester and Philadelphia Railroad Company v. Miles*, 55 PA. 209, 1867; Welke, 292, 299, 307.

73. *North American and U.S. Gazette*, Oct. 12, 1866; *Thirty-Fourth Annual Report*, 16. See Miles's wedding announcement in the *North American and U.S. Gazette*, April 3, 1862, and her appearance in the 1870 Manuscript Census. She may have been related to Mary London, a free woman who was kidnapped from Philadelphia in 1842 to be sold at the slave market in Charleston, South Carolina. See *Pennsylvania Inquirer*, June 27, 1843.

74. Mitchell, "'Lower Orders, Racial Hierarchies, and Rights Rhetoric," 129; Ann D. Gordon, "Stanton and the Right to Vote: On Account of Race or Sex," in DuBois and Smith, 111, 114.

75. Stanton, Anthony, and Gage, 2: 347, 357; Bacon, *But One Race*, 165.

76. Stanton, Anthony, and Gage, 2: 359-60; Charles Robinson to (wife) Sara, Jan. 23, 1869, Charles and Sara T. D. Robinson Papers, 1834-1911, Box 2, Folder January-May 1869, Kansas Historical Society (thanks to Kristen Tegtmeier Oertel for this reference).

77. Elizabeth Cady Stanton, "Address to the Anniversary of the American Equal Rights Association, May 12, 1869, New York City," in DuBois and Smith, 196; Stanton, Anthony, and Gage, 2: 382.

78. LCM to Philadelphia Family, Feb. 1, 1869, in Palmer, 412; LCM to Martha Coffin Wright, June 6, 1869, in Palmer, 419.

79. LCM to Martha Coffin Wright, Jan. 21, 1868, in Palmer, 398.

80. LCM to Martha Coffin Wright, Dec. 3, 1868, in Palmer, 408.

Chapter 12. Peace

1. PFASS Minutes, March 10, 1870, PAS Papers, Reel 30, HSP; LCM to Richard D. Webb, Feb. 24, 1870, in Beverly Wilson Palmer, Holly Byers Ochoa, and Carol Faulkner, eds., *Selected Letters of Lucretia Coffin Mott* (Urbana: University of Illinois Press, 2002), 535. For PFASS finances, see *Thirty-Sixth Annual Report* (Philadelphia: Merrihew & Son, 1870), 26-28.

2. PFASS Minutes, March 24, 1870, PAS Papers, Reel 30, HSP.

3. *Thirty-Sixth Annual Report*, 4. For an analysis of Grew as the historian of the PFASS, see Julie Roy Jeffrey, *Abolitionists Remember: Antislavery Autobiographies and the Unfinished Work of Emancipation* (Chapel Hill: University of North Carolina Press, 2008), 19-20.

4. Anna Davis Hallowell, *James and Lucretia Mott, Life and Letters* (Boston: Houghton Mifflin, 1884), 446, 458; LCM to Martha Wright, Aug. 26, 1872, Mott Manuscripts, FHL.

5. Thomas F. Curran, *Soldiers of Peace: Civil War Pacifism and the Postwar Radical Peace Movement* (New York; Fordham University Press, 2003), 10, 112–13. For antebellum pacifism, see Valarie H. Ziegler, *The Advocates of Peace in Antebellum America* (Macon, Ga.: Mercer University Press, 2001).

6. Quoted in Curran, 112.

7. LCM to Richard D. Webb, Jan. 22, 1871, in Palmer, 452–53.

8. LCM to Webb, Jan. 22, 1871.

9. LCM to Martha Coffin Wright, Nov. 3, 1867, in Palmer, 394; LCM to Martha Coffin Wright, Dec. 3, 1868, Mott Manuscripts, FHL; Curran, 124–25. For an example of the Universal Peace Union's goals, and a letter written on the back of a Pennsylvania Peace Society flyer, see LCM to Pattie, April 20 1873, Mott Manuscripts, FHL. For Mott on arbitration, see LCM to Ulysses S. Grant, Nov. 12, 1873, in Palmer, 487; "Remarks, Delivered to the Executive Committee of the Pennsylvania Peace Society, November 27, 1877," in Dana Greene, ed., *Lucretia Mott: Her Complete Speeches and Sermons* (New York: Edwin Mellen, 1980), 392.

10. Palmer, 128 n 9; "Remarks, Delivered to a Special Meeting of the Universal Peace Union, Camden, New Jersey, September 16, 1877," in Greene, 389–90; LCM to Martha Coffin Wright, May 27, 1872, in Palmer, 470; "Remarks, Delivered to the Executive Committee of the Pennsylvania Peace Society, Nov. 27, 1877," in Greene, 392.

11. *Niles' National Register*, July 4, 1846.

12. "Remarks, Delivered at the Third Annual Meeting of the Women's Peace Festival, June 2, 1875," in Greene, 371, 373.

13. Palmer, 453 n 1; LCM to Martha Coffin Wright, June 6, 1869, in Palmer, 419.

14. LCM to Josephine S. Griffing, Dec. 25, 1869, in Palmer, 429.

15. Quoted in Margaret Hope Bacon, *Valiant Friend: The Life of Lucretia Mott* (New York: Walker, 1980), 215; Curran, 166–67. On Mott's warlike pacifism, see "Remarks, Delivered at the Woman's Peace Festival, Philadelphia, June 2, 1876," in Greene, 383.

16. "Remarks, Delivered at the Abington Peace Meeting, Abington, Pennsylvania, September 19, 1869," in Greene, 346.

17. LCM to Octavius B. Frothingham, May 20, 1867, in Palmer, 387–88.

18. Quoted in Stow Persons, *Free Religion: An American Faith* (Boston: Beacon Press, 1947, 1963), 53.

19. Carol Faulkner, *Women's Radical Reconstruction: The Freedmen's Aid Movement* (Philadelphia: University of Pennsylvania Press, 2004), 60–61.

20. Greene, 291, 293–94, 295, 296.

21. Excerpts in Greene, 359, 360, 363.

22. LCM to Octavius B. Frothingham, May 22, 1874, in Palmer, 489–90; Parsons, 52–53.

23. LCM to Martha Coffin Wright, June 6, 1871, in Palmer, 462; LCM to Martha

Coffin Wright, May 27, 1872, in Palmer, 470; LCM to Martha Coffin Wright, June 1, 1873, in Palmer, 483.

24. LCM to Martha Mott Lord, March 6, 1874, Garrison Family Papers, Smith College.

25. LCM to Martha Mott Lord and George Lord, Nov. 13, 1869, in Palmer, 422; Hallowell, 412, 437; Bacon, 204.

26. Sherry H. Penney and James D. Livingston, *A Very Dangerous Woman: Martha Wright and Women's Rights* (Amherst: University of Massachusetts Press, 2004), 218–19.

27. Palmer, 452 n 5; LCM to Martha Coffin Wright, June 3, 1870, Mott Manuscripts, FHL; LCM to Martha Coffin Wright, July 16, 1870, in Palmer, 448; Penney and Livingston, 187–88.

28. LCM to Eliza Wright Osborne, Jan.12, 1875, in Palmer, 493.

29. Penney and Livingston, 227.

30. LCM to Martha Mott Lord, Jan. 22, 1871, in Palmer, 449.

31. LCM to Elizabeth Cady Stanton, March 25, 1872, in Palmer, 468.

32. LCM to Theodore Tilton, March 18, 1870, in Palmer, 437.

33. LCM to Martha Coffin Wright, April 7, 1870, in Palmer, 438–39.

34. LCM to Martha Coffin Wright, July 16, 1870, in Palmer, 445–46.

35. Quoted in Paulina Wright Davis, *A History of the National Woman's Rights Movement for Twenty Years, with the Proceedings of the Decade Meeting Held at Apollo Hall, October 20, 1870* (New York: Journeymen Printers' Cooperative Association, 1871), 4.

36. Davis, 11–12, 22, 23, 26, 31–32. See also LCM to Paulina Wright Davis, April 7, 1871, in Palmer, 458. For disagreement over Davis's history, see Nancy Isenberg, *Sex and Citizenship in Antebellum America* (Chapel Hill: University of North Carolina Press, 1998), 5–6.

37. There may have been African American women in the audience, see Diary of Susan B. Anthony, October 20, 1870, in Ann D. Gordon, ed., *The Selected Papers of Elizabeth Cady Stanton and Susan B. Anthony*, vol. 2, *Against an Aristocracy of Sex, 1866–1873* (New Brunswick, N.J.: Rutgers University Press, 2000), 368.

38. Davis, 117. See also Amanda Frisken, *Victoria Woodhull's Sexual Revolution: Political Theater and the Popular Press in Nineteenth-Century America* (Philadelphia: University of Pennsylvania Press, 2004).

39. Gordon, 2: 524; see also Appendix C for a national list of female voters in 1868–73. LCM to Elizabeth Cady Stanton, March 25, 1872, in Palmer, 468–69.

40. Quoted in Ellen Carol DuBois, "Feminism and Free Love," http://www.h-net.org/~women/papers/freelove.html; Frisken, 39–40.

41. Quoted in Palmer, 460 n 3; see also LCM to Martha Coffin Wright, May 4, June 6, 1871, in Palmer, 459, 462.

42. LCM to Martha Coffin Wright, Dec. 25, 1872, Mott Manuscripts, FHL; LCM to Martha Coffin Wright, March 18, 1873, in Palmer, 478. See also LCM to Martha Coffin Wright, March 3, 1873, Mott Manuscripts, FHL.

262 Notes to Pages 208–214

43. LCM to Elizabeth Smith Miller, Jan. 23, 1879, in Palmer, 498. See also Andrea Tone, *Devices and Desires: A History of Contraceptives in America* (New York: Hill and Wang, 2001), 22–23, 39–40.

44. "Declaration of the Rights of the Women of the United States," in Ann Gordon, ed., *The Selected Papers of Elizabeth Cady Stanton and Susan B. Anthony*, vol. 3, *National Protection for National Citizens, 1873–1880* (New Brunswick, N.J.: Rutgers University Press, 2003), 235, 238, 239.

45. Elizabeth Cady Stanton to Mathilde Franziska Anneke, July 1, 1876, in Gordon, 3: 233; Diary of Susan B. Anthony, in Gordon, 3: 227.

46. Elizabeth Cady Stanton to Isabella Beecher Hooker, July 5, 1876, in Gordon, 3: 241–42; LCM to Susan B. Anthony, July 21, 1876, in Palmer, 494.

47. *Woman's Journal*, July 27, 1878, in Greene, 393.

48. "Third Decade Celebration at Rochester, New York," in Gordon, 3: 393–94; Bacon, 224.

49. Hallowell, 452–53.

50. "Remarks, Delivered at the funeral of Mrs. [Mary Ann] Johnson," in Greene, 367.

51. Parke Godwin, *A Biography of William Cullen Bryant*. 2 vols. (New York Appleton, 1883), 2: 349–50; "Remarks, Delivered at the Pennsylvania Peace Society, Abington, Pennsylvania, September 19, 1875" in Greene, 378.

52. Maria Mott Davis to Sister, May 17, 1880, Mott Manuscripts, FHL.

53. LCM to Pattie, May 21, 1875, Mott Manuscripts, FHL; see also Chuck Fager, "Lucretia Mott: Liberal Quaker Theologian," *Quaker Theology* 10 (Spring/Summer 2004), http://www.quaker.org/quest/issue-10-mott-CEF-01.htm.

54. Mary Grew to LCM, Sept. 8, 1880, Mott Manuscripts, FHL.

55. Lucy Stone to LCM, Nov. 1, 1880, Mott Manuscripts, FHL.

56. Hallowell, 465.

57. Hallowell, 466. See also Ednah Dow Cheney, "Lucretia Mott," in *Prophets of Liberalism: Six Addresses Before the Free Religious Association of America* (Boston: James West, 1900), 40.

Epilogue

1. "Mrs. Child and Mrs. Mott," *Unitarian Review and Religious Magazine*, Dec. 1880; "The Beatitudes Illustrated," *Friends' Intelligencer*, Dec. 18, 1880; "Lucretia Mott," *Friends' Intelligencer*, Nov. 20, 1880; "Lucretia Mott," *Phrenological Journal and Science of Health*, Feb. 1881.

2. "Tributes to Lucretia Mott," *New York Times*, Nov. 15, 1880.

3. Mary Clemmer, "A Woman's Letter from Washington," *Independent*, Feb. 3, 1881.

4. *Brooklyn Daily Eagle*, Oct. 3, 1920, 14. See also *The Statutory Record of the Consolidated Laws of the State of New York* (Albany, N.Y.: J.B. Lyon, 1909), 807. Two years before the clinic's dissolution, it was almost defrauded of $4,500. See "Nearly Lost Its Money," *New York Times*, Nov. 20, 1890.

5. "O Lord Let This Little Standard-Bearer Go," *Christian Recorder*, May 10, 1883. The poem echoed Mott's last words. For more on Hanaford, see Lisa M. Tetrault, "A Paper Trail: Piecing Together the Life of Phebe Hanaford," http://www.nha.org/history/hn/HNhanaford.htm.

6. Phebe Ann Coffin Hanaford, *Lucretia, The Quakeress, or Principle Triumphant* (Boston: J. Buffum, 1853); Elizabeth Oakes Smith, "Lucretia Mott," *Potter's American Monthly*, March 1881. For other examples, see "Poetry," *Liberator*, Jan. 15, 1841; "To Lucretia Mott," *Pennsylvania Freeman*, March 4, 1852; "Noble Women," *Pennsylvania Freeman*, March 24, 1853.

7. Elizabeth Cady Stanton, Susan B. Anthony, and Matilda Joslyn Gage, *History of Woman Suffrage*, vol. 1, *1848–1861* (New York: Fowler and Wells, 1881), 429–30.

8. Reminiscences of Phebe Couzins, unidentified photocopy, Nov. 22, 1880, Mott Manuscripts, FHL.

9. Mary White Ovington to Alice Paul, Jan. 4, 1921, Mary Church Terrell Papers, Library of Congress (Microfilm, Reel 2, #544), included in Kathryn Kish Sklar and Jill Dias, *How Did the National Woman's Party Address the Issue of the Enfranchisement of Black Women, 1919–1924?* (Binghamton: State University of New York at Binghamton, 1997), http://asp6new.alexanderstreet.com.libezproxy2.syr.edu/was2/was2.object.details.aspx?dorpid=1000688291. See also Marjorie Spruill Wheeler, "Race, Reform, and Reaction at the Turn of the Century: Southern Suffragists, the NAWSA, and the 'Southern Strategy' in Context," in Jean H. Baker, ed., *Votes for Women: The Struggle for Suffrage Revisited* (New York: Oxford University Press, 2002), 102–17; Glenda Elizabeth Gilmore, *Gender and Jim Crow: Women and the Politics of White Supremacy in North Carolina, 1896–1920* (Chapel Hill: University of North Carolina Press, 1996).

10. For example, Judith Wellman, *The Road to Seneca Falls: Elizabeth Cady Stanton and the First Women's Rights Convention* (Urbana: University of Illinois Press, 2004); Jean H. Baker, *Sisters: The Lives of America's Suffragists* (New York: Hill and Wang, 2005). Recent exceptions include Nancy Isenberg, *Sex and Citizenship in Antebellum America* (Chapel Hill: University of North Carolina Press, 1998), 2–6, passim; Sally G. McMillen, *Seneca Falls and the Origins of the Women's Rights Movement* (New York: Oxford University Press, 2008).

11. Julie Roy Jeffrey, *Abolitionists Remember: Antislavery Autobiographies and the Unfinished Work of Emancipation* (Chapel Hill: University of North Carolina Press, 2008), 38–39, 103.

12. LCM to William Lloyd Garrison, March 8, 1870, in Beverly Wilson Palmer, Holly Byers Ochoa, and Carol Faulkner, eds., *Selected Letters of Lucretia Coffin Mott* (Urbana: University of Illinois Press, 2002), 436.

13. Oliver Johnson, *William Lloyd Garrison and His Times; Or, Sketches of the Anti-Slavery Movement in America, and of the Man who was its Founder and Moral Leader* (Boston: B.B. Russell, 1880), 257.

14. William Still, *The Underground Railroad* (Philadelphia: Porter & Coates, 1872), 649–54.

15. For example, John Stauffer, *The Black Hearts of Men: Radical Abolitionists and*

the Transformation of Race (Cambridge, Mass.: Harvard University Press, 2001); Bruce Laurie, *Beyond Garrison: Antislavery and Social Reform* (New York: Cambridge University Press, 2003); Jonathan Earle, *Jacksonian Antislavery and the Politics of Free Soil* (Chapel Hill: University of North Carolina Press, 2003); David Reynolds, *John Brown, Abolitionist: The Man Who Killed Slavery, Sparked the Civil War, and Seeded Civil Rights* (New York: Vintage, 2006). Two important exceptions include Michael Pierson, *Free Hearts & Free Homes: Gender and American Antislavery Politics* (Chapel Hill: University of North Carolina, 2003); Frederick J. Blue, *No Taint of Compromise: Crusaders in Antislavery Politics* (Baton Rouge: Louisiana State University Press, 2005).

16. *Philadelphia Ledger and Transcript*, May 10, 1884; clipping in Mott Manuscripts, FHL.

17. "Sermon to the Medical Students," in Dana Greene, ed., *Lucretia Mott: Her Complete Speeches and Sermons* (New York: Edwin Mellen, 1980), 83.

The abbreviations LCM, JM, and MCW refer to Lucretia Mott, James Mott, and Martha Coffin Wright; they are alphabetized by surname.

herself, 6, 120, 123; LCM supports for others, 201; as protest to churches failing to denounce slavery, 109–10, 132
Comly, John (Hicksite Quaker), 58
Compromise of 1850, 161
Comstock Act (1873), 208
Comstock, Anthony, 208
Congregational Friends, 133, 153
consensus, 66
Constitution, U.S.: Dred Scott decision (1857), 171; Fourteenth Amendment (1868), 191, 194, 206; fugitive slave clause, 68; Nineteenth Amendment (1920), 215–16; political abolitionists claim slavery unconstitutional, 138; seen as hostile to slavery, 130; Thirteenth Amendment (1865), 186. See also Fifteenth Amendment
Constitution of Man. See Combe
contraception, 158, 208
"Convention of the Colored People," 143–44
Cooke, Jay (financier), 181, 200
Cooper, Griffith M. (N.Y. Quaker): on Joint Indian Committee, 134; LCM praises efforts on behalf of Native Americans, 201; Society of Friends (Hicksite) disciplines, 123, 132; White opposes, 133
corporal punishment, 28, 31–32, 199
cotton, 53, 55, 89–90, 190
Couzins, Phebe (suffragist), 215
Cowper, William, 29–30, 155; "The Negro's Complaint," 29; "Pity for Poor Africans," 30; "The Task," 29
Crandall, Prudence, school of, 65, 89
Crèvecoeur, J. Hector St. John de, 11, 13
Curtis, George (women's right's activist), at arbitration between NWSA and AWSA, 205

Dana, Richard Henry, Sr. (lecturer), 146
Dangerfield, Daniel (aka Daniel Webster), 175
Davis, Anna (LCM's granddaughter). See Hallowell, Anna Davis
Davis, David Brion, 130
Davis, Edward M. (LCM's son-in-law), 173; avoids association with Woodhull, 207; business of/and women's employment, 144–46; and Camp William Penn, 181; children of, 87; Civil War participation, 178–79; lives with LCM, 148; marries (1836), 71; memorial to LCM, 213–14; organizes Citizen's Suffrage Association, 207;

at PFASS final meeting (1870), 198; privileges black male suffrage over women's suffrage, 195; support for women's rights, 204
Davis, Maria Mott (LCM's daughter): birth (1818), 40, 52; children of, 87, 143; dramatizes meeting of E. Davis over women's employment, 145; image of, plate 8; lives with LCM, 148, 211; marries (1836), 71; with LCM at death (1880), 212; PFASS membership, 67; resigns from Society of Friends in sympathy with husband, 178
Davis, Paulina Wright (women's rights activist): "History of the Woman's Rights Movement," 205–6; Second Decade Convention (1870), 205–6; visits LCM, 204; Worcester convention (1850), 149–51
death of LCM (1880), 211–12
Declaration of Sentiments of American Anti-Slavery Society (AASS): JM signs, 189–90; LCM prefers to those of Seneca Falls convention, 139; LCM's commitment to, 6, 105, 115–16, 126, 167; LCM's influence on, 64–66
"Declaration of the Rights of Women of the United States" (NWSA), 208–9
Delano, Joseph C. (ship captain), 106
Delaware Free Press (newspaper), 56
Democratic Party: Barnburner Democrats (New York), 131, 132; in New York City/Tammany Hall, 154; Workingmen's Party (New York), 43, 56
descriptions of LCM: as demure, 2; as noble and heroic, 88; phrenological, 102–3; as teenager, 33. See also public image of LCM
Dial (publication), 58
diary of LCM, 92–93
Dickinson, Anna (Republican Party stump speaker), 180, 205
discipline/disownment in Society of Friends: abuse of elder power, 42–43, 46; among Hicksites, 56, 120–21, 123, 132; of H. Barnard, 18; denying authority of Scripture, 45; of Hicksites, 52; marriage of first cousins, 119; LCM laments, 121; on Nantucket, 15–16; for war participation, 178. See also marriage out of meeting
"Discourse on Woman" (speech, LCM), 146–47
disunionism, 171; F. Douglass grows disillusioned with, 130–31; LCM favors

ACKNOWLEDGMENTS

The first spark for this book began in Kathryn Kish Sklar's amazing course on American women's history at Binghamton University, as Kitty discussed the career of Lucretia Mott and asked, "Can you believe there is no scholarly biography of Mott?" Beverly Wilson Palmer offered further inspiration and guidance when I worked as an editing fellow on *The Selected Letters of Lucretia Coffin Mott.* I am grateful to have such incredible mentors.

Since those early days, many people have offered assistance and encouragement. At SUNY Geneseo, President Chris Dahl, Provost Kate Conway-Turner, and Chair Jim Williams enabled a research leave at a crucial stage in this project. I am also grateful to Michael Oberg, who provided timely and essential assistance on the history of the Seneca Indians, and Emilye Crosby, who read the entire manuscript and came up with the title. When I moved to Syracuse University, my new colleagues Subho Basu, David Bennett, Susan Branson, Albrecht Diem, Michael Ebner, Paul Hagenloh, Samantha Herrick, Amy Kallander, George Kallander, Norman Kutcher, Chris Kyle, Elisabeth Lasch-Quinn, Dennis Romano, Roger Sharp, David Stam, Scott Strickland, Junko Takeda, and Margaret Susan Thompson welcomed me and this project. I owe special thanks to Dean Mitchel Wallerstein, Associate Dean Michael Wasylenko, and Craige Champion. I rely heavily on the excellent History Department staff: Patti Blincoe, Fran Bockus, and Patti Bohrer.

I appreciated the opportunity to research and write at some wonderful institutions. At Friends Historical Library, I benefited from a Margaret W. Moore and John M. Moore Research Fellowship. Curator Chris Densmore is a model historian and great ally. The FHL staff, including Barbara Addison,

Charlotte Blandford, Susanna Morikawa, and Patricia O'Donnell, answered my questions with patience and enthusiasm. I am grateful for a Library Company/Historical Society of Pennsylvania research fellowship, and the advice and assistance of Tammy Gaskell, James Green, Nicole Joniec, and Phil Lapsansky. I spent an enjoyable and productive semester at the Gilder Lehrman Center for the Study of Slavery, Resistance, and Abolition at Yale University, with its great director David Blight, assistant director Dana Schaffer, and education director Tom Thurston. The librarians and staff at Syracuse University Library, especially Charlotte Hess, Charles Russo, Suzanne Thorin, Lydia Wasylenko, and Mark Weimer, offer fantastic support for faculty research and teaching. Finally, I am indebted to Diana Carey at the Schlesinger Library, Elaine Grublin at the Massachusetts Historical Society, Mary Huth at the University of Rochester Library, and the staff at the Nantucket Historical Association, especially Marie Henke and Elizabeth Oldham.

Many fellow scholars and biographers contributed their insight and expertise. At the Schlesinger Library's Summer Seminar "Writing Past Lives: Biography as History," Nancy Cott, Lori Ginzberg, Megan Marshall, and all the participants gave me valuable feedback. The members of the Rochester-Area U.S. Historians (RUSH) group read drafts of several chapters, and I am grateful to Jenny Lloyd, Dorinda Outram, Alison Parker, and other regulars for their close readings. Two research assistants, Alexandra Elias and Nicole Sanford, helped me with other projects so I could finish this one. It was a pleasure to meet Sherry Penney and Jim Livingston, scholars and descendents of Martha Coffin Wright. I also want to thank Bonnie Anderson, Margaret Hope Bacon, Lyn Blackwell, Lyn Blanchfield, Kate Culkin, Tom Dublin, Laura Edwards, Claudette Fillard, Ann Gordon, Nancy Hewitt, Kathi Kern, Michelle Kuhl, Linda Janke, Bonnie Laughlin-Schultz, Roderick McDonald, Richard Newman, Kristen Tegtmeier Oertel, Françoise Orazi, Jeff Pickron, Michael Pierson, Hélène Quanquin, Stacey Robertson, Marcia Robinson, Leslie Schwalm, Connie Shemo, James Brewer Stewart, Lisa Tetrault, members of the Upstate New York Women's History Organization, Judith Wellman, Dot Willsey and the National Abolition Hall of Fame, Victoria Wolcott, and Jean Fagan Yellin for their support at various stages of the project.

I am thrilled to be publishing another book with the University of Pennsylvania Press. Peter Agree was an enthusiastic supporter of this biography from the beginning, and I am thankful for his kindness and advice. Alison Anderson, Chris Bell, Robert Lockhart, Julia Rose Roberts, and Mariellen Smith have helped this book along in many ways. Also, I deeply appreciate the thorough review of the manuscript by Lori Ginzberg and the anonymous reader. Their wise suggestions greatly improved the book. Thanks also to Kathryn Simmons of Twin Oaks Indexing for her skill and speed.

I could not have written this book without the help of friends and family. Joanne Landy and members of the X-biking class at the JCC offered laughs and a much-needed workout. I enjoyed good conversation and playdates with Annie and Mike Brandt and family, and Lyn Blanchfield and Paul Batkin and family. Andy and Amy Lutz welcomed me into their home during a research trip to Philadelphia. I also appreciate the continued hospitality of my father-in-law Robert Baer Cohen in Philadelphia. My parents, David and Joanne Faulkner, provide love and a place to stay in New Haven. Unsurprisingly, they are extraordinary babysitters as well. My family, especially my sister Jill, my brother Jim, my Aunt Joan and Uncle Walt, are always interested in what I'm doing. My joyful daughter Mae deserves credit for dragging me away from the computer to play. My greatest love and appreciation is for Andrew Wender Cohen. I am extremely lucky to have his companionship, humor, imagination, and support.